CAESAR
AGAINST ROME

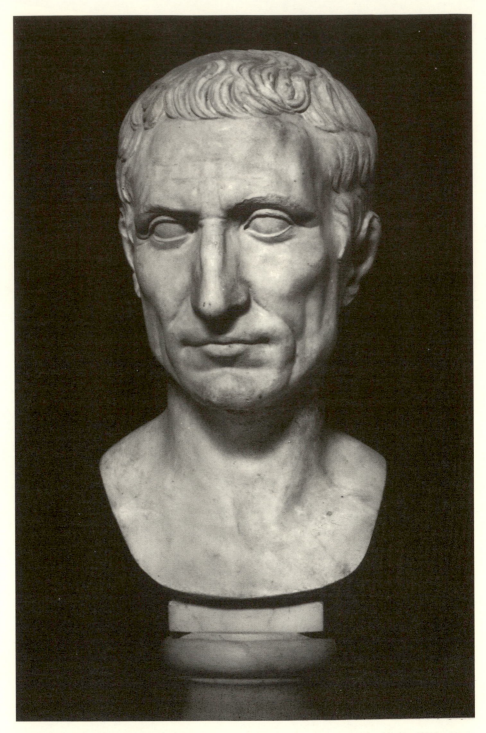

This marble bust of Julius Caesar is an Augustan copy of an earlier work, most likely produced in bronze during the last years of his life. (Vatican Museums, Vatican State. Alinari/Art Resource, NY.)

CAESAR AGAINST ROME

The Great Roman Civil War

Ramon L. Jiménez

Westport, Connecticut
London

Library of Congress Cataloging-in-Publication Data

Jiménez, Ramon L.
    Caesar against Rome : the great Roman civil war / Ramon L.
Jiménez.
      p. cm.
    Includes bibliographical references and index.
    ISBN 0–275–96620–8 (alk. paper)
    1. Caesar, Julius—Adversaries. 2. Rome—History—Civil War,
49–45 B.C. 3. Generals—Rome—Attitudes. I. Title.
DG266.J55 2000
937′.05′092—dc21   99–36592

British Library Cataloguing in Publication Data is available.

Library of Congress Catalog Card Number: 99–36592
ISBN: 0–275–96620–8

First published in 2000

Praeger Publishers, 88 Post Road West, Westport, CT 06881
An imprint of Greenwood Publishing Group, Inc.
www.praeger.com

Printed in the United States of America

The paper used in this book complies with the
Permanent Paper Standard issued by the National
Information Standards Organization (Z39.48–1984).

10 9 8 7 6 5 4 3 2 1

Copyright Acknowledgments

The author and publisher gratefully acknowledge permission for the use of the following material:

From Caesar's *The Civil War*, translated by J. M. Carter (1997). Reprinted by permission of Oxford University Press.

From Lucan's *Lucan's Civil War*, translated by Paul F. Widdows (Bloomington & Indianapolis: Indiana University Press, 1988), p. 1. Reprinted by permission of the publisher, Indiana University Press.

From Plutarch's *Fall of the Roman Republic*, translated by Rex Warner (Harmondsworth, U.K.: Penguin Classics 1958, Revised edition 1972), pp. 67, 104, 171, 225, 226, 241–42, 283, 350–51, 360. Copyright © Rex Warner, 1958. Reproduced by permission of Penguin Books Ltd.

This is for
my mother
Cisna Baun

War, civil war and worse, fought out on the plains of Thessalia,
Times when injustice reigned and a crime was legally sanctioned,
Times when a powerful race, whose prowess had won it an empire,
Turned its swords on itself, with opposing armies of kinsmen—
This is my theme. I shall tell of the compact of tyranny broken,
Huge contention throughout the shattered world, to engender
Universal guilt, and of spears and standards and eagles
Facing each other in battle, of Roman arms against Roman.
—Lucan, *Lucan's Civil War* I, 1–7, Translated by P. F. Widdows

Contents

Maps and Figures

Maps and Figures

Preface

Although the Romans suffered their first civil conflicts during the ninth decade BCE, the war that began with Julius Caesar's attack across the Rubicon River in 49 was the first that had a lasting effect upon their method of government. It had its genesis in the fears and ambitions of Caesar, Gnaeus Pompeius, and a few dozen others of the elite Senatorial class, including its newest member, Marcus Tullius Cicero. This is the story of that war and how it changed the unwieldy Roman oligarchy into a somewhat more efficient dictatorship that fluctuated from benevolent to murderous for the next five hundred years.

From its beginnings, ancient Rome applied itself to war and conquest, as did nearly every ancient society. Such a purpose does not necessarily result in civil war, but in Rome's case the repeated success of its warmaking machine created a strong impetus to internal strife. Its generals used their devastating armies to conquer and then annex territories ever further afield, until the collection of provinces and subject kingdoms reached a size that was almost impossible to govern. The Roman Senate, which had sole responsibility for foreign policy and warmaking, became reluctant to finance the large standing army necessary to police and defend this territory. The result was that control and support of Rome's armies gradually fell to its generals, who began to conscript their own troops, and then maintain and reward them with booty and captives from conquered lands.

This situation led to the rise of millionaire soldier-politicians, of whom Sulla, Caesar, and Pompey were the most notable examples. With great victories behind them, and powerful armies under their command, these generals were wont to have their way when they returned home. The resulting quarrels and confrontations with the Senate led to armed conflicts, of which the Civil War between Caesar and the Senatorial forces led by Pompey was the lengthiest and the most damaging to the shaky Republican government.

Those who are interested in the people and events of the late Republic are fortunate in that this period is among the best documented in all of Roman history. The major political and military figures (one and the same, except for Cicero) have been repeatedly portrayed by poets, historians, and biographers. The Civil War itself was the subject of several narrative histories and epic poems. But we are without what was probably the most comprehensive treatment of the War, another eyewitness account very likely more objective than Caesar's, written by his officer Asinius Pollio.

It is upon the surviving histories, letters, and biographies, and upon the fruits of the best available research and reflection, that I base the following narrative. Where these sources conflict, as they often do, I have chosen the most reasonable alternative or, where there are serious disagreements (as in the case of Caesar's alleged son), tried to present the two or three sides of the question. Where there is speculation or supposition by me or others, it is so labeled.

Within this framework, I seek to refute the adage that Fact is a poor storyteller, and offer a story to be read and enjoyed, rather than a textbook, a survey, or an argument. To help identify and distinguish the many characters, I include an Index of Persons in addition to a standard index. Generally, the modern name of an ancient place, and the meaning of an unfamiliar term, are given at the time it is first mentioned. The book is not intended to be a biography of Caesar, nor a history of the Roman Republic, but readers who want those things will find an extensive list of sources that might be pursued.

Such a project is not accomplished alone, and I am deeply grateful to the following people for helping make it possible: To Tod and Susan Fletcher, Jan Vetter, and Joan Leon for reading and commenting on all or part of the manuscript; to Helga Roth, Tod Fletcher, Sarah Jiménez, and George Cozyris for custom translations; and to John Rigdon, Jonah Jimenez, and William Jimenez for mapmaking assistance. For encouragement, enthusiasm, and support, I owe no greater debt than to my wife, Joan Leon.

Maps and the figure of the Roman catapult by Meridian Mapping, Oakland, California.

NOTE

The Romans customarily used three names to formally identify themselves, such as Marcus Tullius Cicero. In the interest of clarity and brevity, the names and spellings used in the narrative are those most recognizable to the modern reader, such as Mark Antony, Pompey, and so forth.

Unless otherwise indicated, all dates are BCE, and all dates prior to 45 BCE are in accordance with the Roman calendar then in use. Subsequent dates are in accordance with the Julian calendar. Distances given by Caesar are in Roman measurements. The Roman foot (*pes*) was 296 millimeters, or slightly over $11\frac{1}{2}$ inches, five of which made one *passus*. The Roman mile (*mille passus*) was 5,000 Roman feet, equalling 92 percent of an English mile.

Chronology

	(August)	Caesar defeats Pharnaces at Zela
	(September)	Birth of Caesarion; Caesar returns to Rome
46	(April)	Battle of Thapsus
	(September)	Caesar's four triumphs
45	(January)	Introduction of the Julian calendar
	(March)	Battle of Munda
44	(February)	Caesar *dictator perpetuus*
	(March)	Assassination of Caesar
43	(November)	Second Triumvirate
43	(December)	Death of Cicero
30		Suicides of Antony and Cleopatra and death of Caesarion

PART ONE
The Rise of Caesar

Prologue
Three Men

In the waning weeks of a Roman winter, some eight decades before the birth of Christ, a noisy procession of horsemen and chariots, marching soldiers, prisoners in chains, and wagons laden with captured arms and booty filed through the narrow streets of the capital of the Roman Republic. At the head of the spectacle, preceded by marching trumpeters and horn players, walked Rome's new *dictator*, fifty-six-year-old Lucius Cornelius Sulla, a rogue general who had stormed the capital with his own army and taken control of the government less than six months before. Behind him followed the government magistrates and the three hundred members of the Senate. In the middle of the procession, a handsome young general, round faced and curly-haired, stood in a high two-wheeled chariot drawn by four horses, and waved to the crowd.

The twenty-four-year-old Gnaeus Pompeius, known to history as Pompey, was celebrating one of Rome's most ancient rituals, the *triumphus*—an honor granted by the Senate to a Roman general after he defeated a foreign enemy. The son of a despised general who had also been a Consul, Pompey was well known and well liked by the Romans. They could hardly help their fascination with this attractive young man who, in the space of a single year, had become one of the country's leading generals, had divorced his wife of five years, had married Sulla's stepdaughter, and was suddenly now again unattached, his new wife having died giving birth to her former husband's child.

Just weeks earlier Pompey had returned from Rome's province of Africa, a portion of modern Tunisia, where, in the course of hunting down the last opponents of the new regime, he had defeated and put to death the Numidian King, Hiarbus, who had supported them. To symbolize his victory, he had captured and brought back to Rome a number of African elephants, which now lumbered among the marching soldiers. Pompey had wanted two of them to pull his triumphal chariot, but the Porta Triumphalis, the Triumphal Gateway, proved too narrow to let them through in tandem, and he was forced to settle for the traditional horses.

In the crowd, observing the procession as it moved through the Forum, stood another young man, a member of the *gens*, or clan, Julia, one of the few dozen *gentes* that comprised the elite patrician class, the social group that ranked above all others in Roman society. It was their alleged descent from the founders of Rome some seven centuries earlier that distinguished the *patricii* from all other Roman citizens, whether rich and poor—the *plebes*. Reflecting the feelings of many in the crowd, the expression on the face of the eighteen-year-old Gaius Julius Caesar would have been solemn, and his dark eyes might have blazed with disapproval. For more than one reason he felt a strong aversion to the vulgar parade winding through the city. Lucius Sulla, the new ruler of Rome who had ordered the Senate to approve Pompey's triumph, was known to regard Caesar and his family with suspicion. His branch of the Julii had been aligned with the losing faction, and had suffered in the bloody civil war that had just ended.

Furthermore, the notion of the upstart Pompey celebrating a triumph was a slap in the face of order and tradition. He was not even old enough to be elected *quaestor*, a junior officer who customarily served under a legionary commander or governor. Yet Sulla had given him six legions to command and had sent him to hunt down the exiled rebels in Sicily and Africa. More than that, Pompey's family had entered the plebeian nobility only in the previous century, a status earned when a family member was elected a Consul. Now he was the first Roman who was not a Senator, and the youngest Roman ever, to taste the glory of a triumph.

A second spectator in the crowd was Marcus Tullius Cicero, a twenty-five-year-old student of oratory and the law with an intellectual turn of mind. He had been personally acquainted with Pompey from the time when the two of them, as teenagers, had served briefly in the army of Pompey's father. Cicero's own father was a prosperous businessman of the plebeian upper class known as *equites*, literally "horsemen," a word deriving from the ancient obligation of men from wealthy families to serve in the cavalry. Two decades earlier the elder Cicero had moved his family to Rome from their estate near the town of Arpinum, today's Arpino, about seventy miles to the east, a town whose residents had been Roman citizens less than a hundred years. He wanted his sons Marcus and Quintus to take advantage of the superior schooling and political opportunities in the capital to perhaps raise the family from the propertied to the noble class.

Besides studying law, Marcus had written poetry and a treatise on oratory, and had traveled to Greece to study philosophy and rhetoric. Although he was not yet politically active, he would have regarded the triumph of Pompey with much of the same distaste as Caesar, with whom he was also acquainted. As a member of a family still aspiring to nobility, he would have been envious of Pompey and dismayed, as well, by the conduct of the new regime in Rome. His first argument in court would take place later in the year.

The presence of the young Julius Caesar and Marcus Cicero at the triumphal parade of Pompey is not recorded in the histories or letters of the period, nor is the exact sequence of their movements at that time known for certain. But it is highly likely that the two young men stood in the crowd on the twelfth of March in the year we now call 81 BCE and watched the third celebrate the highest honor conferred upon a Roman citizen. It would not be the last time they would do precisely the same thing.

It is certain that none of them knew that they would gradually become linked to each other over the next four decades until they were locked in a struggle that none of them could escape. Nor could they have known that the struggle would radically alter the way Rome was governed, and involve the entire Roman world and beyond.

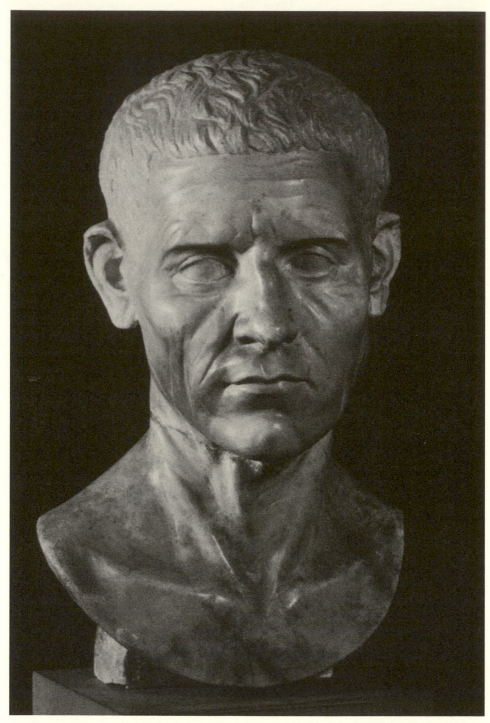

This bust of Lucius Sulla, while not authenticated, bears a close resemblance to his coin portraits. (Museo Archeologico, Venice, Italy. Scala/Art Resource, NY.)

I
Sulla Against Caesar

For the two years just prior to Pompey's triumph, the peninsula of Italy had been riven by rebellion, treachery, armies in battle, and capricious slaughter. What was worse, the fighting was largely among Romans themselves, a murderous conflict between two factions, the Marians, named after their now-dead leader Gaius Marius, Caesar's uncle, and the Sullans, supporters of Lucius Sulla, a flamboyant and erratic general who subjected Rome to one of the strange and terrible episodes in its history.

The seven families of Cornelii, the patrician *gens* into which Lucius Cornelius Sulla was born in 138, boasted a lengthy and glittering history, filled with eminence and luxury, Consuls, priests, and *dictatores*. But by the time of Sulla's youth, his particular family was in eclipse, and the death of his father left him with such a modest income that he was forced to live in a cheap apartment with an ex-slave for a neighbor. It was not until the age of thirty that Sulla, by now a handsome redhead with piercing blue eyes and noticeably pale skin, finally acquired the wealth befitting his class. Both his stepmother and his mistress, each a wealthy woman, died about this time and left him their fortunes. By then, his only achievement was a reputation as a liar, a drinker, and a libertine who took his pleasure with either sex. But he was well connected enough to be elected one of the Republic's eight *quaestores* for the year 107, four of whom were assigned to each of the two presiding Consuls.

One of the Consuls elected for the same year was another native of Arpinum, the veteran soldier Gaius Marius. In addition to his Consular role, the Senate appointed him to take charge of the four-year-old war against King Jugurtha, ruler of the African kingdom of Numidia, modern Algeria. After taking office, Marius made Sulla a cavalry officer and later brought him and his horsemen to Africa to help hunt down the Numidian King. The novice revealed an unknown flair for diplomacy and intrigue. Charged with negotiating with the Numidians, Sulla met secretly with Jugurtha's rivals. When they tricked the King into attending a peace conference, Sulla seized him without a fight, ending the war.

Over the next twenty years the two men distinguished themselves against Rome's enemies, and as their reputations grew, a bitter rivalry arose between them. After leading an army that defeated a pair of German tribes threatening

Italy, Marius was reelected Consul five times. Sulla developed his own popular following after a diplomatic coup against the German Marsi and military victories in the Alps and in Cilicia, a Roman province on the southern coast of modern Turkey.

In 88 Sulla also achieved the Consulship, and he and the sixty-nine-year-old Marius contended for the privilege of leading an army in defense of the Roman provinces of Greece and Asia. The need for this arose out of the actions of the Persian ruler of the kingdom of Pontus on the Black Sea coast of modern Turkey, Mithradates VI, who bore the honorific title Eupator (born of a noble father). His attack and occupation of Asia (the western third of Turkey) was accompanied by the massacre of thousands of Roman citizens, and he now invaded Greece. Because of Rome's previous successes in the East, the war promised to bring an easy victory, with much glory and booty to be had, and neither man nor his supporters would let the other have it.

After much political maneuvering and some street fights and rioting, the fifty-year-old Sulla took a step unprecedented in the history of the Republic. He marched his already-assembled army to Rome, where he threatened the Senate and forced it to vote him the command. It was, in the words of one historian, "the first march on the capital, the first civil war, and the first clear example of troops acting out of loyalty to their commander to defy the government."[1] But Sulla was less interested in the government than in a lucrative war in the East. Early in 87, after forcing legislation through the Assembly that strengthened his conservative supporters, he departed for Greece with six legions.

The next year he won a notable victory over one of Mithradates' generals at the Greek city of Chaeronea and then besieged and sacked Athens. From there he pursued the invaders back to Anatolia (the region of modern Turkey) and finally, two years after setting out, halted the war and made a peace settlement with Mithradates. Although all of Rome's territory was restored, the pact was widely criticized because Mithradates himself had not been pursued and captured. Sulla was saving his troops for Rome.

In the meantime, back in Italy Sulla's military coup had brought on a plague of political chaos, terror, and vengeful killing. On the departure of Sulla, the Marian faction, despite the death of Marius in 86, had taken control of the government, declared Sulla an outlaw, and exiled or murdered hundreds of his supporters. In the spring of 83, while the Marian leaders scurried to raise troops and assemble a fleet, the whole of Italy waited anxiously as Sulla and his legions made their way from Anatolia to Greece and then embarked for the Roman homeland.

The army of forty thousand men landed both at Brundisium, modern Brindisi, and at Tarentum, modern Taranto, on either side of Italy's heel. Not since the Carthaginian general Hannibal, more than a century earlier, had there been a larger invasion of Italy. But this time the army was Roman, and the civil war that followed tore the country from one end to the other. At first there was no appreciable opposition to Sulla's army, and some of the country's eminent men rushed to join him. The twenty-three-year-old Pompey raised a legion from among his father's veterans on his family's estates in the region of Picenum, and marched it to Sulla's side. He was shrewd enough to see that Sulla would prevail, and that now was the time to join him. When they met, he saluted Sulla with the traditional title *imperator*—conquering general—and Sulla, delighted with this influential prize, impetuously returned the compliment.

The invading legions proceeded up the Appian Way as far as the plain of Campania, inland from Neapolis (now Naples), before two Marian armies confronted them. Sulla's veterans, hardened by four years of fighting in the East, easily defeated the first, and Sulla persuaded the other to defect to him. He then sent Pompey back to his region of Picenum on the Adriatic coast to recruit two more legions. Over the next eighteen months, except for the winter, when both sides retired from the battlefield, the Sullans and Marians, and their allies, pursued and fought each other in valleys, along roads, and at city gates all over the northern half of the country. Pompey proved to be one of Sulla's most reliable generals, taking his three legions from one victory to another over Marian armies.

During the second year of the war, two considerations, one personal and one political, brought about a dramatic change in Pompey's life. Sulla's wife Metella desired that the attractive young general marry Aemilia, her daughter from a previous marriage. At the same time, Sulla sought to bind the influential nobleman more closely to his own faction. The only obstacles were that Pompey was already married, and Aemilia was not only married, but far into her first pregnancy. By this time, however, Sulla's authority was such that both couples promptly divorced. Just as quickly, Pompey married Aemilia; but the unfortunate woman died in childbirth almost as soon as she moved into Pompey's home.

In the fall of 82 Sulla's army reached Rome, and after a decisive battle at the Porta Collina, the Colline Gate, he took control of the city and the Roman government in the same way he had in 88, and as the Marians had when he left the country in 87. There had been terror and killings on both previous occasions, but this time the effort the war had cost Sulla seemed to drive him mad with revenge. In the words of Plutarch, he "devoted himself entirely to the work of butchery."[2] His soldiers coursed through the streets, pillaging, destroying, and murdering indiscriminately. Thousands of prisoners were rounded up and executed with volleys of arrows, and the heads of captured generals were impaled on pikes in the Forum, including that of one of the year's Consuls, Marius the Younger, son of Gaius Marius and cousin of Julius Caesar.

By now the fifty-six-year-old Sulla had been embroiled in war or political intrigue, in Italy or in the East, for the better part of ten years. His face had become thin, and the blue eyes had taken on a sharp and dominating glare. He had also by this time developed a severe case of scabies, which caused him to scratch his face in a way that left it disfigured with red blotches. The resulting contrast with his pale skin gave rise to a remark about him that Plutarch reports: "Sulla's face is mulberry with oatmeal scattered on it."[3]

Although Sulla had an iron grip on the city and its terrified citizens, he insisted on a formal meeting of the Senate, ostensibly to give his report on the outcome of the war with Mithradates. When he had finished, those Senators who had survived voted to ratify all his acts, and to place a gilt statue of him on a horse in front of the *rostra*, the speaker's platform, the first such honor accorded a Roman. (The platform was so named because it was ornamented with the *rostra*, beaks or prows, of ships captured in a naval battle with the city of Antium, modern Anzio, in 338.)

There followed a brutal and comprehensive purge of hundreds of prominent Romans, especially Senators and *equites*, who had not supported Sulla in the civil war. When droves of suspects fled the city, the names of those still at large were posted throughout the country, and citizens invited to bring in their heads. No less than ninety Senators perished, including fifteen former Consuls. As many as twenty-six hundred *equites*, the cream of the business and propertied class, were put to death. The homes of Sulla's enemies were confiscated and sold at auction, or deeded over to his supporters. Sulla freed their slaves—the number may have reached ten thousand—and ordered that they subsequently bear the name of his own *gens*, Cornelii, rather than that of their former masters, as was the custom.

During this time the teenaged Caesar (he was born in 100) and his family—his mother Aurelia, wife Cornelia, and daughter Julia—did not venture far from their modest house in the crowded Subura district. They hoped that the age and insignificance of the only male in the family (he had two older sisters) would mask the fact that both his father and his uncle had been among the Marian opposition. Furthermore, Caesar's aunt Julia had been the wife of Marius, and Caesar himself, two years before, had taken as his bride Cornelia, the fifteen-year-old daughter of Marius' comrade Cinna. As it was, Sulla paid little attention to Caesar and his family; they had little influence and less wealth.

Toward the end of the year, Sulla sent Pompey to track down the Marian generals who had fled to Sicily and Africa, both of which were vital wheat-producing provinces. Pompey commandeered a fleet of warships and trapped Gnaeus Carbo, who was serving his third term as Consul, on an island in the Sicilian Channel. When Carbo was brought to Pompey begging for his life, the young man ordered him beheaded and his head sent to Sulla in Rome.

Despite Sulla's successful military coup, and his seizure of every function of government, he chose to indulge in one of the legal niceties so cherished by the Romans by arranging for a constitutional transfer of power to himself. As both Consuls were dead, he ordered the Senate to appoint an *interrex*, a temporary chief magistrate whose job in such situations was to conduct an election. But before he could do so, Sulla sent him a letter saying that what was needed was a *dictator*, a legally appointed magistrate with absolute authority to govern without restraint. The Romans had resorted to this procedure in the past in times of emergency, but the office was nearly obsolete; no *dictator* had been named for more than one hundred and twenty years, and his term had never been longer than six months. Needless to say, the *dictator* that Sulla had in mind was himself, and in the face of his troops, the surviving Senators not only appointed him promptly, but left the term of his office indefinite.

In January 81 Sulla ordered Pompey to transport his army from Sicily to Africa and chase down another Marian general, Gnaeus Domitius, the brother-in-law of Caesar's wife, who had taken control of the province and raised a large army. Pompey landed his six legions at Carthage and Utica, two ancient ports founded by Phoenicians, but subject to Roman rule since the year 200 and part of a Roman province for seventy years. After a delay of several days in which his soldiers occupied themselves with digging for buried coins, Pompey led them against the Marian troops, whom he outmaneuvered during a violent rainstorm, and then watched while his men slaughtered them and their general.

After nearly two years of repeated victories over a series of enemy armies, Pompey's troops eagerly hailed their youthful commander *imperator*, the honorific bestowed on a general after a great victory. From Africa, Pompey led them into neighboring Numidia, where he captured and executed the Numidian King Hiarbus, who had been aiding the Marians, and restored his rival Hiempsal to the throne. After a few days of hunting lions and elephants, he returned to his base in Africa, having taken only forty days to secure the province for Sulla.

Ironically, the competence of Pompey and his army alarmed Sulla to such a degree that he ordered him to dismiss five of his six legions, and await his successor in Africa. When Pompey relayed the order for dismissal to his troops, they reacted as he had anticipated, raising a great clamor and demanding that he remain their commander. When he begged them to comply, finally resorting to tears and threats of suicide, they were moved to hail him "Magnus," in a clear reference to Alexander the Great, who had once used the same tactic in the face of his own mutinous army. Pompey's posturing was an early example of what was to become typical behavior in later years, behavior described by a later historian as "pretending as far as possible not to desire the things that he really wished."[4] The outcome of these histrionics was that both Pompey and his troops had their way. He yielded to their wishes, and early in 81 personally led all six victorious legions back to Italy.

Pompey's return with his army intact was a signal to Sulla that he might have another rebel to put down. But when he was told that Pompey was not in revolt, and when he saw the Romans preparing to welcome him as a hero, he went out himself to meet him and generously addressed him as "Magnus," telling everyone around him to do the same. Now the confident young general asserted that he deserved a formal triumph on the basis of his defeat of the foreign king Hiarbus. Sulla demurred. The boy was not of the patrician class, and not even a Senator. But Pompey persisted with his demand, and Sulla could not ignore his military successes, much less his large army camped outside the capital. Finally, an exasperated Sulla is said to have shouted, "Let him have his triumph."[5]

The *triumphus* originated as a ceremony in which Etruscan kings offered thanks to the gods of the state on their return from a victorious battle. By the time of Caesar and Pompey it had become a spectacular civic event with an elaborate protocol and marked by a splendid procession through the city. It had also become more commonplace. Any general who had the slightest success in battle demanded a triumph, and the Senate was often under political pressure to approve it and to pay for the banquets, shows, and games that followed.

In keeping with the ancient tradition, the participants in Pompey's triumph assembled on the Campus Martius, the Field of Mars, outside the northwest wall of the city. From the Campus Martius the procession entered the capital through the Porta Triumphalis and passed through the Circus Maximus, the huge old stadium built by an Etruscan king. From there it circled the Palatine Hill and followed the Sacred Way, Rome's main street, through the Forum to the foot of the Capitoline Hill.

In the middle of the procession, harpists and flutists marched in time to their own music, followed by singers and dancers, and then by Pompey's chariot, preceded by a line of purple-clad lictors, ceremonial bodyguards who always accompanied the highest government officials. In his slow-moving chariot, Pompey stood with a laurel wreath on his head, and wearing the *toga picta*, a purple toga embroidered with gold thread. Clouds of incense swirled around him, and his face may have been smeared red with lead oxide, a practice intended to reflect the vigor and vitality of Jupiter, an Etruscan god adopted by the Romans. In his right hand Pompey carried a laurel branch and in his left an ivory scepter topped by a wooden figure of an eagle. Behind the *triumphator* marched his soldiers carrying weapons decorated with laurel and shouting, "Io triumphe," an exclamation surviving from the Etruscan language that was echoed by the crowd.[6]

The traditional destination of the triumphal parade was the Temple of Jupiter, a massive structure on the Capitoline Hill, where the *triumphator* made a sacrificial offering to Rome's principal deity, Jupiter Optimus Maximus (Jupiter the Best and Greatest). The customary victims were white oxen that had been part of the procession, and then became part of the feast that followed. It is likely that Pompey made the usual sacrifice, but the grandeur of the event was diminished because the sacred temple, first built by an Etruscan king more than four hundred years earlier, had been destroyed by fire during the first year of the war, and had not yet been rebuilt.

From his first seizure of power Sulla had professed that he wanted only to restore the proper balance to the conduct of government, by which he meant increasing the influence of the Senatorial class, the small group of families headed by Senators. In the previous fifty years various reformers had pushed through laws that strengthened the popular Assembly so that it had begun to challenge the Senate for control of the legislative process. Sulla now stripped the Assembly's leaders, the *tribuni plebis* (tribunes of the people), of much of their authority and gave the Senate the right of approval over new laws. He also barred any *tribunus plebis* from ever advancing to any higher office, thus making the position unattractive to anyone with serious political ambitions. True to his aristocratic bias, he abolished the government's forty-year-old practice of selling wheat to its citizens at cut-rate prices every month, and then doubled the size of the Senate to six hundred members.

Once he had reformed the government to his liking, Sulla sought to weaken his opposition by ordering several prominent men, just as he had ordered Pompey, to divorce their wives from suspect families and marry women more closely aligned with his faction. Justifiably afraid for their lives, those so ordered hastened to comply. Although the eighteen-year-old Julius Caesar was not prominent himself, his family was squarely in the middle of events, and his child-wife Cornelia was the daughter of Cornelius Cinna, who had mercilessly persecuted Sulla's allies less than a decade earlier. When Sulla ordered Caesar to divorce her, the young man refused—the first evidence of the daring that Caesar would display in a lifetime of risk taking, an act that nearly cost him his life. Presumably, what motivated him was his attachment to his wife, but it is possible that there was another factor. Cornelia was not Caesar's first wife. When he was fourteen, he had entered into an arranged marriage to Cossutia, the daughter of the plebeian Cossutii, a wealthy family of architects and builders.[7] Comfortable, but without great wealth, both of Caesar's sisters had married into affluent equestrian families, and it was reasonable that he should do the same.

Within a year of this marriage, Caesar suffered the loss of his father, of whom little is known except that he attained the level of *praetor*, the second-highest rank of magistrates, and served a term as Governor of Asia in 91. The next year the adolescent was jolted again when his mother informed him that he would have to divorce Cossutia and marry someone else.

One of the Consuls for the year 84, the patrician Cornelius Cinna, decided that Caesar was to be the next holder of the unique office of *flamen Dialis*, the special priest assigned to serve Jupiter Optimus Maximus. This lifetime ceremonial post was heavy with restrictions on the incumbent's behavior, including the requirement that he be married to a patrician, whom he could never divorce. The girl Cinna had in mind for Caesar was his own daughter Cornelia, and in the easy way of Roman marriage and divorce, the fifteen-year-old Caesar divorced Cossutia and married Cornelia, who could hardly have been any older. But before Caesar was actually old enough to be appointed *flamen*, Sulla came to power and squelched the idea. When he ordered Caesar to divorce Cornelia after less than three years of marriage in 81, it is likely that the young man was fed up with being pulled about.

Rather than comply, he fled to the Sabine country east of Rome, the home of his mother's ancestors. Sulla confiscated Cornelia's dowry, stripped Caesar of his own inheritance, and added his name to the list of fugitives to be hunted down and executed. Although Caesar was able to buy a hiding place in a different home each night, he eventually came down with quartan fever, a form of malaria, and was captured by one of Sulla's patrols. Even then he was able to purchase his freedom with a large bribe, but remained a fugitive. In the meantime, some of those in Sulla's inner circle, including Aurelia's cousin Gaius Aurelius Cotta, pleaded with him to spare Caesar, and the *dictator* finally relented, but he did so reluctantly. Caesar was in the habit of wearing his belt only lightly fastened around his tunic, and Sulla saw a connections between Caesar's style of dress and his potential danger to the Sentorial class. He is quoted by Suetonius as saying, probably during the same episode, "Beware of that boy with the loose clothes."[8]

Caesar returned to Rome and his family, but remained under suspicion and in danger from Sulla's henchmen. Aurelia and her cousins thought it best that he leave the country, and arranged an appointment for him as aide-de-camp to Marcus Thermus, Governor of Asia. About the time of his nineteenth birthday, Caesar, accompanied by a slave or two, traveled for two days down the Appian Way to Brundisium, and sailed to the East. His destination was the fabled city of Ephesus, capital of Asia.

II

Rome and Its Neighbors

The Roman Republic of Caesar's youth was a vast and untidy collection of provinces, colonies, dependencies, and territories spread over thousands of square miles, and populated by citizens, freedmen, foreigners, slaves, other subjects, *socii* (allies), and *amici populi Romani* (friends of the Roman people). It was easily the largest and most powerful single nation that had arisen in the Western world; its ten provinces stretched from Spain in the west to Cilicia on the southern coast of modern Turkey. Rome had achieved this eminence during the previous six centuries primarily through its skill at making war, the central occupation of all ancient states.

Although the middle of the eighth century before Christ is the traditional date for the founding of Rome, archaeologists have found evidence that the site of the city had been continuously occupied for some eight centuries before that. Its Bronze Age settlers were an Indo-European people who had migrated into Europe from the east over the course of many centuries. It was not until the first millennium, however, that substantial settlements appeared on the circle of hills surrounding a marshy area at a particular curve on the Tiber River—its lowest feasible crossing point. By this time other groups from the area of Latium (the region of modern Lazio south of Rome) had joined the settlers, as had migrants from other parts of the peninsula and from across the Adriatic Sea. Besides its convenient location, the area was especially suited to farming because it was covered with a thick layer of fertile soil, the result of volcanic eruptions of nearby Monte Cavo thousands of years earlier.[1]

The legend of the founding of Rome by the migrant Trojan Aeneas and the traditional story of Romulus killing his brother Remus and becoming the first King of Rome are now regarded as folktales without historical basis. They are a type of origin myth that is common to many societies throughout the world. Similarly, the founding of Rome, that is, the creation of a unified political community, is now thought to have taken place somewhat later than the traditional date of approximately 750 BCE. Archaeological evidence indicates that it was about 625 that the hill settlements adjacent to the Tiber began to organize themselves for religious and political purposes.[2] They were influenced in these matters by a more advanced culture just to the north of them, on the other side of the Tiber. This society was stronger and richer than any other on the penin-

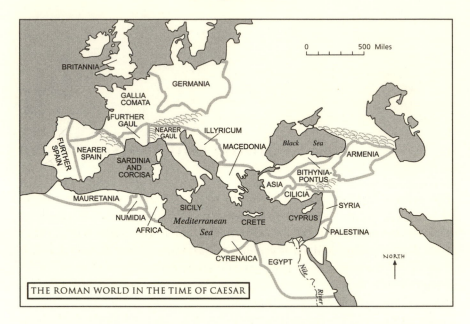

THE ROMAN WORLD IN THE TIME OF CAESAR

sula, and its cities and citizens would be involved in the development of the Roman state for centuries to come. They called themselves "Rasenna." To history they are known as Etruscans.

Etruscan society was organized around a dozen or more city-states scattered over a large area north of Rome and Latium. Because their language is unrelated to any other in Europe, historians and archaeologists have argued about the origin of the Etruscans since ancient times. Some legends trace them to Anatolia, but today it is generally agreed that they are probably the Bronze Age descendants of the indigenous Villanovan culture that dominated northern Italy early in the first millennium, a culture that was possibly influenced by migrants from Asia.[3] The Etruscans grew rich by mining abundant deposits of copper, iron, and tin along the coast of Etruria, modern Tuscany, and on the nearby island of Elba. Their metals and their wealth attracted traders from all over the Mediterranean, including Phoenicians, Carthaginians, and Greeks. From the Phoenicians, the Etruscans imported such new commodities as wine, olive oil, and glassware, and from Greek colonies on the Italian peninsula, an alphabet that they modified for their own language.

As a result of trade, in-migration, and intermarriage, Etruscans became a substantial minority in the new city of "Roma," itself a name of Etruscan origin. By 600 the Roman city-state was fully formed and organized, and resident Etruscans exerted a significant influence on its development. The principal streets of the first Rome that was a city were probably laid out by Etruscan planners, and its first substantial buildings erected by Etruscan builders. Although some historians have recently discounted the importance of the Etrus-

16

cans to Rome, there remains substantial evidence of Rome's debt to its wealthy neighbor. From this more advanced culture, the Romans obtained the essential elements of their religion, their government, their farming practices, their engineering capability, their ceremonies and festivals, their use of gladiators, their chariot races, their personal naming system, their alphabet, their numerical system, the toga, and even the Roman sandal.[4]

Just as the Etruscan city-states were ruled by kings, so the earliest form of Roman government, lasting about a century and a quarter, was a kingship. The King was elected by an Assembly of citizens after being nominated by the Senate, a body of one hundred senior men, *senatores* (those over forty-five), who also continued to advise him. A decade or two before the middle of the sixth century, the choice of the Assembly was Tarquinius Priscus, an Etruscan noble whose family had migrated to Rome and become citizens. From this time on, the elective process began to break down, and the two Kings who ruled during the rest of the century, one of whom was also an Etruscan, seized their thrones illegally. Purporting to act on behalf of the common people, they became autocratic and dispensed with Senatorial advice, gradually alienating and then persecuting the aristocratic class.

In about 509 this aristocratic class overthrew the last Roman King, an Etruscan known as Tarquin the Proud, an outright tyrant who openly murdered Senators who opposed him. In place of the kingship, the Romans established a hitherto-unknown form of government—a hierarchy of unpaid magistrates, or administrators, headed by two Consuls, all elected yearly by a popular vote of an Assembly of all citizens. Each Consul presided over the Senate during alternate months, and controlled how and when its decrees and laws were introduced and discussed. Each also had veto power over the actions of the other. The Senate continued in its advisory function, but now became the originator of all proposed legislation, which became law only if approved by the Assembly.

The Romans called their government *res publica*, "the public business." One of its basic principles was that each citizen could participate in the government by casting a vote in the Assembly. But the Assembly was organized into categories of "centuries" of different sizes based on wealth, and voting was by century rather than by individual. The poorer citizens were crowded into a small number of centuries that voted only if the issue had not been decided by the wealthy centuries, and so rarely voted at all. The result was that the vote of the richest citizens was always the majority. Moreover, eligibility for office was limited to citizens with substantial property, and citizenship to males aged fifteen and over, excluding all slaves as well as women.

By the time of the founding of the Republic, Rome had become a rich and powerful city in which thirty to thirty-five thousand people lived in an area of more than seven hundred acres, surrounded by earthen banks and walls of rough stone.[5] Such defenses were necessary because of the Romans' habit of seizing the land of their neighbors, with the result that they were almost continuously at war. Pursuing this policy of what has been called "predatory militarism," they had gradually overrun the area around them until the *ager Romanus*, Roman territory, extended over an area of more than three hundred square miles, including the Tiber River down to its mouth. Most Romans spoke an early form of Latin, at that time no more than a minor language among a dozen on the peninsula, but Etruscan and Greek were also common in the capital.

Beginning about 400, northern Italy was repeatedly subjected to what the Romans called the *tumultus Gallicus*—invasions over the Alps of various tribes of Celts, another Indo-European people whose ancestors had migrated from the east some two thousand years earlier. Celtic society had developed in the center of the European continent, and as its population increased, tribal bands pushed into nearby territory. Some of those invading Italy sought plunder, and some the attractive farming land of the fertile Po Valley. During the next century these marauding tribes overran a number of Etruscan cities to the north of Rome, and established their own settlements at places now called Bologna, Milan, and Verona.

In about 386, a roving army of about thirty thousand Celts of the Senone tribe, led by their King, Brennus, crossed the Apennines and swept down the Tiber Valley. The Romans hastily assembled their largest army yet—as many as fifteen thousand men—and marched out to meet them, but they were quickly overcome and routed. The Celtic horde poured into the capital and completely occupied it, killing, looting, and burning at will, until they were finally persuaded to accept a large payment of gold to depart. The incident marked the beginning of five hundred years of conflict between Roman and Celt, a conflict in which Julius Caesar would play a prominent role.

Rome recovered from this disaster and continued to expand against its neighbors until, fifty years later, it controlled an area of forty-five hundred square miles in which more than one million people lived under its rule. The keys to this expansion were both military and diplomatic. Roman society was permanently organized for war, with no distinction between civilian and military leadership, and Roman citizens were routinely conscripted into standardized legions organized for efficiency, self-sustenance, and flexibility.

The Romans supplemented this slight military advantage over the less organized cities around them with a diplomatic policy that was rare in the ancient world. The usual aftermath of military victory was devastation of the enemy's lands and death or slavery for the conquered people. But the Romans often made alliances of different types with them, and sought to integrate them into their own culture, sometimes incorporating one or more of the defeated peoples' gods into their own pantheon. In other cases, they extended to them trading rights, partial citizenship, or even full citizenship without, or with, voting rights. Roman citizenship, as well as lesser privileges, became coveted rights that each city and tribe negotiated with the Romans, and in return furnished soldiers or warships against the next enemy, and refrained from any further attack. In this way the Romans assimilated dozens of neighboring cities and territories into a monolithic state that gradually became all but impervious to conquest.

During the third century Rome achieved control of nearly the entire peninsula, which came to be called Italia, after the Itali, the dominant tribe in the toe of Italy's boot. But with the emergence of a powerful Rome, friction developed with other Mediterranean states, especially the Greeks, who had established colonies in Sicily and along the southern coast of Italy even before the founding of Rome. The first foreign invasion was mounted in 280 by the Greek King Pyrrhus, who crossed the Adriatic Sea and attacked Roman settlements in southern Italy, the regions now called Calabria and Apulia. After winning his first two battles with heavy losses, Pyrrhus immortalized his name in the phrase "Pyrrhic victory" when he remarked to a soldier who congratulated him, "One more victory over the Romans and we are completely done for."[6] After a series of campaigns over more than four years, during which they fought for the first time against elephants, the Romans defeated Pyrrhus and took control of most of the Greek colonies in the south.

Later in the century the Romans fought two wars, now called the Punic Wars, with the Phoenician city of Carthage on the North African coast, a city even richer than Rome and one that controlled the entire western Mediterranean and its major islands. For more than six decades Rome and Carthage struggled intermittently against each other on land and sea. The First Punic War, which was fought on and around Sicily and in Africa over a twenty-year period, was probably the most destructive war in the Mediterranean world until then. As a result of its victory in 241, Rome seized Sicily from the Carthaginians and sent a *praetor* to govern it, calling it his *provincia*, Rome's first province. A few years later Rome expelled the Carthaginians from Sardinia and Corsica and established its second province, a form of political expansion it continued for more than three hundred years.

In 218 the Carthaginian general Hannibal launched an overland assault through Spain and southern Gaul and crossed the Alps into Italy. During the next fifteen years his army roved at will over most of Italy, besieging numerous towns and cities, once appearing at the gates of Rome itself. But though the Romans never defeated him in Italy, they had the advantage of fighting in their own country, and their war of attrition finally forced him to withdraw. In the meantime, Roman generals were advancing through Spain, and when Publius Scipio invaded across the Strait of Sicily and defeated Hannibal near Zama in modern Tunisia in 202, the threat from Carthage was removed forever. For his efforts Scipio earned the *cognomen*, or nickname, Africanus, which he and his descendants proudly bore thereafter. Although Rome found it necessary to mount yet another war against Carthage fifty years later, its victory in the Second Punic War gave it complete control of the western Mediterranean.

Between the first two wars with Carthage, the Romans had begun to advance against the Celtic settlements in the Po Valley, and with the end of the Second Punic War they resumed their incursions into northern Italy. After ten years of intermittent fighting against several Celtic tribes, a Roman army defeated the most powerful tribe in Italy, the Boii, and captured their capital, modern Bologna. Behind their conquering armies came Roman citizens to establish colonies throughout the area, which they called "Nearer Gaul."

During the second century before Christ, Roman eyes turned to the East, where King Philip V of Macedon had gradually brought the entire Greek peninsula under his control, except for a few independent city-states. Reacting to his provocations, Rome sent an army into Greece under its Consul Titus Flaminius, who defeated Philip in Thessaly in 197 and took his son as a hostage. Another son, Perseus, later sought to revive Macedonian power, but another Consul, Lucius Paullus, defeated him at Pydna in 168, with the eventual result that Macedonia became Rome's fifth province. Another important territory in the East fell into its hands three decades later when King Attalus III bequeathed to Rome his entire kingdom of Pergamon, modern Bergama, which, with its surrounding territory, became the province of Asia.

It was during the campaigns in Macedonia and Greece that the traditional Greek phalanx faced the newer Roman legion for the first time in large-scale battle. The self-contained legion of five to six thousand heavily armed infantrymen, in which troops were organized by function and experience, proved to be superior in most situations to the tightly packed and relatively immobile phalanx, where troops were deployed in a single mass across a broad front. The legion was further divided into ten self-contained cohorts, and each cohort into six centuries of eighty to a hundred troops under the command of a centurion. (The first cohort in every legion was composed of five double-strength centuries whose centurions were senior to all others.) This system of organization gave Roman generals the versatility to fight on any terrain, and to deploy their infantry in small or large units in different directions, and for different missions. A standardized system of recruitment, training, maintenance, and pay eventually turned the Roman legion into a disciplined war machine without peer in any other ancient state.

In the last decades before Caesar's birth, the Romans again fought with the Celts, this time with a pair of tribes in southern Gaul on whom they inflicted devastating defeats in two battles in the Rhône Valley. To protect their northern frontier, they occupied and then organized the entire southern coast of Gaul and the Rhône Valley as far north as Lake Geneva as the new province of Gallia Narbonensis. It took its name from a new colony at its western end, Narbo Martius, modern Narbonne, which they made its capital. The province came to be called Further Gaul or Transalpine Gaul in a pairing with Nearer Gaul or Cisalpine Gaul, on the Italian side of the Alps.

After two centuries of relentless conquest and expansion, during which it was literally at war every year, Rome had secured its borders, safeguarded its foreign trade, and created several buffer states to protect it from marauding kings and barbarian tribes. Its provinces, colonies, and dependencies ringed the Mediterranean and Aegean seas. In addition to revenue from its actual provinces, which it governed and taxed with varying degrees of efficiency, Rome exacted taxes and tribute from numerous other cities, kingdoms, and tribes. It was the strongest and wealthiest nation in the known world, but its wealth, power, and privilege were concentrated among a tiny minority of citizens in the capital.

Even after four hundred years of what purported to be government by all its citizens, Rome at this time was a badly polarized society in which all but a small number of prosperous families struggled to survive in the meanest of circumstances. Virtually all high governmental, military, and religious offices were held by men of the Senatorial class, one individual often holding two or even three such offices simultaneously.

Senatorial policy was controlled by about twenty of the six hundred or so families in this class, all of whom were property owners living on incomes from large farms, or rents from land or buildings. Senators and aspiring Senators were prohibited from engaging in commerce, but many ignored the ban. The mercantile business of the country was carried on by the *equites*, a class of wealthy citizens comprising no more than two to three thousand families. Equestrian status was a legal designation limited to citizens with assets of at least one hundred thousand *denarii*, the equivalent of a year's pay for four hundred and forty soldiers or working men. Members of the equestrian and Senatorial classes numbered less than thirty thousand of the total in the capital, which in Caesar's youth was approaching one million people, a size unsurpassed in Europe before the early nineteenth century.[7]

Although all citizens were allowed to vote, provided they could appear in person at the polls, only the men in this wealthy group of less than three percent of the inhabitants of Rome were eligible to run for public office. The principle that only men in the small upper class could hold office was so obvious to the Romans that no law was needed to enforce it, and it was not even a matter for discussion.[8] And even though all citizens could vote, it was obvious that only a tiny fraction did so; it has been shown that in the late Republic no more than ten thousand citizens could be accommodated in an Assembly or at the polling place. Nor did public officers or even Senators purport to represent anyone except themselves and their *clientela*—those who were personally beholden to them. In fact, the idea of elected representation in a legislative body was never conceived by any ancient society.

Below this thin stratum of wealthy families, the great majority of Romans lived in a state of continual economic uncertainty. Such a thing as a middle class was virtually absent. Except for a tiny number of *patricii* in the Senatorial class, all Romans were *plebes*, some rich, but most poor and at the mercy of the vagaries of the economy, such as uncertain harvests, a fluctuating money supply, and erratic building activity. Although Roman society was among the most advanced in the world, fewer than one in five men could read, and less than half that many women.

The Romans had not even the luxury of knowing the actual season of the year. The Roman calendar of 355 days required both small and large adjustments at irregular intervals to stay in line with the actual solar year. For centuries, one of the duties of the *collegium pontificum*, the college of priests who supervised the Roman state religion, was to insert at the end of February of every other year a short month of twenty-two or twenty-three days called Mercedonius. This adjustment itself required a small reduction every four years to align the solstices and equinoxes of the calendar with their actual solar occurrences. For various reasons, ranging from carelessness to political pressure, the *collegium pontificum* had often failed to make the proper adjustments, and in the period about a hundred years before Caesar's birth the calendar year was nearly four months ahead of the solar year. This was eventually corrected, but by the middle of the first century before Christ the gap had reappeared, and the calendar was almost two months ahead of the sun.

Aside from the Forum area, the largest and wealthiest city in the Western world was a congested hodgepodge of narrow, winding streets, noisy and dusty in summer, muddy in winter, and unlit and unsafe at night all year round. Except for two main roadways adjacent to the Forum, the streets were no more than passageways two or three yards wide and, more often than not, dirty with trash, garbage, and sewage.

There were, as yet, no marble buildings or temples and no theaters, most structures being built of wood and sun-baked mud brick. The overwhelming majority of Romans lived in cramped and poorly built tenements of several stories that were liable to frequent and disastrous collapses, floods, and fires. They had no running water or heat; in cold weather people wore overcoats indoors and out, and went to bed fully clothed. The few windows in the buildings were either open or shuttered; window glass was not invented until the next century. There were no fireplaces or chimneys, and the only baths, toilets, and sources of water were public ones.[9]

Perhaps the most significant fact about the Roman capital was that fully a third of its inhabitants were enslaved to others, and another third, the *libertini*, were former slaves. Although Romans had always been slaveholders, the population of slaves had been relatively modest until the end of the third century BCE, when large numbers of captives taken in the Second Punic War were brought to Rome and sold into slavery. During the next century, the wars in Macedonia created hundreds of thousands of new slaves, and Caesar's war in Gaul would add a million more. Slaves had no rights of any kind and could not even marry; they were considered property and were bought, sold, and rented just like any other possession.

Because of the loss of so many able-bodied men to the army, slaves were readily absorbed by the Roman economy in a wide variety of occupations. Although many were educated, and practiced as architects, doctors, and teachers, the great majority were employed at the lowest level of labor in mines, factories, and households, and in all types of agriculture. Slaves were often freed at their owner's death or because he could no longer afford to feed and house them. The freedman benefited from a unique Roman practice, which was to assimilate its *libertini* and grant them automatic Roman citizenship on manumission. By Caesar's day a large proportion of the citizenry, including many in the upper classes, had slaves among their ancestors.

The principal nourishment of all but the wealthy was a thick soup or porridge of wheat or millet, and a coarse bread made from unhusked wheat. The balance of the diet was composed of turnips and a few other vegetables, usually cooked in fat, and, now and then, olives, beans, figs, or cheese. The meals of an ordinary person were occasionally supplemented by a piece of pork or by fish caught no more than a day's travel away. In these circumstances, the life expectancy of a typical Roman baby was no more than thirty years, and only a small minority lived beyond fifty.

In the previous century the government had begun selling unmilled grain to the public at a nominal price, but only to citizens: that is, free males over fifteen living in Rome. There being no means test, the law was wildly popular, and by midcentury more than a third of the population was receiving free grain. In addition, the Roman citizen, whether wealthy or poor, paid no direct taxes of any kind. After the victory at Pydna in 168, which yielded enormous booty, even the modest tax that had been levied on Roman property owners in emergencies was abolished.

But even with the abundant wealth that poured into the country in the late Republic, the Senate made the crucial mistake of refusing to finance a standing army, or to provide for veterans discharged after a campaign or retired after long service. About the time of Caesar's birth, soldiers began to look to their own commanders for their rewards and postwar security. The result of this arrangement was that upon induction, a soldier swore an oath of allegiance to his general—more often than not a millionaire soldier-politician—rather than to the Roman government. This became the common practice whenever a new legion was needed, a practice that tended to cede military power to individual generals. During the last century before Christ, victorious generals, especially those returning from foreign wars, were tempted to use their armies to bargain for triumphs and Consulships, or even to stage a military coup. The Republic survived at least three such coups during Caesar's youth, and the next one would bring a civil war that would threaten its method of government, and change the course of Roman history.

III

Pompey and Cicero Conquer Rome

At the time of Caesar's arrival in 81, Ephesus was an important religious and commercial center and the chief city of the province of Asia. It was the site of the gigantic Temple of Artemis, one of the seven wonders of the ancient world, and even then a destination of tourists. Today it is the ruins of the temple and of the ancient city that are the tourist attractions. Its modern descendant, the town of Selçuk, has survived nearby, but its harbor has silted over and the site is now nearly two miles inland.

Marcus Thermus, even though he had been appointed Governor of Asia by Sulla, welcomed Caesar as the son of the Governor of less than a decade before. At this time the Roman army was still mopping up after the peace that Sulla had concluded with Mithradates four years earlier. Several cities in the area that had sided with the King had refused to surrender, the last being the Greek city of Mytilene on the island of Lesbos. The siege of Mytilene required a large number of warships, the best source for which was the navy of King Nicomedes IV of Bithynia, a small country on the Black Sea in northwestern Anatolia. His capital was Nicomedia, modern Izmit, on the Propontis, today the Sea of Marmara, about three hundred miles north of Mytilene. Nicomedes owed Rome a favor, having begged for assistance there a decade before when he was attacked by Mithradates, and having been twice restored to his throne by Roman armies. Caesar's father and Nicomedes had become acquainted when the former was Governor of Asia, and it is likely that the nine- or ten-year-old Caesar had met Nicomedes when the King had traveled to Rome in 90 to make his appeal to the Senate. Thus it was only natural that Marcus Thermus would send the young Caesar to make the deal with Nicomedes.

Caesar's visit to the Bithynian court at Nicomedia gave rise to a piece of scandal that became part of the political rhetoric of his opponents for the rest of his life. The report reached Rome that Caesar had been observed at the court of Nicomedes in the role of royal cupbearer, a function customarily performed by the King's male lovers. Although it was nothing unusual for a Roman aristocrat to have a male lover, the notion of the scion of one of Rome's patrician families in the bed of an Asian King was a salacious tidbit that clung to Caesar all his life. Although he denied any dalliance with Nicomedes, he did his reputation no good by returning to Nicomedia on another matter later in the year.

Whether the story was true or not, Caesar accomplished his mission: the Bithynian fleet was deployed at the successful attack on Mytilene, which fell to the Romans early in 80. Caesar took part in the battle and distinguished himself by saving the life of a fellow soldier. In the way of all militaristic societies, the Romans attached the highest significance to bravery in battle. For his heroic act, Marcus Thermus awarded Caesar the *corona civica*, the civic crown, an important military decoration consisting of a wreath of oak leaves that the recipient was allowed to wear at all public events and celebrations for the rest of his life.

In the meantime, back in Rome, the erratic Sulla, after terrorizing the city for a year, announced that he would give up his office of *dictator* at the end of 81 and be a candidate for Consul for the next year. When he arranged for the murder of his only opponent, he and his colleague Metellus Pius were the easy victors. But this may have been Sulla's last atrocity; he began to relax his grip on governmental affairs and turn his attention to less serious matters. Besides his own two triumphs and that of Pompey at the beginning of the year, he authorized two more to be celebrated before the year was over, both of questionable justification, making an unprecedented five in all for 81.

The last public exhibition of Sulla's year as Consul took place in November when his nephew organized the *ludi Victoriae Sullanae*, Sulla's victory games, to celebrate his success at the Colline Gate two years earlier. To add interest to the games, the promoters conscripted so many performers and athletes from all over Greece that the quadrennial games at Olympia for that year, games that had been staged, by then, for nearly seven hundred years, were reduced to simple footraces.

It was during Sulla's year as Consul that the young Cicero argued his first important case, a defense of one Sextus Roscius against a charge of murdering his wealthy father. The trial was well attended and heavy with political overtones because of the defendant's friendship with several of Rome's noble families, and because the accuser, although only an ex-slave and a Greek, was known as a particular favorite of Sulla's. In his speech *Pro Roscio Amerino*, which has survived in its entirety, Cicero steered a careful course by condemning the Greek as a brazen opportunist trading on his association with a great leader, and by emphasizing the distance between Sulla and the crime. When the jury of Senators acquitted his client, the twenty-six-year-old Cicero was famous overnight.

At the end of 80, Sulla astonished his opponents and supporters alike by refusing a second year as Consul and retiring to private life. During the year, he had taken his fifth wife, and he now retired to his seaside villa at Cumae, today Cuma, just north of the Bay of Naples, giving himself over to hunting, fishing, gossiping with his cronies, and writing his memoirs. But less than two years later his habits caught up with him, and at the age of sixty he suffered a sudden massive oral hemorrhage, followed by delirium and death a few hours later. Modern medical opinion concludes that his liver failed as a result of alcoholism.[1]

The end of Sulla's life did not mean the end of his peculiar flamboyance. He had completed the last of twenty volumes of memoirs, in Greek, just two days before his death, and although they no longer survive, they preserved his version of events for historians for many decades afterward. Some months later, his new wife gave birth to his third child, a daughter, who was given the name Postuma, as was the custom. In the argument over his funeral, his partisans prevailed; his body "was borne through Italy on a golden litter with royal splendor"[2] and then brought to Rome and displayed in the Forum. Enormous crowds, including thousands of Sulla's veterans, followed the trumpeters, dancers, and mimes leading the funeral procession to the Campus Martius; those who were not genuinely grieving pretended to do so for fear of their lives.

In his will, contrary to the custom of the Cornelii, Sulla had ordered that his body be cremated to prevent any possibility that his enemies would do to it what he had done to so many. His tomb bore an epitaph of his own composition, his own succinct description of himself, to the effect that he never neglected to repay the kindness of a friend nor the hurt of an enemy. Among the many friends and bequests appearing in his will, there was one notable omission—the name of Pompey.

With Sulla's death in 78, Caesar welcomed the chance to return to Rome after three years in Asia. Despite the turmoil of the previous decade, in which politicians had lost their heads with every change of government, the lure of Rome was more than that of his birthplace. Elective office was still the surest way to power and wealth, two things for which Caesar had by now developed a craving, and Roman office seekers had to live in or near the capital. Although the Julii Caesares had been politically active for centuries, they were one of the less prominent patrician families. Caesar's great-grandfather, Sextus Julius Caesar, had achieved the rank of *praetor* in 208, during the second of Rome's wars with Carthage, but since then there had been only one Consul in his branch of the family.

Although elective positions were limited to the small number of Romans who met the property requirement, dozens of candidates competed for a limited number of offices, and the first task of the newcomer was to distinguish himself among them. In Caesar's case, both his father and grandfather had borne the same three names as he. In fact, Caesar was such a common name among the Julii that half a dozen of his living relatives called themselves Julius Caesar and were differentiated only by a *praenomen*, such as Lucius, Sextus, or Gaius.

The third name, or *cognomen*, that many prominent Romans bore was originally a private name or nickname based on a distinctive personal characteristic, or on a successful exploit or military campaign. The origin of the *cog-*

nomen Caesar for this branch of the Julii is uncertain. In his *Natural History* Pliny the Elder introduced the mistaken notion that Caesar's birth had been accomplished *a caeso matris utero,* by cutting him from his mother's womb, the belief giving rise to the word "Caesarean" to denote such a surgical procedure. It is faintly possible that an earlier Caesar had been delivered this way, but his mother would have died, as did all women undergoing the procedure until modern times. The stem *caes* is also shared by the Latin words for "bluish gray" (eyes) and for "dark hair," as well as the Punic word for "elephant." The name Caesar is more likely to have been based on *caesaries,* a dark head of hair, and in the first century CE, Verrius Flaccus, a linguist in the Augustan court, asserted that it originated with a Julian ancestor who was born with a shock of dark hair.[3]

The customary method of gaining attention and attracting a popular following was to bring criminal prosecutions or civil suits in the law courts against prominent men. During the late Republic, this practice became especially frequent; more than a quarter of those who became Senators between 80 and 60, for instance, were brought to trial at some time during their careers. Any citizen with the time and money could prosecute anyone else, and an attack on a well-known politician could bring instant notoriety. With this in mind, the twenty-three-year-old Caesar, in the year after his return to the capital, formally charged Gnaeus Dolabella with extortion while he had been Governor of Macedonia in the years 80 to 77.

Such trials were ideal opportunities for a public display of skillful oratory, a talent greatly esteemed and crucial to success in public life. For centuries the Roman government was conducted largely by discussion and debate in mass gatherings, and decisions reached in the Assembly or the Senate were dependent upon convincing oral argument. For this reason, and because oratory had had a historic significance in Greek culture, the art of rhetoric was the centerpiece of the education of upper-class Roman boys.

Aside from the meetings of the Assembly and Senate, civil and criminal trials afforded the best venues for formal public speaking. They provided a kind of political theater, a combination of entertainment and persuasion cloaked in the mantle of justice, in which the orator displayed his talents, and the audience of politicians and idlers, both wealthy and poor, judged his delivery as much as his argument. The spectators at a Roman trial were much more sensitive to the rhythm and cadence of the spoken word than a modern audience, and might applaud the speaker after a well-delivered passage, regardless of its legal merit.

Although in Roman law a death penalty in the late Republic was extremely unusual, a criminal conviction might cost a defendant his office and his property, as well as exile to some remote province. But an acquittal was often a foregone conclusion, the jury having been bribed, or reluctant to convict because of political loyalties. The result was that the oratorical performance of the advocates, for both prosecution and defense, was often of more interest than the outcome of the trial.

Caesar's bold prosecution of Dolabella, an ex-Consul, was one of the notable trials of 77, not only because it was the debut of a young patrician in the courts, but also because Dolabella had been one of Sulla's chief henchmen during the terror of just four years earlier. More than thirty years later, Cicero recalled in his essay "On Oratory" that he was in the crowd of spectators who heard Caesar debate against two of the leading defense counsels of the day. One was Aurelius Cotta, his mother Aurelia's cousin, a skilled and experienced advocate, and the man who had intervened on his behalf with Sulla four years before. The other was Quintus Hortensius, Rome's greatest orator until Cicero displaced him.

During the trial Dolabella mocked Caesar for his alleged seduction by King Nicomedes, sneering that he was "the Queen's rival, the inner partner of the royal bed."[4] The combined firepower of Caesar's two opponents and Dolabella's deep purse convinced the jury to acquit, and Caesar lost his first case. But he was more successful the next year with a civil suit against Gaius Antonius, one of Sulla's generals and uncle of Mark Antony, for his brazen looting in Greece eight years earlier. Although Caesar convinced the jury to convict, Antonius appealed to a tribune of the people, who vetoed the verdict.

It was in these early trials that Caesar essentially launched his public career, testing his ability to debate in public and to sway his listeners to his opinion. He quickly gained a popular following and then a reputation as a superb orator. According to his biographer Suetonius, he delivered his speeches in a high-pitched voice accompanied by impassioned gestures. This was no more than the customary style of Roman oratory at the time; speakers commonly indulged in body movements of all kinds and extravagant displays of emotion. In one of his later essays, Cicero admits that he once concluded his client's defense with a baby in his arms.

There is no record of Caesar's activities during the next three years, but it is likely that he continued to refine his oratorical style in the courts. Well before his later eminence, his *eloquentia* earned him the reputation of the Roman orator second only to Cicero, who himself acknowledged that he knew no more eloquent speaker than Caesar, and that "of all our orators he is the purest user of the Latin tongue."[5] Caesar took the trouble to preserve and publish his speeches, an early sign of his inclination to use his literary work for political purposes. Although none of his speeches survives, if his oratory may be likened to his narrative, his arguments would have been logical and economical, and his use of words limited to the common and ordinary. He avoided the florid "Asiatic" style then popular, and cultivated the "Attic," a sparer and simpler speech that he once referred to as "the plain style of a soldier."[6]

In the earliest surviving description of Caesar we are told that he was "tall, fair, and well-built, with a rather broad face and keen dark-brown eyes."[7] Although this was written one hundred and seventy years after his death, there were numerous eyewitness accounts on which to base it. Coin portraits and busts made while he was alive reveal a broad head, balding at the front, and a face narrowing to the chin. The rigorous physical education in the Greek tradition that was customary among aristocratic Roman boys, along with Caesar's well-known abstemious habits, would have kept him fit even if he had chosen a sedentary life. By all accounts, the military life that he would lead for the better part of his career more closely resembled that of an ordinary soldier than that of a self-indulgent general.

During the same year in which Caesar was prosecuting Dolabella, the political scene in Rome was again thrown into confusion, and another opportunity arose for Pompey to demonstrate his military skills. The death of Sulla had emboldened the Marians and their supporters to return from abroad or emerge from their hiding places to reclaim their land, homes, and positions in government. When Marian leaders recruited two armies in the north, the senate commissioned Pompey to deal with one of them. He promptly crushed it and accepted the surrender of its commander, the plebeian nobleman Marcus Junius Brutus, scion of one of Rome's most notable families, and husband of Servilia, who would later become Caesar's mistress. The day after notifying the Senate that he had Brutus in custody, Pompey ordered him executed, thus earning the enduring hatred of both Servilia and her eight-year-old son Marcus Brutus *filius*. The boy, whose name would forever be linked with Caesar's, was brought up by one of the notable politicians of the late Republic, Marcus Porcius Cato, Servilia's half-brother and a fervent opponent of both Caesar and Pompey. For the rest of his short life, Brutus would be embroiled in the conflict that swirled around his mentor-uncle, his mother's lover, and his father's executioner.

Pompey's success against the Marians in Italy led the Senate to engage him to hunt down the surviving Marians who had fled to Spain and joined the forces of Quintus Sertorius, a brilliant outlaw general who had frustrated every attempt to defeat him. The reputation of Sertorius was such that neither of the sitting Consuls could be persuaded to lead an army against him, but Pompey was eager for further military employment. Not yet forty, he had been on the battlefield for most of the previous twenty years, and had never been bested. His notorious habit of murdering the generals he defeated would later earn him the nickname *adulescentulus carnifex*, the teenaged executioner.

Toward the end of 77 he set out for Spain over the Cottian Alps *pro consule*, with Consular authority, and with an army of more than forty thousand men. He is said to have opened a new passage through the Alps, one that Caesar was to use when he led an army into Gaul nearly twenty years later. In Further Gaul, Pompey's progress was delayed for several months by rebellious Celtic tribes, and he was forced to winter at Narbo Martius. After arriving in *Hispania Citerior*, Nearer Spain, in the spring of 76, Pompey and his colleague Metellus Pius began maneuvering back and forth in the eastern half of the province against Sertorius and his generals. For the better part of the next three years, half a dozen armies assailed each other with every tactic of ancient warfare—sieges, blockades, ambushes, fake retreats, and even a variation of the Trojan Horse. But despite several pitched battles, and at least one massacre, neither side could decisively defeat the other. It was dissension in Sertorius' army and his own arrogance that finally produced an outcome.

In the late summer of 73, a group of Sertorius' officers, led by Marcus Perperna, his jealous second-in-command, lured him to a bibulous dinner party where they distracted his bodyguards, and then murdered him. Perperna took charge of the dwindling Marian forces, but had little of his general's tactical brilliance, and just as much trouble keeping the army together. It took Pompey only a few months to ambush and defeat him. He then sent his horsemen to chase down the fleeing Perperna, who had run from the same Pompey in Sicily nine years before. Dragged to Pompey's tent, the captured general attempted to bargain for his life by offering to hand over secret letters of support that Sertorius had received from leading men in Rome. Pompey, as was his custom, had him put to death immediately; but also had the prudence to burn the letters before anyone could read them, thus averting a new episode of the twenty-year quarrel between Marius and Sulla.

Pompey spent the next twelve months mopping up the remaining rebel forces throughout the province and reorganizing the local government. Then, late in 72, the Senate sent him an urgent summons to return to Italy immediately to help against the slave revolt led by Spartacus. With another figurative scalp at his belt, Pompey and his legions marched back to Rome early the next year on yet another military mission.

In the same year that Pompey was dispatched to Spain, Cicero returned to the capital after a two-year tour of Greece and Asia. He had interrupted his successful practice as an advocate early in 79 to seek further training in oratory at Athens, and to study with teachers of rhetoric in Asia and the Greek city of Rhodes. His purpose was to strengthen his voice and lungs and to rid himself of what he called an "excessive exuberance" that marked his language and delivery.

While in Athens, Cicero visited, and probably boarded with, his boyhood friend Titus Pomponius, a wealthy landowner with literary interests who had taken up residence there several years before, and had given himself an appropriate *cognomen*—Atticus (belonging to Attica or Athens). A few years later Cicero and Atticus would begin the most famous exchange of letters in classical times, a correspondence that extended over the last twenty-five turbulent years of the Roman Republic. Unfortunately, only one side of it survives, Atticus having preserved and later published over four hundred of Cicero's letters to him, a priceless record of Cicero's gossip and opinions about everyone and everything that affected him.

On reaching the age of thirty in the year after his return, Cicero was eligible to run for the lowest public office, that of *quaestor*, twenty of whom were now elected each year to perform administrative work as judges or assistants to provincial Governors. As a member of a plebeian family without a Consul or even a Senator in its ancestry, he campaigned with a disadvantage, but his skill as an orator and his careful cultivation of *amici* were sufficient to win the office, the first step on the traditional ladder to the Consulship. He had also made, just before his trip to the East, an advantageous marriage to one Terentia, who was not only a member of a wealthy and distinguished *gens* (and herself owned substantial investment property), but also had a half-sister of patrician status.

As one of the *quaestores* for the year 75, Cicero was posted to the city of Lilybaeum, modern Marsala, on the west coast of Sicily, the oldest of the Roman provinces. The island was a major supplier of wheat and other foodstuffs to the mainland, and his job was to insure their prompt and efficient shipment. He kept in practice by defending clients at the Governor's court in Syracuse, modern Siracusa, at that time the largest city in Europe after Rome. It was in the cemetery at Syracuse, a Greek colony as old as Rome itself, that Cicero, on one of his idle days, uncovered the overgrown and forgotten tombstone of Archimedes, the Greek inventor and mathematician who had lived there one hundred and forty years earlier.

Cicero's election as *quaestor* entitled him to lifetime membership in the Senate, the elite body of six hundred of Rome's wealthiest and most influential men that was the most important institution in the Roman government. Although the law provided that only the Assembly could enact legislation, the Senate almost always decided what measures the Assembly could consider. It also nominated all candidates for public office, and controlled the treasury, the army, and the conduct of foreign affairs. Aside from the small patrician class, the Senate was the most prestigious group in the Roman world. Cicero was not only the first man in his family to attain Senatorial rank, he was the first *novus homo*, the first "new man," to enter the Senate from outside the nobility for more than a generation. But it would be several years before he would address his fellow members; Senators were called upon to speak only in the strict order of seniority.

Although there is no direct evidence for the date, it is likely that it was in 76, the year of Cicero's campaign for *quaestor*, that Caesar's wife Cornelia gave birth to a daughter who was given the name Julia, the same as given to all women in the *gens* Julia.[8] Like many other aristocratic Roman women, Julia would be drawn, while still a teenager, into her father's political world and become a pawn, albeit a willing one, in one of Rome's historic power struggles.

The next year the twenty-five-year-old Caesar made his second trip to the East, this time to study oratory at Rhodes under Apollonius Molon, Cicero's instructor, and reputedly the finest living practitioner of the art. But his winter crossing of the Aegean Sea was ended abruptly by Cilician pirates, who boarded his ship and captured him near the island of Pharmacusa, only a day's sail from his destination. From the earliest days of maritime travel, fleets of pirates had preyed on ships throughout the Mediterranean and even on coastal towns, which they would attack and plunder, and then kidnap the inhabitants and sell them into slavery. In the decades of Caesar's youth, pirate fleets based in strongholds along the rugged coast of Cilicia in southern Anatolia would routinely intercept merchant ships that were unequipped to defend themselves. After surrounding and then boarding a vessel, they would seize the cargo, the crew, the passengers, and even the ship itself and sell all their plunder wherever they could find a buyer. When they captured someone from a wealthy family, they would hold him or her for ransom, and this was the case with Caesar.

But Caesar was unlike any other captive. Indulging in the hubris that he would display all his life, he ridiculed their ransom demand of twenty talents, about a thousand pounds of silver, as too small, and offered to pay fifty, an enormous sum, enough to pay the wages of a thousand men for a year. Caesar sent all but three of his retinue to the mainland, where they were able to borrow the ransom in nearby cities after accusing the residents of negligent patrolling of their coastal waters. During his nearly forty days in captivity, Caesar taunted the pirates with the promise that he would return one day and have them crucified. Once his ransom was paid and he was released, he promptly set about doing that.

In the same cities that had supplied his ransom, Caesar commandeered a small fleet, led it back to Pharmacusa, and brought the pirates to battle, capturing several ships and their crews. He transported his prisoners to the Roman prison at Pergamon, on the mainland, and then sought out the provincial Governor for permission to execute them. Pirates were so despised that no method of punishment was considered too severe. But when the Governor suggested that they be sold as slaves instead, Caesar hurried back to Pergamon and, before anyone could stop him, had the pirates crucified. In what was later described as a humane gesture, Caesar ordered their throats cut beforehand.

At the end of this episode, Caesar finally proceeded to Rhodes and to the rhetorical studies that had brought him to Asia. But before long his energetic temperament led him to pursue another adventure on the mainland, this time to resist another encroachment into Roman Asia by troops of King Mithradates. In another display of audacity and self-confidence, Caesar, perhaps relying on his standing as a holder of the *corona civica*, recruited a force of volunteers and helped turn back the invading army.

After less than two years in the East, Caesar received word from Rome in 73 that his mother's cousin, Gaius Aurelius Cotta, had once again intervened to change his fortune, this time involuntarily. After serving a year as Consul, Cotta had been assigned the Governorship of Nearer Gaul by the Senate, but soon after taking his post had suddenly died. Even while holding these offices he was also one of the sixteen members of the *collegium pontificum*, the most important college of priests in the Roman religious hierarchy. Such dual, or even triple, responsibilities were not uncommon. The priests themselves selected a successor to Cotta, and their surprise choice for this prestigious lifetime post was the twenty-six-year-old Julius Caesar. Although he was popular in Rome and had distinguished himself in the East, it is likely that he owed this benefaction to the efforts of his mother Aurelia. Caesar may also have owed a debt to his mistress Servilia, who was a wealthy and powerful woman in her own right, and who probably lobbied her cousin, a member of the *collegium*, on Caesar's behalf.

By now Caesar had revealed the qualities that would mark his political success: a personal charm and geniality with anyone in his company, and a generous spirit that indulged the needs and whims of others, men and women alike. More than this, he was an entertainer on a lavish scale and a spender whose excesses ran up enormous debts. His affairs with women are described by Suetonius as "numerous and extravagant," and his name was linked more than once with the wives of some of his closest associates. This playboy style led his opponents to consider him no threat as a politician. But they failed to see that it concealed an utter practicality and a clear vision of the path to power.

Partly because of his affinity with his uncle Marius and Marian causes, Caesar chose to align himself with the political group known as *populares*, or "men of the people." This group was loosely identified with reform, with change, and with appeal to the needs of ordinary voters. It had a history of conflict with the Senatorial oligarchy and was more likely to bring its issues directly to the Assembly. The opposition was the traditionalist *optimates*, "the best men," who championed the aristocracy and resisted any diffusion of the Senate's power. Power was what interested Caesar, and he saw a faster way to achieve it by a direct appeal to the voters rather than by cultivating the Senatorial establishment. Neither group had a stronger claim to integrity than the other, nor was either organized in the way of a modern political party. Personal, familial, and financial alliances nearly always took preference over political philosophy.

Caesar returned to Rome in 73 to take up his priesthood, but it was not long before he found himself in another military role. In the middle of July word reached the capital that several dozen gladiators had broken out of the training barracks where they were confined at Capua, now called Santa Maria Capua Vetere, some eighty miles south of Rome. For nearly two hundred years the Romans had entertained themselves by staging displays of armed combat, usually to the death, among men picked for the task from a pool of foreign captives, slaves, and those condemned to death. Although their name derives from *gladius*, the word for sword, gladiators were given different weapons for different occasions, or none at all in some cases, and their opponents might be other gladiators, convicted criminals, or even wild animals.

The leader of the escapees was Spartacus, a mercenary soldier from Thrace who had turned to crime, been captured, and then held prisoner in a gladiator training school. The episode turned into a full-scale revolt when Spartacus and his band overcame the soldiers sent to pursue them, armed themselves with their weapons, and fled to the heights of Mount Vesuvius. Tens of thousands of slaves, fugitives, and other supporters joined them and began looting country houses and villages, and then taking control of isolated towns. Over the next two years the Senate sent one army after another against Spartacus, and he was pursued all over southern, and then northern, Italy, but always managed to escape.

Late in 72 the wealthy patrician Marcus Crassus offered to supply six legions at his own expense to capture Spartacus if the Senate would put him in charge of the war. The Senate agreed with alacrity, and Crassus recruited the legions, one of which was probably commanded by Julius Caesar, who had been elected to the post of military tribune for the year 71. Within six months Crassus' private army trapped and killed Spartacus in the mountains behind Brundisium. The remnants of the rebel army fled northward toward Rome just as Pompey and his army, recalled by the Senate and sent against Spartacus, were hurrying south. When Pompey's troops set upon the fugitives and massacred them, the rebellion evaporated.

Even though Crassus flaunted his own accomplishment by crucifying six thousand rebels along the Appian Way, Pompey claimed that it was he who had won the war, and led his victorious army into a jubilant Rome. For his success in Spain, Pompey was rewarded at the end of the year with his second triumph; Crassus had to be satisfied with a smaller celebration, an *ovatio*, in which he walked in a modest parade wearing a laurel wreath, and then sacrificed a sheep in the Temple of Jupiter instead of an ox. With the war in Spain and the revolt of the gladiators concluded, a grateful Senate passed a special decree exempting the thirty-six-year-old Pompey from the age and experience requirements for the Consulship; the Assembly responded by electing him and Crassus Consuls for 70.

During the Consulship of Pompey and Crassus in 70, the Assembly elevated Caesar to the office of *quaestor*, and to the Senate, in which his father and grandfather had also served, as had numerous other ancestors. He was assigned to carry out judicial responsibilities for the Governor of Hispania Ulterior, Further Spain, the larger portion of the Iberian Peninsula. Sometime during 69, Caesar's year as *quaestor*, Cornelia, not yet thirty and Caesar's wife for more than fifteen years, suddenly died. Other than the stories of Caesar's womanizing, little is known of their marriage, but Cornelia was the woman for whom Caesar had defied Sulla, and it is likely that the marriage was based on genuine affection. Although it was not the custom at funerals of young women, Caesar took the opportunity to deliver a moving tribute to the bride of his adolescence. The public reaction was one of widespread approval and sympathy.

But Caesar was not one to remain long without a wife. When he returned to Rome in 67, he married Pompeia, a woman with both a notable lineage (she was daughter of a Consul and granddaughter of Sulla) and a substantial dowry. Caesar's social standing needed no enhancement, but the marriage created a strategic alliance with a family in the Sullan faction, and restored his dwindling wealth. Nearly all marriages among the Roman upper class (including all of Caesar's), especially those involving adolescents, were essentially compacts between families for social, political, or financial advantage. Although Pompeia was not related to Pompey, her brother was one of his supporters, and the marriage brought Caesar into a closer connection with the most popular man in Rome.

Pompey's popularity, however, was stronger among the ordinary citizens than with the *optimate* Senators. As Consul in 70 he had helped to restore some political power to the Assembly at the expense of the Senatorial oligarchy. This became an issue in the early 60s when the problem of pirate attacks on ships and on coastal areas assumed enormous proportions. Large areas of the Mediterranean had become unsafe for ordinary travelers and merchants, and the loss of so many of the enormous freighters carrying grain from Africa, Sicily, and Sardinia to Rome had begun to affect the capital's food supply. Pirates attacked and pillaged the coasts of Italy itself, and in 68 sailed their ships into the mouth of the Tiber, burned the government's fleet, and plundered the port of Ostia.

Beginning nearly forty years before, the Senate had several times conferred special authority on one of its generals to pursue and eradicate the pirates, but none had been successful. The obvious choice for the next attempt was Pompey, but the *optimates* in control of the Senate were unhappy with him and suspicious of his ambitions, and thus reluctant to confer on him any further authority. When the Senate refused, the Assembly passed a special law giving Pompey an unprecedented command over the entire Mediterranean, and up to fifty miles inland along its coasts. To dispose of the pirates, he was given five hundred ships, fifteen legionary commanders, and as large an army as he wanted.

The people's confidence in Pompey was not misplaced and, on the mere announcement of his appointment, prices of imported goods fell in the Roman markets. Starting in the early spring of 67, he sent his ships into the western Mediterranean and in less than six weeks cleared it of pirates and placed garrisons in each port to protect it. Then, taking his fleets into the Aegean Sea, he needed only two more months to destroy or seize hundreds of pirate ships and then wipe out the pirate settlements along the coasts of Anatolia. Instead of crucifying his captives or selling them into slavery, something he was urged to do, he resettled them in deserted towns in various places. One of these, on the southern coast of modern Turkey, he renamed Pompeiopolis, only one of dozens of places to which he gave his own name over a long career of conquest.

In the next year, one of Pompey's supporters in the Assembly proposed that yet another special command be given him—the responsibility for Rome's third war with Mithradates Eupator, who had been harassing the Romans in Anatolia for more than twenty years. It was on this occasion that Cicero made his first political speech to the Assembly, a memorable and enthusiastic statement of support for Pompey. Although Pompey was popular with the Roman people, and obviously the best man for the job, Cicero had his own motive for taking the initiative. He had just been elected a *praetor*, and he knew that when

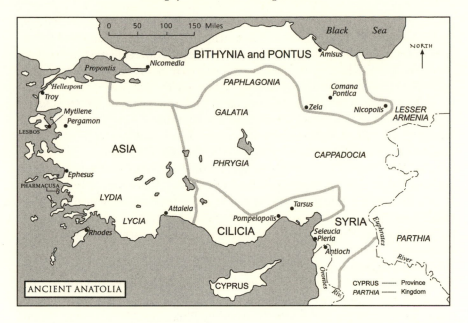

ANCIENT ANATOLIA

he stood for the Consulship in two years, the support of Pompey would be crucial. Cicero's speech, which was probably called "On the Command of Gnaeus Pompeius," was a classic of Roman oratory that turned the vote in Pompey's favor. It was the beginning of a twenty-year political alliance between the two men, one that Cicero was tempted to abandon on more than one occasion.

Pompey set about his task in his usual vigorous and methodical way. After establishing his headquarters in Cilicia, he pursued Mithradates across Cappadocia, the area of east-central Turkey, with an army of forty to fifty thousand infantry and three thousand cavalry. After staging an ambush that shocked the Pontic army, he pursued it northward into Pontus, and then administered a decisive defeat by an unusual surprise attack at night. At the site of the battle, Pompey ordered a new city built—Nicopolis (City of Victory)—and then sent a detachment of troops in pursuit of Mithradates, who had fled around the east end of the Black Sea and over the Caucasus Mountains to his stronghold in the Crimea.

From here Pompey turned to the east along the Anatolian Plateau and took his army up the Euphrates, crossing it near its source in what is now Turkish Armenia. As he approached the Armenian capital at Artaxata, today's Artashat at the foot of Mount Ararat, an area that no Roman army had ever penetrated, the seventy-three-year-old Armenian King Tigranes surrendered himself and his entire kingdom. From there Pompey turned north and for more than a year pursued and defeated tribes and kingdoms in the southern Caucasus who also had never seen a Roman army.

37

As Pompey claimed for Rome one area after another, he set up an administrative structure throughout Asia Minor that supplied enormous sums for the
Roman treasury, and proved durable for decades to come. His customary practice was to allow the reigning King or warlord to remain in power, provided he
promised to serve and defend Rome, and to pay for the privilege.

After spending the winter at the ancient port of Amisus, today Samsun, on
the Black Sea coast, Pompey took his army due south across Anatolia in the
early summer of 64 to Antioch, modern Antakya, in southeastern Turkey, no
doubt mindful that he was marching in the footsteps of his personal idol, Alexander the Great. There he easily forced the surrender of Antiochus XIII,
the last King of the Seleucids, the dynasty that had, for two hundred and fifty
years, ruled the greatest of the empires that emerged after the death of Alexander the Great. On the sole authority of Pompey and his army, the remains
of the Seleucid Empire were reincarnated as the twelfth Roman province,
Syria.

In 63 Pompey entered Damascus, which one of his generals had captured
already, and then proceeded southward into the Jordan Valley and Judaea. The
Romans called this area Palestina, their word for Philistia, the region to the
southwest of Judaea that was the home of the Philistines. While he was camped
at Jericho, couriers brought the news that King Mithradates, when faced with
a rebellion in the Crimea led by his own son Pharnaces, had killed his wives and
daughters, and then himself, thus ending one of the more spectacular and turbulent careers in ancient times. With the death of Rome's most stubborn enemy, Pompey achieved the ostensible objective of the entire campaign, and his
men cheered him as he stood on a makeshift platform to announce the news.
When word reached Rome of the final demise of the Pontic king, the Senate,
on the proposal of the new Consul, Marcus Cicero, declared a ten-day *supplicatio*, or thanksgiving.

Eager to establish a buffer to protect the new province, Pompey called on
King Aristobulus to surrender Hierosolyma, the ancient name for Jerusalem,
the capital of his small Judaean kingdom. Its defenders were split into two factions; one group capitulated, but the other refused and took refuge in the
Temple, where they made a stand behind its walls. Working under a continual
barrage of missiles from the defenders, Pompey's engineers began building
siege towers and filling in the ravine at the northern edge of the Temple. Although Pompey found to his surprise that his men could work unmolested
every seventh day while the Jews observed their Sabbath, it was a full three
months before the Romans, using a battering ram acquired from the coastal
city of Tyre, broke into the sacred Temple and slaughtered some twelve thousand defenders.

Although Pompey, unlike any other Roman general, left the Temple trea-
sures and gold intact, his destruction of Hierosolyma and desecration of its
Temple caused him to be vilified in contemporary Hebrew literature. In a
group of poems titled *Psalms of Solomon* that is dated to the last half of the cen-

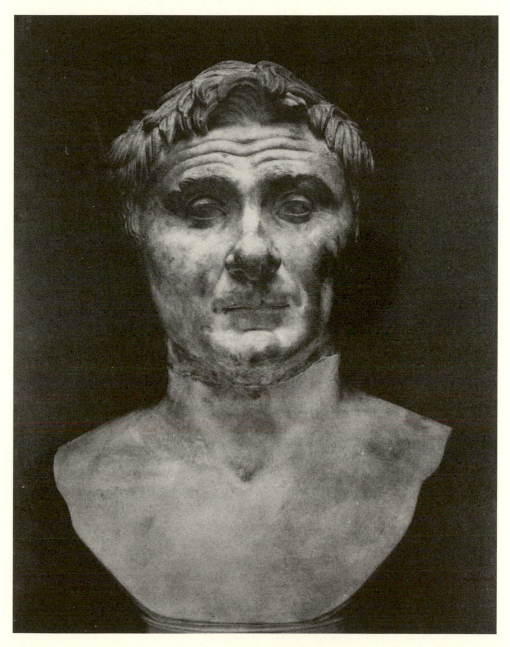

This imperial-age marble copy of an earlier work is thought to be an accurate likeness of Pompey in his last years. (Ny Carlsberg Glyptotek, Copenhagen, Denmark. Foto Marburg/Art Resource, NY.)

tury before Christ, the unknown poet, in an obvious reference to Pompey, begins a psalm about the loss of Hierosolyma with the words "Arrogantly the sinner broke down the strong walls with a battering ram."[9] Pompey's occupation of Hierosolyma marked the beginning of the long and contentious Roman control of the city, which lasted until CE 638, when it was captured by Arabs.

Pompey returned to Amisus on the Black Sea, where Pharnaces supplied him with the body of his father Mithradates. According to Plutarch, he refused to look at it and ordered it buried with those of the previous Pontic kings. From there he began a leisurely nine-month journey toward Italy with considerable pomp and ceremony, taking time to visit the site of ancient Troy, a favorite destination for traveling Romans, the surrounding settlement having been devastated in the recent war for at least the seventh time. At Athens and Rhodes he made large donations for civic restoration and was hailed all along his route as a second Alexander. After spending a few days at Mytilene on Lesbos, he declared the Greek city free of any control from Rome, and then attended a contest of poets whose sole theme was the greatness of his exploits. The city named a month in his honor, and other cities stamped his portrait on coins, revised their calendars to reflect a new Pompeian era, and erected statues to him as savior of the world.

During his four-year campaign he had conquered all of Anatolia and much of the Near Eastern littoral, adding or enlarging three provinces and surrounding them with a ring of client kingdoms, all of whom paid tribute to Rome. According to Plutarch, he had captured nearly nine hundred cities and founded thirty-nine new ones. The immediate spoils from the war amounted to more than twenty-four thousand talents, a stupendous sum, nearly two-thirds of which he distributed among his troops, each legionary receiving a bonus of more than thirteen years' pay, and centurions proportionately more. After deducting enough to make each of his officers a wealthy man, and himself the richest man in Rome, Pompey brought fifty million *denarii*, the equivalent of two hundred and twenty-three tons of silver, back to Italy for deposit in the treasury.

When he landed at Brundisium with his entire army in December 62, it seemed that Pompey had everything any Roman could want, including the widespread adulation of the Roman people. There were those who were suspicious that he would lead his army to the capital and establish his own dictatorship, as his mentor Sulla had, twenty years before. But to everyone's relief, Pompey disbanded his legions shortly after landing and chose to use the normal channels in the Senate to obtain grants of land for his soldiers, and ratification of his Eastern arrangements.

But despite his great and good fortune, Pompey returned from the East with a troubling personal problem. For a long time he had discounted rumors of the infidelities of Mucia, his wife of twenty years and mother of his three children. But when he returned to Italy after a four-year absence, he became convinced that they were true, and sent her notification of his intent to divorce her. Marriage in the Roman world was a private act requiring the sanction of no public authority. Thus Pompey effected his divorce simply by announcing it and then sending Mucia and her dowry back to her family. Although he never made his reasons public and made no accusations, several sources identify her lover as Julius Caesar. Suetonius later wrote that Pompey had, in the way that many Roman aristocrats likened themselves to the ancient Greeks, despairingly called Caesar his Aegisthus, the legendary seducer of the wife of Agamemnon while he was besieging Troy. Ironically, Caesar had, in the same month, divorced his own wife Pompeia for alleged infidelity after a young aristocrat, Publius Clodius, was found in their home disguised as a woman during the all-female celebration of the goddess Bona Dea, patroness of chastity. It was on this occasion that Caesar made the notorious remark that his wife must be "above suspicion."

During the subsequent trial of Clodius for sacrilege, Cicero testified for the prosecution and refuted the defendant's claim that he had been out of town on the night in question. When Clodius was acquitted by a jury that had probably been bribed, Cicero took it as a personal affront and taunted him in the Senate about the bribery. The hotheaded Clodius later proved to be one of the most dangerous enemies that Cicero ever made.

Meanwhile Pompey returned to the vicinity of Rome, where he busied himself with plans for the construction of a gigantic theater-temple and pavilion on the Campus Martius, patterned after one he had seen in Mytilene. What else occupied him during the next nine months were preparations for his third triumph, just twenty years after his first. But he refrained from entering the capital because of a law that required a *triumphator* to remain outside the *pomerium*, the city boundary, and enter the city only on the day of his ceremonial parade. At the end of September 61, on his forty-fifth birthday, he celebrated a two-day extravaganza more spectacular than any ever witnessed in Rome. Walking in the usual parade of notables, soldiers, musicians, and dancers were hundreds of captives from the fourteen nations he had subdued, including kings, queens, generals, and tribal chiefs, the wife and son of King Tigranes of Armenia, and five sons and two daughters of Mithradates himself.

Pompey rode in a gem-encrusted chariot, wearing a golden crown, also set with gems. According to one historian, he also wore a cloak that had belonged to Alexander the Great, suggesting that his exploits had now earned him the title of the Roman Alexander. Although his conquests fell short of those of Alexander, he was more admired because he never sought a personal empire or to rule as a monarch. Nor did he aspire to divinity by allowing himself to be declared a god, as Alexander had in Egypt and Arabia. He appeared to desire admiration and affection more than political power. But his undeniable achievements and overwhelming popularity with the public made him the focus for those in the shallow upper stratum of Roman society for whom political power was more important than anything else. Although many of them admired him, their attitude toward him was more likely to be envious, and even hostile. The political struggles in Rome for the next several years would take place between those who opposed him and those who used him.

IV
The Road to Gaul and Back

During the second year of Pompey's extended campaign in the East, Caesar advanced to the next level of political power by winning the office of *curule ae-dile*, an official responsible for, among other things, organizing the public games held on religious holidays. He made the most of this by staging, partially at his own expense, the most lavish and elaborate displays ever seen in the city, including wild-beast hunts and gladiator fights. When he brought in three hundred and twenty pairs of gladiators, all with armor and weapons of glittering silver, the Senate became so alarmed that it hurriedly made a rule limiting the number of armed men that anyone might bring to Rome. With this direct appeal to public favor, Caesar gained the influence and popularity to compete in 63 for the recently vacated position of *pontifex maximus*, the chief priest of the Republic. After an expensive campaign, he defeated two other candidates of far greater seniority by spending freely on votes and by invoking his patrician lineage—unbroken from the time of his supposed ancestor Iulus, reputed son of the Trojan Aeneas, and founder of the Julian house.

In the prestigious and lifetime position of *pontifex maximus*, Caesar would exercise control over the entire Roman state religion and decide important questions of sacred law. (The Latin title has been retained into modern times by the Bishop of Rome, the Catholic Pope.) But the duties were light enough that they did not interfere with any other activity the incumbent might undertake, and the office carried with it an official residence, the *domus publica*, situated just beyond the southeast edge of the Forum adjacent to the *regia*, the home of the ancient Roman kings. Although Caesar was notorious for his lack of any religious beliefs, he cultivated a public conformity with ritual and tradition and remained in the post (and when in Rome lived in the *domus publica*) for the rest of his life.

Meanwhile, in 64 Cicero reached the age of forty-two, the minimum required to compete for the Consulship. His successful campaign made him the first Consul without a Senator among his ancestors, the first *novus homo*, in three decades. It was the climax of many years of careful attention to politics, and he was justifiably proud to have won, especially without the direct help of Pompey, who would not return to Rome for two more years. Cicero and Caesar had each spoken in support of Pompey's special commands, and were op-

Cicero was said to have retained his health and vigor into his later years through regular exercise. (Vatican Museums, Vatican State. Alinari/Art Resource, NY.)

posed by the principal advocate of the *optimate* Senators, the young plebeian Marcus Cato, one of the most unusual men in the Senate. A fierce defender of the rule of law and the primacy of the Senate, he was almost unique in his unbending moralism, tending to rigidity, that often left him the single proponent of a given position. Cato's reaction to freewheeling politicians like Caesar was one of stern disapproval, and he fought him on every issue, large and small, for the rest of his life.

Toward the end of Cicero's year as Consul, he was confronted by the case of Lucius Catilina, known in English as Catiline, a patrician Senator and a loser in the Consular elections, who organized a group of discontented noblemen to assassinate Cicero and seize control of the government. Acting on a tip from an informant, Cicero called a meeting of the Senate to expose the plot. When Catiline boldly took his usual place, Cicero burst out against him with the first of the four speeches he called *In Catilinam* (Against Catilina), perhaps the best known of all Roman speeches. They are striking examples of both Cicero's rhetorical power and the violent invective that was common in Roman oratory.

Catiline left the building without a word and fled to the countryside outside Rome, where he had assembled an army of twenty thousand men. A few weeks later, five Senators were caught with incriminating letters, and Cicero brought them to face the Senate. After a few vain denials, all five conspirators confessed, and a debate began over their punishment. Caesar and Cato were the principal adversaries, Caesar arguing for imprisonment and Cato for the death penalty.

In his biography of Cato, Plutarch has preserved a dramatic moment during the debate between these two bitter antagonists. In his call for the death penalty, Cato had insinuated that Caesar was part of the plot, and when a messenger approached Caesar with a note, Cato demanded that he read it out to the Senate. Caesar instead looked at it quickly and then handed it to Cato. In Plutarch's words: "But when Cato read the note, which was a lewd letter from his half-sister Servilia to Caesar, who had debauched her and made her his lover, he threw it to Caesar, saying, 'Take this, you drunkard,' and went back to his speech."[1]

Despite his embarrassment, Cato won the argument and the Senate imposed an unprecedented death penalty and confiscation of property on the conspirators, all Senators and one an ex-Consul. Cicero ordered the executions carried out promptly, and the next day the five men were led to the *carcer*, the prison in the northwest corner of the Forum, and into an underground chamber, the Tullianum, where the public executioners summarily strangled them. The deed had a cathartic effect in the capital; Cicero was accompanied home by a celebrating crowd, and hailed as the savior of his country. Early in the new year the Senate's legions confronted the rebel army and crushed it, Catiline dying in the battle. Cicero was credited with preventing another dictatorship, but his decision to proceed with the executions, so admired at the time, would return to haunt him. One of those he put to death and stripped of all his property was Lentulus Sura, stepfather of the twenty-year-old Mark Antony. Caesar's opposition to the death penalty, and Cicero's insistence on it, were very likely the basis for Antony's later adherence to Caesar and his life-long enmity toward Cicero.

During the year of Cicero's Consulship, Caesar campaigned successfully to win election as one of the Republic's eight *praetores*. After serving during 62 as a judge in Rome, he was sent to govern Further Spain for the next two years. There he carried out a series of military operations against various rebels, pirates, and local warlords. Although he had seen army service in Asia, his tour in Spain was his first chance to command large numbers of men and to direct military operations in an entire province. Besides gaining this valuable experience, he plundered the country of so much booty that he was able to pay off his own debts, share some with his officers, and still deliver a substantial amount to the treasury in Rome.

After regaling the Senate with dispatches describing his conquests in Further Spain, Caesar returned to Rome in June of 60, six months before the end of his term, and petitioned the Senate for a triumph. His growing popularity was such that the Senate approved it, the first for the thirty-nine-year-old Caesar. But he also wanted to stand for the Consulship, and the deadline to declare his candidacy was only a few days away. One law required candidates to appear in Rome to declare themselves, but a potential *triumphator* could enter the city only on the day of his ceremonial parade. Caesar asked the Senate to waive the personal-appearance requirement, which it was inclined to do, but a day-long filibuster by Cato, whose son-in-law was also a Consular candidate, prevented it from acting in time. Faced with the choice between a triumph and a chance to be the next Consul, Caesar did not hesitate to forgo the symbolic for the actual; he entered Rome and announced his campaign.

Caesar immediately saw an opportunity to improve his election chances, and his success as Consul, by making a deal with the popular and influential Pompey. In the months since his return from the East, Pompey had labored to persuade either the Senate or the Assembly to ratify his various treaties and settlements in the East and to make grants of public land to his thousands of veterans. But the *optimate* politicians, led by Cato and Marcus Crassus, were reluctant to add to the luster of his victories, and frustrated all his efforts. Caesar proposed to Pompey that he throw his support to him in the election and that, once Caesar was Consul, they cooperate to push through the legislation they each wanted. Although Pompey may still have borne some resentment toward the seducer of his wife, he saw the merits of a bargain with the shrewd and popular Caesar, and the deal was made. They agreed to secrecy while Caesar sought yet another ally.

Approaching Marcus Crassus, Pompey's longtime rival, Caesar offered him the same arrangement—legislation that would increase the profits of the private tax collection companies in which both he and Caesar had interests, in return for support at the polls. The result of these negotiations was later called the "First Triumvirate," a secret agreement that Pompey and Crassus would support Caesar's candidacy, and that once he became Consul, none of the three would take any political action that did not suit each of the others.[2]

On election day in July of 60, Caesar won more votes than any other candidate and thus became the senior Consul for the next year. He was the first Consul in his branch of the family in one hundred years. But his *optimate* enemies had pooled their resources to elect Cato's son-in-law, Marcus Bibulus, as the other. It appeared that Bibulus, with his veto power, would be able to block any action by his co-Consul, and that the year ahead would be one of wrangling and deadlock between the two factions. But no one was prepared for what Caesar would do once he was in office.

On the first day of his term, January 1, Caesar brought his measure before the Senate to redistribute land to the urban poor and to Pompey's veterans. The *optimate* Senators on whom Caesar called to speak limited themselves to trying to put off the vote. Although they were unable to make any cogent counterarguments, they were unwilling to add to the popularity of either Caesar or Pompey. Cato alone spoke against the bill, and demanded simply that nothing be done and nothing changed. When he refused to stop speaking and threatened to hold the floor with a filibuster until the required adjournment at sunset, Caesar, in a fit of anger, ordered him removed from the Senate and taken to jail. But when most of the Senators left to join him, Caesar was forced to release him.

The hidebound Senate, headed by its Consuls elected by the nobility, had always been the graveyard of reform, and Caesar would not have been surprised that it rejected his popular measures. He now used his Consular authority in an unprecedented way to bypass the Senate and bring his legislation directly to the *concilium plebis*, the Plebeian Assembly, which also had the power to enact legislation. There he scheduled a *plebiscitum*, a direct vote of all citizens except patricians.

When several of the people's tribunes pronounced the *veto* (I forbid) over the bill, which was their legal prerogative, Caesar simply ignored them. When Bibulus attempted his own *veto* of the measure, which was his right by law and tradition, Caesar's henchmen threw dung over his head and physically threatened him. Finally, when both Pompey and Crassus spoke in favor of the measure, the full nature of the Triumvirate was revealed. Despite an outcry against what was called the "three-headed monster," there was sufficient support committed to the three Senators, and the Assembly passed the bill.

The law to benefit Crassus was pushed through with similar tactics, and the manifest strength of the Triumvirate, as well as the threat of violence, cowed the Senate into allowing Caesar to enact the rest of his program. When Bibulus, perhaps encouraged by his strong-willed wife Porcia (Cato's daughter), sought to adjourn the Senate by invoking his authority as co-Consul, Caesar ignored him. By February, Bibulus had virtually abandoned his office and had retired to his home, prompting the opposition to complain that the year's

Consuls were Julius and Caesar. But even Cato felt obliged to vote with the Triumvirate out of fear for his personal safety.[3]

Although modern historians agree that Caesar's measures were reasonable and affordable, and that the opposition was obstinate and inflexible in rejecting them, these tactics left bitter feelings among many influential Senators. Traveling on the Appian Way, Cicero wrote to his friend Atticus, "You say that men are keeping quiet at Rome. I thought as much. Still, they are certainly not in the country. The very fields cannot abide this tyranny."[4] Although Consuls in office were immune from prosecution, Caesar could be brought into court at the end of the year for what were considered treasonous acts. There he would be at the mercy of a possibly hostile judge, as well as a jury subject to either intense political pressure or bribery, or both. Feelings ran so high against him among the *optimates* that conviction, forfeiture of his property, and exile were real possibilities. It was this threat, more than anything else, that colored his course of action over the next ten years.

It was the custom for the Senate to assign each of the Consuls to the Governorship of a province in the year after his Consular term. As a provincial Governor, he remained immune from prosecution as long as he held the office. One of Caesar's agents pushed a measure through the Assembly that allotted Caesar both Illyricum (portions of modern Bosnia, Croatia, and Albania) and Nearer Gaul, and the three legions that accompanied them, not for the customary one or two years, but for five. The effect of this was to give Caesar five years of immunity from prosecution, as well as control of the two provinces closest to Rome, and a substantial army to do with what he pleased. Furious at being bypassed, the *optimate* Senators railed against Pompey and Caesar, calling them the King and Queen of Bithynia, but Caesar's support was sufficient to sustain the measure, and he shouted them down.

The year also saw another round of political marriages that struck even the Romans as beyond the bounds of propriety. As a confirmation of their agreement, Caesar and Pompey arranged for the latter to take Caesar's daughter Julia as his fourth wife, cancelling her imminent marriage to Servilius Caepio, half-brother of Caesar's mistress Servilia.[5] Caepio was consoled with the hand of Pompey's daughter, whose engagement to Faustus Sulla, son of the *dictator*, was also broken. Besides supplying Julia's dowry, Caesar, who had no close male relatives, changed his will to make Pompey his principal heir. In the spirit of things, he then married Calpurnia, thus gaining the allegiance of her father, the wealthy and respected Calpurnius Piso, whom he then helped to win the Consulship for the next year.

Historians have addressed the question of why Caesar did not at this time marry Servilia, his longtime mistress, who had been widowed the year before. Aside from the possibility that she was not interested, the opportunity to make a political alliance with an influential family (and an electable Consul) may have been Caesar's first preference; or it may be that he still hoped to have a son, and the eighteen-year-old Calpurnia was more likely to produce one than the forty-year-old Servilia. Some have speculated that the pearl costing sixty thousand gold pieces that Caesar is said to have given Servilia about this time was meant to soothe her feelings.[6]

As it was, the marriage that made the forty-six-year-old Pompey the son-in-law of the forty-year-old Caesar might not have come about if Pompey's own attempts to create a family alliance with Cato the previous year had not failed. After his divorce of Mucia, Pompey had offered himself and his son Gnaeus as husbands to two of Cato's nieces (Servilia's daughters), hoping to remove Cato's objection to the legislation he wanted. In accordance with the Roman custom, the proposal was made to the ranking male in the family rather than to the two women or their mother. Not wanting to be muzzled in the Senate, and despite the wishes of the two nieces, Cato turned down the deal. Even more frustrating to Cato was the marriage of his own father-in-law, Lucius Marcius Philippus, to Caesar's niece Atia, the recently widowed mother of a four-year-old named Octavius (the future Emperor Augustus), a marriage that effectively removed him from Cato's faction. Cato protested that it was intolerable that the government had become a marriage office where wives and daughters were bartered for provinces and armies.

The last insult came when the Senate was forced to name a new Governor of Further Gaul when the incumbent took ill and died. Pompey and Crassus promoted a resolution in the Senate that Caesar should have this province also, and the threat of another loss in the Assembly induced the Senators to grant him the third province and another legion, but only for one year.

The unprecedented coalition among Caesar, Pompey, and Crassus, as well as Caesar's creative use of the Assembly to bypass the Senate, marked a turning point in Roman politics. Coalitions were not unusual, but none had placed such power in the hands of three men, and none held together, as this one did, for nearly ten years. Cicero's opposition to it cost him the support of Caesar and Pompey and allowed one of his enemies to mount a campaign against him that proved to be the most painful episode of his career.

Near the end of 59, Publius Clodius, who had been waiting to avenge Cicero's slurs, finally succeeded in becoming a tribune of the people, and promptly introduced legislation aimed directly at him. He proposed reviving an old law against putting Roman citizens to death without a trial. Even though four years earlier the senate had voted that the five Catilinarian conspirators suffer the death penalty, Cicero's order for their execution put him in jeopardy of exile if the bill now became law and he were convicted. Since the new Consuls were unfriendly to Cicero, and neither Caesar nor Pompey would speak against the bill, it passed early in March of 58. Cicero chose to depart the country voluntarily rather than endure the humiliation of a trial over his most decisive act as Consul. The next day Clodius pushed through a bill that declared Cicero an outlaw and ordered his property confiscated. Even as his Palatine mansion was set on fire and one of his country estates looted, Cicero fled Rome and then Italy. He traveled as far as Thessalonica, at the eastern edge of

Macedonia, where he took refuge with an old acquaintance from Arpinum, Gnaeus Plancius. Depressed and in poor helath, he would be safe there until there was a change of the political winds.

Meanwhile the first few months of 58 were far easier for Caesar than for Cicero. Despite the insurance of two friendly Consuls taking office in January, Caesar took up his provincial commands by moving to a residence outside the city, thereby guaranteeing his immunity from prosecution, just as his opponents began a futile attempt to indict him for treason. His main objective now was to maintain sufficient support in the capital so that he could not be dislodged from his Governorships and lose his immunity. To pay for this, and to indulge his taste for the trappings of the aristocrat, he needed large amounts of money. Caesar's expensive tastes for costly works of art, jewelry for his women, extravagant homes, and the finest slaves were a constant drain on his income. The Governorship of a province was one customary way to amass wealth, but none of Caesar's provinces held much prospect for substantial booty. Another was to lead a conquering army into a rich country in the way that Pompey had captured the treasure of the Eastern kingdoms. One of Caesar's persistent ambitions was to wrest the mantle of Alexander from the man who called himself Pompeius Magnus, Pompey the Great.

Within three months of taking up his duties in Nearer Gaul, Caesar found the opportunity to accomplish all these objectives. For several hundred years the various tribes of Celts and Germans who controlled the lands to the north of the Romans had been among Rome's most feared enemies. It had been only forty years since Caesar's uncle Marius had defeated tribes of invading Germans who had threatened Rome's first Transalpine province, Further Gaul, and in 61 the Allobroges tribe had mounted a revolt in the same province that had taken Rome a full year to put down. Now a group of Celtic tribes in the area of modern Switzerland, led by the Helvetii (whose name survives in Helvetia, the traditional name of Switzerland), announced their intention to seek more land for their burgeoning population in western Gaul by migrating across the northern neck of the Rhône Valley. Caesar saw a chance to take the popular role of protector of Roman territory by preventing barbarians from crossing Further Gaul.

Setting off early in April of 58 with a troop of cavalry, Caesar reached the Rhône in a week and then hurried up its valley to Lacus Lemannus, modern Lake Geneva, where the Roman garrison was manned by a single legion of less than five thousand men. On arriving, he first burned the bridge across the Rhône leading into the Roman province, and then summoned the Celtic leaders to explain their intentions. When they asked for permission to cross a small portion of Roman territory, he refused, and then fortified the southern bank of the Rhône along a fourteen-mile stretch with ditches and palisades of stakes. When they attempted to ford the river anyway, his legionaries fought them off, and they were eventually forced to take a roundabout route through the Jura Mountains, and then travel across the plain of the Saône River.

Although the Helvetii and their allies, said to number three hundred and sixty thousand, were traveling outside the Roman province, Caesar made a surprise night attack with three legions on the rear of the migrant column as it was crossing the Saône. According to his later report, his legionaries slaughtered fully a quarter of the hapless Celts, and the rest retreated northward into the region of present-day Burgundy.

After a futile peace conference and several weeks of maneuvering across the countryside, the mass of migrating Celts turned and faced Caesar's army, which had now grown to six legions comprising perhaps thirty thousand men. The Romans took up positions on what is now the plateau of Armecy near the Arroux River in southern Burgundy, while the Helvetii gathered in a mass on the plain below in their customary phalanx formation. It was Caesar's first large-scale pitched battle, and he faced the largest Celtic army any Roman had engaged for more than fifty years.

It was early on an August afternoon when the Helvetii organized themselves and then charged pell-mell up the hill against Caesar's troops, who were spread along the slopes in three thick lines of eight ranks each. After several hours of fierce hand-to-hand fighting, the Romans were still in control of the hill, and had begun to push the Celts back toward its base. By sundown the Helvetii had retreated across a small valley and barricaded themselves behind their wagons and carts at the top of the next hill. The Romans pressed after them well into the night, until at midnight the defeated horde of Celts fled from the hill and into the woods, leaving thousands dead on the battlefield.

Within a few weeks Caesar took his legions northward into modern Alsace and defeated an army of German invaders led by an ambitious chieftain, Ariovistus, who fled back across the Rhine. In both battles Caesar used the tactics that enabled him to defeat Celtic armies again and again over the next eight years all over the area of modern France, Belgium, and Holland. His careful maneuvering to obtain the most favorable field position, and the surprise and speed of his movements, almost always gave him the upper hand even before the battle had begun. Once in battle, the Roman legions usually had the advantage over their unorganized enemies because of their centuries-old practice of physical conditioning, rigorous training, and stern discipline. Caesar's well-drilled and heavily armed infantry lost only one or two battles throughout the entire conflict that came to be called the Gallic War.

At the end of the warmaking season in the fall of 58, Caesar billeted his six legions at Vesontio, modern Besançon, the principal *oppidum*, or fortified town, of the Sequani tribe, located just outside the border of Further Gaul. He returned to his headquarters in Nearer Gaul, probably Ravenna on the Adriatic Sea, a five-hundred-year-old city founded by Etruscans, then taken from them by the Celtic Boii, and finally occupied by the Romans around 200 BCE. From there he arranged for his two hand-picked Consuls in Rome to have the Senate extend for another year his term as Governor of Further Gaul. His Governorships of the two other provinces, Nearer Gaul and Illyricum, had four more years to run.

Historians think that about this time he began reworking his battlefield dispatches to the Senate into the opening chapter of the plainspoken narrative that has been preserved as *The Gallic War*, the first part of a larger work that has come to be titled *Commentaries*. He would eventually complete seven books of this work, each describing a year's warmaking against the Celtic tribes of Gaul and Britain, leaving the last two years to be covered by his aide Aulus Hirtius. A model of simple and vigorous Latin prose, *The Gallic War* is among the finest military narratives surviving from the ancient world.

At the opening of Book II, describing the events of 57, his second year in Gaul, Caesar writes that during the winter his sources informed him that the Belgae, a group of Celtic tribes even more barbaric than those he had just defeated, were threatening to march south from their territory in northern Gaul and attack the Roman garrison at Vesontio. Within a few weeks he had added two legions to his army and led all eight as far north as the Marne River, the southern edge of Belgic territory. Over the next several months Caesar's army fought and defeated every Belgic tribe that resisted him, sweeping through the valleys of the Aisne and the Somme and capturing tribal capitals later to be called Soissons, Beauvais, and Amiens.

While Caesar was thus occupied, Cicero was at last reaping the fruits of his tireless efforts over the past year to get the Senate to reverse the law that had outlawed him. His pleading letters to Pompey and others, combined with political chicanery and violence on the part of Clodius, brought about a change in attitude in the capital. Once Pompey was convinced that Cicero should be restored to his office and to Rome, he persuaded Caesar, who probably gave his assent from his camp in Gaul. More than four hundred Senators participated in a historic vote on a decree to recall Cicero, the only dissenter being Clodius. Already on his way back from Macedonia, Cicero landed at Brundisium in August of 57, where he was greeted by a large crowd, and then traveled to Rome surrounded by well-wishers. His speech of thanks in the Senate early in the next month, and public compensation for his property losses, marked the conclusion of this ugly episode, the most humiliating of Cicero's career.

Meanwhile the last battles of the fighting season were taking place at the northern edge of modern France and in Belgium. Caesar's army suffered an ambush and a close brush with defeat by the Nervii, reputedly the fiercest tribe in Gaul, but Caesar ran onto the battlefield himself to regroup the scattered legions, and they eventually overwhelmed the Nervii, but not without heavy losses. A week later, arriving at a Belgic stronghold protected on three sides by sheer cliffs, Caesar ordered his *fabri*, his engineers, to build a siege tower on rollers, a wooden structure of several stories, that the Romans then moved up to the outer wall. The sight of this device so astonished the defenders that they offered to surrender immediately.

Although the Romans' advanced engineering technology was often the deciding factor against the unsophisticated Celts, it was less successful against the Veneti, a maritime tribe that lived in settlements on rocky promontories along the coast of Brittany. In the summer of 56, Caesar took his legions to northern Gaul and penetrated several of their fortified towns using siege towers and water barriers, but the Veneti always escaped by boat to another stronghold. Caesar's response was to build a navy and attack their merchant fleet, which they used to conduct trade with tribes on the island of Britain.

In the first recorded naval battle on the Atlantic coast, hundreds of Roman and Venetic ships faced each other in Quiberon Bay in Brittany, probably opposite the inlet to the Gulf of Morbihan. The Romans' lack of skill at sailing led them to fit their ships with oars, which the Veneti did not use. The result was that during the battle the Romans were able to move freely among the Venetic ships and pull down their sails and rigging with a device they had invented for the purpose, a sharp hook attached to a long pole. When the wind suddenly died and left both fleets becalmed, the Romans moved in and burned or captured all but a few vessels in the Venetic fleet. A little of Caesar's self-proclaimed luck and a modest advantage in technology gave Rome its first victory in the Atlantic.

Caesar returned to Gaul with his devastating army in each of the next six years, citing the need to protect Roman interests or to punish tribes that had attacked Roman settlements. Although each year brought new efforts in the Senate to recall him, the Triumvirate remained in control, and in January of 55, after delaying the elections for six months and then sending thugs to beat up the only candidate willing to oppose them, Pompey and Crassus were elected Consuls for the year.

Within a few weeks they had engineered five-year appointments for themselves as Governors of Nearer and Further Spain, and of Syria, respectively, for the next year. In a bitter debate in the Assembly, Cato opposed the measure with such fervor that the Consuls' henchmen finally removed him forcibly from the podium and threw him out of the building. At the same time Pompey and Crassus sponsored a measure that extended Caesar's control of his three northern provinces for five years, but exactly when this command would terminate was left unclear. The result was that for the foreseeable future the *tres homines* would govern half of Rome's dozen provinces and command all twenty of its legions.

Later in the same year Caesar found himself on the banks of the lower Rhine after attacking and massacring two tribes of Germans that had ventured across the river. In an obvious bid for favorable attention in Rome, he ordered his engineers to build a bridge over the river in the area between modern Coblenz and Bonn. When he and his cavalry rode across the five-hundred-yard span ten days later, he became the first man to bridge the Rhine and the first Roman general in Germany. He was also the first to tear down a Rhine bridge, which he did after a two-week episode of burning German fields and villages.

From the Rhine, Caesar hurried across northern Gaul late in the summer of 55 to launch his most spectacular effort to win public acclaim, an ill-advised and dangerous expedition across the English Channel to Britannia, an island that was not yet present on the Roman map. Even though he managed to land two legions on the Kentish coast in the face of furious opposition by the Britons, a late summer storm wrecked his ships and blew his cavalry transports back to Gaul. He repaired his ships, but without his cavalry he was unwilling to advance inland, and so brought his men back to Gaul after only a few weeks on the island.

Caesar's two military escapades in 55 may have been attempts to match the public attention given in August to the dedication of Pompey's spectacular theater-temple, the first stone theater in Rome and an architectural marvel that stood for more than four centuries. In addition to a vast open-air theater seating fifteen to twenty thousand spectators in front of a stage a hundred yards wide, the main building included a small temple dedicated to Venus Victrix (Venus the Goddess of Victory) placed at the center of the top row of seats. Extending behind the stage were several public buildings, including a new Senate House (the Curia Pompei) and an open pavilion fully two hundred yards long (eventually dubbed Pompey's Portico), the first public park in Rome. Throughout the complex, statues filled every niche and arch, and paintings and murals covered every wall. The outline of the sweeping curve of the back of Pompey's theater can be seen today in the rounded façade of buildings in the Via di Grotta Pinta in the Campo dei Fiori district.

The dedication was followed by five days of public entertainments, including athletic games, stage performances, horse races, and battles between men and wild beasts. Among the participants were hundreds of lions and leopards, twenty elephants, several baboons, a lynx, and Rome's first rhinoceros, most of which perished fighting each other or against African spearmen. "The public gaped at all this," wrote Cicero to a friend. "But what pleasure can a cultivated man get out of seeing a weak human being torn to pieces by a powerful animal or a splendid animal transfixed by a hunting spear?"[7]

Cicero was more impressed, as were many others, when news reached Rome in October of Caesar's transit of the unknown waters of Oceanus and his landing on the mysterious island that no Roman had ever seen. When word reached Rome of his return from his three-week expedition to Britannia, the amazement and enthusiasm were such that the Senate, with the single dissenting vote of the persistent Cato, voted a *supplicatio* of twenty days, longer than any previous thanksgiving period.

Caesar was quick to take advantage of the public's fascination with the skin-clad *horridi Britanni* and their strange country. In 54 he mounted a full-scale invasion of Britain with the largest fleet to cross the English Channel until the First World War—an armada of over six hundred ships carrying five full legions and as many as thirty thousand infantry and cavalry. After landing again on a Kentish beach, this time unopposed, Caesar marched with four legions across Kent and Surrey to the Thames. The Britons organized themselves under the leadership of one of the Celtic Kings in Kent, Cassivellaunus, the first Briton to be named in a written history. After fording the Thames, probably in the vicinity of Brentford, a borough of modern London, the Romans pursued the retreating Britons northward, finally overrunning a massive *oppidum* usually identified with the plateau of Wheathampstead in present-day Hertfordshire.[8]

In two months on the island, Caesar defeated everyone he faced, but had too little time and too few men to take control of it or station any garrison there. On top of that, the Romans found little or none of the gold, silver, or tin they had expected. Caesar brought his five legions and dozens of captive Britons back safely to Gaul, but he was stunned to learn when he arrived that his twenty-two-year-old daughter Julia, Pompey's wife, had died the previous month while giving birth to his grandchild (the ancient sources disagree as to its sex), who survived only a few days. The loss of Julia fell heavily on Pompey, who had doted on her (and she on him) during their five years of marriage, and especially since her miscarriage a year earlier. After her funeral in the Forum, a crowd took up her corpse and carried it outside the city wall for burial in sacred ground on the Campus Martius. From his camp in Gaul, Caesar showed his gratitude by ordering gladiatorial games at his own expense, and a public banquet in her honor.

The loss of this bond between Caesar and Pompey was perhaps the start of the unraveling of the Triumvirate, which had now endured for almost six years. All three members had sought allies wherever they could, and their deliberate cultivation of Cicero with favors and support had brought about his reconciliation with them in 56. Caesar had even made a large loan to Cicero and had taken his brother Quintus with him to Britain as an officer in his army. Cicero responded at the end of the year with an epic poem —"a delectable piece," he called it in a letter to Quintus—celebrating Caesar's expedition across the English Channel.

But Caesar's continual extensions of the war into Germany and Britain, and his repeated successes in Gaul, aroused his opponents to fury, and they were more determined than ever to topple him. Among the most prominent of these was the man Pompey and Crassus had frightened off in 55, Lucius Domitius, the ranking member of a distinguished family of the plebeian nobility, and a brother-in-law of Cato. The men of this branch of the Domitii bore the *cognomen* Ahenobarbus, or Bronzebeard, because of a legend from the early Republic that the Roman gods Castor and Pollux had once appeared in Rome to announce a victory over an Etruscan army. They came upon a certain Lucius Domitius and, in order to authenticate themselves, changed the color of his black beard to bronze. With seven Consuls among his ancestors and an Emperor among his descendants (Nero was his great-grandson), Lucius Domitius was born for high office, and mounted a new campaign for Consul for 54. The main plank in his platform was a promise to strip Caesar of all three of his provinces and disband his army. Even though Domitius was elected, Caesar's supporters put their own man in as his colleague, and he prevented Domitius from carrying out his promise.

The following year Marcus Crassus, eager to make the most of his Governorship of Syria, undertook a military expedition against the Persian kingdom of Parthia, the northern portion of modern Iran. After only a short campaign, the Parthians inflicted a crushing defeat on his army, and he was lured to peace talks and then murdered. His son, a cavalry officer, perished with him, leaving a young widow, Cornelia, a beautiful and accomplished patrician who would not long remain unattached. Crassus' death left the Triumvirate suddenly bereft of its third leg, and dependent upon the remaining uneasy alliance between Caesar and Pompey.

In an effort to restore the familial tie between them, Caesar now proposed that he divorce Calpurnia, his wife of nearly seven years, and marry Pompey's daughter Pompeia, who had been widowed since she had been forced to exchange Faustus Sulla for Servilius Caepio six years before, and who was again betrothed to Sulla. At the same time he broached the idea that Pompey marry Octavia, Caesar's grandniece and sister of the future Augustus, even though she was already married to Gaius Marcellus, a leading *optimate* politician. Pompey rejected both suggestions, a move that heartened Caesar's opponents, who began pressuring Pompey to bolt the Triumvirate.

When Caesar returned to Italy in January of 52, Rome was in turmoil over the increasing corruption, bribery, and violence that accompanied the annual elections. The magistrates in the previous year had served only six months because new elections had been delayed, and the Senate was unable to agree on even temporary Consuls by the time the new year started. In the middle of January one of Caesar's most prominent supporters, Publius Clodius, a candidate for *praetor*, had been murdered in the street by a Consular candidate, and his funeral turned into a violent riot that ended only when the Senate House was burned to the ground.

An alarmed Senate declared a state of emergency and approved the *senatus consultum ultimum* (final decree of the Senate), a rarely used measure that charged all public officers, including any provincial Governors in the vicinity, to "take steps to see that the State suffer no harm." Unable to break the political stalemate, and unwilling to name a *dictator* the Senate turned again to Pompey and appointed him the first sole Consul in Roman history. This not only violated the fundamental Roman law of dual magistracy, but also ignored the law that made Pompey ineligible for the Consulship until ten years after his previous term. But he was the only Senator with sufficient authority and broad-enough support to command a majority. The Senate ordered all citizens of military age to register for military service, and instructed Pompey to safeguard the capital.

Pompey immediately mobilized scores of troops from among his veterans and deployed them around the capital, putting an end to the rioting. Then he promoted new laws against violence, corruption, and bribery, appointed a new jury pool, and obtained convictions of the worst offenders. A few weeks later he took as his fifth wife the recent widow Cornelia, who also happened to be the daughter of the ardent anti-Caesarian Metellus Scipio. Later in the year Pompey appointed his new father-in-law to serve with him as co-Consul. But he continued to support his partner in Gaul and pressured the Assembly to pass a law that gave Caesar, and only Caesar, the privilege of competing for the Consulship without appearing in Rome. Although this was the exemption that Caesar wanted, the precise date that he would have to give up his command remained unclear, as did the date when he could return to the Consulship. Was it 49, ten years after his first term, as current law provided? Or was it whenever the Senate wished, as it had just shown by allowing Pompey to return only three years after his previous term?[9]

The immediate political turmoil in Rome, and Caesar's preoccupation with his own political future, emboldened dozens of Celtic tribes in Gaul to unite under the leadership of Vercingetorix, a nobleman of the Arverni tribe, and mount the most significant revolt of the entire Gallic War. Caesar could not break away until late in February, and then had to make a dangerous journey across hostile territory to join his ten legions about sixty miles southeast of Lutetia, modern Paris. From there he took an army of more than forty thousand infantry and cavalry southward and began assaulting the capital towns of the rebelling tribes. Among them was Avaricum, modern Bourges, the *oppidum* of the Bituriges, which was said to be "perhaps the most beautiful town in the whole of Gaul,"[10] but one that required a full month to subdue.

Continuing south in pursuit of the army of Vercingetorix, Caesar made an abortive assault on Gergovia, the Arvernian capital, a fortified mountaintop a few miles from modern Clermont-Ferrand. After his troops had dislodged a line of defenders from their camp partway up the slope, Caesar ordered the trumpet signal for a halt. But when his troops ignored it and continued their charge against the town's ramparts, Vercingetorix attacked from the flank and swept the Romans off the hill, killing many of them and forcing a wholesale retreat. It was Caesar's worst defeat of the entire Gallic War, and gave the Celts of Gaul new hope that they could drive him out of the country. After his clear victory at Gergovia, Vercingetorix and his followers moved north and gathered on the plateau of Alesia, now called Mont Auxois, about thirty miles northwest of Dijon in upper Burgundy.

Caesar brought all ten of his legions to the area and surrounded the plateau with an eleven-mile ring of ditches, barricades, and ramparts, the most extensive siegeworks ever seen in Gaul. After Vercingetorix sent out a call for help, dozens of tribes from all over Gaul formed an enormous relieving army, said by Caesar to number a quarter of a million men, and brought it to the plain to the west of Alesia. The Romans then constructed an even larger ring of defenseworks outside their own positions to protect themselves against the relieving army's attack.

Over the next several days the Gallic army outside the ring and Vercingetorix's men on the plateau made three separate attempts to break through Caesar's defensive barricades, but none succeeded. The Romans were hard pressed at times from both directions, and though they were able to fend off every charge against their lines, they could not deliver the decisive blow that would settle the battle. Finally, Caesar sent several cohorts of cavalry and infantry around and behind the advancing Gauls to attack from the rear. When this tactic succeeded in trapping and killing a large number of the enemy, the defenders of the plateau retreated into their stronghold, and those on the plain who observed the slaughter began to panic. The huge relieving army, no doubt laboring under several commanders, had not the leadership or experience to hold its position in the face of such a reversal. It turned and fled the field.

Vercingetorix surrendered the next day, and the Romans took him and thousands of Gallic troops prisoner. Making the most of the moment, Caesar staged a formal ceremony in which Vercingetorix was led before him as he sat on a platform that had been erected in front of the Roman fortifications. After the Celtic chieftain had been suitably humiliated, Caesar ordered him taken to Rome under arrest to await the privilege of marching in his triumph. Caesar allowed the members of two tribes to return to their homes on the assurance of their loyalty and future cooperation; the remaining prisoners he distributed among the legions, one slave to each soldier.

Although various Celtic tribes mounted sporadic attacks during the next two years, the defeat of Vercingetorix marked the end of any large-scale resistance in Gaul, and Caesar's faction in the Senate persuaded it to declare another twenty-day *supplicatio*. His seven-year command of three provinces and his extension of Roman hegemony as far as the Atlantic now exceeded Pompey's successes in the East, and were unprecedented in Roman history. Ironically, the *supplicatio* gave Caesar's enemies in the Senate another opportunity to call for an end to his command, and throughout the following year they argued that a Roman army in Gaul was no longer needed. Pompey continued to block all attempts to recall Caesar, but finally, in September of 51, agreed that the Senate should discuss the issue the following March.

During the year after his victory at Alesia, Caesar began distributing booty from the war in places where it was likely to bring the best return. To insure his soldiers' continued service and allegiance, he doubled their pay and granted them special allowances, at the same time settling considerable fortunes on each of his officers. To communities throughout Italy he donated funds for municipal buildings, and in Rome he paid supporters' debts, gave lavish presents, and made gifts of slaves wherever political favor was to be had. When the new Consuls took office the following January, Caesar was able to persuade one of them to support him, probably on the promise of a future Governorship. But the other was Gaius Marcellus, a member of one of the families most opposed to him, and husband of his grandniece Octavia, the woman whom Caesar had proposed two years earlier be handed over to Pompey.

In February the Senate was astounded by the sudden about-face of a long-time enemy of the Triumvirate, Scribonius Curio, who now took up Caesar's cause with the same skill and energy that he had previously used to oppose him. A compelling speaker and a popular politician with a large following, Curio apparently decided, perhaps at the urging of his new wife Fulvia, that his own political future was best served by siding with Caesar and taking a hard line against Pompey. On his election as a tribune of the Assembly in the previous December, he was empowered to veto any of the Senate's proposals or decrees for the following twelve months. And it was in the Senate that the three-way battle over the issue of Caesar's provincial commands, his prospective Consulship, and his immunity was played out over the course of the year.

Each at the head of his own circle of supporters, each commanding large armies in his provinces, and by ancient law thereby barred from entering the capital, Caesar and Pompey continued to maintain the uneasy balance of their decade-long partnership. Working to dismantle it and to restore the traditional oligarchy of the Roman nobility were four ancient and eminent families, aided by Cato and his supporters.[11] The remaining Senators, over whom the factions contended, were simply intent on keeping and augmenting their property and their privileged status. Above all, they wished to avoid an armed conflict that would disrupt commerce and require them to fight or flee.

Early in 50 Caesar proposed that his provincial commands be extended until the end of 49, and that during that year he be allowed to compete for the Consulship of 48 without having to appear in Rome. It may have been about this time, some historians argue, that he ordered hundreds of copies of *Bellum Gallicum, The Gallic War,* to be made and distributed in the capital. Besides preserving a detailed record of his achievements in Gaul, he hoped to convince the moderates in the Senate that those exploits entitled him to retain his command and his immunity until he could stand again for the Consulship and the protection it provided.[12]

In reaction to Caesar's proposal, Pompey, under increasing pressure from the *optimate* faction, gave his support to a counterproposal, introduced by Gaius Marcellus in March, that Caesar wrap up things in Gaul during the next seven months and lay down his command by the Ides of November. This was the first time he agreed to an actual date after which Caesar would lose his immunity and become a *privatus* (private citizen). But this was unacceptable to Caesar, and Curio vetoed it. By now Pompey was exasperated by Caesar's recalcitrance, feeling that he had supported his partner to the limit of his ability, and that any further concessions would be an affront to his own *dignitas*, his honor and personal standing.

In July or August Curio brought a proposal from Caesar that "in order to relieve Rome of unnecessary anxiety" both he and Pompey immediately give up their armies. To Pompey and his conservative allies, this was unacceptable, and they mustered enough support to defeat it. In November Marcellus moved that successors be appointed to take over Caesar's Gallic provinces, but when the motion was rejected, Curio used the opening to propose again that both *triumviri* resign their Governorships and discharge their armies. Although Caesar had made no threats and had only a single legion in Italy, the majority of Senators were genuinely afraid of armed conflict and ready to make concessions to him to avoid it. On December 1 more than ninety percent of the Senate agreed to Curio's motion that both commanders down their commissions and disband their armies.

In reaction to this, the presiding Consul, Gaius Marcellus, abruptly adjourned the Senate and, with the two Consuls-elect for 49, went to Pompey and authorized him to defend Rome against Caesar. Although the Senate's vote was not a decree, Marcellus was on dubious legal ground. Nevertheless, Pompey, so long accustomed to responding to such calls to arms, began recruiting more troops and preparing for war. A few days later he told Cicero that he no longer saw any hope of reconciliation with Caesar.

Early in December Curio's term as tribune ended, and among those newly elected were two of Caesar's closest aides, Mark Antony and Quintus Cassius. From Ravenna, Caesar directed the maneuvering in the Senate by means of couriers traveling back and forth to the capital. Toward the end of the month he proposed that he give up his Governorship of Further Gaul, keep his two other provinces, and relinquish all but two of his legions until he took office as Consul. When Curio delivered this proposal to the new Senate and new Consuls on January 1, they rejected it promptly. Caesar then offered to give up all his legions and provinces and take his chances unprotected if all other Governors and commanders would do the same, specifically Pompey, who still had seven legions in Spain. But Cato and the other *optimates* would have none of this proposal, and even tried to prevent his messengers, Mark Antony and Quintus Cassius, from reading it out to the Senate.

Instead the Senate voted that Caesar must dismiss his troops and lay down his command by a date they would fix, or be considered an enemy of the state. When Antony and Cassius vetoed this measure, which was their privilege as tribunes, the Senate exploded in uproar, and the new presiding Consul, Cornelius Lentulus Crus, adjourned the session. That night Pompey summoned the Senators to his home outside the capital and praised the zealous and encouraged the hesitant.

A few days later, on January 7, Lentulus brushed aside the veto and convinced the Senate to approve the *consultum ultimum*, legally authorizing the full mobilization of an army. In a melodramatic gesture, Caesar's tribunes Antony and Cassius fled the city disguised as slaves, and the Senate promptly appointed new Governors for the provinces. Nearer Gaul—Caesar's flagship—went to Marcus Considius, and Further Gaul to Lucius Domitius, the most prominent leader of the *optimate* Senators. Now, after a lifetime of hating Pompey, the noble-minded Marcus Brutus decided that it was Caesar who was threatening the Republic, and he sided with the murderer of his father against his mother's lover. The Senate sent him to Cilicia as an aide to the new Governor, and gave his brother-in-law Gaius Cassius a naval command. His uncle Cato was ordered to secure Sicily, one of Rome's important granaries, and Cicero was given the job of defending Campania, where he had a villa on the coast.

The *optimate* faction had finally succeeded in prying apart the last two members of the Triumvirate, aided in large part by the *triumviri* themselves, each of whom stubbornly refused to give way one inch to the other. But the Triumvirate had become too large to simply disappear, and the deadly duel on the horizon now threatened the Republic itself.

PART TWO
Caesar and Pompey

V

Across the Rubicon

For an unplanned and chaotic war of twenty centuries ago, the great Roman Civil War of the mid-first century before the Christian Era is unusually well documented. It is helpful that a master of prose narrative and the Republic's most prolific letter writer were both principals in the conflict, and that they wrote about it in detail, occasionally to each other. Dozens of Cicero's speeches have been preserved, and hundreds of his letters. Only a handful of Caesar's letters are extant; his literary reputation stands on the two *Commentaries*, the second of which is *The Civil War*—on the surface a simple narrative, but in reality one of the most artful and accomplished works in Latin literature.

Caesar's own account of the war came to light only in the aftermath of the Ides of March some five years later, when Mark Antony made a hurried nighttime visit to Calpurnia, Caesar's grieving widow, and took charge of the letters and papers of the general he had served for more than a decade. What he found, among other things, was a manuscript of some fifty thousand words that may have already borne the title *Bellum Civile, The Civil War*, Caesar's version of events that began with his crossing of the Rubicon in January of 49 BCE. For more than fifteen centuries the text of this manuscript and that of *The Gallic War* were preserved in copies made by hand until they were printed in Rome, as Caesar's *Commentaries*, in 1469, on the first printing press in Italy.[1]

The Civil War is marked by the same plain style and economy of expression as *The Gallic War*, and the appearance of objectivity in both is enhanced by Caesar's unusual practice of referring to himself in the third person. Caesar's *Civil War* is the only remaining eyewitness account of the first two years of the war, and it is the eye, and the voice, of the commander himself.

In the ancient world no news traveled faster than a horse, and the news of the Senate's *consultum ultimum*, its final decree ordering the mobilization of its defensive army, took a full three days to reach Caesar at Ravenna, two hundred and forty miles away. When it arrived, he had two alternatives. He could risk his freedom and his fortune at a trial controlled by his enemies, or he could use his army to frighten the Senate into letting him retain his immunity until he was reelected Consul, in which position he could not be prosecuted.

Caesar does not say what decision he made, only that he addressed his troops, complaining of the wrongs done him by his enemies, and of the illegal

suppression of the vetoes of his tribunes. When he exhorted them to defend the reputation and *dignitas* of the general under whom they had "pacified all of Gaul and Germany," their response was to shout their enthusiastic assent. What follows is the single sentence he devotes to his armed incursion across the southern boundary of his province—across the Rubicon: "Having discovered the feelings of his men, he set out with this legion for Ariminum [modern Rimini, the next large town below Ravenna] and there met the tribunes who had fled to him; the rest of the legions he called out from winter quarters and ordered to follow after him."[2]

In the way of many ancient icons, the Rubicon River has enriched our languages and our symbolism. Possibly no other metaphor from the ancient world has achieved such standing in modern discourse. But the famous figure of speech—to cross the Rubicon—has survived even as its inspiration has receded into obscurity. The narrow Rubicon (the root of the word denotes redness), flowing from the Apennine foothills into the Adriatic Sea about twenty miles south of Ravenna, divided the Roman homeland from Caesar's province of Nearer Gaul. It remained an important political boundary for hundreds of years, but during the Middle Ages the name became separated from the river and then disappeared from the map entirely, so that by the eighteenth century no one knew which of the three or more modest rivers in the area had been the ancient Rubicon. A controversy arose among the towns along each river's banks over which deserved the storied name that had slipped from the grasp of geographers. Inevitably the Church became involved, and in 1756 Pope Clement XIII issued a bull asserting that the Uso, a river about seven miles north of Rimini, was the Rubicon.

In the next century, however, the question made its way into the courts, and in the 1920s Mussolini took up the issue as part of his campaign to revive the grandeur that was Rome for the glory of modern Italy. He decided that the modern Fiumicino River, two miles north of the Uso, was the ancient Rubicon, and ordered its name changed to Rubicone. On its bank, near the town now called Savignano-sul-Rubicone, he placed a stone slab carved with the text of the Senate's decree: "Let the Consuls, praetors, tribunes and those proconsuls who are in the neighborhood of Rome take action to see that the state suffers no harm" (*The Civil War* 1.5.3). The slab and the eighty-five-foot limestone bridge that carried the Via Aemilia over the Rubicon at the same spot were destroyed in a bombing raid in 1944. Today the Rubicone, unequivocally identified along its fifteen-mile length, reaches the Adriatic between a campground and a trailer park in the nondescript resort town of Gatteo a Mare.[3]

Caesar not only fails to mention the Rubicon, he refers to no river at all, and simply omits the fact that he has crossed the boundary of his province and thus violated the law against bringing an army into the Roman homeland. Although he describes his incursion in a matter-of-fact way, it is certain that he knew it was a momentous step. According to both Suetonius and Appian, he shouted at the time, "The die is cast,"[4] or some similar phrase, meaning that it was an irrevocable gamble.

Caesar also fails to reveal that the night before the crossing he had sent a small squad of legionaries disguised as travelers to gain entrance to Ariminum and open the town gates for the legion the following morning. At least two other chroniclers of the Civil War include this incident, and although they wrote in the next century, they had access to another history, now lost, by Asinius Pollio, an officer in Caesar's army and eyewitness to the events.[5]

It was sudden and surprise marches by Caesar's troops that led to his successes in the Gallic War, and he saw no reason now to change his tactics. Perhaps on January 10, or more likely on the eleventh, he ordered Quintus Hortensius (son of the orator) to take the XIIIth Legion on the twenty-mile march south on the Via Popillia from Ravenna to the Rubicon River and camp on its north bank. By the end of the day, the legion of perhaps five thousand infantry and several hundred cavalry reached the Rubicon, and the party in mufti proceeded on to Ariminum during the evening. Caesar himself remained in Ravenna, where he concealed his intentions by attending the theater and then dining with the usual numerous guests. But he is said to have slipped away at dusk and quietly set out toward Ariminum in a hired carriage, accompanied by several aides and officers. He would have reached the Rubicon a few hours later and then, before dawn on the twelfth, crossed the river and led the XIIIth the final nine miles to Ariminum.

The advance party having unbolted the city gates, Caesar's thousands of troops easily took control of Ariminum before noon. Within hours the two tribunes, Mark Antony and Quintus Cassius, arrived, still disguised as slaves. It was then, on the basis of the best evidence, that Caesar addressed his troops, using the legally elected tribunes, now posing as fugitives, as props to support his accusations.

In his narrative, Caesar implies that he began repositioning his legions only after the Senate's ultimatum. What he fails to mention is that he had ordered significant movements of all eleven legions under his control well before the Senate acted, and even before the turn of the year. Of the four legions quartered in the region of modern Burgundy, he had, in the previous December, sent three into Further Gaul under his general Gaius Fabius and stationed them at Narbo Martius to defend against a possible attack by Pompey's seven legions in Spain. At the same time he had moved his four most distant legions down from northern Gaul to replace them.

Also in December, or possibly before that, he had ordered his two legions in winter quarters in Further Gaul, the VIIIth and the XIIth, to begin marching toward him in Italy. Lastly, Caesar implies that he did not order his XIIIth Legion to march to the Rubicon until he received the Senate's ultimatum. This is no doubt technically correct, but to have had this legion at Ravenna on January 10, a legion consisting of five thousand or more infantry quartered in garrisons throughout the province, plus several hundred Gallic and German cavalry, he cannot have given the order to mobilize later than the previous month, at least a week before the Senate acted.

On the basis of these facts, it is clear that Caesar was preparing for a military operation many weeks before the Senate challenged him, but it should come as no surprise that in his narrative he would hurry over these preparations and omit any suggestion that he was planning an armed challenge to the Senate's authority. In the genre of military memoirs, ancient and modern, this is the rule rather than the exception.

Within a day Caesar dispatched Antony on an ancient road over the Apennines with half the legion to occupy Arretium, modern Arezzo, another former Etruscan city that dominated the upper Arno Valley. He also sent a single cohort, a tenth of the legion, to both Pisaurum and Fanum, the two towns just south of Ariminum on the Via Flaminia along the Adriatic coast. By the fourteenth, Pisaurum, modern Pesaro, and Fanum, modern Fano, where the Via Flaminia turned from the coast to Rome, were in the hands of Caesar's troops. A third cohort occupied the port city of Ancona a day later, the same day that Antony captured Arretium and took control of the Via Cassia, just four days' march from the capital.

When news of these events, and rumors of even worse, reached Rome on the seventeenth, panic and confusion swept the city. Pompey, commander of the government's army, issued a declaration of civil war and abandoned Rome the same night, Cicero the next day. At the urging of Pompey, most *optimate* families and thousands of others fled south from the capital on the Appian Way into Campania and beyond. To the north and east of Rome, towns and farms along the main roads emptied overnight, and thousands sought refuge in the city from the threat of Caesar's troops. Cato announced his despair of the Republic and swore to never again shave or cut his hair, no matter what the outcome of the fighting.

At about the same time the news of Caesar's advance reached Rome, a secret message from Pompey to Caesar arrived in Ariminum. It was carried by Lucius Roscius, a former officer in Caesar's army, and young Lucius Caesar, a supporter of Pompey whose father, a distant cousin of Caesar's, had remained on his staff after serving in Gaul. According to *The Civil War*, the only remaining source, the message was a patronizing admonition from Pompey about the duties that each of them owed the state; none of the issues at hand was discussed.

In his reply Caesar recounted the unfair and illegal treatment he had suffered at the hands of the Senate, but said that nonetheless, he was "ready to descend to any depths and put up with anything for the sake of the republic. Pompey should go to his provinces, they should both disband their armies, everyone in Italy should lay down their arms, the community should be liberated from fear, and the Senate and people of Rome should be permitted free elections and complete control of the state" (*The Civil War* 1.9.5). Roscius and Lucius Caesar left the next day with this offer, to which Caesar added his own admonition that to speed the process and guarantee its authenticity, he and Pompey meet in person.

In the meantime, Cicero, who was depressed about the threat of a full-scale war, retreated to his villa on the coast at Formiae, today's Formia, some ninety miles south of Rome, and fretted over what Pompey would do. To Atticus, who remained in Rome, he wrote, "As for your request that I should let you know what Pompey is about, I don't think he knows himself; certainly none of us knows."[6]

But the news was not all bad. In the same letter Cicero revealed that a rumor he had heard a few days earlier had proved to be true—that Titus Labienus, Caesar's second-in-command throughout the Gallic War, had suddenly defected from Caesar's camp and traveled to the town of Teanum Sidicinum, today's Teano, just north of Capua, where he joined Pompey and the Senate on January 22. Because of the valuable information he brought, he was warmly welcomed, and the defection of such a high-ranking officer was a sharp boost to morale.

Labienus' decision surprised both Cicero and Pompey. It must have been a sudden one; he left his baggage and valuables behind. After the fact, historians have found several reasons for his defection, the most obvious being his reported unhappiness as Caesar's second-in-command. He had become quite wealthy, as well as arrogant, according to contemporary reports, and resented the fact that under Caesar he had never been given an independent command. It is true, as some have pointed out, that he had once served under Pompey, and that they were from the same region, Picenum, the precise area that Caesar was approaching. But it is more likely that he thought that Caesar and his single legion would be promptly defeated in Italy, especially if he, Labienus, joined the opposition. In the first of many similar gestures during the Civil War, Caesar expressed his contempt by ordering that Labienus' baggage and valuables be packed up and sent after him.[7]

Although Cicero had reservations about the latest proposal brought by Roscius and Lucius Caesar from Ariminum, Pompey and most of the Senate gave it serious attention. When even Cato announced that he preferred slavery to war, they agreed to accept Caesar's terms, with the stipulation that he first remove his troops from Italy proper. Cicero was encouraged by this condition, and for a few days carried the hope that it would end the argument over Caesar's sincerity and, if accepted, begin the process of restoring order.

But in the meantime, that is, at the same time that Roscius and Lucius Caesar left his headquarters in Ariminum, Caesar ordered two of his cohorts there and another at Pisaurum to march southward on the Via Flaminia toward Rome. As their commander, he chose the mercurial Scribonius Curio, who had switched sides and joined his faction less than a year before. His mission was to capture the important inland city of Iguvium, modern Gubbio, which was defended by Quintus Thermus with five cohorts— more than two thousand men. But when Thermus learned of the approach of Curio, he led his army out of the city in the opposite direction. Before going very far, however, many of his troops deserted him, returned to the city, and surrendered it without incident. With Curio's occupation of Iguvium on January 21, Caesar's army was fifty miles closer to Rome.

The Senatorial forces at Iguvium were the largest yet faced by any of Caesar's generals, and their prompt surrender typified the reaction of many in northern Italy to the appearance of Caesar's troops at the town gates. There was a general understanding that Caesar's veterans were a fearsome lot, but there was also substantial support for Caesar himself, outlaw or not. This support he enhanced with an unprecedented policy of *clementia*—orders that forbade any looting, burning, or unnecessary killing. And his policy went beyond avoiding destruction and bloodshed; he forgave and freed those he captured, and invited them to join him. In the struggle with the *optimate* government for the public favor, Caesar's *clementia* was an astute tactic that served him well throughout the war. It perhaps had its origin three decades earlier when he was a witness to the beheadings and other atrocities of Marius, and then Sulla. As a result, he was able to recruit many new troops in the areas he occupied. In the words of Appian, "He . . . either by force or kindness, mastered all whom he fell in with."[8]

After occupying the three coastal towns below Ariminum by January 14, Caesar remained in the area for the next two weeks, not allowing his troops to advance beyond Ancona. The only exception was Curio's thrust over the Apennines to Iguvium. On the surface it appears that this pause was to allow the two emissaries to deliver his proposal to Pompey and the Senate, and await their answer. But it is much more likely that Caesar, now having captured and occupied six towns, four of them substantial, and controlling the two most important roads between Umbria and Rome, as well as the coast road, was unwilling to spread his single legion any further until reinforcements arrived. Also, he needed to know what military response Pompey and the Senate were making and if they would advance against him, and along what route. When he received the news around January 20 that they had abandoned Rome, it was clear that there would be no move against him along the Via Cassia or the Via Flaminia, nor even any defense of the capital. It appeared that Pompey intended to make a stand somewhere in southern Italy, or even depart the country entirely.

To counter this strategy, Caesar moved to consolidate his army and confront Pompey further south. By the twenty-eighth he would have known that the XIIth Legion was only a few days away, after marching more than five hundred miles from its winter quarters in Further Gaul. As soon as Curio notified him that he had taken Iguvium, Caesar sent him orders to leave a small garrison and bring the balance of his troops back to the coast at Ancona. The same orders went to Antony at Arretium. When Curio arrived at the coast a week later, Caesar, without waiting for Antony or the approaching legion, moved the rest of his army—perhaps two to three thousand legionaries—ten miles farther south to the inland town of Auximum, modern Osimo.

It was only now, on January 29 or 30, based on the evidence of Cicero's letters, that Roscius and Lucius Caesar returned to the coast and to Caesar with the Senate's counterproposal that he immediately withdraw all his troops from Italy. But ten days after sending his own proposal, Caesar had continued his advance, had captured another inland city, and was now seventy miles into Italy with two more legions marching to join him. His success so far, and the lack of opposition from the general population, no doubt persuaded him that withdrawal would gain him nothing.

Auximum, the northernmost town in Picenum, Pompey's native region, was defended by several cohorts of government troops commanded by Attius Varus. But when the members of the town council heard that Caesar was approaching, they advised Varus that they welcomed Caesar, and that the commander might want to be out of town when he arrived. Varus and his troops fled, just as Thermus and his had fled from Iguvium, with the same result. When Caesar's troops caught up with them, many simply disappeared into the countryside; the rest came over to Caesar, bringing with them their ranking centurion as a prisoner. Pursuing his policy, Caesar praised the deserters, thanked the town council, and released the prisoner.

From there the army continued south twenty-five miles to Firmum, modern Fermo, where Antony joined it with most of the men he had taken to Arretium. As he neared Asculum, modern Ascoli Picenum, the next town south, Caesar's XIIth Legion, on the march for more than a month from the other side of the Alps, finally reached him. The XIIth was another battle-hardened legion, one that had survived the ambush by the ferocious Nervii in 57, and had fought between Caesar's double ring at Alesia. But these reinforcements were hardly necessary at Asculum, where most of the ten cohorts of Senatorial troops reacted in the same way as the defenders of Iguvium and Auximum. What little resistance Pompey's generals were able to organize seemed to melt away as Caesar approached. Worse than this, Pompey himself seemed to be in a state of confusion and indecision. A frustrated Cicero wrote to Atticus from Campania on February 8: "As for our Gnaeus, it is a lamentable and incredible thing. . . . No courage, no plan, no forces, no energy. I won't dwell on what is past—the disgraceful flight from Rome, the craven speeches in the towns, the ignorance of his own forces, let alone the enemy's."[9]

His incredulity rose another notch later in the same letter when he added that Pompey had sent a message to the Consuls to return to Rome and remove the large sum of money that had been left behind three weeks before in the *aerarium sanctius*, the Inner Treasury. This cache of money was kept in the Temple of Saturn at the foot of the Capitoline Hill as a reserve for extreme emergencies, and had apparently been forgotten in the haste and confusion of the *optimate* evacuation of the capital. According to Cicero, the Consuls' reply was that before they went to Rome Pompey should first go to Picenum, his presumed stronghold, and confront Caesar, who had overrun the entire area. The next day, Cicero gave up all hope for the country, saying, "Clearly, there is not a foot of Italian soil that is not within Caesar's grasp."[10]

But even as Cicero was writing these words, those troops loyal to the government who had been fleeing Caesar were moving toward the important city of Corfinium, a mountain stronghold in the Abruzzi region, a hundred miles east of Rome. Today what remains of it is only a protected ruin, its name surviving in the village of Corfinio a few hundred yards away. It was here that Caesar would face his most determined opponent—Lucius Domitius, the man who six years before had won a Consular election on the promise to dethrone him, and who still had not done it.

Domitius had begun recruiting troops as soon as he was named Caesar's successor in Further Gaul early in January, and in the first week of February he arrived in Corfinium with a small army of several thousand men. He was joined there a few days later by two of Pompey's fleeing *legati*, who brought several thousand more on the retreat from Picenum. Domitius took command of them all and sent contingents to two nearby towns, keeping about seven thousand men to defend Corfinium. In the meantime, after a four-day march down the coast, Caesar was approaching up a river valley toward the city with two veteran legions at full strength and a few extra cohorts—more than twelve thousand men. It had been just a month since he had crossed the Rubicon.

It was only now that Pompey gave the first hint of his strategy to his generals in the field, and to Caesar, and it was not what Domitius, or Cicero, wanted to hear. Although he had been reassuring the *optimate* Senators and generals for several months that he had, or would have, enough troops to defend Italy against Caesar, he now sent a message to Domitius to abandon Corfinium and bring his entire army to the south. He was to join Pompey at Luceria, present-day Lucera, a remote town in the region of Apulia on the eastern side of the Apennines, to which he had withdrawn only a week after departing Rome.

As early as the previous fall, when he had moved his two legions from Capua, near Rome, to Apulia on the southern Adriatic coast, Pompey had apparently decided that if Caesar attacked, he could not defeat him in Italy and would have to retreat to the East. The wisdom of this decision has been the subject of a modest debate among historians, but most agree that Pompey's position was poor for several reasons. Although he had seven full legions in Spain, they were too far away to help him in Italy, and could easily be denied passage through Gaul by Caesar's army. The two legions he had, the Ist and the XVth, he considered less than trustworthy. Although they had fighting experience, one had been raised by Caesar a few years before, and the other had fought under him for years until he transferred them both to Pompey to help him defend Syria, a use to which they were never put. Any other troops Pompey could round up would have little or no experience, and would be just as likely to favor Caesar as him. This was Pompey's dilemma. A large fraction of the country, including its fighting-aged men, either supported Caesar or were unwilling to oppose him.

In the long run, a quick withdrawal would put him in the best position to regroup and return to reconquer Italy. Besides his seven legions in Spain, he had the support of nearly every political entity east of Italy. Among them, they could deploy tens of thousands of fighting men, and their naval power alone would allow Pompey to control hundreds of fighting ships in every part of the Mediterranean. He was already sending messengers and emissaries to various foreign capitals to arrange for support, and would soon send his son Gnaeus to Egypt, where, in the course of negotiating for ships and troops, he was reportedly captivated, and perhaps seduced, by a young queen named Cleopatra.

It is true that Caesar had the reputation of an invincible general, but Pompey had the same reputation, had had it twice as long, and had never been beaten on the battlefield. Among the many who thought that Pompey should have stayed and defended Italy, the retreat was a serious psychological letdown. Cicero was not only disheartened, but offended when Pompey, even before he urged Domitius to retreat, wrote to him in Formiae, "I advise you to join us at Luceria, as you will be safest there." To Atticus Cicero wrote indignantly that he was replying "at once . . . that I am not just looking for the safest place I can find."[11] He had, however, taken the precaution of arranging for a boat to stand by at Caieta, today Gaeta, a few miles from Formiae, and another at Tarentum, modern Taranto, on the southern coast. But a few days later he decided that Pompey was right; he packed up and left Formiae by land to join him, only to turn back after a day on the road, fearful of being captured, when he heard that Caesar had reached Corfinium.

Pompey's reluctance to engage Caesar at this time captures their striking differences on the battlefield. Caesar was the obvious risk taker, Pompey the careful planner and a master of logistics, two skills that led him to avoid battle unless the odds were heavily in his favor. To rely on Domitius to hold Caesar at Corfinium with his hastily recruited troops was a gamble he was unwilling to take. A strategic withdrawal would preserve more than two legions until the right time and place for a stand.

But the proud and stubborn Domitius, whose family history was far more illustrious than Pompey's, had waited more than a decade for the chance to confront Caesar on the battlefield. Furthermore, although he and Pompey were now allies, he had fought the Triumvirate in the Senate only a few years earlier, and surely had not forgotten Pompey's execution of his older brother and annihilation of his army in Africa thirty years before. His antagonism toward both generals aroused him to stand and fight and not let Pompey dictate a retreat. He ordered Corfinium barricaded against attack, and sent five cohorts of troops three miles north of the city to tear down the bridge that carried the road from the coast across the Aternus River and into the city.

Approaching Corfinium after a two-day march, Caesar was told that the bridge he needed to cross was being torn down, and immediately sent his advance guard to prevent this. His troops found Domitius' men destroying the bridge and attacked them, forcing them back into the city. The rest of his army hurried across the bridge and set up its camp in front of the city walls. Domitius addressed his soldiers and promised them free land from his own estates and other rewards if they would hold the city. But within a day or two he was stunned to learn that the nearby town of Sulmo, modern Sulmona, to which he had sent seven cohorts of troops for its defense, had opened its gates to Antony. All the defenders had switched sides and then marched to Corfinium with Antony to join Caesar's army.

Now Caesar's third legion, the VIIIth, another veteran legion that had fought all over Gaul, arrived at Corfinium after a march of more than six hundred miles from Further Gaul. With the VIIIth came an additional twenty-one cohorts that had been recruited in Nearer Gaul. With more than five legions of infantry, perhaps twenty thousand men, and hundreds of horsemen, Caesar surrounded Corfinium and prepared for his first siege of a Roman city. Although Pompey had urged him to abandon the city, Domitius was convinced that a move to the north by Pompey, if only a modest one, would draw troops away from the siege, and possibly attract Caesar himself. In a message carried at top speed the one hundred and forty miles to Luceria, Domitius reported that he was surrounded and begged Pompey to bring an army north, trap Caesar between the mountain passes, and cut off his food supplies.

Pompey's response was to say that what he had predicted had come true, and that Caesar had accumulated too large an army to be halted by him or Domitius. Citing his lack of confidence in the loyalty of his two standing legions, he refused to come north, and again exhorted Domitius to extricate himself and bring his troops into the safety of Apulia. At the same time Pompey revealed the full extent of his plan to the Consuls and the rest of the *optimate* leaders in Campania. He was withdrawing his army even further south to Brundisium, and they should join him there. From Brundisium they could all be taken across the Strait of Otranto to Macedonia. Within a day or two he moved another fifty miles south to Canusium, modern Canosa, and from there again wrote to Cicero, urging him to meet him in Brundisium "so that in concert we may bring aid and comfort to our afflicted country."[12]

Even before Domitius received Pompey's last reply, Caesar's legionaries had dug a ditch, piled up a bank of earth in front of it, and then built a rampart and towers on the bank around most of the five-mile perimeter of Corfinium. Siegeworks of this magnitude were nothing unusual for his veteran engineers; the double ring they had built around Alesia just three years before had been twice the length. Now surrounded by the largest army in Italy, and with no help approaching, Domitius was suddenly and ignominiously trapped. In *The Civil War*, Caesar allows himself several pages to detail what happened next: "After reading [Pompey's] . . . letter, Domitius pretended to his council of war that Pompey would quickly come to their aid, and encouraged them not to lose heart and to make whatever preparations would serve to defend the town. He himself spoke secretly to a few of his intimates and decided to make a plan of escape. . . . [But] the thing could not be hidden nor the pretence maintained for very long" (*The Civil War* 1.19.1–3).

According to Caesar, Domitius' own troops arrested him and sent word to Caesar toward nightfall that they were ready to hand him over and surrender Corfinium. Caesar, no doubt surprised at his good fortune, but concerned that he could not control his troops if they entered the city after dark, decided to let the town's defenders stew overnight. Before dawn the next morning, Lentulus Spinther, a former Consul who had earlier fled from Asculum to Corfinium, shouted from the wall that he wished to meet with Caesar. After he was conducted to the commander's tent, he reminded him of their long-standing friendship (Caesar had supported his election as Consul in 57), and begged for his life. Caesar assured him that he had no quarrel with him, that he was only trying to preserve his own *dignitas* and protect the Roman people from domination by a small clique, and sent him back behind the walls.

At dawn Caesar conducted a ceremony in front of the gates of Corfinium similar to the one he had imposed on Vercingetorix at Alesia three years before. He ordered all the Senators and their families, the military tribunes, and other important men to be brought before him. Among the group were five Senators, including the two ex-Consuls Lucius Domitius and Lentulus Spinther (who had celebrated a triumph only two years before), all of whom had ample reason to believe that they would be summarily executed. Instead, Caesar addressed them briefly, admonishing for ingratitude several he had helped, and set them all free. The entire defensive army readily switched sides and took an oath of allegiance to him. When the city officials handed over a large sum of money that Domitius had brought to pay the troops, Caesar returned it to him, in his words, "in order not to seem greedier of men's money than of their lives" (*The Civil War* 1.23.4). The unrepentant Domitius, unexpectedly still in possession of his life, his freedom, and even his money, set out immediately for his estate on the Tuscan coast, where he began requisitioning merchant vessels from private owners to use as warships against Caesar.

Before noon on February 21, after a week at Corfinium and hardly any bloodshed, Caesar was on the road again with the entire army, now the equivalent of eight legions. Anticipating a campaign in Sicily against Cato, he ordered his young officer Asinius Pollio to advance promptly to the island province with the three legions that had just defected. With the rest of the army Caesar began a rapid march toward Apulia in pursuit of Pompey, who had just hurried out of Canusium, some two hundred miles to the south.

According to Caesar, Pompey had created a corps of three hundred cavalry by arming *servi* and *pastores*, slaves and shepherds, and giving them horses. If true, this would have been seen as a desperate measure. Slaves were traditionally barred from serving as legionaries or cavalrymen, although many accompanied the army in their usual capacities. But regardless of what recruiting had been done, it was now clear to Caesar that Pompey would not attempt to hold territory in Italy, and that he would assemble whatever troops he could at Brundisium, and either try to hold the port or evacuate them by boat to Macedonia, which was under the control of a Pompeian Governor.

The same day that Caesar left Corfinium, Cicero, still waiting at Formiae for some decisive move by Pompey, heard that Sulmo had gone over to Caesar, Corfinium was locked in a siege, and that Pompey was on his way to Brundisium. "[C]onfecta res est," he wrote before dawn on February 22; "it's all over."[13] Despite his frequent misreadings of Pompey's strategy, as well as Caesar's, his judgment this time was correct. There would be no defense of Italy, and the opening campaign of the Civil War had turned into a race to the sea. The question became: Would Pompey's troops, and Pompey himself, be able to escape Italy before Caesar and his unstoppable army caught up with them?

From Corfinium, Caesar pushed his men at top speed along the hilly backroads into Apulia and then to the coast road, which they followed toward Brundisium. For more than two weeks the army of perhaps thirty thousand infantrymen, thousands of slaves, servants, and camp followers, and hundreds of horsemen, traveled an average of seventeen miles a day. Along the way, Caesar's troops captured one of Pompey's staff officers, Numerius Magius, whom he sent immediately to Pompey with a message urging that the two of them meet in the interests of the Republic, as they were both in the neighborhood. Still waiting at Formiae, Cicero thought such a meeting the only chance to avert a prolonged conflict. "My whole mind is fixed in expectation of news from Brundisium," he wrote to Atticus on March 1. "If Caesar has found our Gnaeus there, there is a faint hope of peace, but if he has crossed over beforehand, there is the fear of a deadly war."[14]

But there would be no meeting and no peace, even though Pompey was still in Brundisium when Caesar arrived at the city gates a week later. The harbor was nearly empty, the Consuls having commandeered every suitable vessel and sailed for Macedonia a few days before with dozens of Senators and their families, as well as about fifteen thousand troops. Pompey had taken a surprising risk in putting most of his troops and the entire *optimate* government on the open sea in the dead of winter. Although the month was early March by the traditional Roman calendar, the actual date according to the modern solar calendar was closer to mid-January.

Sailing on the open sea was considered dangerous for the eight months of September through May, and was undertaken during winter only in emergencies. Even more threatening were the fierce gales and strong currents that were common at the mouth of the Adriatic in winter. But once Pompey decided to

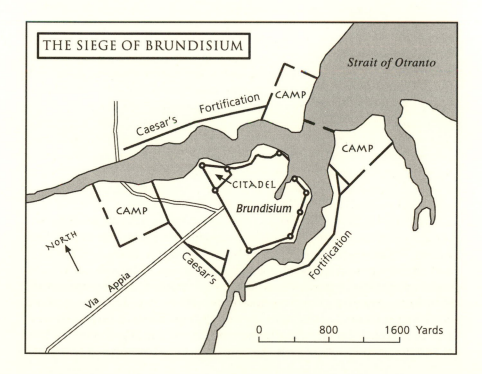

77

quit Italy, he had to take the risk, and his first good luck of the war was that his convoy made it across and back without incident.

While he waited for the empty ships to return, Pompey had barricaded himself inside the city and was directing its defense with twenty cohorts. Without ships, Caesar could do nothing to intercept the departed army, and he was unsure of Pompey's plans. Did he intend to hold the city and frustrate his pursuit by denying him Italy's best Adriatic harbor? Or was he only waiting for the ships to return to evacuate himself and the rest of the army? In either case, once Pompey's army made it safely out of Italy, it was certain that he would reinforce and prepare it for an invasion of the homeland. One modern strategist has been critical of Caesar for moving so quickly that he hastened Pompey's decision to abandon Italy. This "excess of directness," according to B. H. Liddell Hart, "robbed Caesar of his chance of ending the war in one campaign."[15]

We cannot know if Pompey could have been induced in some way to stay and fight, but we do know that Caesar's forte was the swift, surprise attack, and once he reached Brundisium, he immediately ordered the city surrounded and put under siege. Because of the configuration of land around the city, he had access to both sides of a channel that connected its harbor to the sea. He decided to close off the channel, thus blockading the harbor and preventing Pompey from escaping or using it as a naval base. Over the course of the nine-year Gallic War, Caesar had made frequent use of his *fabri* to build siege towers, tunnels, and bridges, but this was his first attempt to block a waterway. At its narrowest place the channel was a fifth of a mile across, somewhat less than the length of his bridge over the Rhine, but most of it was too deep for driving pilings.

Just as he had for the bridge, Caesar carefully describes the method and details of putting a barrier across the channel. From the shore on each side of it, his engineers rolled large boulders into the water and then covered them with earth to form two breakwaters, topped by roadways, that extended about eighty yards into the channel from each side. To obstruct the remaining deep-water passageway, they built heavy rafts, thirty feet square, which they floated at the ends of the breakwaters, anchored to the bottom at each corner, and then covered with earth. On the rafts they erected screens and barricades and then put up a two-story gunnery tower on every fourth one, so that they could be manned much like stationary warships.

To foil the blockade, Pompey fitted out several cargo vessels remaining in the harbor with three-story towers and *catapultae*, the artillery devices of classical times that used energy produced by torsion to fire missiles of all types, much like modern field guns. He manned them with archers and slingers, and sent them into the channel to ram the rafts and attack Caesar's construction crews. From their positions on the breakwater and the rafts, Caesar's legionaries fought back with the same weapons, and the ensuing naval battle may have been the most spirited fighting of the war until then. Caesar writes that he sent yet another envoy to Pompey at this time to propose a mediated peace and again ask for a meeting. But the reply came that the Consuls were no longer available, and without them nothing could be decided.

When the fighting in the channel had gone on for nine days, and Caesar's crews had managed to block only half the deep-water passageway, the fleet of transports returning from Macedonia appeared on the horizon, and Pompey immediately prepared to evacuate his troops. They had, in the interim, sealed off the city gates, and cut trenches across streets, built walls and fences, and planted booby traps all over the city to obstruct Caesar's pursuit.

Early on March 17, the transports and accompanying warships, under a barrage of missiles from Caesar's artillery, moved carefully in single file through the middle portion of the channel that was still open, and entered the harbor. By nightfall Pompey's last twenty cohorts, perhaps ten thousand men, were on board ship, with only a few light-armed infantry remaining to man the city walls. The people of Brundisium had not taken well to Pompey's military occupation. As the last defenders retreated in the early darkness, and Caesar's advance troops put ladders to the walls, they hastened to warn them of the traps and led them quickly through the city to the docks, but the remaining government troops had escaped in small boats at the last minute. Caesar's men took after them in what boats they could find, and eventually boarded and captured two transports that ran afoul of the breakwater, but Pompey and the rest of his troops slipped out of the harbor and made for the Macedonian coast, fifty miles away. The first campaign of the war—just over sixty days in length—ended with Caesar the master of Italy. But Pompey's army was intact.

VI

The First Spanish Campaign

The shock of Pompey's flight from Italy, and the abdication of the government of the most powerful state in the known world, rippled through the capital, across the country, and into the provinces and foreign states around the Mediterranean. Among the shortest campaigns of such consequence, it was all the more striking because it was nearly bloodless, and the victor did not seem inclined to beheadings or mass executions.

If there was a Roman more disturbed by Pompey's departure than Cicero, his story has not survived. In a series of letters to Atticus during a single week in March of 49, he revealed a range of strong and bitter feelings about the event. "I am not merely distressed," he wrote, "I am consumed with grief." He was doubly upset at Pompey's retreat because he had failed to join him. "I grieve that I am not participating." "The one thing that tortures me is that I have not followed Pompey." On top of this, he complained that Pompey had ignored him: "Meanwhile not a line to me, not a thought except for flight." Finally, he expressed anger at Pompey's abandonment of Italy: "This dishonor our Gnaeus contemplated two years ago."[1] His ambivalence toward Pompey would continue all his life, but now there was another man to deal with.

Within a day or two of Caesar's capture of Brundisium, Cicero sent him a fawning (and misleading) letter, praising his wisdom and kindness and assuring him that "when arms were taken up, I had nothing to do with the war, and I judged you therein to be an injured party."[2] He thanked him for sparing his friend Lentulus, and offered to act as an intermediary between him and Pompey.

But the slim chance that Caesar and Pompey would even meet face to face, much less settle their differences, had already evaporated, and the flight of Pompey and his army was a clear sign that the war would continue, and a clear victory for Caesar. If he was surprised by the ease of his success, he made no mention of it in *The Civil War*, saying only that there was not time to bring more ships to Brundisium or to build new ones to pursue the fleeing army, and that the most pressing danger was from Pompey's legions in Spain.

Before proceeding to Spain, however, he needed to safeguard Italy. He sent Mark Antony's younger brother Gaius into Illyricum with two legions to guard against a Pompeian invasion from that direction, and ordered Publius

Dolabella, Cicero's patrician son-in-law, to assemble a fleet of warships for duty in the Adriatic. To patrol the Tyrrhenian Sea and protect the west coast, he gave the same orders to Quintus Hortensius. Knowing that he would eventually have to pursue Pompey into Macedonia, he also ordered every port in Italy to begin building transports and to send them to Brundisium.

His other objective was to insure that shipments of wheat to Rome from the provinces were not halted or interrupted. Because of the high cost of transporting Italian wheat to feed the capital's growing population, Rome had turned to imported wheat, which could be shipped by water more cheaply than it could be transported by land. Eventually the capital became dependent on massive shipments of wheat from Sicily, and smaller amounts from Sardinia, Africa, and Egypt.

Pompey's navy could easily intercept cargo vessels from Africa and Egypt, making Sicily and Sardinia critical to the country's needs. After the fall of Corfinium, Asinius Pollio had begun marching with three legions toward Sicily, the source of half of Rome's imported wheat. Caesar now sent Quintus Valerius with a single legion to seize Sardinia, but it would be several weeks before an army would reach either island.

Leaving two newly recruited legions to garrison Brundisium, Tarentum, and Sipontum, modern Siponto on the Adriatic coast, Caesar set out along the Appian Way to Rome with his three veteran legions. Before long, he pulled ahead of them, most likely in a *raeda*, a four-wheeled carriage drawn by mules that allowed him the luxury of dictating to his amanuensis while on the road. He took the opportunity to respond to Cicero's flattering letter with a preening letter of his own, expressing his pleasure at his *clementia*, and professing no chagrin that many of Pompey's troops whom he had freed would return to fight him again. He even arranged for Cicero's letter to be taken to Rome and distributed among the influential people still in the capital. Having just driven the government out of the country, he was eager to gain the support of what remained of the governing class, as well as the general population. His intent was to maintain some semblance of the Republican system, and he counted on Cicero's participation to add to its legitimacy. As a first step, he instructed the tribunes Antony and Cassius to call a meeting of the Senate on April 1 in Rome, as was their legal prerogative.

A few days later, he stopped at Formiae, where Cicero was waiting nervously with his entire family, including his wife Terentia, son Marcus, and pregnant daughter Tullia, the wife of Dolabella. Cicero was determined to take a firm position against Caesar's military coup, but he was undecided about joining Pompey, and genuinely afraid that he would become Caesar's prisoner, or at least be prevented from leaving Italy. Although he and Caesar had known each other since adolescence, and had corresponded all their lives, they had not met in person for nine years. Moreover, Cicero still owed Caesar a large sum of money that he had borrowed five years before.

As they began their conversation, the central conflict between them quickly became clear, Caesar pressing Cicero to attend the Senate's meeting in Rome, and Cicero resisting. In his letter the next day to Atticus, Cicero expressed his dismay about the argument that ensued and his surprise that Caesar was so insistent. When Caesar suggested that Cicero come to Rome "to discuss peace," Cicero replied "On my own terms?" " 'Who am I,' he answered, 'to dictate to you?' 'Then,' said I, 'I shall take the line that the Senate objects to your going to Spain or transferring forces to Greece; and I shall express deep sympathy for Pompey.' " Caesar's answer was abrupt: "I cannot have such things said."[3] He told Cicero to think it over and ended the conversation. The entire matter is unmentioned in *The Civil War*. It would be another two months before Cicero made up his mind.

When Caesar reached the outskirts of Rome on April 1, it was his nearest approach to the city since he had hurried away at the end of his turbulent year as Consul nine years before. Although his legions were still on the road behind him, he remained outside the city limits in punctilious compliance with the law that prohibited a general from entering Rome with his army. Although his supporters welcomed him, the general reception was guarded. Those Senators who remained—a minority, including only two ex-Consuls—reluctantly convened a session to hear him out. They knew that they had made a fateful decision by remaining in Rome; Pompey had threatened severe sanctions for those who failed to join him. Even Calpurnius Piso, Caesar's father-in-law, was absent.

Addressing the uncomfortable Senators at length, Caesar reminded them that the Assembly had legally granted him the right to campaign for Consul *in absentia*, and that a clique of *optimate* Senators had prevented him from doing that. He recounted his offers to give up his provinces and his army, and to meet with Pompey, all of which had been spurned. He proposed that the Senate send delegates to negotiate with Pompey, and it duly voted to do so, but no one was willing to go. The next day he spoke along the same lines to a crowd of ordinary citizens, assuring them that there would be adequate supplies of grain, and promising each citizen a cash reward at the war's end.

With that he entered the capital and, after two more days of wrangling with the Senators, urged it to join him in administering the government, adding that if they did not, he would do it himself. He proceeded on his own authority to appoint Marcus Lepidus, Servilia's son-in-law, as Prefect of Rome, and placed Mark Antony in command of Italy. To Marcus Crassus *filius*, son of his former partner in the Triumvirate, he assigned his province of Nearer Gaul.

When he ordered the confiscation of the gold and silver bars and coins in the *aerarium sanctius*, the tribune Lucius Metellus attempted to bar the doors. Caesar himself confronted him and angrily threatened to have him killed if he persisted, adding that he disliked saying it more than he would doing it. Metellus retreated, and the doors were broken open. That his opponents had left their treasure in Rome was a stroke of *fortuna* for Caesar, but opportunism put it in his hands to use against them. Although this episode drew criticism, Romans had reason to be relieved. There were no murders or purges, and even the property of Pompey's supporters was left intact.

Nevertheless, it was an angry Caesar who departed Rome for Spain only a week later. Despite his seizure of the capital and the treasury, he had expected that a general who had served the interests of the Republic for so long, and who had refrained from harming his countrymen in the assertion of his rights, would be greeted by something other than resentment, fear, and hostility. Before he left the city, nearly five years after the death of his daughter Julia, he removed from his will the name of Gnaeus Pompeius.

His route to Spain was along the Via Aurelia on Italy's northwest coast, one of the oldest of Roman roads. The Via Aurelia had been built during the third century by Caesar's mother's ancestors, the Aurelii Cottae, and then extended as far as the vicinity of Savona in 109. From there the route into Further Gaul followed a narrow ancient track on the edge of the rugged Maritime Alps where they plunge toward the sea along today's Italian Riviera. At this point Caesar would have transferred to a *cisium*, a two-wheeled carriage, or more likely to horseback. At the Var River, the traditional boundary between Gaul and Italy, he would have found a century-old Roman road that took him to Aquae Sextiae, today's Aix-en-Provence, and then to the Greek city of Massilia, modern Marseilles. This trip of over five hundred miles he accomplished in about ten days, accompanied by a bodyguard of cavalry.

In the meantime, Quintus Valerius had occupied Sardinia without incident, and Asinius Pollio and his army had completed their march from Corfinium to the toe of Italy, just across the narrows from Sicily. A friend of the poets Catullus, Virgil, and Horace over the course of his long life, Pollio, not yet thirty, had already made his reputation as an orator when Caesar invited him to be one of his officers. In his history of the Civil War, now lost, he recorded the messages that passed between him and Cato at Sicily's capital city of Syracuse. They survive in the account of Appian of Alexandria, a later historian who had access to Pollio's work: "When Cato asked him whether he had brought the order of the Senate, or that of the people, to take possession of a government that had been assigned to another, Pollio replied, 'The master of Italy has sent me on this business.' "[4]

As Pollio had brought three legions with him, perhaps fifteen thousand men, Cato answered that in order to spare the province and its people he would not resist, and immediately departed by boat to join Pompey, leaving Sicily and its grain in Caesar's hands. Pollio was now joined by Curio, whom Caesar had directed to take an army across the Strait of Sicily and capture Rome's province of Africa, now held by the Pompeian general Attius Varus. Curio would be the first of Caesar's generals to undertake a major campaign by himself.

By April 19 Caesar was at the gates of Massilia, an independent city-state of less than a fifth of a square mile in area and perhaps five thousand inhabitants; it straddled a series of hills on a peninsula extending into what is now the Gulf of Lion. Along the southern side of the city, between it and a larger peninsula, lay a sheltered, deep-water harbor, now called Vieux Port, that had attracted Greek colonists from Phocaea, an Ionian city, some six centuries earlier. Since that time Massilia had become a naval power in the western Mediterranean and had founded its own colonies along the coasts of Gaul and Spain. It was a center for the exchange of the products of Gaul—grain, amber, and tin—for the wine and luxury goods of Italy and Greece. Rome and Greek Massilia were allies during the Punic Wars against Carthage, and when Rome created its province of Further Gaul in about 123, it left the city an independent state.

Massilia was governed by a council of six hundred men appointed for life, and was administered by a smaller group known as the Fifteen, the *quindecemviri*, on whose orders the city gates were now locked. Caesar summoned the Fifteen from Massilia to his camp and urged them not to involve Massilia in the hostilities. He must have suspected that he would be barred from Massilia. The Celtic tribes in its vicinity had been subdued in the last century by none other than the grandfather of his antagonist Lucius Domitius, and the province created afterward, the province that Caesar had governed for the past ten years, had been assigned by the Senate to the same Domitius just three months before.

While the Fifteen retreated behind the walls to discuss the issue, the persistent Domitius sailed into the harbor with the seven merchant vessels he had rounded up and outfitted himself, and then manned with his own slaves and tenant farmers. He was admitted to the city immediately and placed in command of what Caesar quickly perceived would be an energetic resistance to him. His scouts reported that food supplies were being rushed into the city, repairs were being made to the city walls and docks, and all available ships were brought into port for outfitting. Obviously, Massilia's spacious harbor and its position on his supply line between Italy and Spain were too important to be ceded to Pompey. "Roused by these hostile moves," he writes tersely, "Caesar brought up three legions against Massilia" and gave orders to prepare for a siege (*The Civil War* 1.36.4).

Within days, three legions that had spent the winter in Further Gaul under the command of Gaius Trebonius, the VIth, Xth, and XIVth, arrived in Caesar's camp, and he put them to work cutting trees and preparing timbers for the protective sheds and siege towers to be used for the attack on the walls of Massilia. But so long as Domitius and the Massiliots controlled the harbor, the city could be supplied and reinforced at any time by sea. To prevent this, Caesar prepared to impose a naval blockade, and sent a crew of shipbuilders up the Rhône to the port of Arelate, modern Arles, more than fifty miles away, where they began building a dozen war galleys. According to him, these were finished and equipped in thirty days and then brought down to the coast through the Fossa Mariana, the canal built some fifty years earlier by his uncle, Gaius Marius, to skirt the shallow, sediment-filled Rhône delta.

To the post of *praefectus classis*, commander of this extraordinary makeshift flotilla, Caesar appointed Decimus Brutus, the young officer who had led the Roman fleet to victory against the Veneti off the coast of Brittany five years before. Brutus brought his ships along the coast and stationed them at the island now called Île Ratonneau, three miles off Massilia's harbor. With these twelve warships carrying heavily armed marines, he was able, for the time being, to prevent any vessels from entering or leaving the port.

The blockade and siege of Massilia were the longest and most elaborate of the entire Civil War, and a severe test for even Caesar's experienced engineers. But they were undertakings for which Caesar himself had no time. With each passing week, Pompey's armies in Spain and in Macedonia, not to mention his naval forces, were gaining strength and gathering allies. To counter the threat of the Spanish legions from the west, Caesar had sent orders to Gaius Fabius at Narbo Martius, near the western end of the province, perhaps as early as March, to take his three legions, the VIIth, IXth, and XIth, toward Spain and secure the passes across the Pyrenees Mountains. But he knew that it was urgent that he deal with Pompey's army there himself.

At the end of May his three veteran legions, the VIIIth, XIIth, and XIIIth, arrived at Massilia. Caesar substituted them for the three legions that had been working on the siegeworks, and immediately dispatched the original three toward Spain. A week later he put Gaius Trebonius in command of the siege and started westward on the Via Domitia with an escort of nine hundred German cavalry.

At about the same time Cicero finally decided what he would do with himself during the course of the war. Caesar had written him while en route to Massilia about the rumor that he was about to leave Italy and join Pompey: "I appeal to you in the name of our friendship not to do this. . . . [W]hat more suitable part is there for an upright man and a good, peace-loving citizen than to keep aloof from civil dissensions?"[5] Cicero had taken this to mean that he might retire to some neutral place, such as Malta, and maintain his amity with Caesar. It is likely that he would have left immediately, except that a voyage into the middle of the Mediterranean in late April (actually early March) was all but impossible because of the weather. Because of his network of friends and correspondents (letters to or from over ninety different people have survived, including men in the inner circle of both factions), Cicero may have been the best-informed man in the Republic. His correspondents and his family urged him to wait for the outcome in Spain before committing himself.

What else caused him to hesitate was the pregnancy of his only daughter Tullia, of whom he was extremely fond. He was still waiting when she gave birth to a premature boy on May 19, whom Cicero described to Atticus as "a puny creature" who did not survive. At the end of the month he sent his wife and daughter back to Rome to the care of Atticus and finally, on June 7, despite warnings and threats from Mark Antony not to depart Italy, he left the country by boat from Formiae's port, Caieta. With him were his brother Quintus, his son, and his nephew. In his last letter from Italy, written on board ship to his wife Terentia, he said, "I shall at last be fighting for the commonwealth alongside my peers."[6] Nothing is known about his voyage, and very little about his subsequent movements, except that he eventually joined Pompey in Macedonia.

In the meantime, after spending several months at Narbo Martius, Gaius Fabius and his three legions, all veterans of the Gallic War, began their march to Spain along the Via Domitia. To the local inhabitants, the departure of this army from its camp outside the city—as many as fifteen thousand infantry, perhaps fifteen hundred slaves and servants, two to three thousand pack mules, and at least three thousand cavalry—would have been a remarkable spectacle. Over several centuries the Roman army had developed into a highly organized institution centered on the individual legion as a self-sufficient unit that quartered, fed, and transported itself according to a standard pattern. By Caesar's time the routine of breaking camp and the order of march had remained unchanged for more than a hundred years.

Before dawn on the day the legion was to march, a call on the *tuba*, the three-foot-long Roman trumpet, would alert the troops to strike their tents and prepare their baggage. At the second trumpet call they would dismantle any artillery they had, load it onto wagons, and load their pack animals. When the entire legion was ready to march, a herald at the commander's side would call out three times to the troops, asking if they were ready for war. Their response each time would be to raise their right arms and shout loudly "Sumus paratus" (We are ready). At the third trumpet call each unit of cavalry and infantry, as well as the mule train and the special cadres of troops, would file out the camp gate in a prescribed order.

Even though Fabius was marching on the seventy-year-old Via Domitia through a Roman province, he could not be sure that Pompeian troops had not crossed into Gaul to intercept him. Therefore, the usual contingent of cavalry rode at the head of the line to guard against an ambush. It was followed by the vanguard legion, chosen by lot and led by its *aquilifer*, a soldier picked for his experience and bravery, who carried the legion's standard, the *aquila*, a sculpted wooden eagle painted silver and mounted on a long wooden staff. As a sign of his status, and to convey the appropriate ferocity, the *aquilifer* wore the head and skin of a bear or a wolf over his head and shoulders. The *aquila* he carried marked the legion's location on the march or on the battlefield, and symbolized its pride and honor. Needless to say, it was fiercely defended, and its loss to the enemy was a rare disgrace that every soldier dreaded.

Marching behind the first legion were the *mensores*, the measurers or surveyors responsible for laying out the camp, and a pioneer corps that was responsible for clearing or bridging any natural obstacles. Next in line was the commanding general, on horseback, his cavalry bodyguard, and his baggage. Following them was the mule train, carrying the legionaries' tents and other *impedimenta*, as well as artillery and any other siege equipment. Behind it were the *legati legionum*—the individual commanders of the legions, and the *tribuni militum*, the military tribunes, six of whom reported to each *legatus*.[7]

The rank and file of the remaining legions, led by their *bucinatores* and *tubicines*, buglers and trumpeters, and their *aquiliferi*, followed by their baggage trains and servants, made up the bulk of the line. Each cohort of infantry was divided into six centuries of about eighty men each, and commanded by a centurion who had the duties of a modern captain and first sergeant. The sixty centurions who marched in each legion were promoted from the ranks on the basis of their courage, experience, and judgment, and were often in their fifties. Bringing up the rear of the line were the camp followers—prostitutes, common-law wives, and *mercatores*, merchants who peddled goods to the soldiers, all protected by both infantry and cavalry. In wars against barbarians and other non-Romans, another group would follow the army, slave dealers who purchased captives on the spot and transported them to Rome or another market city for auction.[8]

Moving briskly along the Via Domitia, an unpaved roadway perhaps fifteen to eighteen feet wide, the line of Gaius Fabius' three-legion army would have stretched for several miles. All three legions, as well as their commander, had fought under Caesar for nearly a decade and had survived the ambush of the Nervii in northern Gaul in 57. They had seen no action since the siege of Alesia in 52, after which Caesar had doubled their pay and rewarded each of them with a single Gallic slave. Their mission now was to capture the passes through the Pyrenees, and then hold Pompey's generals in northern Spain until Caesar's arrival.

The two Spains, Nearer and Further, at this time composing all but the northwestern part of the Iberian Peninsula, had been wrested from Carthage in 206 and had been made Rome's third and fourth provinces. During Pompey's second term as Consul in 55, the Senate appointed him Governor of both provinces for five years. But he chose to remain in Italy (his new theater was about to open) and delegated the provincial commands to three loyal *legati*, Lucius Afranius, Marcus Petreius, and Terentius Varro, all of whom had served with him for more than twenty-five years.

This trio was still there in the spring of 49 when the news arrived that Pompey had abandoned Italy, and that Caesar and his Gallic legions were on their way to Spain. Among them, only Petreius, son of a centurion, an officer for thirty years, and now over sixty, was a skilled commander. Varro, also in his sixties, though he had been in the army much of his life, was a prolific writer and scholar, and eventually became Rome's greatest antiquarian. Although he was a friend of both Cicero and Pompey, his loyalty to their cause was in doubt. Afranius, the youngest of the three, had been such a cipher as Consul in 60 that Cicero, in a letter to Atticus, had called him a "gutless, witless warrior." His reputation was as an expert dancer and, for a reason that remains unknown, he was the senior commander in Spain.

The three generals reasoned that because Caesar had served twice before in Spain and had a substantial following there, it was urgent that they prevent him from advancing very far into the peninsula. Varro agreed to stay behind with two legions and defend *Hispania Ulterior*. Afranius and Petreius combined their five legions of infantry and five thousand cavalry and marched toward the northeastern corner of *Hispania Citerior*, intending to bring Caesar to battle in what is now Catalonia.

They stationed their army in a secure position on a long knoll, now called the Mont de Gardeny, just to the south of the town of Ilerda, today the Catalan city of Lleida, but widely known as Lérida, less than ninety miles south of Spain's northern border. From the time of its founding in the late Iron Age by a Celtiberian tribe, Ilerda has commanded one of the main routes into northern Spain, and the modern city is the capital of one of the four provinces making up the autonomous region of Catalonia. The ancient town was situated on a rocky hill at the edge of a highland plain and overlooked the Sicoris River,

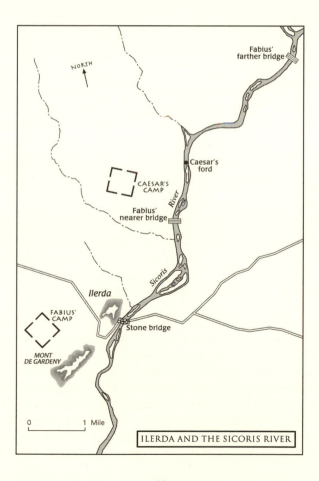

ILERDA AND THE SICORIS RIVER

now the Segre, a large, swift-moving river originating in the Pyrenees. Just opposite the town a stone bridge, the foundations of which support the present one, spanned the river, here some three hundred yards across and too deep to ford.

The Pompeian army took control of the town and stocked it with food supplies and fodder collected from the surrounding countryside. By now it had been augmented by thirty cohorts of auxiliary infantry, that is, light-armed native soldiers conscripted in the provinces, bringing its total to about forty thousand infantry and cavalry.

Afranius and Petreius sent cadres of troops to block the two eastern passes over the Pyrenees, as well as the Via Domitia, which ran along the coast toward Barcino, modern Barcelona. But after learning the position of the Pompeian encampment at Ilerda, Gaius Fabius turned off the Via Domitia near modern Perpignan and marched inland some eighty miles and up more than five thousand feet into the Pyrenees. There his cavalry dislodged the Pompeian troops and captured the main pass, now called Col de la Perche, leading directly into the valley of the Sicoris, and to Ilerda. Fabius brought all three of his legions through the pass down the right bank of the river, and built a camp north of the town on a hill about two miles upstream from the Pompeians, who were on the same bank.

It is certain that both armies constructed the elaborate field camp used by all Roman armies while on the march whenever they stopped, even for a single night. The camp was laid out in a gigantic square crisscrossed by several roadways according to a prescribed design that hardly varied over several hundred years. Around the perimeter, the legionaries dug a continuous ditch, as much as three yards deep, piling the earth in a bank just inside it. On top of the earth bank they built a palisade of sharpened stakes interwoven with lateral branches, each also sharpened at its ends. It was for this daily job that each ordinary soldier carried in his kit a shovel and a wicker basket (the wheelbarrow had not yet been invented). Also in his kit were spare clothing, food rations, and cooking and eating utensils. The troops' personal pack animals carried *dolabrae* (pickaxes), saws, *tabernacula* (tents), and heavy cooking pots. The finished camp was a secure compound, perhaps one hundred and fifty acres in area, that could be breached only with difficulty, even if there were no armed defenders.[9]

About a month after he reached Ilerda, Fabius was reinforced by the three other Gallic legions, the VIth, Xth and XIVth, which had begun the siege of Massilia, had been relieved by the three from Italy, and then had made a rapid march to Spain. Fabius now had a six-legion army of perhaps thirty thousand infantry and three thousand cavalry, and more were on the way. Armies of this size had not been seen in this area for more than two decades, and the sudden demand on the farms, gardens, and grazing stock in the countryside around Ilerda was severe. In fact, it was the scarcity of food supplies for both men and animals, rather than military strength, that was the crucial factor in the cat-

and-mouse game that decided the Spanish campaign. It was a game that Caesar was ready to play.

He was still traveling from Massilia, however, when the first fighting took place, triggered by Fabius' need for grazing land for his thousands of animals. Although the two armies had been camped within sight of each other for more than two months, neither was inclined to attack the other's well-defended position. Under orders to wait for Caesar, Fabius had improved his situation by building two bridges across the Sicoris four miles apart, one on either side of his camp. The Pompeians, with an open route by the stone bridge at Ilerda for supplies and reinforcements from the south, and easy access to good pasturage across the river, were content to block any further advance by Fabius, and perhaps hopeful that he would soon run out of food and fodder.

By the third week of June the dwindling forage in the vicinity of both camps caused each army to send its pack animals across the river each day to graze, accompanied by cavalry and a pair of legions for protection. Occasionally the cavalry from each army skirmished on the plain, but there was no serious fighting. Heavy spring rains had caused the river to rise, and one day while one of Fabius' *legati*, Lucius Plancus, was making this daily crossing with two legions, a strong gale suddenly blew up, and the bridge was swept away, leaving most of his cavalry unable to cross.

Camped downstream from Fabius, Afranius and Petreius saw the debris from the bridge in the swollen river and realized that part of Fabius' army was isolated on the far shore. Their trumpeters hastily summoned four legions and thousands of horsemen, who raced across the stone bridge to attack Plancus' troops. Outnumbered and bereft of his cavalry, Plancus could only retreat to a nearby hill, where his two legions were soon sustaining fierce attacks from two sides. But the collapse of the bridge had also alerted Fabius. He understood the tactical opportunity presented to the Pompeians and immediately ordered two legions to march northward, cross the river on the upper bridge, and relieve Plancus. When their *aquilae* appeared on the horizon, Afranius chose not to risk a full-scale battle and returned to his camp.

When Caesar arrived at Ilerda two days later, the repair of the lower bridge was under way, and he ordered it completed that night. He quickly saw that Ilerda would not yield readily to a siege, and that to defeat the Pompeian army he would have to detach it from its magazine in the town and from the stone bridge across the Sicoris—its single route for reinforcement and retreat. The next day he assigned six cohorts to guard the bridge and the baggage in the camp, and led his entire army down past the town and to a flat plain northwest of the Pompeian camp. There he formed the six legions in the traditional three lines of infantry facing the Mont de Gardeny, in effect, offering immediate battle. Afranius brought his legions out of camp under arms and halfway down the hill, where they drew up in battle formation, but advanced no further.

Seeing that Afranius was unwilling to engage him, Caesar ordered his first two lines to stay in place, concealing the third line of legionaries, fully a third of his infantry, who then dug a long trench behind them to form the front of a fortified camp. By the time Afranius realized what was happening, it was too late to attack, using the advantage he would have had. That evening Caesar withdrew all six legions behind the ditch, where they camped for the night *sub armis*, without disarming. With this simple deception, Caesar was able to take a protected position practically under his enemy's nose. Over the next two days half the troops completed the ditch and bank on the other three sides of the camp, and brought in the army's baggage while they were guarded by the other half.

Caesar's next move was to try to occupy a small hill between the town and the Pompeian camp. This led to an extended battle of more than five hours during which Caesar's men were nearly surrounded, then retreated in a panic, and then regrouped and fought their way to the walls of the town. Finally, after heavy losses in both armies, they were forced to retreat to their camp, leaving Afranius in control of the disputed hill.

Hard on this setback, the weather now caused a new predicament: "So great a storm arose that it was generally agreed there had never been more extensive flooding in the area. On this occasion it in fact melted the snow from all the mountains and overflowed the banks of the river and broke down on a single day both the bridges which Gaius Fabius had constructed. This brought great problems for Caesar's army" (*The Civil War* 1.48.1–3).

Caesar's supply and reinforcement line from Further Gaul was severed, and his access to grain and fodder from the countryside to the west was blocked by the Cinga River, now the Cinca, which ran southeast out of the Pyrenees and into the Sicoris about twenty miles south of Ilerda. Since Afranius had stripped the area bare, and what grain was left standing was not ready for harvesting, Caesar was stranded between the rivers with no source of food for his thousands of men and animals. He tried desperately to rebuild one bridge once the flooding subsided, but his men were thwarted by the strong current and by the hail of missiles from the Pompeians controlling the far bank.

Before he had left Gaul, Caesar had called on friendly Celtic tribes to support him in the Spanish campaign, and now a large convoy of reinforcements and supplies, including thousands of Celtic auxiliaries, cavalry, and archers approached from the northeast. As was their custom, their families, slaves, servants, and wagonloads of possessions trailed behind them. But they were forced to halt at the swollen river a few miles upstream and, when Afranius sent three legions at them, obliged to retreat into the nearby hills.

There they remained for the next two weeks, during which Caesar's army began to suffer for lack of supplies and food, and his legionaries started to show signs of weakness. In his after-the-fact narrative Caesar notes that the growing confidence among the Pompeians, who were well supplied and situated, was conveyed in their letters to Rome, delivered some weeks later. "When these letters and reports reached Rome, there were great gatherings at

Afranius' house and great demonstrations of joy; numbers of people started out from Italy to join Gnaeus Pompeius" (*The Civil War* 1.53.2).

In a determined effort to get his bridge-building crews across the river, Caesar ordered his *fabri* to construct a type of boat he had seen the Celts use during his campaign in Britain five years before. This was the Celtic curragh, a light, elongated craft made with a frame of small saplings interlaced with woven reeds and pliable branches, and then covered with hides. Because of its easy handling and economical construction, Welsh and Irish fishermen continue to use it in modern times.[10]

To forestall any interference by the Pompeians, Caesar's workmen built several large curraghs in secret and transported them at night on pairs of wagons to a spot twenty-two miles upstream. There they used them to float a small party of legionaries across the Sicoris, where they occupied a solitary hill on the opposite bank and fortified it without being detected. Modern investigators have identified this hill, precisely thirty-three kilometers, or twenty-two Roman miles, north of Ilerda. Caesar then ferried across an entire legion to protect his bridge-building crews, who, building from both sides, completed the bridge at the spot in two days.

When the Gallic convoy, with its long-awaited supplies and reinforcements, streamed across the bridge and joined Caesar's camp, *celeriter fortuna mutatur*, as Caesar puts it (fortune swiftly changed). It had become apparent by now that Pompey would not be seen in Spain, and a number of nearby towns, including Tarraco, modern Tarragona, a Roman port on the coast, as well as several tribes in the area, declared their support for Caesar. On his request, they supplied him with grain, animals, and soldiers. Also, his six to seven thousand armed horsemen, both Gallic and German, were now able to protect any foragers and grazing animals that he sent to the left bank of the Sicoris. But they were all forced to travel more than twenty miles upriver to use the bridge, and Caesar knew that even in his improved situation, time favored the enemy. He could not afford a lengthy standoff.

To remove the disadvantage of the distant bridge, Caesar undertook another of the remarkable engineering feats for which he is justly famous. About three miles above Ilerda, where the river's banks were low, he had his legionaries dig several thirty-foot-wide trenches—diverting enough water from the river into the flood-plain so it could be forded by a horse and rider. Afranius and Petreius quickly realized that if Caesar's cavalry, which outnumbered their own, could cross the river here, their own use of the left bank and their access to the south might be cut off. Although their army was slightly larger than Caesar's, they were not confident that they could defeat the conqueror of Gaul in a pitched battle.

They decided to gradually retreat about twenty-five miles south to the far bank of the Iberus River, now the Ebro, where they would be less vulnerable and closer to supplies and reinforcements. They sent instructions to their allies in the vicinity to lay a bridge of boats across the Iberus, then and now the largest and longest river in Spain. At the same time, they sent two of their five legions across the Sicoris, where they built a heavily fortified camp on a rise overlooking the stone bridge.

Meanwhile, Caesar's engineers continued their job of diverting water through the trenches until, after a week of work, the river had fallen enough so that his horsemen could barely get across. The Pompeians became alarmed that he would soon do the same with his infantry, and that they would be attacked by tens of thousands of legionaries on both sides of the river. Leaving just enough troops to hold the town and its access to the stone bridge, they led the rest of their army across the Sicoris and joined the camp on the other side.

At this point in his narrative, Caesar introduces a favorite type of anecdote intended to impress the reader with the bravery of his troops and their loyalty to him:

But all over the camp the soldiers gathered in groups, sorry that the enemy had slipped from their grasp and that the war was inevitably being prolonged, and they approached the centurions and military tribunes and begged them to tell Caesar not to shrink from exposing them to toil or danger; they were prepared, and had the capability and the courage, to cross the river at the spot where the cavalry had crossed. Caesar was stirred by their words and enthusiasm, and although afraid to expose his army to such a powerfully flowing river, thought he ought to make the attempt and see what happened. (*The Civil War* 1.64.2–3)

To have his troops spontaneously demand the most dangerous mission was a high compliment to the leadership and inspiration of any Roman general. Caesar no doubt intended his Civil War narrative to serve the same propaganda purpose as *The Gallic War*, and both books are sprinkled with tales of his soldiers' heroism. To top off the story, true or not, Caesar writes that after excusing the weaker men, he stationed a line of pack animals in the river both above and below the ford to slow the current, and led the rest of the infantry himself through the water to the opposite bank. Nearly all the pack animals and all the heavy baggage, that is, tents, tools, and supplies, were left behind. With the river at their chests or higher, the legionaries could carry no more than their weapons, clothing, and temporary rations on their shields above their heads. Whether Caesar was on horseback or on foot, he does not say.

With the transfer of both armies to the left bank of the Sicoris in late July, the final week of the Ilerdan campaign now unfolded in the twenty-five miles of dry and mountainous country between Ilerda and the Iberus. Although Caesar's bold fording of the river substantially improved his position, it left his infantry with practically nothing but their weapons and a little food. But it was the type of chance that he was prone to take, this time in the hope that the mission would be a short one.

After leaving a single legion behind to guard his camp, Caesar prepared to pursue Afranius with five of his veteran legions and the equivalent of one more of Celtic auxiliaries; in the Pompeian army were almost eight legions of both

Roman and native infantry. Although he had fewer foot soldiers, Caesar had nearly seven thousand horsemen to his opponents' five thousand.

The cavalry of Caesar's day, however, was not the fearsome mass of shock troops that it became in later centuries; at that time neither the horse nor its equipment was suited to the cavalry charge. Although the horse was of prime importance to both Celts and Germans, and they bred it for strength and size, it was still much smaller than the stout charger of Napoleonic or even medieval times. Also, the stirrup was not part of a horseman's equipment, and it would be another seven hundred years before it reached the West from the Orient.[11]

The Romans learned the use of the saddle, the bit, the horseshoe, and other equine gear from the Celts, who were far more expert with the horse than they were. Caesar notes that the German cavalry used no saddles at all; he preferred German horsemen to Celtic, and both to Roman. With or without their saddles, however, even the best cavalry had limited use in a pitched battle. The customary three lines of heavy infantry, armed with spear, sword, and shield, could usually turn back a cavalry charge, either by stabbing the unprotected horses or jolting the riders off them. For this reason, cavalry were most often sent against their counterparts and were better used, as Caesar used them, for scouting, for escorts, for carrying messages, for chasing down foragers and retreating troops, and for harassing the ends and edges of marching legions.

It was for this last purpose that Caesar now deployed his thousands of cavalry against the rear guard of the Pompeian army as it struggled across the hot and dusty countryside. Several miles ahead was a range of low and rugged hills that lay in front of a high ridge, beyond which was the Iberus and its valley. Both sides had observed that the nearest route over the ridge, at least for the armies they commanded, lay through several narrow passes, in front of which lay a broad plateau. Afranius' objective now was just to take his army to the Iberus intact, and to dismantle the boat bridge after crossing; Caesar had not only to prevent his doing this, but also to defeat him promptly, one way or another, so that he could resume his pursuit of Pompey.

For several days Afranius and his army moved ahead by fits and starts, marching for several hours, then stopping to fight off Caesar's cavalry. One night they tried to sneak away during the third watch, between midnight and 2 A.M., but Caesar's scouts detected them, and his trumpets sounding through his camp caused them to abandon the attempt.

Two days later, just at dawn, Caesar and his infantry, pretending to leave the field and retreat to Ilerda, circled back into the hills undetected, and laboriously made their way over a chain of rocky bluffs and steep ravines—"He had to struggle across very deep and difficult gullies" (*The Civil War* 1.68.2)—until they were finally seen, far out on the flank, clambering through the jagged hills toward the high plateau behind the Spanish legions. Afranius and his men, who had been jeering at their enemy's retreat, quickly formed up and rushed to reach the plateau first, leaving a few cohorts behind to guard their baggage. But the trademarks of Caesar's tactics, *celeritas* and *improvisum*, quickness and surprise, had caught them flatfooted. Out of the hills streamed his legionaries and down to the plateau, where they drew up their battle lines in front of the passes. Afranius was blocked from the route over the ridge to the Iberus and to safety.

The disorganized and frightened Pompeian army was now at Caesar's mercy, and the campaign was all but over. His officers crowded around him, eager to give battle, urging him to attack even though the enemy was on higher ground. At this point in his narrative, Caesar stops to consider the issue, and to pose a few rhetorical questions:

Caesar had conceived the hope that he would be able to bring matters to a conclusion without fighting or shedding his men's blood, because he had cut his opponents off from food. Why should he lose any of his men, even if the battle were to go his way? . . . Why should he tempt fortune, especially when it was a true general's duty to secure victory as much by strategy as by the sword? He was swayed too by pity for his fellow citizens, whom he was aware had to lose their lives; he would much prefer to gain his ends by preserving them safe and sound. (*The Civil War* 1.72.1–3)

He moved his troops back from the hill "so that his opponents should feel less threatened," and both armies built the usual fortified camp. He did not surround the Pompeian camp, but posted detachments in the mountains, blocking routes to the Iberus.

Despite the great effort expended and blood already shed, Caesar chose to frame the conflict as a Roman quarrel, not a struggle to the death against foreigners, to whom he routinely showed no mercy. Although he admits that this policy was unpopular with his men, his next few paragraphs describe a remarkable scene on the following day that leaves little doubt of its wisdom. With both Afranius and Petreius temporarily away from their camp to see about their water supply, numerous Pompeian soldiers, including some officers, made their way into Caesar's camp and, being welcomed there, thanked everyone for sparing them the day before. A delegation that included Afranius' own young son approached Caesar and got his assurance that if they surrendered, Afranius and Petreius would not be killed. When they sought out friends and townsmen, and Caesar's men did the same in the Pompeian camp, the scene was one of "general rejoicing and congratulation" (*The Civil War* 1.74.7).

But when Afranius and Petreius returned, the mood changed abruptly. Petreius denounced all fraternization and ordered his bodyguard to hunt down any of the enemy visitors they could find and kill them. He made an emotional appeal to his troops, begging them not to betray the cause of Pompey, and then demanded that every soldier take an oath that he would never surrender or desert his leaders. Even Afranius, who had been inclined to accept the truce, agreed to the oath, and the entire army prepared to continue fighting. Caesar, on the other hand, ordered all enemy visitors in his camp sent back unharmed; a number of tribunes and centurions, who would have suffered severely had they returned, chose to remain with him.

But the restored resolve of the Pompeian army did nothing to improve its situation. Both water and animal fodder were scarce, and the lack of food among the auxiliary troops caused a great number of them to desert to Caesar. Afranius and Petreius decided that their best alternative was to return to Ilerda, where food and fodder had been stored, and water was plentiful. But after advancing only four miles, all the time harried by Caesar's cavalry, they were forced to stop and build a camp to protect themselves. Over the next two days they started out again, then stopped and camped, then slaughtered their remaining pack animals to preserve fodder and water, and then formed up outside their camp and offered battle. But Caesar would not fight. He simply kept his legions close, using his German and Gallic horse to nip at their edges and keep them from foraging or finding water.

Finally, on August 2, the two dispirited generals sent word to Caesar that they were ready to talk, but wanted to meet with him out of sight of both armies. When he rejected this condition, they were forced to negotiate in public, a scene that Caesar does not shrink from painting in detail:

Afranius spoke in front of both armies: he said that neither they themselves nor their soldiers ought to be the objects of anger because they had wished to remain loyal to their general Gnaeus Pompeius. But they had done their duty and had suffered enough punishment: they had put up with lack of everything; and now, almost as though they were wild beasts, they were walled in, kept from water, and kept from moving, and their bodies could not stand the suffering, nor their spirits the disgrace. And so they admitted they were beaten; they begged and entreated, if there were any place left for pity, that it would not be necessary for Caesar to apply the ultimate punishment. (*The Civil War* 1.84.3–5)

In response to this pitiful appeal, Caesar delivered a lengthy oration to the same audience, perhaps fifty thousand men, though most would not have heard him. To Afranius' claim of duty done, *officio satisfactus*, he replied that everyone had done his duty except the Pompeian generals, who had murdered men their own army had invited into their camp, and then had stubbornly refused to surrender until they had no choice. Now they "passionately seek what they have just spurned" (*The Civil War* 1.85.4). He added that he had declined to attack the helpless army in order to improve the prospect of peace. Now, rather than punish the army he had captured, he wanted only to insure that it would no longer be used against him. He ordered that those with homes or property in Spain be discharged at once; the others his army would escort through Further Gaul to the border with Italy and there release.

As expected, the Spanish legions responded with enthusiasm, but then complained that they had not been paid. After some negotiation, Caesar agreed to make good their claims against Afranius and Petreius, as well as reimburse his own soldiers for valuables taken from the enemy army, which he ordered returned. Such magnanimity was almost unprecedented in the ancient world, and although Caesar was too immodest to omit it from his commentary, *The Civil War* went unpublished while he lived, and its full propaganda value was unrealized.

Ilerda has been called Caesar's finest hour, and there are few better examples of his persistence and ingenuity on the battlefield. He also achieved that rare result in warfare—eradication of his enemy without a destructive battle. Some credit must be given to Afranius and Petreius, who, perhaps at odds over tactics, had managed to lose an army of nearly forty thousand foot and horse in less than six weeks. Caesar rewarded them with their lives and their freedom; to repay him, they found another time and place to fight him.

Varro and his two legions remained at large and in control of Further Spain, but Caesar had removed the main Pompeian threat from the peninsula. While at Ilerda, he had received the first dispatches from Massilia, and it was there, where his army was besieging the city and his navy blockading the port, that the next episode of the Civil War took place.

VII
The Siege of Massilia

Old as warfare itself, the siege was the endgame in countless ancient conflicts. The specialized devices and machines of the siege have a shorter history, but were used by Egyptians and Babylonians, and then by Assyrians early in the first millennium before the Christian era. Greeks and Carthaginians brought the ancient siege to its acme in their wars among themselves and with their neighbors, especially around Sicily at the end of the fifth century BCE. From them the Romans learned to execute the stunning feats of construction and mechanical engineering that typified the siege in its most advanced form. They also learned the value of perseverance, and became known for never abandoning a siege, no matter how long it took, as they demonstrated in their siege of Veii, an Etruscan city-state on a rocky plateau only twelve miles from Rome, which held out for more than seven years before it fell in 396.

Caesar's land and sea blockade of Massilia was the last of the great sieges of the Hellenistic age, the three centuries between the death of Alexander in 323 and the beginning of the Christian Era. During this period Roman aggressiveness, wealth, and ingenuity produced a host of successful sieges, and Caesar's assaults on Celtic *oppida* in Gaul were notable for their grand scale and resolute consummation. But the Greek Massiliots were better prepared and far more sophisticated than the Celts and Britons he had faced during the previous decade. At Massilia, after laying out his plan of attack, Caesar delegated its execution to Gaius Trebonius, a general who had participated in Caesar's prodigious assaults on Aduatuca, Avaricum, and Alesia during the Gallic War.

Trebonius was one of Caesar's most experienced *legati* and, like his commander, was another soldier-politician with a literary bent. As a Senator and tribune in the 50s, he had served the interests of the Triumvirate, then had fought under Caesar in Gaul and Britain, and had distinguished himself at the siege of Alesia. He was a friend and correspondent of Cicero's, and is most likely the original author of the detailed account of the siege of Massilia with which Caesar opens Book II of *The Civil War*. In its final form, it is the most exact report of such a siege that has survived from antiquity.

A siege was undertaken to capture a fortified place by undermining, breaking through, or getting over its walls in some way, or by depriving the defenders of food or water until they surrendered. Aside from this, the circumstances of each siege could differ markedly. At Massilia Trebonius' advantages were that the city, as long as Brutus maintained his blockade, could not be supplied by sea, and there was no serious threat to him from the surrounding area. On the other hand, the city had a natural source of drinking water, and had laid in substantial food and supplies. More important, Massilia was a Greek city with centuries of experience in the art of warfare; it was prepared to fight back with an arsenal of artillery devices and other antisiege techniques.

As a single, small colony at the edge of a region filled with barbarian tribes, Massilia had, long before, fortified itself against an attack by land. Across the neck of their hilly peninsula the Massiliots had constructed a massive stone wall more than twelve hundred yards long and thirty to forty feet high. Circular towers forty feet in diameter and rising another ten feet flanked the main gate, and other towers stood at intervals along the wall. When French archaeologists uncovered a portion of this wall in 1967, it was found to be ten feet thick, the interior being filled with rubble, and faced with large blocks of pink limestone from a quarry thirty-five miles west of the city.[1]

Just outside the middle part of the wall lay a deep ravine, beyond which, at a distance of five to six hundred yards, stood another hill that overlooked the entire city and harbor. On this hill, the site today of the St. Charles railway station, Trebonius built his main camp, surrounded by the ditch and palisade common to all Roman camps. Partway down this hill and on another nearby,

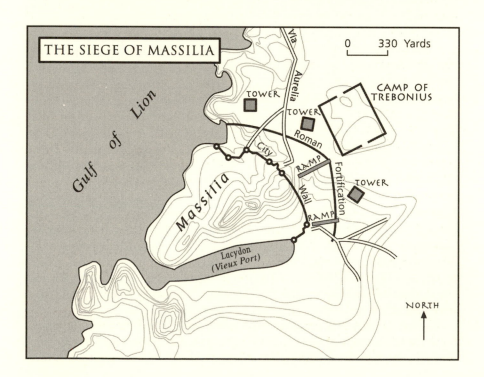

THE SIEGE OF MASSILIA

Gulf of Lion

Massilia

Via Aurelia

TOWER

TOWER

Roman City Wall

RAMP

Fortification

TOWER

RAMP

CAMP OF TREBONIUS

0   330 Yards

Lacydon (Vieux Port)

NORTH

his legionaries constructed at least three towers, each of several stories, in which they placed their own artillery. Although Caesar does not say so, it is highly likely that the Romans then linked these towers by a deep protective ditch, behind which they built up a continuous mound of earth surmounted by a palisade of stakes and saplings. Thus they enclosed the Massilian wall within their own outer one, some three hundred to three hundred and fifty yards in front of it, which protected the besiegers moving between the towers and prevented any escape from the city.

Once this work was complete, Trebonius was ready to make his assault on the city wall proper. His objective was to get his engineers across the ravine to the wall to break through or undermine it, and then to bring his heavy infantry to the breach in such numbers that they could enter the city in force. For this purpose, he had conscripted laborers and collected animals from all over the province, and he now put them to work building two sixty-foot-wide earth ramps up to the wall at right angles, one across the ravine near the main gate, and another across the lower ground near the harbor.

As the Massiliots watched the Romans prepare to constrict them by land, they hurried to build a fleet of warships to break the sea blockade and open their harbor to supplies and reinforcements. By converting merchant vessels into warships and constructing new ones, they were able to assemble a fleet of seventeen *naves longae*, the long, low warships of antiquity that were usually propelled by triple banks of oarsmen on each side. Eleven of them were built with decks that could accommodate fighting troops and artillery and protect the oarsmen sitting below. Lucius Domitius took personal command of several and manned them with his own slaves and tenant farmers whom he had brought from Italy. At the end of June, when Brutus had maintained the blockade for about a month, the Massiliots completed their work and put out to sea against his squadron of twelve ships. Among the marines on board the Massilian ships were *sagittarii*, mercenary archers from the Albici, a Gallic tribe who were noted for their skill with the bow and arrow.

The Romans had copied the design of the *navis longa* from the Carthaginians two hundred years earlier, and had used it to defeat them off the coasts of Sicily and Africa. They were substantial vessels, at least forty yards long, with beams of ten to twelve feet, and decks four to five feet above the waterline. A huge square sail made of sections of linen, with a full set of rigging for working it, hung from a mast set amidships, and some ships had a second mast and sail. Large eyes were customarily painted on each side of the bow. Attached to the front of the hull at the waterline was a massive bronze ram projecting a blunt tip that was used to ram enemy ships. A typical ram on a warship of this period was a single bronze casting three feet in height, more than seven feet long, and weighing half a ton.[2]

The configuration of ancient warships has long been a fertile field of study for naval archaeologists, but there is no precise description of those used in the sea fights off Massilia. It is likely that both the Romans and Massiliots used tri-

Cross-section of a model showing the oar arrangements of an ancient trireme. (National Maritime Museum, Greenwich, England. Courtesy of J. S. Morrison.)

remes and quadriremes, and possibly quinqueremes, in their fleets, the numeral prefix denoting the number of files of oarsmen on each side. The typical trireme had three banks of oars on each side, twenty-seven to thirty in each bank, with oarsmen seated at three levels, one to an oar, and one above the other in diagonal lines. Other trireme arrangements used only one bank on each side, each oar being pulled by three men, or two banks in which half the oars were manned by two men, and the rest by one. Outfitted for battle, a trireme carried one hundred and seventy oarsmen, fifteen officers and crew, and another fifteen fighting troops, for a total of about two hundred men.[3]

The quadrireme and quinquereme used about sixty and a hundred and twenty additional rowers, respectively, and were usually limited to one or two banks of oars to keep the center of gravity lower and reduce the danger of tipping. The quadrireme had four files of oarsmen on each side, either two to an oar arranged in two banks, or four in one bank. The quinquereme was similar, except for an additional file of oarsmen on each side. In *Pharsalia*, his epic poem about the Civil War, written about one hundred years later, Lucan described Brutus' flagship as a *hexeris*, a "six," with six files of oarsmen on each side.

The Roman method of fighting at sea was to duplicate, as far as possible, the circumstances of an infantry battle on land. They sacrificed speed and maneuverability in favor of a heavier warship that could carry more troops, and they concentrated on closing with the enemy vessel and then boarding it with legionaries carrying sword, shield, and dagger. It was precisely for this purpose that Caesar had ordered the *fortissimi viri*, the toughest men, selected from each legion and put aboard his warships. These marines, but not the crew, were also armed with the same heavy and light javelins that they used on land.

According to Caesar, the oarsmen Brutus had recruited were handicapped not only by their inexperience and ignorance of naval matters, but also by the slowness of their vessels, which had been built with green timber, which retained moisture. A well-built and properly manned trireme could reach a speed of eleven knots for short spurts, but a more common speed was no more than two knots.[4] Although the Massiliots sent many vessels, including fishing boats, carrying the Albici *sagittarii* against Brutus' fleet, the crux of the battle took place between their seventeen warships and Brutus' twelve: " The Massiliots . . . relying on the speed of their ships and the skill of their helmsmen, slipped out of our way and absorbed our attacks, and so long as they had plenty of searoom they extended their line further and attempted either to surround us or to make attacks in groups against individual ships or, if they could, to break off our oars by passing close alongside" (*The Civil War* 1.58.1).

But the Romans were confident enough of their tactics that they steered between the enemy ships, threw their javelins into them, and then used *manus ferreae*, "iron hands" (grappling hooks), to hold them alongside, sometimes one on each side. The hired *sagittarii* and the slaves and farmers Domitius had conscripted, were no match for Caesar's veteran infantry, who jumped aboard their ships, slashing and stabbing with their swords from behind their shields.

From the heights within their city walls, the Massiliots saw a brief and bloody battle in which three of their ships were sunk, having been rammed or swamped (the trireme was notoriously unstable), and six others captured with their crews. The Romans drove the remaining half of Massilia's fleet back into the harbor, and the blockade remained intact, but Domitius was one of the survivors and had no intention of giving up.

It was a stunning naval victory for Brutus, and he sent a courier racing down the Via Domitia to take the news to Ilerda, where Caesar had just completed his bridge over the Sicoris, allowing the Celtic convoy to cross. Caesar writes that the report from Massilia, combined with the arrival of reinforcements, food, and fodder, greatly heartened his discouraged army.

It is likely that the Romans besieging Massilia also witnessed the sea fight from their camp and towers, but it would have been a diversion of only a few hours from the laborious work of constructing the two ramps leading up to the wall. The Roman crews used teams of oxen to drag huge tree trunks to the site, and then rolled them into the ravine or laid them across the marshy ground to make a base for the ramps. At intervals they covered them with dirt and clay brought up in baskets to stabilize them and make them fireproof. But anyone within two or three hundred yards of the wall was exposed to a constant barrage of missiles—arrows, metal-tipped bolts or javelins, and stone shot—coming from the defenders on the wall and behind it.

During the Gallic War Caesar's troops had been accustomed to protecting themselves against the rocks and arrows of the Celts with portable screens made of the light branches of willow and other bushes. But the Greek Massiliots possessed far more powerful weapons, and the Romans were astonished to see twelve-foot-long steel-tipped javelins pierce four layers of screens and bury themselves in the ground. It was the first time Caesar's army had faced the powerful artillery used by the armies of the advanced Mediterranean states.

Aside from ordinary arrows shot from bows, which were used by Celtic *sagittarii* on both sides, the Massiliots and Romans both used torsion *catapultae*, missile-firing machines of a type known as *tormenta*—so called because they used torsion produced by the twisting of thick ropes of sinew or hair. The torsion *catapulta* revolutionized ancient warfare after it was invented by Greek engineers midway through the fourth century BCE, and by Caesar's time it had developed into a highly accurate device with remarkable throwing power.

The *catapulta* consisted of a heavy tripod supporting a seven-foot-long trough fitted at the back end with a windlass and hook. At the front of the trough a sturdy upright frame about two feet square was fixed in a vertical position. Within the frame, two thick coils of hair or animal tendon were stretched between the top and bottom beams. These coils were then twisted tightly, producing a strong torsion, and wooden arms inserted into the middle of each of them at right angles. A bowstring of stout rope was attached to the other end

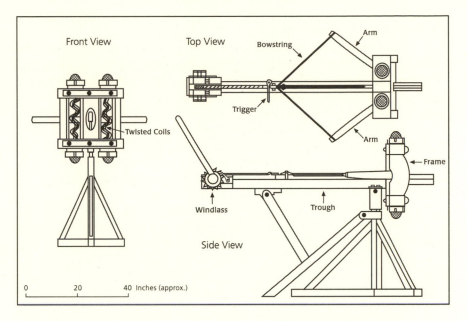

Diagram of Erwin Schramm's reconstruction of *scorpio*, the catapult used by Caesar's army in the first century BCE. In the decade before World War I, Schramm built a working catapult solely from specifications in Book X of Vitruvius Pollio's *On Architecture*.

of each arm and passed through a trigger mechanism. When the bowstring and the arms were drawn back by us of the windlass, and the trigger released, the rapid untwisting of the coils yanked them forward, driving the arrow or javelin out of the trough with tremendous force. Depending on the size of the *catapulta*, a missile could be flung in a nearly flat trajectory as much as several hundred yards.[5]

Caesar equipped each of his legions with these torsion *catapultae*, which his men called *scorpiones*, possibly because the sudden, sharp forward thrust of the missile resembled the attack of a scorpion. Also, the upright handle of the windlass at the rear of the *scorpio* may have reminded them of the raised stinger at a scorpion's back. Once set up, these machines could be loaded and fired by two gunners in less than a minute, and they were light enough to be carried in two pieces on mules. *Scorpiones* could be built to fire small or large javelins, as well as egg-sized rocks or even larger ones. On the hill of St. Charles, the location of Trebonius' camp, archaeologists have found numerous round stones of basalt weighing about seventeen pounds that were probably used by both sides. *Catapultae* were accurate enough to bring down a man at a hundred yards, and a horse at two hundred, a better performance than the early musket some sixteen centuries later. Another feature of the arrows and javelins used by the Massiliots was that they could be smeared with pitch and wood shavings and set on fire just before launching.

To protect themselves against these missiles, the Romans were forced to construct a variety of devices that had also enjoyed long use in ancient warfare. The crews filling in the ravine to form a base for the ramp worked behind a sixty-foot-wide *testudo*, or tortoise, a sort of mobile armored hut with a sloping roof, built of heavy timbers that the men pushed in front them. To prevent flaming missiles from igniting it, the outside of the *testudo* was covered with fresh hides that had been soaked in water. Other crews were protected by a series of wooden sheds, also built of heavy timbers and sheathed with wet hides, that were placed one in front of the other to form a covered passageway that extended along the length of the ramp.

From any point of view, this was slow work, and word of the siege and then the blockade would have reached Pompey in Macedonia within a few weeks. Nevertheless, it was not until the end of July, nearly a month after the rout of their navy, and three months after the start of the siege, that the defenders of Massilia got word that help was on the way. A rescue fleet of sixteen ships sent by Pompey, several of them warships, approached the city under the command of Lucius Nasidius after a nine-hundred-mile journey from the Adriatic coast of Macedonia, modern Albania.

After putting in at Tauroentum, today the harbor of Le Brusc about twenty-six miles southeast of Massilia, Nasidius managed to get a small boat through the blockade with a message to Domitius and the Massiliots urging them to join him in another attack on Brutus' fleet. The Massiliots had repaired their remaining ships in the meantime, and had outfitted some fishing boats with decks, and then loaded them all with archers and *catapultae*. Slipping out of the harbor, possibly at night, and evading the Roman patrol boats, they made their way along the coast to rendezvous with Nasidius at Tauroentum.

Brutus had added the six captured ships to his own fleet and, when the escape was discovered, boldly took it down the coast to confront the Pompeians. The two fleets most likely engaged within sight of the French city of Bandol, Brutus approaching from the west against a line of enemy ships, the Massiliots facing him on the inshore side and the reinforcements from Pompey on the opposite end. According to Caesar's account, Brutus' ships drifted apart, and when they grappled and held an enemy vessel, the Pompeians were quick to row to its support, while a stream of arrows and javelins flew from each navy against the other. Caesar's description of the climax of the battle suggests that Brutus and his crews had improved their seamanship considerably:

Two triremes, spotting Decimus Brutus' ship, which was recognizable by its flag, raced from opposite directions towards it. But as Brutus was on his guard against the maneuvre, his ship was quick enough to slip from between them with only a few moments in hand. The triremes, traveling fast, collided with each other so heavily that they both suffered severe damage from the impact, and one of them had her ram broken off and was in a state of collapse. Observing this, the nearest ships of Brutus' fleet attacked them in this tangle and rapidly sank them both. (*The Civil War* 2.6.4–6)

Combining this kind of nautical agility with their superior grappling and boarding skill, Brutus' fleet sank five Massiliot ships and captured four others. When Nasidius saw the way the battle was going, he signaled his entire fleet to follow him and escaped to the west, and eventually to Nearer Spain, without a loss. Caesar makes the point that the Pompeians, unlike the Massiliots, were not defending their homes and their freedom, and thus had no incentive to risk their lives.

From their hilltop camp overlooking the city and the harbor, Caesar's legionaries had a clear view of the return of the first Massiliot ship after the disastrous battle with Brutus' fleet. A great crowd had gathered at the dock, and when they heard the news, "their grief was so great that one might have thought the city had been captured that very moment by the enemy" (*The Civil War* 2.7.3). On board the last ship to limp into port was the enduring Lucius Domitius.

With the chance of outside help nearly erased, the Massiliots sought to disrupt the work on the ramps by sending large numbers of Albici tribesmen out of the gates to harass the Roman engineers. Besides attacking the protecting infantry, they tried to ignite any exposed wood in the siegeworks with firebrands and flaming arrows. Trebonius sent additional troops into the ravine against them, and in the violent hand-to-hand fighting that took place, many Albici were killed and the rest forced back into the city. However, when these attacks continued, and the siegeworkers came under increasing fire, Trebonius ordered a brick shelter built next to the ramp, just sixty feet in front of the city wall, in which his men could take cover from the missiles, and begin using their own *catapultae* at closer range.

Under cover of several *plutei*—portable protective sheds with timber roofing—the Roman engineers laid out a thirty-foot square redoubt that they enclosed with brick walls more than five feet thick. After building up the walls to the height of one story, they constructed a sloping roof covered with bricks and clay, and with heavy timber beams projecting from the three sides that were vulnerable to enemy projectiles. From these beams they hung four-foot wide mats of "anchor rope," probably hemp, across the width of the walls, effectively protecting them against missiles. Roman brick was shaped like modern tile, flat and relatively thin. What was used at Massilia was unbaked, and had to be protected by padding so that it would not be weakened and eroded by the streams of water pumped directly against it by the Massiliots.

After completing the roof, the engineers removed the *plutei* and then, using levers, gradually raised it and its hanging mats, building up the walls on each side at the same time. Using this technique, they slowly built a fortresslike tower of six stories, with windows facing the city for their *catapultae*, all the while under a barrage of stones, spears, and water from the Massiliots.

Once the brick tower was complete and the main ramp had been built across the ravine and up to the base of the city wall, Trebonius was ready to assault the wall itself. For this he used another favorite Roman siege device, the *testudo arietaria*, the ram tortoise, the adjective *arietaria* deriving from *aries*, the Latin for ram. Mobile battering rams had first appeared in ancient warfare more than a thousand years earlier, and it has even been suggested that the "wooden horse" used by the Greeks to enter Homer's Troy was actually a type of battering ram on wheels.[6] The variety of ram tortoise used at Massilia is described by Vitruvius Pollio, a Roman architect and engineer, in the tenth book of his *On Architecture*, the most complete description of Greek and Roman architecture and siegecraft that has survived from the ancient world. As a young man, Vitruvius was employed by Caesar as an engineer, and may have actually participated in the siege of Massilia.

The ram tortoise resembled the modern tank, except that it was commonly much larger, being nearly fifty feet wide and twenty-four feet from its floor to the top of its sloping roof. It rolled on six huge wheels and carried on its roof a six-foot-wide tower of up to three stories, in which were stored a supply of water to extinguish fires, and as many *catapultae* as could be accommodated. The ram itself, a squared timber or just a tree trunk, might be as long as one hundred feet, and rested on two or three rollers finished on a lathe, according to Vitruvius, and mounted on the tortoise floor. The tortoise crew, which might be several dozen men, pulled the ram backwards with ropes and then quickly forwards so that its tip, encased in hardened iron, was brought with great force against the wall. Every exposed wood surface of this remarkable machine was covered with wet hides for protection.

The ram tortoise at Massilia, built on the spot with the time and materials available, may not have reached the dimensions recorded by Vitruvius, but its size was sufficient that the Massiliots could not ignore its pounding at their unmortared limestone defenses. On the other hand, the Romans may not have regretted their modest investment of time and energy in their ram tortoise when they saw the Massiliots counter it with a device that was simplicity itself. As the caretakers of Greek culture in the western Mediterranean, the Massiliots may have had a finer grasp of the niceties of siege warfare than the Romans gave them credit for. From the top of the wall they lowered a noose of stout rope, caught the head of the ram in it, and, using a winch, raised it high enough that it was rendered useless. Although it is easy to doubt this marvelous tale, surviving accounts of other sieges, some of them centuries before Caesar's time, describe just such a battering-ram technique, and the same response by the defenders.

Presumably the Romans abandoned this attempt, but Trebonius also tried another traditional method of defeating the walls—tunneling under them. As it was difficult to conceal this work from the watchers in the towers, the Massiliots were quick to counter it by digging a deep ditch behind their wall, even lower than the bottom of the ravine, where they calculated the tunnels would emerge. Those sappers that did break through found themselves far down in the ditch, and were quickly slain with whatever weapons the defenders chose. At other places where the Romans tunneled, where it was impossible to dig such a ditch, the Massiliots simply dug a broad moat and filled it with sea water. Those luckless sappers who broke into the moat were either drowned or buried, or both.

Neither the ram-tortoise incident nor the tunneling attempts appear in Caesar's narrative, and it is possible that he, or Trebonius, omitted them because they were such conspicuous failures. Instead, Caesar follows his account of the successful completion of the tower with a description of the next Roman initiative. Using the protection of the tower, Trebonius' engineers now built another structure, similar to the covered passageway on the ramp. This was a *musculus*, a narrow gallery, sixty feet long, built with a gabled roof of timbers two feet square, on which were placed bricks and wet hides, and on top of them, padded quilts. In Caesar's words, "They completed this whole work close by the tower under the shelter of screens; then when the enemy were off guard, they put rollers underneath it and suddenly moved it up to the enemy tower so as to abut it" (*The Civil War* 2.10.7).

With direct access to the wall, and with a solid protective roof overhead, the Romans now used crowbars to loosen the soft limestone blocks at the base of it. At the top of the wall, the desperate Massiliots levered up the largest boulders they could, and dropped them on the *musculus*. When these failed to break through the roof, they set fire to barrels full of pitch and dropped them onto it. These rolled off the slanted roof and lodged at the side of the *musculus*, but the Romans pushed them away with forked poles they had prepared for this purpose. When Trebonius ordered his *catapultae* operators to concentrate their missiles against the defenders just above the *musculus*, the Roman sappers were gradually able to loosen enough blocks so that a portion of the wall collapsed.

It was now clear to the Massiliots that they could not prevent further destruction of their wall and that the Romans were on the verge of breaking through. Once they were in, they would loot and burn the city, and slaughter or capture everybody. Massilia's navy was crippled, and there was no prospect of the blockade being broken. Finally, earlier in the month the news had reached the city that the Pompeians had been defeated at Ilerda, and that more Roman legions were marching toward Massilia. Caesar reports the moment of Roman triumph: "The enemy, terrified by the thought of a sack of their city, all poured out of the gate, unarmed and with the sacred ribbons of suppliants tied around their foreheads, stretching out their hands for mercy to the officers and army" (*The Civil War* 2.11.4).

The startled Romans abruptly stopped what they were doing and stared at the crowd approaching them. Archers and artillerymen held their fire as the Massiliot spokesmen reached a group of officers and men and threw themselves at their feet. They begged that they and their city be spared the fury of the infantry, and that the Romans wait for Caesar to decide their fate. As Trebonius was, in fact, under strict orders from Caesar not to let his men sack the city, he agreed to a truce and ordered the engineers to halt their work. Although many of the soldiers were angry at this and had to be restrained from rushing into the city, the officers enforced the truce across the whole battle line, posting pickets on the siegeworks and withdrawing their troops to await Caesar's arrival.

It would be some time yet, however, before Caesar reached Massilia. Although he had defeated the army of Afranius and Petreius in early August, and had freed a third of it and sent the rest back to Italy, Terentius Varro, with two more legions, was still a threat in Further Spain. But when popular opinion swung in favor of Caesar after the Pompeian surrender at Ilerda, Varro decided that rather than march out against him, he would hole up with his legions in the island city of Gades, modern Cádiz, the largest harbor on the Atlantic coast. (The narrow sandbar between the island and the mainland has now built up enough to support a road.) He sent word to the city to begin building ships and laying in supplies; he could hold out there until the war forced Caesar to return to Italy.

From Ilerda, Caesar had dispatched two legions to Further Spain under Quintus Cassius, the tribune who had fled Rome with Mark Antony just seven months earlier. Eager to wrap up things in Spain, Caesar writes:

He himself went ahead with six hundred cavalry by forced marches, sending on an edict announcing the day on which he wished the magistrates and leading citizens of every community to be ready to meet him in Corduba. After this edict had been published all over the province there was not a community that did not send members of its council to Corduba at the right time, not a single Roman citizen of any standing who did not gather on the day. (*The Civil War* 2.19.1–2)

Even allowing for some Caesarean exaggeration, this is strong evidence of the tepid support for Varro and Pompey among the Roman residents of Further Spain. Caesar had, of course, served twice in Spain, as *quaestor* in 69 and as Governor just ten years before the war, and his reputation for harshness toward the native tribes was well balanced by one for support of Roman citizens. On his way to Gades, Varro attempted to garrison Corduba, modern Córdoba, but found himself barred from the city by its citizens.

Varro's prospects were not improved by a letter he received from the leading citizens of Gades while he was marching there with his two legions. They informed him that the commander he had appointed to defend them had left town with his troops at their invitation, and that they were preparing to hold the town for Caesar. Varro's last humiliation came when an entire legion of recent recruits marched out of his camp and deserted to Hispalis, modern Seville, where the townspeople offered to put them up. He sent word to Caesar that he was ready to surrender, and the first Spanish campaign came to a bloodless end.

At a second public meeting in Corduba, Caesar took the opportunity to make another magnanimous speech, and "expressed his thanks to all in their various categories: to the Romans . . . to the Spaniards . . . to the people of Gades . . . to the officers and centurions" (*The Civil War* 2.21.1). In the manner of the astute politician that he was, he restored money and property to those who had been forced to contribute, and gave rewards and promises to others. After freeing an embarrassed Varro, he appointed Quintus Cassius Governor of both Spanish provinces, assigning him Varro's two legions and the two he had sent from Ilerda.

Caesar then commandeered the ships that Varro had ordered built in Gades, filled them with his bodyguard, and sailed back through the Strait of Gibraltar, called by the Romans Fretum Herculeum, the Strait of Hercules. After several months on horseback on dusty roads and trails, each week hotter than the last, he was perhaps in the mood for a short and scenic sea voyage before he returned to the battlefield. Sailing was faster than any land trip; a voyage from Gades to Rome could be made in seven days and was reasonably safe in summer. After leading his convoy northward along the coast, he made a final appearance in Nearer Spain, conducting the same postvictory ceremony before the cheering citizens of its capital, Tarraco, modern Tarragona on today's Costa Brava.

Near the end of September, Caesar and his bodyguard of German cavalry proceeded by land from Tarraco up the Spanish coast and into Further Gaul, and started toward Massilia on the Via Domitia. It had been just a month since the four Pompeian legions captured at Ilerda, escorted by four of Caesar's Gallic legions, had taken the same route, bypassing Massilia (perhaps about the time the city surrendered), on their way to Italy.

Meanwhile, a great calm had settled over Massilia in the days after its capitulation. With no missiles flying, no shouts of alarm and pain, and no work being done, the scene had been transformed from a noisy and dangerous construction site to something more typical of a summer on the coast of southern Gaul. Caesar describes this unusual aftermath:

After an interval of a few days our men were relaxed and unconcerned, and one midday, when some soldiers had gone off duty and some were resting from their daily tasks at the siege-works themselves, and all their weapons and armour were laid aside and wrapped up, the enemy suddenly burst out of the gates and in a strong and favorable wind set fire to the siege-works. The wind spread the flames to such effect that a ramp, siege-sheds, the "tortoise," a tower, and artillery caught fire simultaneously and were all destroyed before anyone realized how it had happened. (*The Civil War* 2.14.1–2)

The Romans scrambled to get their helmets, armor, and weapons, but the Massiliots quickly retreated behind the walls and resumed their artillery barrage, preventing even any feeble fire-fighting efforts. In a few hours the work of months was undone, and the Romans could only watch while their wooden structures and devices burned and collapsed and then turned to ashes. (It was one of the wooden towers in the Roman outer palisade that burned, not the brick tower.) To their credit, the Romans were prepared the next day when a similar wind prevailed, possibly the mistral, the Fierce north wind that bears down on the coast from the mountains of southern France and is known to strike in summer as well as winter. This time the Massiliots made a second attack on the other ramp and another tower, setting them on fire in several places; but the Romans drove them back behind the walls after killing many of them, and were able to douse the flames before they did extensive damage.

Even though the Massiliots failed in their second surprise attack, Trebonius had to mount a new effort to subdue the city before Caesar arrived from Spain. Another ramp with a base of tree trunks was impossible, according to Caesar's account, because the Romans had stripped the land around Massilia of all its trees for what they had already built. Instead, Trebonius' engineers now began construction of a new type of ramp by laying two brick walls six feet thick and about fifty feet apart, pointed directly at Massilia's wall. At a height of one story they laid a roof of timber between the walls, then covered it with woven branches and plastered it with clay. In the walls they left doorways so as to be able to get out and in again anywhere along their length. By pushing a portable *pluteus* ahead of them while under this roofed passageway, the Romans were able to extend it right up to the city's wall, and resume prying out the facing blocks. The Romans gained an unexpected advantage when they found that they were able to work within a few yards of Massilia's wall unmolested, the enemy's *catapultae* being positioned on the wall in such a way that they could not be fired downward.

According to Caesar, the Massiliots were dismayed at the Romans' new tactics and realized that similar ramps, as well as walls and towers, could be built very close to their own wall. From these the Romans could propel any type of missile at them, and they would be helpless to respond. At the same time, their wall, for the same reason, was vulnerable to dismantling and undermining, and one of their towers had already partially collapsed. There seemed to be no way they could defend themselves any longer, and after such a long period without new food supplies, they were suffering the effects of eating old millet and rotting barley. Moreover, as it was clear that they could not expect any outside assistance by either land or sea, they decided to again signal the Romans that they were ready to surrender.

Lucius Domitius, however, learning of the plan in advance, secretly got three ships ready for himself and his retinue, and slipped out of the harbor during a storm. Brutus' patrol boats, which were keeping watch on the port, spotted them, hoisted anchor, and gave chase. The crews of two of the fleeing ships were terrified by the war galleys bearing down on them and turned back to port. But on board the third, Domitius ordered his oarsmen to redouble their efforts, and, helped by the rough weather, they managed to get away and down the coast. Domitius and his crew were the only escapees from Massilia.

At about the same time—in the latter half of October—Caesar arrived from Spain and took charge of the surrender. He immediately gave orders that the city was to be occupied peacefully and the Massiliots spared, "more in accordance with the fame and antiquity of their state than with what they deserved." (*The Civil War* 2.22.6). But he ordered them to turn over their artillery and weapons, to remove their ships from the harbor and dry docks, and to hand over everything in their treasury. For a city that had resisted a siege as long as Massilia, this was gentle treatment in the ancient world. But Caesar was not a destroyer of cities, at least not Greek or Roman cities. However, he is careful not to use the word *clementia* here or anywhere else in *The Civil War*. As the ostensible defender of Republican institutions, he was astute enough to foresee the hostile reaction its hint of the forgiving monarch would bring.

The siege of Massilia was one of the hardest fought in Roman military history. No Greek city, not Mytilene in 77, not even Athens against Sulla in 82, had held out so long against a Roman army. But for Caesar, Massilia was a side issue, a distraction from his urgent need to pursue and defeat Pompey. With both Spanish provinces in safe hands and his route through southern Gaul secure, he left two legions to garrison the city and set out for Rome with Trebonius.

VIII
Curio in Africa

Following his terse account of the surrender of Massilia, Caesar brings Book II of *The Civil War* to a close with his narrative of the first campaign in Africa, which he had entrusted to Scribonius Curio in April. After their decisive defeat of Carthage in the Second Punic War in 202 BCE, the Romans had confined what had been the Carthaginian Empire to the region they called Africa, comprising at that time the northeastern third of modern Tunisia. In the course of expanding its trade and influence during the following fifty years, Carthage was provoked to war by neighboring Numidia, whose King appealed to Rome for assistance. In the Roman Senate Cato the Elder, leader of the most conservative faction, lobbied untiringly against Carthage, ending every speech he made on whatever subject with the solemn intonation *that*, Carthage must be destroyed. In 150 the Senate obliged him and declared a third war against Carthage, this time expressly to destroy it.

After a conflict of nearly four years, Scipio Aemilianus, adoptive grandson of Scipio Africanus, the first conqueror of Carthage, brought his army to the outskirts of the capital, which lay on a peninsula projecting into the great Bay of Carthage, now the Gulf of Tunis. The final subjection of the city was accomplished in 146 only after a difficult six-week siege culminating in a fiery battle, fought house-to-house for seven days, that brings to mind the desperate street fighting in European cities at the end of the Second World War. After razing and burning the city and selling its fifty thousand survivors into slavery, the Romans forbade any occupation of its site, annexed Africa as their sixth province, and established its capital at Utica, its next-largest city, thirty miles away.

Since then, Africa had become wealthy and important as a supplier of grain, fruit, wine, and other commodities to Rome. In a fast ship it was only a two- or three-day sail from the capital, as Cato the Elder once demonstrated in the Senate by holding up a fig that had been picked at Carthage only three days before. As Rome's southernmost possession, it had the quality of a tropical frontier, filled with exotic people, plants, and animals. Even in the next century, Pliny the Elder would write, "The names of its people and towns are completely unpronounceable except by the natives."[1] Speculators, developers, and colonists flocked to it, as did politicians and generals fleeing coups and revolutions. In the first month of the Civil War, the Pompeian general Attius Varus made his way to Africa after his flight from Auximum and, finding no one in charge, installed himself as Governor.

Caesar had his own plan for Africa and, during his brief week in Rome in April, had appointed Curio *legatus pro praetore*, general acting as *praetor*, for Sicily and Africa. On his way south from Rome, Curio had stopped to visit Cicero, and the two of them had an excited discussion about the momentous events of the past three months. Cicero had just met with Caesar, and was concerned that he would not be allowed to leave Italy if he wished; Curio spontaneously assured him that he would, and offered to intercede for him.

By the time Curio arrived in Sicily toward the end of April, Marcus Cato had already left to join Pompey in Macedonia, and Asinius Pollio had brought his three legions across to the island. But it was not until early August that Curio set out with his army for Africa, escorted by a dozen warships. Of the four legions available, he took the two that had defected from Domitius at Corfinium and supplemented them with five hundred Gallic cavalry. What delayed him is not known, but it may have been the lack of ships; he would need more than a hundred transports for his army, and the demand for all types of ships by both Pompey and Caesar had soared since the start of the war. It is possible that word of the surrender at Ilerda reached him by boat just before he left, and perhaps that is what he was waiting for. Among his officers was Pollio, whose account of the African campaign, along with Curio's dispatches, was the probable source of Caesar's narrative.

Curio led his convoy into the Bay of Carthage and landed at an unidentified spot on its eastern coast. A two-day march westward along the southern coastline took him past the site of modern Tunis and within a few miles of the ruins of Carthage, which remained uninhabited a century after its destruction. After crossing the Bagradas River, now called the Medjerda, he proceeded a further ten miles to a promontory overlooking the bay, from which he could see the busy port of Utica about a mile away. A Phoenician colony supposedly founded in 1100 (archaeological evidence suggests the eighth century), Utica had survived the Punic Wars and had succeeded Carthage as Africa's most important city. The site of Utica today is occupied by the Tunisian city of Bordj bou Chateur, and is separated from the bay by six miles of silt deposited at the mouth of the Medjerda River.

Attius Varus had conscripted two legions in the province, and as Curio approached, they were setting up their camp in a protected spot just outside Utica's wall and its adjacent theater. While his men were constructing the usual ditches, gates, and ramparts, Varus had put the local people to work preparing for a siege by bringing in food, supplies, and animals from the nearby countryside. In addition, he had just been reinforced with six hundred cavalry and four hundred infantry sent a few days earlier by King Juba of neighboring Numidia.

Numidae was one of the names the Romans gave to the semi-pastoral nomads, now identified as Berbers, who had migrated, probably from the Far East in the third millennium, into the region of North Africa. Long after Phoe-

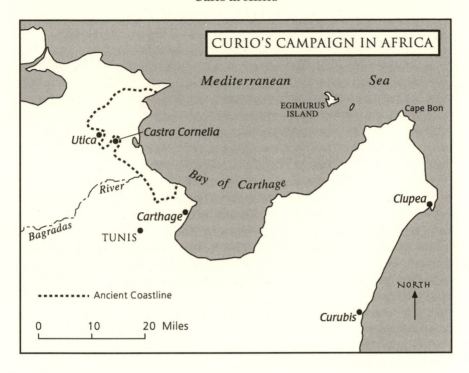

CURIO'S CAMPAIGN IN AFRICA

Mediterranean Sea

EGIMURUS ISLAND

Cape Bon

Castra Cornelia

Utica

River

Bay of Carthage

Clupea

Bagradas

Carthage

TUNIS

NORTH

········· Ancient Coastline

0   10   20 Miles

Curubis

nician colonists had founded several ports along the coasts of modern Tunisia and Algeria, the Berbers established their own kingdom in the northern region of Algeria, which the Romans called Numidia. The Numidians were expert horsemen and their kings found it profitable to hire them out as mercenaries both to the Phoenicians at Carthage, and then to the Romans.

King Juba was a willing supporter of the Senatorial forces; his father, Hiempsal, had been restored to his throne by the young Pompey more than thirty years before. More than that, it was none other than Curio who had, in the previous year, introduced a proposal in the Senate, subsequently defeated, that Rome annex Numidia to make room for veterans and other colonists.

Varus' supply line was an easy target, and when Curio ordered his Gallic cavalry to attack it, Varus responded by sending out all his Numidian reinforcements. A vicious battle ensued between the mercenary horsemen, and the Gauls quickly routed the Numidians, killing more than a hundred and twenty and forcing the rest back into the camp. In the meantime, Curio's warships had arrived off Utica's harbor, and he sent orders to all the merchant ships inside, which were promptly obeyed, to move around the promontory to the river mouth and hand over all their cargo to his troops.

These first two auspicious episodes, as Caesar dryly reports, caused Curio's army to hail him *imperator*. The next day he moved both legions closer to Utica, and had begun fortifying a camp when word arrived that another contingent of cavalry and infantry from King Juba was on its way. At the same time a cloud of dust appeared on the southern horizon, and the head of a column came into view. Curio, a man who "does nothing except on impulse,"[2] according to an acquaintance, sent out his cavalry again and ordered his legions to prepare to march. But before his infantry could reach the Numidians, who were marching unprepared, the cavalry had set upon them and slain a great number, and the rest had fled.

In spite of these successes, an attitude of fear and discontent seemed to take hold among Curio's legionaries, all of whom had originally been recruited by Lucius Domitius, and had then switched allegiance to Caesar at Corfinium. The great majority had been in service only since January and had done nothing but march since then. One commander had already tried to desert while they were under siege, and now, after surrendering and agreeing to fight for Caesar, they had been transported for three days across the water to a strange country and had been threatened, and then defended, by barbarian cavalry.

Curio had kept them organized in the same units and with the same officers as they had had under Domitius, and now a few of them changed their minds again and deserted to the Pompeian army. They told Varus that many of their comrades were not loyal to Curio and might be persuaded to change sides. This led one of Varus' officers who had also been at Corfinium to make his way into Curio's camp and encourage his former troops not to abandon the oath, the *sacramentum*, they had sworn to Domitius, and not to allow themselves to be forever labeled deserters. He told them that they were merely tools being used by Caesar, and hinted at a cash reward if they returned to the Pompeian army. Although there were no further desertions, many expressed fears about the loyalty of their colleagues, and wondered how they would be received in their home towns, regardless of who won the war.

When Curio heard what was going on, he called a general meeting and addressed the men himself, praising them for their courage to side with Caesar, reassuring them that they were on the winning side, and asserting that he would never desert them. Here, for the first time in *The Civil War*, Caesar reports direct speech, and whether they are his words or actually those of Curio, the rhetoric is worthy of the master himself:

Perhaps you have not heard of Caesar's exploits in Spain? Two armies defeated; two generals overcome; two provinces gained; and this done in forty days from the time Caesar set eyes on his opponents. Or do you think that men who could offer no resistance when they were fresh, can resist now they are finished? Are you who followed Caesar when his victory still hung in the balance really going to follow the loser now that the result of the war is settled and you ought to reap the reward of your services? They say they have been deserted and betrayed by you, and make mention of your previous oath. But did you desert Domitius, or did Domitius desert you? . . . When he had betrayed you, were you not saved by Caesar's kindness? (*The Civil War* 2.32.5–8)

To this he added a list of his own successes so far in Africa, ascribing them to both his *diligentia*, his thoroughness, and his *fortuna*, the good luck that every Roman general claimed to favor him. Then, after asking if they were "attracted by the disgrace of Corfinium, the flight from Italy, and the surrender of the two Spains," he added that if they regretted saluting him *imperator*, "I give you back your gift" (*The Civil War* 2.32.13–14). Son of a Consul and a protégé of Cicero, Curio had been an active politician for more than a decade, a Senator for five years, and one of Caesar's most forceful spokesmen in the months before the war. His reputation for cleverness was matched by one for eloquence, and his unsophisticated audience was not accustomed to the histrionics common in the Roman Senate. Stung by this rebuke, they responded with shouts that they were ready to fight, and ready to show their loyalty and courage.

Taking advantage of this change of attitude, Curio the next day led out both legions and drew them up in battle formation, and Varus did the same. The two armies faced each other from either side of a small, shallow valley about two hundred feet across, a dozen feet deep, and with sharply rising sides. Although both commanders adopted the usual tactic of waiting on the high ground for the other to attack, Varus finally sent all his cavalry and a few infantry into the valley. When Curio responded by sending down his Gallic cavalry and two cohorts of infantry, Varus' Numidian cavalry fled and Curio's infantry massacred their enemy counterparts—a grisly scene that the rest of Varus' army witnessed from the opposite ridge.

Curio now shouted to his remaining troops to remember what they had promised, and to follow him, and rode down the steep slope into the valley. The legionaries surged after him, but before any of them could get across and up the other side, Varus' entire army, fearing that they were being surrounded, turned and ran in a panic back to their camp under the city wall. So complete and sudden was the retreat that the fleeing soldiers reached the camp in a crowd and choked the narrow gates so that dozens were trampled and killed, and hundreds injured. According to Caesar, by the time the gates were closed against the pursuing troops, there were more casualties from the rush to retreat than from the battle itself. When many of Varus' men, in their panic, continued out the back gate and took refuge in the city, Varus ordered the camp abandoned and moved the entire army into Utica.

Although the claim can hardly be believed that Curio lost only a single soldier, it was the third clear victory for Curio and his army since their landing in Africa. The site of this particular episode was identified by nineteenth-century German archaeologists at a spot about a hundred and fifty yards south of Utica's walls, where they found a sinklike depression such as that described by Caesar in this chapter of *The Civil War*.

The next day Curio prepared to lay siege to Utica. In this effort he had the advantage of knowing that the inhabitants of the city were well disposed toward him because of various favors Caesar had done them. According to Caesar's narrative, "They all now openly talked of surrender, and approached Attius [Varus] to persuade him not to ruin them all by his obstinacy" (*The Civil War* 2.36.2). But before a decision could be made, a message arrived from King Juba saying that he was on his way with an even larger rescue army, and that they should defend the city until he arrived. Curio at first did not believe this, but when he later received more specific information that Juba was only twenty-five miles away, he withdrew his army to the secure and easily defended promontory he had visited a few days before, and began making preparations to withstand a siege.

The site Curio chose, Castra Cornelia, or Scipio's Camp, was already legendary among the Romans, having been the camp of Publius Cornelius Scipio, later surnamed Africanus, in the final days before he brought Hannibal to bay at Zama in the Second Punic War. Even a century and a half later it was ideally suited for defense, having a plentiful water supply and access to the bay. Curio ordered supplies of grain brought in and trees cut for fortifications (the area was still heavily wooded). At the same time he sent a fast boat back to Sicily with orders for his other two legions and the rest of his cavalry to embark for Africa immediately.

It is in the next paragraph of *The Civil War* that the campaign in Africa is decided, and the sympathetic Caesar does his best to soften what will be the verdict of history on his young commander:

When things had been thus organized . . . he was told by some deserters from the town that Juba had been called back by a border invasion . . . and had stayed behind in his kingdom, while Saburra, his general, had been sent on with a modest force and was approaching Utica. Rashly believing this source of information, he changed his plan and decided to proceed by giving battle. In thinking this the correct course, he was much affected by his youth, his nobility of spirit, his previous successes, and his self-confidence. (*The Civil War* 2.38.1–2)

Curio sent all his cavalry southward into the Bagradas Valley at dusk, and before dawn led out his entire army in the same direction, leaving five cohorts behind to guard the camp. After six miles on the march, he was met by the returning cavalry, who reported that they had surprised the Numidians, unprepared in their camp, killed many of them, taken prisoners, and driven off the rest. An excited Curio questioned the prisoners and confirmed that it was indeed Saburra whom the cavalry had routed. Encouraged by this news, and confident that it was only the small army of Saburra that was retreating up the valley, he ordered the entire army forward, horse as well as foot, at an even faster pace. The cavalry, however, exhausted from riding and fighting all night, began to fall behind and stop, one after another.

As the infantry proceeded further into the valley, the forward units began to encounter Saburra's troops, which on his orders gradually retreated. Unknown to the Romans, he had been reinforced with two thousand additional Spanish and Gallic cavalry that Juba had released from his own bodyguard, along with a contingent of his best infantry. The King himself, far from retiring from the scene, was slowly following them with sixty war elephants and the rest of his army, toward which Saburra was steadily luring Curio. After advancing several more hours under the fierce summer sun, Curio halted his exhausted troops, now some sixteen miles from his camp.

Saburra chose this moment to give battle and drew his men up in formation, placing his fresh cavalry at the front. Curio formed up his legionaries, exhorting them to bravery, and they responded as best they could. By now he had only two hundred cavalry at the front, and though they attacked the enemy with great courage, they and their animals were too tired to pursue them with any vigor. Even so, Curio's troops pushed back the enemy cavalry, who retreated nimbly and then spread out and got behind the Romans, picking off stragglers and isolated groups from behind. Numidian reinforcements now began to join Saburra's army, and his cavalry's encirclement of Curio's depleted and stumbling infantry prevented them from retreating or carrying out their wounded. Caesar does not shrink from rendering the scene: "These men, despairing of escape, behaved as men do in the last moments of their lives, either bewailing their own deaths or commending [the care of] their parents to anyone whom good fortune might be able to save from this danger. Fear and grief were everywhere" (*The Civil War* 2.41.8).

Curio desperately signaled his *aquiliferi* to lead a retreat to a nearby hill, but Saburra's cavalry had already occupied it. Gnaeus Domitius, Curio's cavalry commander, begged him to save himself, and promised to stay with him until he was safely away, but Curio, saying that if he lost the army entrusted to him by Caesar he could never face him, refused to flee, and so died fighting. A few horsemen managed to get away and, with the stragglers, made it back to camp. "Milites ad unum omnes interficiuntur" (*The Civil War* 2.42.5): the infantry were killed to a man.

It is not known if Asinius Pollio was with Curio in the valley of the Bagradas, only that he survived the campaign and escaped Africa, and probably supplied Caesar with the eyewitness account that we have today. The final paragraphs of Book II of *The Civil War* report that those who had remained at Scipio's Camp, when the fleeing cavalry brought the news, hurried to escape from their now-untenable position. The *quaestor* in command ordered the ship captains in the harbor to send their small boats to the beach for an orderly withdrawal, but the troops were so frightened that King Juba was about to appear, or that Varus' legions were coming against them, that every man rushed to the beach in a panic to save himself. Those boats that arrived were soon swamped, causing the others to draw back. Seeing this, the captains of the remaining ships in the harbor pulled away, with the result that "only a few soldiers and fathers of families, being those who could make a claim on the good will or pity of others, or could swim to the ships, were taken on board and reached Sicily safely" (*The Civil War* 2.44.1).

The remaining legionaries, perhaps two to three thousand, as well as hundreds of servants and slaves, fled toward Utica to surrender to Varus, hoping to get some protection against Juba. But the victorious King would not be denied his revenge on Curio and Caesar, and when he came upon them gathered outside the city, he declared all of them his spoil. After picking out a few for slaves, he ordered, over the impotent protests of Varus, the remaining men of Curio's African legions stabbed to death. Caesar extracts the last bit of outrage from the scene by remarking that in the entourage of King Juba as he entered the city were two Pompeian Senators.

The death of Curio was surely a blow to Caesar, who would have heard of it while returning from Spain. His high valuation of him may have extended to avuncular affection (he was fifteen years older), and in his narration of the next episode of the war, when he is recounting the losses until then on both sides, he writes that he himself had "suffered the death of Curio" (*The Civil War* 3.10.5). Also, he had lost not only a protégé, but an army and a province. The legions had been a virtual gift from Domitius and could be replaced, but it was certain that the province would eventually have to be captured, and an end put to King Juba, this time by Caesar himself. Pompey and the exiled Senate voted honors to Juba, and Caesar countered by declaring him an enemy of the Roman people and recognizing as Kings two of Juba's antagonists, Bocchus and Bogud, in neighboring Mauretania.

About thirty-five at the time, Curio was the first commander and the first member of the aristocracy to lose his life in the Civil War. He had married the wealthy Fulvia, the widow of Clodius and one of the Republic's most prominent women, less than two years earlier, and their son was born in the early months of the Civil War. At the time of his death, Curio had been in Africa only ten days.

The end of the African campaign coincided with the end of a naval encounter in the Adriatic Sea in which two other lieutenants of Caesar's, Gaius Antonius, brother of Mark Antony, and Publius Dolabella, son-in-law of Cicero, collided with a pair of Pompeian admirals. After Caesar's capture of Brundisium in March, Dolabella spent the next two months assembling a fleet of forty warships and then proceeded into the northern Adriatic to engage Pompey's navy. He was promptly defeated and captured with all his ships by a Pompeian naval force under the command of Marcus Octavius and Scribonius Libo. In an attempt to rescue him, Gaius Antonius brought fifteen cohorts of troops to the northern coast of Illyricum near the port city of Rijeka in modern Croatia. It is not known if Antonius reached the area by sea or by marching around the northern Adriatic coast. By some unknown misfortune he and his army were forced by Pompeian troops to retreat to the nearby island of Curicta, today called Krk, in the Kvarner Gulf. There they were trapped by hostile natives on the island and by the fleet of Marcus Octavius off the coast. When the lack of food and water made their situation desperate, they built three huge rafts of planks lashed to empty barrels and attempted to break through the blockade and reach the shore, which was held by Caesarian supporters.

Although two rafts crossed successfully, a third was caught by means of a heavy cable strung underwater across a narrow inlet and attached at both ends to rocks on the shore. Pompeian warships surrounded and attacked the raft, but Antonius' troops held them off until dusk, when the attack was halted. During the night their tribune Vulteius persuaded them that because they were certain to be defeated, they should kill themselves rather than suffer the disgrace of capture. At dawn the Pompeians called for them to surrender, but they refused and, when the raft was attacked again, fought until they were about to be boarded and then, led by Vulteius, turned their swords on each other.

However, despite all their attempts to escape, all the survivors in Antonius' fifteen cohorts, including Antonius himself, were captured and conducted to Pompey, who incorporated them into his own army. The outcome of the episode was that Caesar lost two commanders, a legion and a half, and forty warships.

The misadventure in the Adriatic and the destruction of Curio's two legions in Africa were Caesar's only significant losses in the first nine months of the war. Pompey had lost three legions at Corfinium and another six in Spain, although as many as twenty cohorts from his Spanish legions, having been repatriated to Italy, would eventually rejoin him. In an early chapter of Book III of *The Civil War*, Caesar catalogs these losses on each side in a candid admission of "quantum in bello fortuna posset" (how great the power of fortune was in war), a theme that he returns to frequently throughout the *Commentaries*. Although his claim that Fortuna, the Goddess of Fortune, favored him seemed evident over the course of his career, he was never so confident that he left her unassisted.

If Caesar had reason to be pleased with his progress so far—control of Italy, Sicily, Sardinia, the two Spains, and the western Mediterranean—he knew that Pompey was augmenting his forces in Macedonia with thousands of auxiliary troops and warships from Rome's Eastern provinces, and from numerous Eastern kingdoms friendly to him. Once he had organized his army, he would certainly invade Italy, and his navy was large enough to bring the army all at once, possibly landing in several places. Rather than defend hundreds of miles of Italian shoreline, Caesar sought to deliver a fatal blow to the opposition by chasing and attacking Pompey himself. Even before leaving Massilia for Rome, he had ordered all his legions that were not defending conquered territory to gather at Brundisium and prepare for an invasion of Macedonia.

Although the prosecution of the war was his paramount objective, Caesar now had responsibility for the functions of government and for the restoration of the country's political processes. Marcus Lepidus and Mark Antony held Rome and Italy under military rule, and Caesar was anxious to remove any appearance of illegitimacy. Elections of magistrates were customarily conducted by the Consuls in office, but since those for 49 had left the country, Caesar had, before leaving Spain, instructed his supporters in the Assembly to pass a law allowing the appointment of a *dictator* (from *dico*, "I say," through *dictum*, "command").

In the distant past, the Romans had occasionally resorted to a legally named *dictator*, who was given sweeping but temporary powers to conduct elections or deal with other urgent matters. The ancient title of the office was *magister populi*, Master of the Infantry, and the incumbent traditionally appointed a second-in-command, a *magister equitum*, Master of the Horse. The only recent *dictator* had been Sulla, who had coerced the Senate into appointing him for an indefinite period. On reaching Massilia, Caesar "heard that a law had been passed . . . and that he had been named *dictator* by the *praetor* Marcus Lepidus" (*The Civil War* 2.21.5). With this tactic, unusual but legal, Caesar secured the authority to take any action he wished, to rule by decree, without fear of veto.

Despite this legal dictatorship, however, Caesar's control of the country depended on his legions, and now one of his oldest and best gave him cause for alarm. At Placentia, modern Piacenza, in his own province of Nearer Gaul, a substantial mutiny arose among the four legions that had just returned to Italy after the arduous six-month campaign in Spain. It apparently originated with the IXth Legion, another legion that had fought its way out of the ambush by the Nervii eight years before, and one that Caesar had described in *The Gallic War* as a veteran legion with "outstanding fighting ability."[3]

The legionaries' complaint was that the war was being prolonged unnecessarily and that they were overdue to be discharged. Also, they had not been allowed to plunder their defeated enemies, as was the custom, and they had not been paid the five hundred *denarii* they had been promised at the siege of Brundisium. On his way from Massilia to Rome, Caesar turned off the Via Aurelia and hurried to Placentia. Calling all four legions together, he delivered a lengthy tongue-lashing, accusing them of breaking their oath to him to fight until the end of the war. He made the gratuitous point that he was pursuing his opponents with his usual speed, and that it was they who were prolonging the conflict. Asserting that it was his affection and respect for them that required him to punish them according to the ancient custom, he ordered the entire IXth Legion disbanded and subjected to the *decimatio*, the execution by stoning or beating of every tenth man, selected by lot.

A cry of despair at once went up from the entire legion and when its officers fell to their knees and begged for mercy Caesar gradually and reluctantly gave way. He relented to the extent that only 120 men, thought to be the ringleaders, were to draw lots, of whom the twelve selected would be executed. Of these twelve it transpired that one had not even been in the camp when the mutiny occurred, and in his place Caesar put to death the centurion who had reported him.[4]

Although Caesar faced a rebellious army on at least three occasions during his military career, this was the only time that he imposed multiple death penalties. As it was, he reinstated the IXth immediately, and it remained one of his key legions throughout the entire war, earning favorable mention by him in the next two battles. Nevertheless, the incident must have embarrassed him, and in *The Civil War* he makes no reference to it, suggesting by his silence that nothing interrupted his journey to Rome from Massilia.

Entering the capital in early December as a legally appointed *dictator*, Caesar was quick to demonstrate that he would be nothing like Sulla, the last one, who was still remembered, more than thirty years later, for the wave of proscriptions, confiscations, and killings that he and his henchmen had carried out. Abstaining from any repressive measures, Caesar ordered immediate elections of the magistrates for the next year and placed his own name on the list of candidates for Consul. His election only a few days later culminated three years of effort, albeit by a circuitous route, to return to the most coveted post in the Republic. As he writes in the opening sentence of Book III, the following year, 48, was "the year he was legally permitted to become Consul," a pointed reference to Pompey's third Consulship in 52, which he entered only three years after his second. As Caesar's colleague the voters chose his hand-picked nominee Publius Servilius, son-in-law of his mistress Servilia.

Other affairs of state Ceaser dealt with swiftly. He arranged for a law to be passed recalling from exile and rehabilitating the sons and grandsons of men who had been proscribed by Sulla, and others who had been banished or deprived of property in recent years by *optimate* juries. Requiring more complicated measures were the economic disruptions brought on by the war—deflation, a scarcity of money and credit, and a virtual standstill of overseas commerce. To increase the money supply, he revived an old law against hoarding, and also put a ceiling on the interest rate. Creditors and bankers expected to be penalized by an abolition of all debts, while debtors, pinched by falling real-estate prices, demanded it. Caesar steered a moderate course with a decree requiring creditors to accept in settlement land and other goods at their prewar value (as determined by a government assessor), and reducing all outstanding debt by the amount of interest already paid, up to a quarter of the total. Anxious to avoid any identification with Sulla, who had abused the dictatorship and remained in it for more than a year, Caesar ostentatiously resigned the office after spending only eleven days in the capital. Departing Rome with a flourish, he made a free grain distribution to the people, and started immediately for Brundisium.

Caesar's confidence and natural aggressiveness were not the only factors in his decision to pursue Pompey across the Adriatic. As a practical matter, he could not hope to prevent a massive invasion from the east, especially as Pompey had already assembled a substantial navy. Another consideration became apparent when he arrived in Italy and received reports from spies and travelers about his opponent's whereabouts and plans. After escaping Italy in March,

Pompey had taken his five Roman legions across Macedonia to the eastern part of the province, where he had set up a huge training camp at the city of Beroea, today Veroia, to organize his invasion army. The two hundred or so Senators who accompanied him, including Cicero and the magistrates and Consuls for the year, convened in the provincial capital, the ancient city of Thessalonica, now Thessaloniki on the Gulf of Thermai, and designated it the temporary seat of the Roman government. Taking a page from Caesar's book, they issued a decree on the motion of Cato that "no Roman should be killed except in battle and that no city subject to Rome should be plundered."[5]

In the year since the start of the war, and especially in the nine months after he landed in Macedonia, Pompey had worked diligently to assemble the resources he would need to defeat Caesar and restore the Republican government. More than a dozen cities and states in the Eastern provinces and beyond owed him debts and personal allegiance because of his defeat of Mithradates in the 60s. From the provinces themselves he had extracted large sums and had established a mint at Apollonia on Macedonia's west coast, where coins were struck on the order of the two Consuls who accompanied him. He had then pressured and cajoled a variety of kings, dynasts, and tetrarchs, as well as free communities, to supply him with troops, ships, money, and food. In *The Civil War* Caesar carefully enumerates these reinforcements to illustrate the superior forces against him, and to emphasize Pompey's use of foreigners to fight against Romans.

The core of the Pompeian army consisted of the five legions of infantry he had brought from Italy, plus another four he had raised among Roman army veterans in Macedonia, Crete, and Asia. To these he had added three thousand archers from Crete, Sparta, Pontus, and Syria, and twelve hundred slingers from Thrace. Among his seven thousand cavalry were more than a thousand Gauls from three Galatian tribes in Anatolia (descendants of Gallic invaders), six hundred from Cappadocia, and the same number from Thrace, all commanded by their own kings or princes.

The remaining cavalry included eight hundred of Pompey's slaves and shepherds, five hundred Gauls and Germans from the Roman forces garrisoned in Egypt, and hundreds more from Thessaly, Macedonia, Lesser Armenia, Pamphylia and Pisidia (in southern Anatolia), and minor tribes in the southern Balkans. From the tiny kingdom of Commagene on the Euphrates River in modern south-central Turkey came another two hundred mounted archers—Caesar uses their Greek name, *hippotoxotai*—who were contributed by King Antiochus I. In the same way, Pompey had commandeered warships from Athens, Bithynia, Pontus, Asia, Phoenicia, and Egypt, and had ordered grain shipped from Asia, Egypt, and Crete and turned over to him in Thessaly.

The assembly and preparation of a great military expedition was exactly what Pompey was supremely qualified to undertake, and the training camp at Beroea became a spectacle itself that people flocked to see, especially his military exercises. Plutarch describes Pompey's personal attention to the training of his heterogeneous army:

Far from just watching it, he took an active part himself . . . as though he were still at the height of his own powers. And certainly it was a most encouraging and inspiring sight to see Pompey the Great, who was only . . . [one year] short of the age of sixty, wearing full armour and vying with all the rest as an infantryman; and then again on horseback drawing his sword with no trouble at all while his horse was at full gallop and putting it back with perfect ease. . . . He showed too that in throwing the javelin he was not only accurate but vigorous. There were many of the young men who did not throw as far as he did.[6]

During December the Senate-in-exile finally named Pompey commander-in-chief of the Republican war effort, with full authority over all Rome's legions, warships, and generals. He had already put Marcus Bibulus in command of his five to six hundred warships (not all of them fully armed), and had deployed them in five squadrons throughout the Adriatic and Ionian seas. Their three objectives were to prevent Caesar from crossing to Macedonia with his troops, to intercept any grain ships attempting to reach Italy, and to provision the garrisons that Pompey had left to guard the Macedonian coast.

Toward the end of the month Pompey sent his wife Cornelia and a contingent of wives and children of his Senatorial colleagues to the safety of the city of Mytilene on Lesbos, and started westward from Beroea toward the Adriatic coast of Macedonia. His enormous army—larger than those the Romans had used to conquer Macedonia in the previous century—comprised thirty-five to forty thousand legionaries, numerous auxiliary troops, slaves and servants, and seven thousand cavalry. Their march across the province took them along the Via Egnatia, the three-hundred-mile road built by the Romans at the time they overran the area to link the Adriatic and the Aegean seas. Pompey was not yet aware that Caesar had returned to Italy, but he knew that Caesar was desperately short of transports, and he was confident that even if he had enough, he would not risk his army at sea until the spring.

Caesar had not been able to assemble an army the size of Pompey's. After leaving two legions in Spain and two at Massilia, he now had available only five veteran legions from his Gallic army, plus the two remaining from Curio's four. Two others had been recruited in Italy during the first months of the war, and three to five more during the summer and autumn of 49. Even though it is certain that they were all well below normal strength, Caesar found on reaching Brundisium that enough ships had been procured to transport only seven of them, comprising twenty thousand infantry and five hundred cavalry.

He gave orders that no personal belongings, no baggage. and no slaves could accompany the departing soldiers. In his address to them he suggested that since they had "almost reached the end of their toils and dangers," they should be happy to make such sacrifices in order to allow more troops to embark. He writes that when he added that they could look forward to his generosity after their victory, "they all shouted," as Caesar's troops were wont to do, "for him to give what orders he liked and they would gladly carry them out" (*The Civil War* 3.6.1). Despite this enthusiasm, stormy weather forced Caesar to wait several more days, and he finally impatiently put to sea on January 4 (early November by the modern calendar), well past the end of the safe sailing season, and despite Pompey's patrolling warships. A northerly was still blowing when the convoy of more than a hundred transports and twelve escorting warships, tightly packed with troops and horses, departed just at dusk from Brundisium for the coast of Macedonia. The war in the East had begun.

IX

The Campaign in Macedonia

Of all the risks that Caesar had taken during his eleven years at war since his year as Consul, his daring thrust across the Strait of Otranto with more than half his army was the most dangerous, and the most surprising. Moreover, once he put himself and seven understrength legions in Macedonia, he was obliged, if he was not to put himself at even greater risk, to promptly bring over the rest by the same method. His overloaded and clumsy transports and his twelve escorts nearly bereft of artillery would have been easy prey for Pompey's warships, stationed in ports all along the Macedonian coast. Sailing on the open sea was dangerous enough in midwinter, and sailing at night was avoided at all times, but a night voyage to transport an army was unheard of. Nevertheless, despite the routine self-serving themes that appear throughout Caesar's narrative—his treatment of prisoners, the loyalty of his troops, the immorality of his enemies—his laconic description of this perilous escapade could hardly be more modest: "postridie terram attigit" (on the next day [he] made his landfall) (*The Civil War* 3.6.3).

The fact that not a single Pompeian warship challenged the convoy on its eighty-mile trip supports Caesar's calculation that it was only during the sailing season that the enemy navy would be on the sea. During the winter it would keep to its ports because of the weather, and because no one else was sailing. Following the lights on Caesar's flagship, the huge convoy drifted far to the south during the night, and the next day entered a small cove below the village of Palaeste, today Palasë, one of the few accessible spots along the mountainous coast of what is now southern Albania. Although eighteen Pompeian warships were berthed in the harbor at Oricum, today Orikum, twenty-five miles north of the cove, the crossing and landing went unnoticed because none of them had put out to sea.

Caesar claims that he deliberately steered away from harbors, but it is likely that his course was determined by the wind and current, which took him dangerously near the island of Corcyra, now Corfu, the site of Pompey's main naval base on the Macedonian coast. There, Caesar's old enemy Marcus Bibulus commanded a fleet of one hundred and ten warships, but they were all in port, and by the time the convoy was finally sighted, put out to sea too late to catch it.

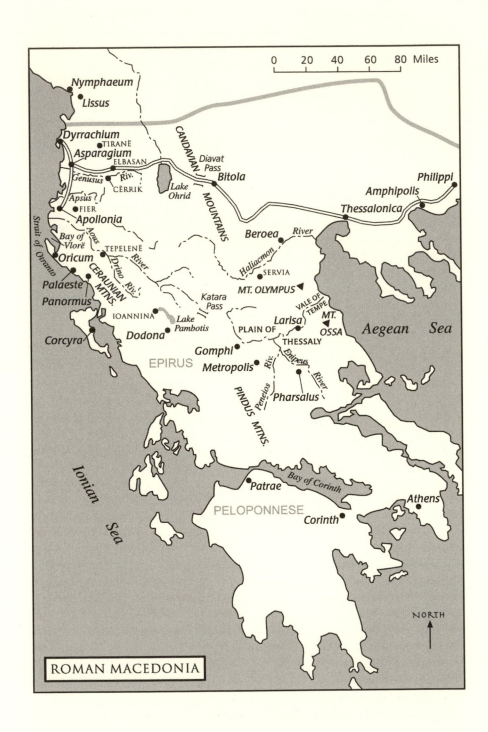

ROMAN MACEDONIA

Bibulus was not too late, however, to intercept the empty transports that Caesar, anxious to bring over the balance of his army, dispatched immediately on the return voyage to Brundisium. Hurrying north some fifty miles from Corcyra with a squadron of warships, Bibulus caught up with about thirty of the transports that had put out too late to catch the evening breeze off the mountains. In what Caesar describes as an angry and vengeful gesture, Bibulus set fire to them all and watched them burn and sink with their crews. He then deployed his warships along the approaches to Oricum and other ports in to-day's Bay of Vlorë to prevent any more of Caesar's vessels from reaching the mainland.

What was uppermost in Caesar's mind was reinforcement by his cavalry and the six or seven legions still at Brundisium, now the responsibility of Mark Antony. But even more urgent was his need for food, fodder, and supplies for the large army and hundreds of horses that were now perched on a narrow beach at the foot of the Ceraunian mountain range. He had been unable to bring much with him but men and horses, and there was no food or fodder to be had in the area because of the season and the terrain. He knew, however, that Pompey had garrisoned and provisioned several towns along the coast, and that his main supply base was at the large seaport of Dyrrachium, modern Durrës, on the central coast of Albania, about one hundred and ten miles north of him.

Seeking to capture these towns before Pompey arrived, Caesar hurriedly disembarked his army and before nightfall began the march to Oricum. He was forced to divide his legions into smaller units so they could negotiate the narrow, steep track that led nearly thirty-five hundred feet up from the beach to what is now called Llogara Pass. From there it was a march of about seven hours through a pine forest and down to Oricum at the foot of the Bay of Vlorë.

Caesar's position was now extremely vulnerable. With only a toehold on the literal cliff edge of a province controlled by his opponent, with food and supplies for only two or three days, he was also outnumbered on the ground and hemmed in by sea. He chose this moment to make another peace overture to Pompey, and sent Vibullius Rufus, a Pompeian officer whom he had captured twice, with a proposal that they both lay down their arms and submit their differences to a vote of the Senate and the Roman people. He recounted the losses that each side had suffered, and suggested that since their military strength now seemed to be about equal, this would be a good time to halt the fighting. Vibullius left immediately, rushing eastward day and night on the Via Egnatia until he reached Pompey, and delivered not the proposal, but the news that Caesar had landed in Macedonia.

Traveling westward with his enormous army through the Candavian Mountains near Lake Ohrid, some seventy miles from the coast, Pompey was astonished to hear of Caesar's successful crossing, and immediately aware of the threat to his garrisons and supply depots on the coast. He ordered the march accelerated and his forward cavalry to make for Apollonia, the site of modern Pojani, a large city at the end of the Via Egnatia, just forty miles north of Oricum. At the same time he sent a courier back along the Via Egnatia and all the way to Ephesus with a letter to his father-in-law, Metellus Scipio, who had been appointed Governor of Syria at the beginning of 49, and had taken charge of two Roman legions left in his province by previous Governors. He warned him that Caesar was in Macedonia with an army and urged him to drop everything and bring his legions into the province. Suddenly the entire situation had changed drastically, and although Pompey was confident of his military superiority in Macedonia, Caesar's potential control of the coast and the harbors could make it difficult to dislodge him.

In the meantime, Caesar and his army had scaled the mountain range behind Palaeste and had reached Oricum at the head of the Bay of Vlorë on the day following his landing. When the Pompeian commander was unable to get his Greek auxiliaries to defend the town, he was forced to open the gates and surrender without a fight. In the harbor two Pompeian admirals hastily scuttled the grain transports they were guarding, and took their eighteen warships up the gulf toward Dyrrachium. After occupying Oricum and pointedly sparing the commander, Caesar detached a legion to hold the town and left the next day for Apollonia on the Aous River, now the Vijosë, forty miles to the north.

At Apollonia two or three days later, the Pompeian commander also attempted to organize a defense of the city, but Caesar writes that its residents "refused . . . to close their gates against a consul, or take a decision that went against the judgement of all Italy and the Roman people" (*The Civil War* 3.12.2). His capture of Apollonia and Pompey's supply depot without a fight was a tactical coup in that the ancient city was situated near the mouth of an important river, and controlled a pass through the mountains behind it. Apollonia had been founded in the sixth century by colonists from Corinth and was known in Caesar's time for its outstanding school of rhetoric. The river now bypasses the site miles to the south, and what is left of the city lies in ruins, scattered on a hill behind today's Pojani. Caesar made Apollonia his headquarters for the rest of the campaign in western Macedonia, and later received delegations there from surrounding cities and towns.

Hurrying toward the coast at top speed, Pompey was approaching the north-south fork on the Via Egnatia at Asparagium when he received the news that Apollonia had fallen to Caesar. He ordered his army to march night and day in an effort to put it between Caesar and his own main supply depot at Dyrrachium. When Pompey finally reached Asparagium he was relieved to find that Caesar was still far to the south, and he confidently placed his enormous army in a position to bar Caesar from Dyrrachium. Asparagium cannot be identified with any modern place, but was known as the point where the Via Egnatia branched into a road to Dyrrachium to the north, and another to Apollonia to the south, each just over a day's march away.

Once Pompey had halted his tired and agitated army, Titus Labienus sought to restore the troops' morale by swearing "an oath that he would not desert Pompey and would share with him whatever fate had been allotted him by fortune" (*The Civil War* 3.13.3). His reputation as a general and his standing as a former officer of Caesar's now fighting for Pompey carried great weight, and the other *legati*, the tribunes, and the centurions readily took the same oath, followed by the entire rank and file. After detaching enough troops to reinforce Dyrrachium, Pompey the next day took his revitalized army down the south fork of the Via Egnatia toward Apollonia.

No more than a day later, when Caesar learned that Pompey had blocked his way to Dyrrachium, he halted his own march and ordered a fortified camp built on the south side of the Apsus River, today called the Semeni, which meanders across the coastal plain of Albania north of modern Fier. He sought the protection of the river because his army was only half the size of Pompey's and his cavalry was outnumbered more than ten to one. He had garrisoned troops in all the nearby harbors and had posted others along the coastline to prevent any Pompeian ships from coming ashore for food, fuel (for cooking), or water, but he was desperate for the rest of his army to get across the strait and reinforce him. He had sent Fufius Calenus back to Brundisium with the empty boats and orders to bring the remaining five legions across as soon as possible. But after losing thirty transports on the return trip, Calenus had only enough to load four legions and some cavalry, and it was with this cargo on board dozens of transports that he put out from Brundisium about the middle of January.

The modern reader may well be startled by the next sentence in Caesar's narrative: "When he was a little way out from port, he received a letter from Caesar telling him that the harbors and the entire shoreline were held by enemy fleets. As a result of this information he put back into port and recalled all his ships" (*The Civil War* 3.14.1–2). One of Caesar's fast warships had slipped through the Pompeian blockade and across the strait, reaching Calenus' flagship in time to warn him that the fleet had no chance to get through. Caesar notes the "remarkable chance" that saved the balance of his army, but reveals the cruelty of his opponents in a sobering aftermath. One ship carrying supplies but no troops, apparently a merchantman under contract, ignored the command to return and continued toward Macedonia until it was intercepted off Oricum by Bibulus. According to Caesar there was again no mercy, and Bibulus had the entire crew massacred, even *impuberes*, "mere boys."

The deep antipathy between Caesar and Bibulus had a history of more than fifteen years, beginning when they were *aediles* together in 65, and continuing when they were both *praetores* in 62, and co-Consuls in 59. On top of this, Bibulus had married Porcia, daughter of Cato, the leader of the *optimate* faction most hostile to Caesar. Some historians suggest that Pompey's appointment of Bibulus as his naval commander had less to do with his competence as a leader, for which there was no evidence, than with his position as a leading

Caesar-hater. In either case, the emotional Bibulus brought a large grudge to the war, and his great need to reverse his failure to stop Caesar from slipping through the blockade may have been his undoing. He came down with an illness, perhaps pneumonia, and "lacking medical attention, and unwilling to abandon the task he had undertaken, he was unable to withstand the force of the disease" (*The Civil War* 3.18.1), and died on board ship.

By this time Pompey had brought his army down the south fork of the Via Egnatia to the point where it crosses the Apsus River and had built his camp on the north bank opposite Caesar's camp on the south. For the first time since Brundisium the previous March, the two generals faced each other, but the circumstances this time restrained Caesar from attacking. Vibullius chose this opportunity to present Caesar's peace proposal to Pompey and his closest advisors. But before he got very far, Pompey angrily interrupted him, saying that since he had been driven out of Italy, any agreement that resulted in his return would look as if he did so with the permission of Caesar, and that was unacceptable to him. Caesar writes that he learned of this conversation after the war from those who were present, but at the time he also sent Publius Vatinius down to the river's edge where he could easily speak to Pompey's troops on the other side.

The next day a large number of troops from both armies gathered on both banks of the river, and Vatinius began talking with Titus Labienus and others about arranging for peace negotiations. "In the middle of this discussion they were interrupted by missiles suddenly thrown from all directions; Labienus, protected by his soldiers' armor, escaped them, but several people were wounded. . . . Then Labienus said: 'Well then, stop talking about peace; there can be no peace for us unless we get Caesar's head' " (*The Civil War* 3.19.7–8).

Perceiving that Caesar was negotiating out of weakness, Pompey, with a clear superiority of arms, determined to force him to battle on the spot. He brought up his legions and sent an advance guard across the bridge, but so many tried to cross at once that the bridge, perhaps weakened by Caesar's men, broke down under their weight. Some of Pompey's troops were trapped on the other side and quickly perished, and he called off the attack. He made no further attempt to bring Caesar to battle, "discouraged," according to the historian Cassius Dio, "because he had failed in the first action of the war."[1]

Well into the winter the two armies watched each other from opposite sides of the river. Pompey was apparently waiting for his father-in-law, Metellus Scipio, to arrive from the east with two more legions. Caesar, with an outnumbered army, was stalling, and growing frustrated that the rest of his legions had not yet arrived from Italy. Pompey's admirals ventured out less often and stayed closer to their ports, even though he admonished them in frequent letters not to let another convoy through. In Caesar's camp the situation was more serious, and he says that when the troops had not arrived more than two months later, he wrote sharply, *severius scripsit*, to Antony and Calenus, ordering them not to lose the first opportunity to catch a favorable wind and bring the men across. But he is silent about an incident in the latter half of March that is reported by several later writers.

According to a composite of the accounts, Caesar disguised himself as a courier on official business, and persuaded a local boat captain to take him and a few aides across the strait to Brundisium so he could bring the ships over himself. Setting out at night from Apollonia, the crew had to row against a brisk west wind to force the boat down the Aous River to its mouth, where the wind and waves became so strong that the captain gave the signal to turn back. Caesar chose this moment to reveal himself. "Be brave," he shouted to the captain, "face the waves. Your cargo is Caesar and his luck."[2] Afraid and astonished that a Consul of Rome was in their boat, the crew bent again to the oars and tried to bring the boat out of the river's mouth. But with the wind, waves, and current all against it, they could make no headway, and when they started to swamp, Caesar finally ordered the boat back to the dock.

Within days of this escapade, on a night late in March (midwinter by the solar calendar), Antony decided that he had the right weather to get his convoy of reinforcements across the strait. He had assembled four legions of infantry, one of them newly recruited, a cadre of slingers, and eight hundred cavalry, as large an army as Caesar's, its four legions being fully enrolled at five thousand men each. His fleet, however, was larger, the thirty lost ships having been replaced and augmented. Caesar had urged him to sail due east and to make for one of the beaches near Apollonia (he was camped nearby) because there were no harbors in the vicinity, and Pompey's warships were staying close to port. It is possible that Antony misjudged the weather, or perhaps it changed suddenly, because as his transports and warships neared the Macedonian coast the next day, they found themselves buffeted by a strong wind from the south that prevented their landing and gradually pushed them northward toward Dyrrachium.

Both Pompey's and Caesar's scouts on the coast spotted the fleet off Apollonia about noon, and then saw it blown even past Dyrrachium and out of sight to the north. In the harbor at Dyrrachium Gaius Coponius, in command of twenty warships sent to Pompey's navy by the Greek city of Rhodes, saw the fleet go by and immediately gave chase. Antony's transports carried only a single, square linen sail and, without oars, could only steer as the gale drove them more than twenty-five miles past Dyrrachium. As the pursuing warships, under full sail and driven by dozens of oarsmen, steadily pulled up to them, Antony's artillerymen and slingers opened fire.

By this time the fleet was directly in front of the small bay at the town of Nymphaeum, now called Shëngjin, at the northern border of modern Albania. Reasoning that shipwreck on the beach was preferable to being rammed, sunk, or boarded, Antony ordered the convoy steered around a headland and into the protected bay. When all the transports but two had cleared the headland, what Caesar calls *incredibilis felicitas*, amazing luck, caused the wind to suddenly turn and come from the west, leaving the fleet undamaged and becalmed in the bay. But the pursuing warships, still in the path of the gale now blowing onshore, were driven due east and against the rocky coast just below Nymphaeum. Sixteen of the Pompeian vessels were wrecked, and all the seamen and marines who were not drowned were taken prisoner by Antony's troops. Caesar writes that he later ordered them all released.

With some help from *fortuna*, Antony had duplicated Caesar's feat, with the exception that two of his transports had fallen out of the convoy and, finding themselves alone at nightfall, had anchored off the town of Lissus, now Lezhë, about three miles south of Nymphaeum. Before long they were surrounded by Pompeian boats sent out by the local commander, and Caesar draws a pointed contrast to his own magnanimity as he describes this aftermath. One boatful of two hundred exhausted and frightened recruits agreed to surrender on an oath that they would be spared, and when they did so, were promptly massacred. The veterans on the other boat dragged out negotiations and managed to put off surrendering until they were able to bring their transport to the beach, and then, after fighting off four hundred cavalry, found their way to Antony's camp. Sending most of the empty boats back to Italy to pick up more troops, Antony dispatched a courier ahead and promptly began a march southward along an inland route through what is now Tiranë, Albania's capital, to find Caesar.

It was a day or two before Pompey, still at his camp on the Apsus, learned that Antony had landed safely at Nymphaeum, and that Caesar's army in Macedonia had now doubled in size. Knowing that Antony would march directly to join Caesar, he broke camp the same night and moved his army by forced marches in a northeasterly direction in an effort to engage Antony before he and Caesar met. With the same objective of reaching Antony, Caesar, from his camp on the south side of the Apsus, marched upriver the next day to a place where he could ford it, and then hurried in the same direction. With the information he had about Antony's route, Pompey intended to ambush him where he emerged into the plain in the neighborhood of the Albanian city of what is now Cërrik, just off the Via Egnatia. But his plan was foiled when Antony halted his march and remained in his camp after being warned of the ambush by local travelers. The next day, some three months after Caesar had landed in Macedonia, he and Antony consolidated their armies in the foothills some twenty-five miles from the coast, and between Pompey and his allies in the eastern part of the province.

Moving to protect his supply base at Dyrrachium, Pompey took his army due west on the Via Egnatia and constructed a camp near Asparagium on the north bank of the Genusus River, now called the Shkumbi. The two generals had in effect reversed their positions, and Caesar, now in command of almost eleven legions (he had recalled all but three cohorts from Oricum) totaling perhaps thirty-four thousand infantry, sent a legion and a half and two *legati* to secure the territory to the south and arrange for grain shipments. He also dispatched Domitius Calvinus, a former Consul whom he had brought back from exile, to the east on the Via Egnatia with the XIth and XIIth Legions and five hundred cavalry to intercept Metellus Scipio, who had entered eastern Macedonia with his two Syrian legions. Caesar then turned to Pompey and followed him westward to Asparagium, keeping to the south bank of the Genusus, where he positioned his seven legions in sight of Pompey's nine just across the river, and prepared for battle.

In the meantime, Pompey's son Gnaeus *filius*, who commanded several dozen warships furnished by Ptolemy XIII and Cleopatra, forced his way past a blockade of the harbor at Oricum, burned eight of Caesar's warships in the inner harbor, and towed off four others. From Oricum he sailed up the coast to Lissus, where Antony had left thirty merchant ships in case they should be needed for a return to Italy. Gnaeus burned all of these, and then tried to occupy Lissus, but was repulsed by the local militia and troops placed there by Caesar. The outcome, however, was that Caesar was left with no warships or transports along the whole western coast of Macedonia.

Without an escape route by sea, and with his only food supplies coming from far inland, Caesar was all the more anxious to capture Pompey's supply depot at Dyrrachium. With three more veteran legions, he was confident that his army was now equal to Pompey's, and he sought to provoke a battle by leading it out of his camp opposite Asparagium in fighting formation. But even when, as Caesar puts it, he "offered Pompey the chance of a decisive engagement" (*The Civil War* 3.41.7), Pompey refused to budge. With his own supply line secure, he saw greater benefit in a stalemate than in risking a battle. Caesar no doubt expected that Pompey would refuse to cross a major river to engage an enemy on the opposite bank, especially in the dead of winter. But the gesture improved his men's morale and underlined the fact that after fifteen months of war his principal opponent still refused to fight. The next morning he struck his camp and led all seven legions back the way they had come, eastward toward modern Elbasan.

Before the day was over, however, Pompey's scouts reported that Caesar was not retreating to the east, but had crossed to the north bank of the Genusus a few miles upriver, and had set out northward through the foothills toward Dyrrachium. His legions followed a roundabout route along a difficult and narrow track that even today is no more than a footpath. Pompey led his own army out of camp the same day and started north on the Via Egnatia toward Dyrrachium at top speed. But Caesar had a day's head start and allowed his troops a nighttime halt of only a few hours on a forced march of about forty-three miles. He reached the coast the next day just ahead of Pompey's advance guard, and constructed a heavily fortified camp on a hill off the Via Egnatia two miles south of Dyrrachium.

With access to his supply depot at Dyrrachium blocked, Pompey had no choice but to entrench his army about two miles south of Caesar on a rocky plateau the Romans called Petra, now Shkumb (or Rock) of Kavajës, overlook-

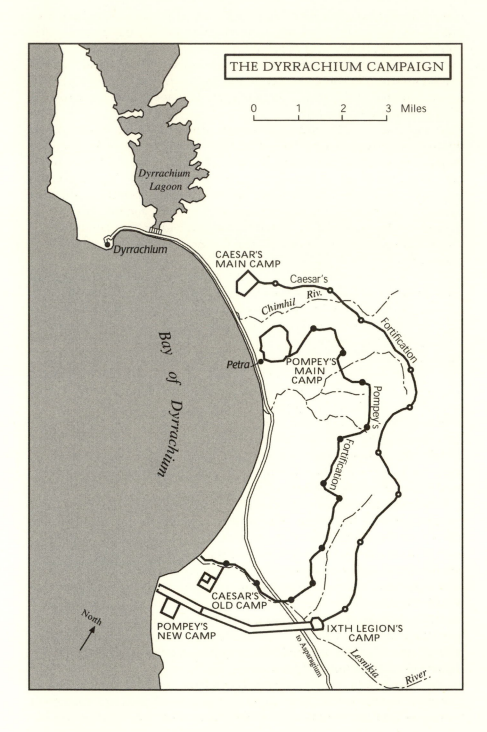

THE DYRRACHIUM CAMPAIGN

0   1   2   3   Miles

Dyrrachium
Lagoon

Dyrrachium

CAESAR'S
MAIN CAMP

Caesar's

Chimhil Riv.

Fortification

Petra

POMPEY'S
MAIN
CAMP

Pompey's

Bay of Dyrrachium

Fortification

North

CAESAR'S
OLD CAMP

POMPEY'S
NEW CAMP

IXTH LEGION'S
CAMP

to Aspragium

Lesnikia River

ing the beach. But because he was able to resupply his army by sea at the base of the cliff and move it anywhere along the coast, he preserved his tactical advantage. Caesar was even farther from his sources of grain than he had been at Asparagium. With Pompey right behind him, Caesar was also prevented from attacking Dyrrachium, and could not even stop it from being reinforced by sea. His seven legions now amounted to no more than about twenty-five thousand men, and he had only a few hundred cavalry; Pompey still commanded nine legions of more than forty thousand infantry, numerous auxiliary troops, such as archers, slingers, and javelin throwers, and at least five thousand cavalry. The two generals had eighty thousand men under arms within two miles of each other and almost nowhere to go and no choice but to fight the long-delayed battle that could decide the war.

Caesar writes that in these circumstances his best strategy was to surround and besiege Pompey's army by pinning it against the coast. This would cut off his flow of supplies by land and allow Caesar to resupply himself more easily from the interior. He would also derive propaganda value from the fact that Pompey—the invincible Pompeius Magnus—was under siege and refused to fight. To this end, he deployed his legions along a chain of steep ridges, some as high as nine hundred feet, and ordered them to build a series of forts, linked by palisades and ditches, in a huge semicircle around Pompey's army at Petra.

Pompey's response was to seize as much land and as many hills as he could, and thus require Caesar's troops to extend their own enclosure of ditches and forts. For several weeks the two armies fought a running battle to demarcate the front line, Pompey's to keep it as far inland as possible, and Caesar's to keep it closer to the sea. Pompey's troops fiercely contested each hill and ridge, his archers and slingers sending thousands of missiles against Caesar's legionaries, who resorted to wearing quilts and hides, and to bringing up bundles of wicker to protect themselves.

Caesar records a lengthy battle that surged back and forth between a Pompeian legion and his own IXth, under the command of Mark Antony, in which both sides used *catapultae* as well as mercenary slingers, or *funditores*, who wielded an ancient weapon with deadly effectiveness. The *funda*, or sling, originated in prehistory as a hunting weapon, but was quickly adapted to warfare. It consisted of a simple cord of hide or sinew about three feet long with a flat pouch in the center in which the slinger placed a rounded stone the size of an egg. He grasped the two ends of the cord, whirled it around his head, and released one end, propelling the stone as far as two hundred yards with tremendous force. Depending on the size of the stone, the sling commonly had a greater range than the bow, and could be used with astonishing accuracy. Slingers from the Balearic Islands were specially trained in the use of their weapon, some from childhood, and were used by both Caesar and Pompey throughout the Civil War. (The weapon David used to fell Goliath in the Old Testament book of I Samuel was a sling.)[3]

With more men available and a fortification line of shorter circumference, Pompey forced Caesar's engineers to extend their line further inland and then miles to the south, where it crossed the Lesnikia River, now the Gesnike, before turning back west to the coast, enclosing an area of approximately twenty-one square miles. Its total length of more than fifteen miles was several miles longer than Caesar's encircling fortifications at Alesia four years earlier, and was probably the most extensive fortified line constructed in classical times. It may also have been the most sparsely manned, Caesar being able to deploy fewer than fifteen hundred soldiers per mile. Pompey's defensive line, along which he built twenty-four fortified towers, was about eight miles long, enclosing about sixteen square miles.

Behind Caesar's fortifications his engineers worked to dam or divert any mountain streams flowing into Pompey's territory, with the result that Pompey's army, and his animals, soon began to suffer from a lack of fresh water. His men were forced to dig numerous wells and rely on water hauled from the Lesnikia, eight miles from his camp. His other serious problem was a lack of pasturage for his horses and pack animals, each of which required at least ten pounds of fodder and three to four pounds of grain a day. Even if he had only five thousand of his cavalry with him, he needed twice that number of pack animals, officers' mounts, and replacements, for a conservative estimate of fifteen thousand animals requiring a hundred tons of food each day, virtually all of which had to be delivered by merchant ship. According to Caesar, Pompey's army was also suffering from being confined in a small space and from the stench of dead animals.

Caesar's army, on the other hand, was well supplied with fuel and water, but lacked sufficient wheat to make the bread and porridge that were the basis of the legionaries' diet. For a time the grain shortage became so severe that they subsisted on barley or the edible seeds of wild plants, normally the diet of slaves and animals, or punishment rations for soldiers. It is unlikely that either army resorted to killing and eating its horses, a practice that Romans found revolting. Eventually Caesar's soldiers took to digging up a root called "chara" that relieved their hunger when chopped up and mixed with milk. "There was plenty of it," writes Caesar. "Our men made loaves of it, and when in verbal exchanges with the Pompeians they were taunted for being hungry, they threw these in handfuls at them to undermine their hopes" (*The Civil War* 3.48.2). This plant has not been authoritatively identified, but may be a tuber from which a bread is made that is still occasionally eaten in Albania. A later historian records that when Pompey was shown the loaves, he exclaimed "Look at the kind of wild beasts we are up against."[4]

Whether Caesar's soldiers were wild beasts or not, Pompey's situation was becoming embarrassing as well as uncomfortable. He had not only to contend with Caesar, but was surrounded in his own camp by a flock of generals and Senators, including Cato, Labienus, Varro, and Lentulus Spinther, some of whom had already been bruised by Caesar, and all of whom had urgent advice about how to conduct the campaign. By now the indefatigable Lucius Domitius, as well as Marcus Petreius, the loser in Spain, had also joined Pompey's camp at Petra, and two extant letters from an anxious and dispirited Cicero reveal that he was also there.

Cicero's sharp tongue and his criticism of the campaign did not make him popular, and his advice to make peace went unheeded. He had made a large loan to Pompey "in the expectation that when things settle down it will be creditable . . . to have done so."[5] At the same time Cicero was being urged by Dolabella, who wrote from Caesar's camp two miles away (reportedly at Caesar's instigation), to abandon Pompey, who was as good as lost, and make peace with Caesar, or at least retire to Athens, or some similar place. Cicero's reply, if any, has not survived, but he stayed in Pompey's camp. The three ex-Consuls had not been in the same vicinity for more than ten years, and would never be again.

In the meantime, Scipio's two legions, traveling from Thessalonica on the Via Egnatia, and those of Domitius Calvinus, marching from the west, approached each other in central Macedonia, while Caesar's XXVIIth Legion and two hundred cavalry under Lucius Cassius took a southeastern route across the Pindus Mountains toward Thessaly. Domitius and Scipio reached the Haliacmon River at about the same time and chose to camp on either side of it, possibly in the neighborhood of today's Servia. Both took postures threatening battle, but aside from some minor ambushes of each other's cavalry, no serious fighting occurred. Their armies were about equal in size, and their main responsibilities were to keep each other away from the main forces of Caesar and Pompey.

Under siege in his camp at Petra, Pompey's problems had begun to worsen by late June. Although he had supply ships that could carry a hundred tons of fodder and grain, they could not get enough to keep up with the needs of his thousands of animals. When his pack animals began to starve, he had many of them slaughtered, and then shipped his cavalry horses across the bay to Dyrrachium, where they were taken to forage in the pastures north of the city. Also, the lack of fresh water and generally unsanitary conditions in his camp caused an outbreak of what may have been typhus among his soldiers. Unwilling to retreat to Italy, he decided to make a serious attempt to break the siege.

The plan he devised, his first offensive move since the aborted attack over the Apsus in February, was to have a message sent to Caesar from a supposed traitor inside Dyrrachium offering to betray the city and secretly open its gates to his troops. Caesar gave enough credence to the offer to personally bring a force of troops on the appointed night to a wooden bridge spanning a narrow lagoon that lay between the city and the mainland. When he had crossed the bridge and was approaching the city wall, Pompey's troops suddenly rushed out of the gates and attacked him, and a seaborne detachment landed on the shore behind him. Caesar and his troops were nearly captured as they fought desperately to retreat across the bridge, while arrows and stones rained on them from Pompeian warships in the bay. With the missiles coming from their right flank, Caesar ordered his infantry to transfer their shields from their left hands to their right, but before they were able to fight their way back to their camp, he had lost many of them and was nearly killed himself.

At the same moment he was luring Caesar into a trap at Dyrrachium, Pompey sent almost all his troops in a mass attack against Caesar's lines at three different locations, including one assault by four legions against a fort defended by a single cohort of the VIth Legion, no more than five hundred men. But Pompey's grand offensive, which resulted in six separate battles during a single twenty-four-hour period, did not achieve what he hoped it would. Although outnumbered, taken by surprise, and without their general, Caesar's veterans beat back the offensive all across the front. They no doubt benefited from holding superior, fortified positions that forced Pompey's troops to attack uphill. Also, Pompey's army had done nothing but march and camp for more than a year, and for the great majority this was their first time under fire.

In no place was Caesar's line breached, and the single cohort under attack held fort long enough to be rescued by two legions under the command of Publius Sulla, nephew of the *dictator*, who beat back the Pompeians, forcing them to retreat to a nearby hill, out of artillery range. The four legions, under Pompey's personal command, were still on the hill at nightfall, and had to construct a new camp and then screen one side of it against missiles. Caesar's dry phrases do not conceal his disdain for Pompey's reluctance to fight: " Five days later he took advantage of another somewhat overcast night, blocked all the gates of the camp . . . at the start of the third watch [midnight] silently led his army out and retired to his old fortifications" (*The Civil War* 3.54.2). Caesar acknowledges only a handful of dead, against more than two thousand in Pompey's army, but he admits that many of his men had been wounded, and it is likely that fatalities in both armies were substantial.

Although Caesar's encirclement of Pompey's army remained intact, he still sought the decisive battle to bring the stalemate to an end. On each of the next several days he led his army out in battle formation on level ground in front of Pompey's camp, but just out of range of his artillery. Although Pompey brought his troops out of camp in the same way "to preserve his public reputation" (*The Civil War* 3.55.2), he kept them close enough to his ramparts to be protected by missile fire, and still refused a head-on fight.

About this time Pompey gained two advantages that put him in a better position to break out of the blockade. The size and experience of his army improved markedly with the arrival of Lucius Afranius with several thousand veteran legionaries, as many as twenty cohorts, who had remained with him after being freed by Caesar after the Spanish campaign. Also, two of Caesar's Gallic cavalry commanders, after quarreling with their subordinates and being reprimanded by Caesar, borrowed what money they could and then defected to Pompey with their retinues and a large number of horses. The two commanders—sons of the chieftain of the Allobroges tribe—had led cavalry wings in Caesar's army throughout the Gallic War, and he had rewarded them liberally. According to him, they were the only soldiers of any rank to desert his army, and Pompey delightedly paraded them in front of his troops at all his outposts. Besides their propaganda value, they supplied him with details about weaknesses and gaps in Caesar's fortified line.

One thing they told him was that the southern end of the blockade was unfinished and vulnerable, besides being a full fifteen miles from Caesar's main camp. Caesar's engineers had just been able to bring the last section of his ditch and bank entrenchment down from the foothills and across the two-mile plain to the beach. This section of the entrenchment was manned by Caesar's IXth Legion, which had constructed a fortified camp at the base of the foothills. To guard against a seaborne Pompeian army landing south of them, they had built a second fortified line two hundred yards below the first, and facing southward, for the last four miles before it reached the sea. But they had not yet completed a transverse barricade facing the sea and extending between the two fortified lines, and this was what Pompey knew when he launched a three-pronged attack during the first week of July against Caesar's blockade where it reached the beach.

During the night Pompey brought six legions of infantry along the beach to the southern terminus of his defense line. After fording the Lesnikia River at dawn, they sent a barrage of artillery and arrows against Caesar's ten-foot-high bank and palisade, and began filling in his fifteen-foot-wide ditch just where it reached the beach. At the same time a large force of Pompey's archers, slingers, and light infantry landed further down the beach and attacked Caesar's outer fortifications from the south. Then, while his troops were attacking Caesar's inner and outer lines, Pompey landed a third contingent of infantry on the beach between them, effecting a simultaneous assault on Caesar's line at the front, the rear, and, from the sea, at the flank.

The two Caesarian cohorts manning the wall were taken completely by surprise, and at dawn found themselves retreating from the beach at a fast pace under a missile barrage, and pursued by charging infantry. They fled nearly two miles inland between the inner and outer lines until they collided with the rest of the legion—the IXth—that was racing toward the beach to relieve them. But the relieving troops were unable to stop their fleeing comrades or the advancing Pompeian infantry, and in the panic of the moment scores of Caesar's legionaries were trampled to death, and more were cut down by Pompey's troops.

After the remainder of the legion had retreated into its camp and was in danger of being overrun, another twelve cohorts under the lead of Mark Antony came rushing down from the hill behind it and joined the battle. As these reinforcements brought the attack to a halt, Caesar himself appeared with another dozen cohorts he had rounded up from the forts along the line, after being called to the rescue by a series of smoke signals transmitted from fort to fort. His reinforced army pushed the Pompeians back through the enclosed corridor to within a mile of the beach, and immediately started building a second transverse barrier between the inner and outer fortifications. But Pompey had taken complete control of the southern end of the line of blockade, and his troops now built a camp just to the west of Caesar's second transverse barrier, and within a half mile of the beach. Caesar could do no more, as the first phase of the battle ended, than set up a temporary camp a few hundred yards inland from Pompey's.

Later in the day Caesar's lookouts observed that a single Pompeian legion was moving to occupy a camp that Caesar had built at the time he was completing his entrenchments down to the beach, and then abandoned. Pompey had subsequently occupied the camp, which was between the river and Caesar's line to the south, enlarged it considerably, and then abandoned it himself. While Pompey's troops were busy fortifying their new camp, Caesar secretly assembled more than three legions, including the much-reduced IXth, for an attack on the single legion, leaving only two cohorts "busy on earthworks, to give the impression that fortification was in progress" (*The Civil War* 3.67.2). Hoping to restore the morale of his army and to cancel the reverse he had just suffered, he led his troops northward by a roundabout way and assaulted the camp with a double line of infantry and a few hundred cavalry on the right wing.

Unobserved by Pompey's scouts, Caesar's troops reached the rampart, overcame the defenders, breached the gate, and swarmed into the larger camp, forcing the remainder of the legion to retreat into the original, smaller camp. But his right wing came upon a four-hundred-yard-long ditch and bank that the Pompeians had built from the camp to the river to protect themselves while getting water. This barrier, about fifteen feet wide and ten feet deep, they followed for its full length, looking for a gate, until they realized that it had none and was undefended, and so they clambered across and broke through it. After filling in the ditch in several places so the cavalry could get across, the entire column, perhaps five to six thousand legionaries and a few hundred cavalry, attacked the Pompeian camp on its north side.

But by this time Pompey realized what was happening and ordered the trumpet signal to alert the troops working on the camp fortifications. He sent his cavalry around the sea side of the camp under attack and behind it against Caesar's right column, and then used the five legions in a direct assault across the old lines of fortification against the southern side of it. When the Pompeian legion that had been forced back saw its rescue coming, it surged forward with renewed confidence, leaving Caesar and his troops on the left wing caught between it and the Pompeian troops bearing down on them from the south. At the same time, Caesar's cavalry and troops on the right wing, seeing Pompey's cavalry in front of them and his infantry coming up behind, feared their retreat would be cut off, and rushed to get back across the ditch. Many of those who could not get to the few causeways that had been built jumped into the ditch and then, before they could climb out, were crushed to death by hundreds of terrified men jumping in after them who "used their bodies to provide a way out to safety for themselves" (*The Civil War* 3.69.3).

Caesar's troops on the left wing, which he commanded himself, seeing the enemy both in front and behind, behaved no better. In Caesar's words: "They attempted to save themselves by a retreat in the direction from which they had come, and there was such confusion, panic, and flight all around that although Caesar seized the standards of his fleeing men and ordered them to halt, some abandoned their horses and ran off . . . others in their fear even threw away the standards, and not a single man halted" (*The Civil War* 3.69.4). In Plutarch's account of this incident, Caesar grabbed the arm of a soldier running past him and ordered him to turn around and face the enemy, but the man, "in his panic-stricken state of mind, raised his sword" and would have cut him down had not Caesar's shieldbearer lopped off his arm at the shoulder.[6]

Unable to halt the retreat, Caesar could only direct his badly frightened troops back to the IXth Legion's camp at the base of the foothills three miles from the beach. His quick decision to counterattack, perhaps more emotional than rational, had only compounded the success of Pompey's land and sea offensive, and had left his own army confused and demoralized. But Caesar's *fortuna* had not deserted him entirely, for despite the disarray and vulnerability of his badly mauled legions, Pompey failed to pursue them, suspecting that the headlong flight was an ambush. To his officers, Caesar hinted that the war had almost been lost, remarking that "today the enemy would have won, if they had a commander who was a winner."[7]

But he was under no illusion about who had won the battle of Dyrrachium. With his blockade broken and his dispirited army in danger of being flanked on the south and bottled up in the mountains, Caesar ordered his original camp above Petra and the entire fortification line abandoned. By his own admission, he had lost a thousand men in a single day, including four legionary tribunes and thirty-two centurions, a large proportion of them unwounded, but trampled to death or suffocated in the ditches under the bodies of their fellow soldiers. According to Plutarch, he lost two thousand troops, and the number of wounded, many of them unfit for further service, may have been twice as many. Among the dead were all the prisoners taken by Pompey, who was persuaded by Labienus to turn them over to him. According to Caesar, Labienus, "deserter that he was" (*The Civil War* 3.71.4), paraded the prisoners, taunting them by asking if veteran soldiers usually ran away, and had them all killed. It is likely that Pompey's soldiers stripped the corpses of equipment and valuables and then, following the Roman custom, burned them on pyres, those in the ditches perhaps being burned where they fell.

Bringing his entire army into the camp, Caesar mounted a platform and spoke at length to as many as could hear him, urging them not to be discouraged and reminding them of their good luck and many successes over the past year. Even as he reprimanded and demoted several *signiferi*, bearers of the cohort's standards, he told the army that victory had been snatched from them by bad luck or some other force beyond their control. Thirty years of speech-making had prepared Caesar for the task of rousing his troops after a stinging defeat. He writes that "the whole army was so hurt by defeat and so eager to restore their reputation" (*The Civil War* 3.74.2) that they voluntarily set themselves to the hardest work, even clamoring to counterattack. But Caesar knew he could do nothing more at Dyrrachium. He needed time and space to regroup, more food for his troops and animals, and another place to do battle. It would need to be away from the coast so as to neutralize Pompey's navy, and to the east where Caesar had two more veteran legions.

In the first hour of darkness he sent one legion quietly out the back gate with the army's baggage and equipment south on the Via Egnatia, with orders to occupy their old camp at Asparagium, twelve miles away. During the night another four legions departed in silence along the same route. At dawn Caesar allowed the first trumpet call to be sounded for the breakup of the camp, "to observe military routine" (*The Civil War* 3.75.2), and then led his last two legions out immediately. It was only then that Pompey realized that he was escaping, and ordered his army after him, but Caesar's legions, with a long head start and traveling without baggage or equipment, stayed ahead of him easily.

Caesar had saved his army, but Pompey controlled the Via Egnatia, and his navy barred any retreat to Italy. Caesar's best choice was to retire to the south into friendly territory, and then make his way up one of the river valleys into the Pindus Mountains. Once over them, he might be able to find the two legions he had sent east under Domitius Calvinus and reinforce his depleted army. Among Pompey's troops and supporters, the news of Caesar's defeat produced a wave of celebration, and "they made that day's victory famous, by letter and by word of mouth, to the whole world" (*The Civil War* 3.72.4). The one-and-a-half-year war had come down to a scene in which Caesar's seven defeated and demoralized legions, carrying numerous wounded, hurriedly retreated by night from a larger army pursuing them with thousands of cavalry. Caesar had not been in such a precarious position since he had been trapped on the Sicoris River without food or supplies just a year earlier. If his troops were not to be hunted down and killed in the mountains of Macedonia, he would have to avoid a battle until he was ready, and then find a way to counter Pompey's great advantage.

X

The Battle of Pharsalus

If it was Pompey's hesitation that allowed Caesar to survive Dyrrachium, it was his own resourcefulness that enabled him to execute the speediest and most desperate retreat of his career. Six of his seven legions made it safely to the Genusus River, some twelve miles down the road, and forded it successfully, but troops in the last legion were caught and attacked by Pompey's cavalry as they tried to negotiate its steep banks. Caesar sent four hundred infantry and his own cavalry against them, and beat them back after a vicious battle.

By midmorning his entire army reached the vicinity of Asparagium, and occupied the camp it had constructed on the south bank three months earlier, after the arrival of Antony and his army. The rest of the pursuing Pompeian troops arrived the same morning, and took possession of their old camp on the north side of the river, placing each army in precisely the same position it had occupied in early April. Although both sides had suffered significant losses since then, Pompey had augmented his army with two veteran legions, and Caesar's was decidedly much worse off.

After entering the camp, Caesar sent his few hundred cavalry out the front gate to forage, and gave every appearance to the Pompeians across the river that he intended to stay the night. But his cavalry circled around the camp and entered it by the rear gate, whereupon the whole army hurried out the back about midday and marched another eight miles before stopping. Again Pompey was caught unawares. Many of his troops were far from the camp, foraging or gathering firewood, and some others, after setting up their tents, had left their weapons and returned to their previous camp to get the baggage they had left behind in their hasty departure that morning. By the time they could take up the pursuit, Caesar again had half a day's march on them, and they were unable to catch him over the next three days as he maneuvered his legions through the coastal mountains, forded the Apsus, full-flowing with spring rains, and brought them all into the temporary safety of Apollonia.

It was about the middle of July (mid-May by the modern calendar) that Caesar completed arrangements for the care of hundreds of wounded men at Apollonia and paid his troops the seventy-five *denarii*, minus the cost of food, clothing, and weapons, that was due them three times a year—about eleven ounces in silver coins. (Centurions received five times as much.) Leaving small garrisons at Apollonia and Oricum, he then took his troops southward at a fast pace up the valley of the Aous River and into the hinterlands of Epirus—a Greek word denoting mainland—the name used in antiquity for the western portion of the Greek peninsula. With his two legions in the eastern part of the province in grave danger from Pompey, he sent messengers along several routes with warnings and instructions to Domitius Calvinus to travel south and meet him at Aeginium on the western edge of the Plain of Thessaly.

By dropping the blockade and retreating south to Apollonia, and then further inland into Epirus, Caesar forced Pompey to decide among three courses of action. He could return to Italy and defend it against a Caesarian invasion, follow Caesar into the mountains and attempt to defeat him there, or march directly east on the Via Egnatia to join ranks with Scipio, and then pursue Caesar. Many of Pompey's lieutenants, especially Afranius, urged him to return to Italy, from which he could control the wheatfields of Sicily and Sardinia, and set up a legitimate government, forcing Caesar to come to him. But Pompey was too proud to be seen running from Caesar a second time, and he knew that he must pursue and defeat him to bring the war to a decisive end. Also, he was unwilling to abandon his allies and friends in the East and allow Caesar to chase them out of their countries, confiscate their wealth, and sack their cities.

Not the least of his concerns was for his father-in-law in central Macedonia, and for the wives and children he and his colleagues had sent to Lesbos. But he would not struggle after Caesar into the wild and rugged country to the south. Instead, he left a strong garrison of fifteen cohorts at Dyrrachium, including Cato and Cicero (who had become ill), and took nine legions and several thousand cavalry at top speed along the relatively easy Via Egnatia into central Macedonia. His objective was to find Domitius Calvinus and eliminate his two legions, and then, accompanied by Scipio and his legions, come to grips with Caesar.

Although Caesar's army by now numbered less than twenty thousand infantry and a few hundred horse, it was still a substantial caravan that followed the Aous southward to its junction with the Drino River about forty miles up the valley. Here the army entered a hilly, westward-sloping region rising sharply to the long range of the Pindus Mountains on the east. Even today Epirus is a wilderness of thick forests, swift rivers, and remote villages. Its narrow upland pastures were famous for producing outstanding horses and cattle. (Cicero's friend Atticus owned a farm near the coast.) Evidence from burial mounds and religious shrines in the area suggests that Epirus was the original home of the founders of the Mycenaean civilization, which flourished in the last half of the second millennium BCE. Epirus achieved the status of an independent state under King Pyrrhus in the third century, but in 167 the Romans overran it, and later made it a part of their province of Macedonia.

Reaching the Drino in the neighborhood of modern Tepelenë in southern Albania, Caesar most likely changed course and followed it across the modern border between Albania and Greece. Continuing thirty-five miles further into the foothills, he reached Lake Pambotis, now the site of Ioannina, capital of the modern province. From there the army climbed upward into the steep mountains of the Pindus range and through the historic Katera Pass, at nearly six thousand feet, which may at that time of year have still been clogged with snow. Another day's march brought them to Aeginium, now the drab town of Kalambaka overlooking the Plain of Thessaly to the east. Caesar offers no details about this difficult march of more than a hundred and eighty miles, which his army, still short of food, apparently accomplished in about twelve days.

In the meantime, in central Macedonia Domitius Calvinus had moved north away from Scipio and toward the Via Egnatia in search of grain and supplies for his two legions. He had camped in the vicinity of modern Bitola, preparing to march west to join Caesar or simply to prevent Scipio from joining Pompey. Neither his nor Caesar's couriers had been able to find the other's army, so he had not heard of the calamity at Dyrrachium. But while Caesar was struggling through the mountains of southern Epirus, Pompey was traveling quickly east along the Via Egnatia and may have needed only seven or eight days to come very close to Domitius Calvinus' position near the border between Greece and modern Macedonia. There, by chance, his advance cavalry came upon some of Calvinus' scouts. It happened that Pompey's cavalry were Gauls from the Allobroges tribe who had only weeks before defected to him, and they, "whether from old acquaintance, because they had fought together in Gaul, or from elation over their great achievement, recounted the whole story of what had happened, and told them that Caesar had left and that Pompey was about to appear" (*The Civil War* 3.79.6).

Calvinus decamped immediately and with only four hours' head start eluded the Pompeian army and hurried south toward Thessaly at a fast march. Although Calvinus' two unprotected legions were right in front of him, Pompey chose not to pursue them, perhaps because the bulk of his enormous army was still on the western side of the five-thousand-foot Diavat Pass that takes the Via Egnatia over a northern spur of the Candavian Mountains. Instead he continued eastward on the road for several more days, until he turned off to the south toward the fortress city of Larisa at the northern edge of Thessaly, where Scipio awaited him. Calvinus most likely escaped into the upper Haliacmon Valley and, after one of Caesar's couriers finally reached him, continued south and joined Caesar at Aeginium at the western edge of Thessaly near the end of July.

Surrounded by mountains and drained by a single river system, the vast Plain of Thessaly, once a prehistoric lake bed, dominates the geography of the modern Greek mainland. Supposedly named for the legendary Thessalus who migrated from Epirus with his people, the Thessali, it is an area steeped in myth and history. At its northeastern edge stands Mount Olympus, home of the gods of the Greeks, and at its southern end lies the region of Phthiotis, Homer's Phthia, the birthplace of Achilles, and home of the Hellenes, a small tribe that eventually gave its name to the whole of the Greek people. Today it is a nearly treeless landscape, subject to extremes of climate, and dotted with dusty villages amid fields of wheat and corn, as well as a modern crop—tobacco.

To Caesar's limping and hungry army, Thessaly was a welcome sight, famed as it was for an abundance of wheat, which by now was just beginning to ripen in the fields. Most of his troops had been in camp or on the march throughout the winter and spring, and they were badly in need of the amenities of a well-supplied town, several of which were within a single day's march. But the news from Dyrrachium, suggesting that it would soon be Pompey who headed the Roman state, had traveled ahead of them, and as they approached the fortified town of Gomphi, today's Palaeo Episkopi, they found that everyone in the area had fled behind the town walls, and had shut and barred the gates. To Caesar this was a double affront, since only a few months earlier the people of the same town had sent a delegation "to invite him to make use of all the help they could give" (*The Civil War* 2.80.1), and had asked for the protection of his troops from Pompey. Now, the chief magistrate of Thessaly, who resided in Gomphi, had not only shut up his town, but had sent to Pompey and Scipio for protection. Caesar wasted no time before ordering preparations for an assault. "When these were ready, he fired the soldiers' enthusiasm by pointing out how advantageous it would be to alleviate their desperate shortage of everything by capturing a rich and well-provisioned town, and at the same time terrify the remaining communities by its example" (*The Civil War* 3.80.6).

Caesar's troops put their ladders to the walls and, the town having no artillery or soldiers to speak of, captured it before sunset. To reward them for their months of deprivation, he let them plunder the town, but he does not mention, as other historians have, the discovery of a quantity of wine and the debauch and massacre that followed.

The next day the rejuvenated army marched about twelve miles to Metropolis, now the village of Paleo Kastro, where the townspeople also barred the gates and posted soldiers on the walls. But when Caesar brought out some of the unfortunate prisoners he had taken at Gomphi and had them tell their tale at the foot of the wall, Metropolis saw the wisdom of surrender and opened its gates. As he led his troops into the town, Caesar forbade them to do violence to anyone, an act that secured the submission and cooperation of all the nearby towns and assured him adequate food and supplies for the rest of the campaign in Thessaly.

After a night in Metropolis, Caesar took his army on a two-day march to the east and to the vicinity of the walled city of Pharsalus, modern Pharsala, one of the oldest and most important cities in southern Thessaly. Between Pharsalus and a low range of hills to the north lay a five-mile-wide plain roughly bisected along its ten-mile length by the westward-flowing Enipeus River. After crossing to the north bank of the river, Caesar built his camp adjacent to a field of wheat, astride the road from Pharsalus to Larisa, "and decided to wait for Pompey there and to make this the centre of his whole campaign" (*The Civil War* 3.81.3).

In the meantime, Pompey had joined Scipio at Larisa and, according to Caesar, addressed the combined army, expressing his gratitude to his troops for their valor at Dyrrachium, and welcoming Scipio's Syrian legions to share in the spoils of the coming victory. He was heartened by the appearance in his camp of Marcus Brutus, who had found little to do in Cilicia and had traveled to Macedonia to join the fight against Caesar. But Pompey did not seem to be moving fast enough for many of his generals:

[T]hey used to say that although the business needed no more than a day, he took pleasure in exercising command and liked to count among his slaves men who had been consuls and praetors. Some were already competing among themselves for rewards and priesthoods, and allocating Consulships for years ahead, and others were asking for the houses and property that belonged to the men in Caesar's camp. (*The Civil War* 3.82.2–3)

Finally, after several days at Larisa, Pompey assembled his eleven legions, and his thousands of archers, slingers, and cavalry, and began the thirty-three-mile march to the south and to the plain of Pharsalus, where Caesar awaited him.

For Pompey it was the opportunity to finally bring his entire army, far superior in numbers, face-to-face with Caesar's on a battlefield with enough space for him to utilize it fully, the venue most favored in classical times for a decisive outcome. Although Caesar had earned his military fame by rapid marches and surprise attacks, he welcomed the chance to engage Pompey in a head-on, set-piece battle, even though his veterans were outnumbered by Pompey's

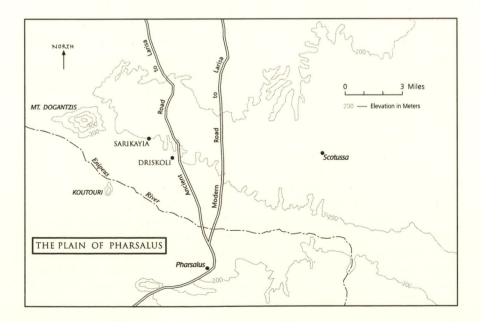

greener troops. By drawing Pompey far inland, he had at least removed the advantage that Pompey's navy gave him near any coast.

Of all the storied battles that punctuate Roman military history, none was more painful and self-destructive than the three they fought among themselves in Macedonia in the last half of the century before Christ. At Pharsalus, and twice at Philippi six years later, the Romans dealt themselves the death blows that sealed the end of the five-hundred-year-old Republic. Had any of the battles gone the other way, Roman history would have been profoundly different.

The actual location of the Battle of Pharsalus has never been precisely identified, and archaeologists and historians have been divided between those who place it on the north bank of the Enipeus River and those who place it on the south. Even within these two factions, the supposed locations of the camps and the battle lines vary by as much as twelve miles. The single surviving eyewitness account is that of Caesar, who gives a detailed description of the battle and of the surrounding topography, but in his typical way never names a place. Other ancient sources, some based on another eyewitness report now lost, are almost evenly divided between north and south banks.

Since at least 1835 dozens of scholars and travelers have personally investigated the site—the upper valley of the Enipeus —excavating, measuring, calculating, photographing, and questioning residents about ruins, roads, rivers, marshes, and the names of ancient places. The most comprehensive modern investigation of the question, that of archaeologist J. D. Morgan in 1983, concludes that the battle took place adjacent to the town of Palaepharsalus, or Old Pharsalus, which had been on the site of the village of Driskoli, today called Krini, on the north bank of the Enipeus, and on the road to Larisa.[1]

When Pompey emerged from the foothills at the northern edge of the plain in the first week in August, and passed through Palaepharsalus, he found Caesar camped on the road directly in his path about three miles ahead, and in control of the only nearby bridge across the Enipeus. It appears that he turned off to the west about two miles and built his main camp on a low hill above the village of Sarikayia, now called Ayra. With Scipio's added troops, he now commanded eleven legions and between six and seven thousand cavalry, as well as several thousand archers and slingers. Even after he placed detachments on two other nearby hills, a camp for an army this size, which would have included as many as twenty thousand slaves and servants, and thousands of horses and pack animals, would have to have been at least a mile square.

In his camp about five miles away, Caesar had about twenty-four thousand infantry in eight understrength legions, plus a thousand cavalry and a few auxiliaries. He writes that despite their smaller numbers, the morale of his men was high, and to test Pompey's willingness to fight, he led them out and formed up battle lines across the plain about halfway between the camps. Pompey's response was to do the same, except that he placed his front line only at the base of his hill, a full two miles from Caesar's army, thus inviting him to fight uphill.

Caesar naturally refused, but on successive days brought his troops closer to Pompey's front.

For several days the two generals postured and maneuvered, Pompey seeking to maintain the advantage, Caesar pressing for a battle, knowing that time was against him. Finally concluding that Pompey would not be tempted off his hill, he decided to move off to the northeast, toward the town of Scotussa in the foothills, where provisioning his army might be easier. He might also lure Pompey into battle along the way. He writes that by marching every day he would exhaust Pompey's army, "which was unused to hard effort" (*The Civil War* 3.85.2). Early the next morning the trumpets sounded the first signal for departure, and Caesar's troops struck their tents. At the same time Pompey's troops emerged from their camp and took their usual positions at the bottom of the slope.

But as Caesar's army began to form the column that would march out the gates, his lookouts reported that Pompey's legions had moved off the hill and onto the plain between the two camps. Caesar ordered the preparations halted and gathered his commanders around him. For the only time anywhere in his published writings he reports his own direct speech: "We must delay the march for the moment and put our minds to a battle, as we have always wanted. We are mentally prepared to fight; we shall not easily get the chance again" (*The Civil War* 3.85.4). He then had a purple flag displayed, the signal for battle, and led his army out of camp in battle formation.

According to Caesar, in the preceding days Pompey's generals had finally convinced him that the time had come to descend far enough into the plain to provoke a battle. Once he had made up his mind, he became confident of success, and predicted that his cavalry would flank Caesar's infantry and rout his army even before the battle lines met. Relying on information he obtained after the battle, Caesar also reports that Labienus assured the Pompeian officers that the enemy army was but a shadow of the one that had conquered Gaul, and that he thought Pompey's plan could not fail. He swore an oath, as did all the others, that he would not return to camp without a victory.

After leaving seven cohorts behind to guard his camp, Pompey deployed his enormous army in a line across the plain facing east, with its right edge at the Enipeus, a river with "difficult banks" (*The Civil War* 3.88.6) and at the time still running with spring rains. On the river bank he placed Lucius Afranius and the troops he had salvaged from his defeated army in Spain. His father-in-law Metellus Scipio and his two Syrian legions held the center. On the left, where Pompey himself took his post, Lucius Domitius, in his fourth engagement of the war, commanded two veteran legions from Caesar's Gallic army that the Senate had ordered transferred to Pompey two years earlier to repel a supposed invasion by Parthia. On either side of his legions in the center, Pompey placed his remaining six legions of veterans and new conscripts from Crete, Macedonia, Asia, and other Eastern states. Each legion was arrayed in three massive lines, each two to three hundred yards across and ten ranks (about twenty yards) deep. Between each line the officers kept an open space of eighty to a hundred yards.

Of his nearly seven thousand cavalry, Pompey assigned about a tenth to support Afranius on the right, and placed the remainder on his left wing under Labienus, where there was additional level ground in front of the foothills. Also on his left wing, behind his infantry and cavalry, he stationed his three to four thousand Greek and Syrian archers and Thracian slingers, where they could loft their missiles over their front lines and into Caesar's ranks.

Estimates of the size of Pompey's army vary widely among both ancient and modern historians, those of his legionaries alone, his core force of heavy infantry, ranging from thirty-six to forty-seven thousand, the latter being Caesar's figure. On close to seven thousand cavalry most authorities agree, but the few estimates of auxiliaries, including slingers, archers (mounted and on foot), javelineers, and other light-armed foreign troops, fall in a vague range of five to fifteen thousand. Interspersed among his eleven Roman legions and bringing up the rear, his foreign auxiliaries included soldiers and horsemen from a score of states and tribes, garbed in every kind of uniform, and wielding every sort of weapon. Beneath a hundred bobbing flags and standards rode kings and petty rulers, dictators, and mercenary generals, Bithynians, Armenians, Paphlagonians, Phrygians, Ionians, Pamphylians, Rhodians, Lydians, Pisidians, Arabs and Jews, and Spartans and Athenians. Pompey's front line has been calculated as at least two and a half miles long and about two hundred and fifty yards deep.

The army that Caesar led out of camp was less than half the size of Pompey's. His nine legions averaged no more than twenty-seven hundred men, and after leaving seven cohorts to guard his camp, he was able to muster only twenty-two thousand infantry, less than a thousand cavalry, a handful of archers and slingers, and, at most, a few thousand light-armed Greeks he had recruited in Epirus. He deployed them in the standard three lines, each no more than five ranks deep, placing the VIIIth and IXth Legions on his left wing along the river under the command of Mark Antony, and several others in the center under Domitius Calvinus. The remainder, including his premier legion, the Xth, he put on his vulnerable right wing under Publius Sulla, and took a position himself on the same wing, directly opposite Pompey.

When he saw where Pompey had placed his thousands of cavalry, he put his own Gallic and German horse opposite them, and then, at the last minute, took an extra precaution to foil Pompey's obvious plan to flank him at the northern edge of the battlefield. Quickly removing selected cohorts from the third line of each legion, he created a short fourth line of three thousand infantry and placed it at an oblique angle behind his right wing so that it was hidden by his cavalry. Caesar was familiar with the writings of the Greek general Xenophon, in which this particular tactic had been described. Pompey himself had used it more than fifteen years earlier in his campaign against Mithradates. To this fourth line Caesar explained how he wanted them to use the *pilum*, the seven-foot spear tipped with iron barbs that all Roman legionaries carried.

154

They were not to throw it on approaching the enemy, as was the custom, but to use it against the cavalry as a spear, stabbing upward at the faces of the riders, who carried only a small shield. Caesar's last instruction, as he rode among the troops in his third and fourth lines, was to caution their tribunes and centurions not to bring them into battle until they received a specific signal from him.

Besides the *pilum*, the infantryman in both armies was armed with a *gladius*, a two-foot, two-edged sword with a long point that hung at his right side on a belt that passed over his left shoulder. In his left hand he carried a *scutum*, a sturdy, oblong, curved wooden shield about four feet by two feet that was covered with heavy leather, and weighed a full twenty pounds. On it was written his name and the number of his legion, as well as the number of his cohort, and often his century, identified by the name of his centurion, in effect, his military address, at which he received mail.[2]

To protect himself, the typical infantryman wore a heavy leather jerkin, sometimes reinforced with a small metal breastplate, a *pectorale*. If he could afford one, he wore a *lorica hamata*, a waist-length coat of mail (interlocking rings of iron wire). His legs were bare, but his calves were often protected with greaves, shin guards of metal or leather. On his feet he wore *caligae*—heavy leather sandals with thick soles studded with hob nails, and tied with thongs to his shins. Over a padded cap of cloth or felt he wore a close-fitting bronze helmet with metal cheekguards and secured with leather straps that passed under his chin. In a metal knob at the top of the helmet were a hole and crest pin that often held a plume of horsehair or, for officers, red or black feathers.

Having arranged their armies to their satisfaction, the two commanders addressed them with the obligatory exhortations that Roman generals delivered before major battles. Caesar's speech, which he summarizes in two sentences, would have been delivered from horseback, perhaps four or five times, as he rode in front of his battle lines wearing the *paludamentum*, the red cloak of the commander-in-chief. At the same time that he urged his men to fight with courage, he stressed his reluctance to shed their blood, and reminded them of his strenuous efforts to seek peace. His troops responded with the usual clamoring to fight, and here Caesar introduces the customary anecdote about the valor of his troops, this one about the *primus pilus*, or leading centurion, of the Xth Legion, Gaius Crastinus, a retiree who had returned to the army for the Macedonian campaign. Caesar writes that Crastinus shouted encouragement to his men, and then exclaimed to Caesar that he would earn his general's gratitude today, whether he survived or not. He then took his place where every Roman centurion fought, at the right end of the front rank of his century, the elemental Roman army unit, ordinarily eighty men, but that day in Caesar's line no more than fifty.

The positioning of the two vast armies and the *adlocutiones*, perorations to the troops, would have taken until midmorning—necessary preludes to the set-piece battle that ancient armies and their opponents customarily arranged between themselves, unless they were barbarians. Although there were exceptions, Roman armies observed a standard set of military courtesies, especially in battles with each other: fighting took place during the day; no battles took place in winter or during inclement weather; and each army waited until the other was ready.

Because summer comes early in Thessaly, the ninth day of Sextilis, later renamed August (June 7 by the modern calendar), would be a hot day, and in a few hours the Battle of Pharsalus, fought in the Roman year 706 (48 BCE) *ab urbe condita*, since the founding of the city, would take its place in history as the largest battle ever fought between Romans. Men in both armies faced their fellow citizens and townsmen, even their uncles, brothers, sons, and fathers. Some followed a cause, some a leader, and for some the army was simply their occupation, but most had suffered great hardship to be at this place, a full six hundred and fifty miles from Rome. It is likely that few on the battlefield did not think the Civil War would end by sunset.

When Caesar's troops were ready, his gesture to the leading trumpeter brought the blast to begin the charge, a signal repeated by the trumpeters in every legion across the army's two-mile front. In Caesar's first two battle lines, fifteen thousand legionaries started forward in silence at a fast trot toward Pompey's army, now waiting some two hundred yards in front of them. The Roman practice was to advance at a steady pace without a sound until they were nearly upon the enemy, a more intimidating tactic than the noisy, headlong rush of the Celts and Germans. "But when the signal was given and our soldiers ran forward with their spears ready to throw, they saw that the Pompeians were not running to meet them; being experienced and practised from previous battles, they spontaneously checked their charge and halted approximately half-way, to avoid being in a state of exhaustion when they came to close quarters" (*The Civil War* 3.93.1).

Pompey had instructed his troops to hold their formation and stand and take the charge, thinking that the *pila* would fall on his troops with less effect, and hoping that they could then move forward without breaking formation and overwhelm the scattered enemy. Caesar's troops, as they neared the Pompeian line, broke into shouts and yells and, after halting briefly, again ran forward, those in the first line hurling their *pila* from as far as eighty feet into the Pompeian army.

Crouching behind their shields, Pompey's infantry threw their own *pila*, and the two mighty walls of men collided with a crash of shield on shield, then sword on sword and helmet, every legionary straining and shoving forward with his shield and stabbing with his sword at any human part exposed in front of him. The thud and clang of iron striking wood and bronze rang above the plain, and the piercing blast of trumpets, the shouts and desperate screams of the living and the dying, drifted upward through the warming morning air. Within seconds the next line of infantry on both sides ran up and threw their *pila*, plunging into the mass of thousands of shouting, struggling men. Neither side gave way as they rushed up behind and between their *commilitones*, their fellow soldiers, into the killing zone, pushing, slashing, and thrusting against the enemy.

At the same moment the infantry engaged, Pompey's thousands of motley cavalry rushed against Caesar's on the northern end of the battle line, wielding spear and sword, while thousands of archers and slingers moved up behind them, launching their stones and arrows over the front. Caesar's cavalry, even though supported by an equal number of light infantrymen moving among them, was badly outnumbered and, as he had expected, began retreating along a rather narrow front. As the sheer mass of Pompey's horse pushed forward, small units began to break through and flank Caesar's right wing. Caesar now ordered a *vexillum* displayed, a rectangular colored banner mounted on a pole, the signal for his fourth line of infantry, which had been concealed behind his cavalry, to make its charge. Trumpets blared again, and each cohort's *signifer* raised its standard as the three thousand legionaries, most likely in ten ranks no more than five hundred yards across, swung around like a giant gate and rushed against Pompey's advancing cavalry. Running among the rearing and wheeling horses, Caesar's troops held up their shields to block the horsemen's swords, and thrust upward with their spears at the riders and their horses. Those who fell they converged upon and finished off with swords.

Fighting under many commanders, and unmotivated by any special loyalty or cause, Pompey's foreign horsemen failed to stand their ground before this attack. They would have been unprepared for a head-on clash with heavy infantry, and their horses would have balked at charging into a line of shielded foot soldiers wielding swords and spears. In Caesar's terse words, "They all turned round and not merely retreated, but immediately proceeded to gallop on in flight towards some very high hills" (*The Civil War* 3.93.6).

The next victims were Pompey's Greek and Asian archers and Thracian slingers, nearly all of them advancing on foot behind his cavalry. Left exposed and weaponless, as well as outnumbered by Caesar's combined fourth line and cavalry, they were easy prey, and by all accounts were slaughtered to a man.

Now Caesar's juggernaut of four to five thousand cavalry and infantry wheeled to the south, flanked Pompey's left wing of infantry, and attacked it from behind. At the same time, Caesar signaled his third line of infantry, which had been waiting in the rear, to move up and relieve his first and second lines. Although it is unclear how old the battle was by now, those who had been fighting hand-to-hand would have been exhausted in no more than twenty minutes. They would have fallen back, dragging out their wounded, as the third line ran forward to take their places.

Caesar says here simply that on Pompey's left wing, "now that fresh, unwounded men had taken the place of those who were exhausted, and furthermore others were attacking them from the rear, Pompey's men were unable to hold out and all turned and fled" (*The Civil War* 3.94.2). But he has speeded up the action considerably, as the fighting went on at least two more hours. Details of the battle are scarce, but some accounts record that the Pompeians made a slow and organized retreat. Even so, after the flight of Pompey's cavalry, the outcome of the battle was not in doubt. His eleven legions and thousands of auxiliary troops were completely routed, a startling result for an army so much larger than its opponent.

Pompey himself, once he saw his cavalry repulsed, fled the battlefield and galloped to his camp, giving orders for its defense before retiring to his tent. By midday those of his troops who had not been killed or captured, or had not fled into the countryside, had also retreated behind the ditch and bank that surrounded the camp. Only four of his legionary commanders, including Lucius Domitius, returned to camp, the others disappearing into the nearby hills.

Out on the plain, where the thousands of dead and wounded lay in a thick, two-mile-long ribbon between the river and the hills, Caesar's troops stood in their cohorts, exhausted from the heat and effort of the morning. What they wanted was water, rest, and a chance to scavenge weapons and equipment from the enemy dead. But unlike Pompey at Dyrrachium, Caesar wanted more than just a battle; he wanted Pompey and his whole army. Every man who could be spared from tending prisoners or the wounded he dispatched to the hill above the village of Sarikayia to lay siege to Pompey's camp.

Burdensome as it was, this turned out to be the work of only a few hours. Although the defending cohorts put up a vigorous fight, the weary and frightened infantry who poured into the camp were bent on flight, and were little help. Caesar's troops pelted the camp with a barrage of stones, arrows, and spears until the defenders abandoned their posts and rushed out the rear and into the hills to the north. As his camp's front gate was breached and his men streamed past him, Pompey discarded his *paludamentum* and all other evidence of his rank, seized a horse, and, accompanied by several Senators, galloped past his fleeing troops toward Larisa, twenty-five miles away.

Caesar's capture of Pompey's camp was a moment of triumph that he pauses to describe in detail:

In Pompey's camp could be viewed artificial bowers, great quantities of silver laid out, tents floored with freshly cut turf, the tents of Lucius Lentulus and some others wreathed with ivy, and much else to indicate gross luxury and confidence of victory. It was easy to deduce from their pursuit of inessential pleasures that the other side had no misgivings about the outcome of the day. (*The Civil War* 3.96.1)

It was perhaps at this moment that Caesar, surveying the huge camp strewn with bodies, turned to his officer Asinius Pollio and uttered the famous remark beginning *hoc voluerunt*, "Thus they would have it. I, Gaius Caesar, would have been condemned despite all my achievements, had I not appealed to my army for help."[3] Having made the powerful enemies he had, no doubt he was correct. One of the most persistent of those enemies, Lucius Domitius, was at that moment fleeing across the hills, but in Caesar's terse words, "when he succumbed to exhaustion he was killed by the cavalry" (*The Civil War* 3.99.5). Cicero later claimed that it was Mark Antony himself who dispatched him.

Allowing his troops no pause, and ordering them not to be distracted by looting, Caesar led them in pursuit of the main body of the Pompeian army, which had taken a position on a nearby hill. When he immediately ordered work to be started on a ditch and bank to surround the hilltop, the fleeing army, realizing that it would be trapped without a source of water, began to withdraw along an adjoining ridge. Caesar pursued it with four legions, after sending several to occupy Pompey's camp and the rest back to his own. Following the Pompeian army along an easier route on a nearby ridge for about six miles, he brought his troops in front of it and deployed them in battle formation. The bedraggled army, now led only by its tribunes and centurions, retreated to a nearby hill, at whose foot ran a stream.

Caesar exhorted his troops one more time, even though night was falling and they were exhausted from an entire day of fighting and marching. They dutifully constructed a fortified ditch and bank that cut off the hill from the stream, leaving the Pompeian army, still some twenty thousand men, without a source of water. The same evening negotiations began, and at dawn Caesar sent orders that those on the hill should come down and throw down their weapons.

This they did without protest, and cast themselves on the ground with hands outstretched, weeping and begging him to spare them. He offered them consolation and told them to stand up, and said a few words about his leniency to them, to lessen their fear, and granted all of them their lives; he entrusted them to his soldiers, saying that none of them should suffer violence or be the recipient of demands from his men. (*The Civil War* 3.98.2)

The Battle of Pharsalus was over, and with it the entire campaign in Macedonia. It has been rightly called the most brilliant and decisive victory in Caesar's career, especially as it took place in his enemy's backyard, only a month after a crushing defeat, and against an army more than twice the size of his own. More than that, it was won against Pompeius Magnus, Rome's most successful general and winner of an unprecedented three triumphs—a general who had never been defeated.

No doubt the key factor in Caesar's victory was his immediate understanding of Pompey's plan for a cavalry encirclement, and his deployment of a concealed fourth line of troops, a rare tactic in Roman warfare. Once his cavalry attack was frustrated, Pompey seemed to have no other plan, offensive or defensive, a result, perhaps, of overconfidence. The failure of both Pompey and his commanders to redeploy their troops to counter Caesar's moves meant that they were taken completely by surprise.

Because of poor communication, lack of discipline, or weakness of command, armies in classical times did not react quickly to surprises or sudden changes in the traditional routine of battle, and so were prone to panic and disintegration. Nevertheless, even with his cavalry lost and his left wing flanked, Pompey still had many more infantry available than Caesar, and might yet have saved the day, had he not inexplicably left the field. In a long career of unbroken successes, he may have been unprepared for adversity.

The mighty army he had assembled was virtually destroyed. A full twenty-four thousand of his troops surrendered, most of them Roman legionaries. Caesar claimed that fifteen thousand of Pompey's Roman infantry were killed, but a more accurate source says six thousand, the great majority of the many thousands of other Pompeian dead being slaves or foreigners, who were held in such low regard that they were not counted. Thousands more, including Afranius, Brutus, Scipio, and Labienus, escaped into the hills. Nine Pompeian *aquilae*, the legions' eagles, and one hundred and eighty other unit standards were brought to Caesar.

Caesar writes that he lost thirty strong and brave centurions and two hundred infantry, but another report of twelve hundred dead from the rank and file is more likely to be correct. The wounded in each army would have numbered at least twice the dead. Among the dead centurions, a group with the highest casualty rate because they always led their units into battle, was the exemplary Gaius Crastinus, whom Caesar reports as having sustained "a sword-thrust full in the mouth" (*The Civil War* 3.99.2). Although there must have been many heroes at Pharsalus, Caesar mentions only Crastinus, citing his courage and his own substantial debt to him. According to Appian, Caesar had a tomb built for him, and left it on the plain. If so, he was the only soldier so honored, the remaining dead having been burned, along with the dead animals, in giant pyres on the battlefield.

Pausing hardly an hour or two after the surrender, Caesar ordered a single legion, the VIth, to follow him and hurried in pursuit of Pompey, reaching Larisa with a troop of cavalry the same day. Pompey and his retinue had passed through the city the day before, warning the inhabitants against reprisals by Caesar, and then continuing along the Peneios River to the coast through the fabled Vale of Tempe, the narrow defile between Mounts Olympus and Ossa. One important fugitive absent from his party was Marcus Brutus, who apparently had lost his way in a marsh before reaching Larisa and there surrendered to Caesar, who readily forgave him for his opposition. Although Caesar spared all Roman captives at Pharsalus, Plutarch notes that he gave special orders that no harm come to Servilia's son.

On every route in every direction, the news from Pharsalus spread from Thessaly at the speed of the fastest horseman, reaching Cato and Cicero at Dyrrachium in two or three days, and Rome a few days later. Caesar's generals organized most of Pompey's captured infantry into three new legions, and Mark Antony began the march back toward Italy with the bulk of the army. Preceding him by only a few days, Labienus rode at the head of several hundred Gallic and German cavalry that he had managed to extricate from the battlefield, and brought them to the Pompeian camp at Dyrrachium, which Cato had been holding with fifteen cohorts. Determined to continue fighting as long as Pompey was alive, Cato put all the infantry and cavalry on board ship and sailed down to Corcyra, where they were met by Scipio, Afranius, Pompey's son Gnaeus, and the troops who had escaped with them.

In Sicily word of Caesar's victory caused a Pompeian blockade of Brundisium to be abandoned, and deterred Gaius Cassius from pursuing an attack on Messana, now Messina, after he had destroyed a Caesarian fleet. Further abroad, the news of Pompey's defeat prompted a host of foreign kings, independent cities, and those who had been neutral to take Caesar's side. Pompey himself could not be sure of his reception anywhere, and when he and his companions reached the Aegean Sea, they spent their first night as fugitives hiding in a fisherman's hut. The next day they traveled by merchant vessel to the port of Amphipolis in eastern Macedonia, where Pompey issued an edict, perhaps only to deter Caesar's pursuit, that all men of military age report for service. But he remained in the area only a single day, on board a ship anchored in the bay, before sailing for Lesbos and Mytilene, where his wife Cornelia waited.

According to Plutarch, the messenger who brought the news from Pompey's ship to Cornelia could not bear to speak of the calamity when he approached her, and instead burst into tears. Cornelia rushed to the dock, where she and Pompey embraced, she confusedly blaming herself, he reassuring her that just as he had fallen low, so might he rise again. But even though Mytilene welcomed him, Pompey knew there was no future for him there. Cornelia and their son Sextus, who had remained with her, joined his small retinue, and they sailed to the south, along the coast of modern Turkey. After several more days they reached Attaleia in Pamphylia, modern Antalya, where warships and troops arrived from Cilicia in support of Pompey, and he was joined by some sixty Senators who had fled in the same direction.

While Pompey was fleeing by sea, Caesar and a troop of cavalry were traveling by land along the coast of eastern Macedonia and to the Hellespont, the narrow waterway now called Dardanelles that separates modern Turkey from the Gallipoli Peninsula. There he commandeered some ferries to carry them across, but in the middle of the channel suddenly found himself among ten Pompeian warships on their way to the Black Sea. Although he was clearly at their mercy, Caesar boldly directed his boat to the commander's flagship and demanded his surrender. The news of his victory at Pharsalus had so stunned the Pompeian forces everywhere that this unknown commander, who might easily have captured him and restored everything Pompey had lost, quickly capitulated and gave up his warships for Caesar's use. Caesar does not mention this hairbreadth escape, but it is attested by three other writers. Nor does he mention, as others do, his short visit to the nearby ruined citadel of Ilium, the site of ancient Troy, which overlooked the Hellespont at its mouth. Throughout his life Caesar asserted that Troy was a sacred place for the Julii because they were descended from Iulus, a son of the Trojan wanderer Aeneas.

Just a few days ahead of Caesar, and still undecided about where to take refuge, Pompey sailed east along the coast to Cilicia, where he raised money and enlisted more recruits, and then crossed to the island of Cyprus. After much hesitation he decided to sail for Egypt, where he hoped that his previous support and ties of friendship with King Ptolemy XII, now dead three years, would gain him the hospitality of his son, the present ruler. Another reason for Pompey's optimism was that Ptolemy XIII, a boy of thirteen strongly influenced by his chief minister, a eunuch named Pothinus, had supplied him with fifty ships and five hundred men just a year earlier for the war against Caesar.

In the meantime, at Corcyra, the Pompeian base on the coast of Epirus, Cato called on Cicero, in accordance with custom and his senior rank as ex-Consul, to take command of the remaining Pompeian troops and the still-considerable Pompeian navy. When Cicero refused to have anything more to do with the war, Pompey's son Gnaeus angrily threatened him with his sword, and only the intervention of Cato kept him from injury, or worse. Cato then took part of the army and continued southward along the coast of Epirus and occupied the city of Patrae, modern Patras, on the northern edge of the Peloponnese peninsula. There they were joined by Marcus Petreius, Faustus Sulla, and other fugitives from Pharsalus. After a futile attempt to take control of the area, they abandoned the idea, and Cato led his ships into the eastern Mediterranean with the hope of joining Pompey.

It was late in September when Pompey's small fleet appeared off the coast of Egypt. After messages passed between ship and shore, he received an invitation to land. The King and his army were camped near the busy port city of Pelusium at the eastern edge of the Nile Delta, a city that today lies under the elongated mound of Tell el-Farama. In the small boat sent out to meet Pompey were Achillas, commander-in-chief of the King's army, several servants, and two Roman soldiers in the King's service, one of whom addressed Pompey as *imperator*. A nervous Pompey embraced his tearful wife and went aboard the King's vessel, accompanied by two servants and two of his centurions.

Recognizing the man who had saluted him as a centurion who had served under him in his war against the pirates, Pompey said, "Don't I know you, fellow-soldier."[4] The centurion, Lucius Septimius, merely nodded, turning away, and as the boat approached the shore, moved behind Pompey and plunged a sword through his body. Two others in the boat did the same with their daggers, and the fifty-eight-year-old Pompey fell down dead on the deck. The boat continued to the shore while his horrified family and supporters watched helplessly from their ships. In the end they could do nothing but withdraw, and find another place of refuge.

For the second time in sixty days a shocking message was borne to cities, towns, and royal courts around the Mediterranean. A lifetime of honors and acclaim, and of leading great armies into war, had been ended by assassination—on the whim of a foreign King. Some could not believe it, but others, including the disheartened Cicero, the most knowledgeable man on either side, thought that after Pharsalus the death of Pompey would not have long to wait. Two months later he wrote: "As to Pompey's end I never had any doubt, for all rulers and peoples had become so thoroughly persuaded of the hopelessness of his cause that wherever he went I expected this to happen. I cannot but grieve for his fate. I knew him for a man of good character, clean life, and serious principle."[5]

Caesar is not so generous, and in fact has nothing to say in *The Civil War* about Pompey's murder except to coolly report how it was done, and to add that he only learned of it later in Alexandria. Had there been no Caesar, Pompey would have been the late Republic's greatest general. But without Caesar, Pompey's Eastern settlement and the land grants for his troops might never have gained Senate approval, and he might have lost most of his authority and influence in the capital. He was rarely an effective politician (when first elected Consul, he asked the scholarly Terentius Varro to prepare a handbook of procedures for him), and on the battlefield he was always one step behind one of the geniuses of ancient warfare. Consumed by pride all his life, by middle age he had tempered his tendency to cruelty. He is historically identified as an opponent of Caesar—in a series of worthies, perhaps the greatest. With three Consulships, three triumphs, five wives, three children, and a stinging defeat of Caesar to his credit, he was a Roman hero for thirty-five years.

Pompey's death and Caesar's arrival in Egypt bring Book III of *The Civil War* nearly to its end. Modern historians must rely on other sources for an account of what happened in Alexandria, the most bizarre episode of the Civil War, or of any war in Roman history.

PART THREE
Caesar and Cleopatra

XI

The Alexandrian War

Two hundred and seventy-five years before the Battle of Pharsalus, a young Macedonian King who had spent half his life at war, and had conquered half the world then known, lay in a fever, possibly malaria, at Babylon on the Euphrates, in the palace built by Nebuchadrezzar three centuries earlier. Over a period of ten days during May of 323 the fever intensified, finally bringing on a coma and then death to the thirty-two-year-old Alexander the Great. The ancient world had seen no one like him, and nothing like the enormous empire he had created. In the usual way, a series of wars ensued among his survivors for control of it. His ablest general and lifelong friend, Ptolemy, who later wrote a history of Alexander's campaigns, claimed the ancient kingdom of Egypt for himself, and successfully defended it against another of Alexander's generals two years later.

Ten years earlier, Alexander had defeated the Persian King Darius near the small town of Issus, on the southwestern coast of modern Turkey. From there he had swept down the coast of Phoenicia, through Gaza, and into Egypt, which he captured without bloodshed, the Persian satrap simply ceding it to him two years later. On a tour of his new acquisition, Alexander had ordered a new city built on the site of a fishing village that lay along a narrow strip of land between the sea and Lake Mareotis, now Mariout, near the western tip of the Nile Delta. He is said to have laid out the main streets himself in simple right angles in the Greek style, and then employed the architect Dinocrates of Rhodes to complete the plans for the city and two spacious harbors sheltered by an offshore island. It was Alexander's first new city, the first of many to bear his name, and the first city known to be named after its founder rather than a god or mythological hero. It was also his greatest city—surpassing all others he founded, perhaps a hundred in a dozen countries—but he did not live to see it.

When Ptolemy, later known as Ptolemy I, took Egypt as his own kingdom after Alexander's death, he declared himself a god and took the surname of Soter, Savior. He moved the capital from Memphis to Alexandria, and devoted himself to the construction of the city and its port. He created the two harbors by building a permanent breakwater, topped by a roadway, from the mainland to the middle of the island of Pharos, a limestone ridge that lay parallel to the city's waterfront less than a mile offshore. At each end of this Heptastadion, so

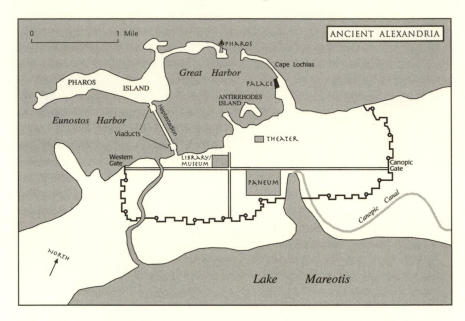

called because it was seven *stadia* in length, about three-quarters of a mile, a viaduct carried the roadway over a channel through which vessels could pass between the Great Harbor on the east and the Eunostos, or "Safe Return," on the west.

To accommodate the scholars and writers inspired by the nine Muses of Greek mythology, Ptolemy Soter founded the Mouseion, a type of ancient think tank that evolved into "the greatest single center for Greek culture that had ever existed and would ever exist again."[1] Adjacent to the Mouseion he established what was called the Great Library at Alexandria, a royal institution that eventually gathered and preserved several hundred thousand papyrus rolls of the most important writings in the ancient world. Finally, at the center of the city he built a marble mausoleum that came to be called the Soma (body) to house the sarcophagus of carved gold in which Alexander's embalmed body, wrapped in sheets of gold, was placed after Ptolemy hijacked it on its journey to Macedonia. Unfortunately, no trace remains of any of these ancient wonders.

Because of its sheltered harbors and its location on the east-west trade route at the mouth of the Nile, Alexandria flourished over the next two centuries, its heterogeneous population of Greeks, Egyptians, and Jews growing to more than half a million. By Caesar's time it had become a cosmopolitan city of unsurpassed wealth, with a reputation for scholarship as well as elegance and luxury. During this period the city had been home to Euclid, Callimachus, Apollonius of Rhodes, and the polymath Eratosthenes, who was also at one time Chief Librarian. It had also become the largest Jewish community in the ancient world and the chief center of Jewish culture. It was in the walled city of

Alexandria that a translation of the Old Testament from Hebrew and Aramaic into Greek, the Septuagint, was completed, according to tradition, by seventy translators brought from Jerusalem for the purpose.

It was partly due to Roman intervention that the dynasty that Ptolemy had founded in 323 still occupied the royal palace when Caesar arrived in the first days of October of 48. The Ptolemies had maintained their rule for nine generations by a combination of deception, treachery, and murder, but had kept it in the family by handing down their personal kingdom from father to son, or to an occasional brother. Just as the old Egyptian Pharaohs had married their sisters to forestall ambitious in-laws, so did the Ptolemy sons, and in several cases the sisters had reigned as queens with their brothers.

The twelfth Ptolemy, known as Auletes, the Flute Player, because of one of his hobbies, had been installed on the throne in 80 by the Alexandrians after they had murdered his predecessor. But twenty years of corruption, idleness, and luxurious living had gradually made him the target of dissension and revolt. His subjects also blamed him for the deterioration of Egypt's prestige and loss of its possessions, and he never quite overcame the stigma of his illegitimate birth to one of his father's concubines. During Caesar's Consulship in 59, Auletes had sought the assistance of Rome to strengthen his position, and had paid Caesar and Pompey an enormous fee, borrowed from Roman financiers, to induce the Senate to declare him the rightful King of Egypt, and a friend and ally of the Roman people.

By the early 50s Auletes had aroused so much hostility in Alexandria that he exiled himself to Ephesus and sought Roman arms to reestablish his authority in Egypt. He found a champion in Aulus Gabinius, the Roman Governor in Syria at the time, and a creature of Pompey. Gabinius brought an army into Egypt in 55 and, for another large fee, also borrowed, forcibly restored Auletes to his throne, leaving a garrison of Roman troops in Alexandria to support him. It was on this foray into Egypt that Gabinius' twenty-seven-year-old cavalry commander, Mark Antony, was first attracted to the King's daughter Cleopatra, then fourteen.

When Ptolemy Auletes died in 51, his will revealed his wish that his oldest son and oldest daughter marry (he had murdered an older daughter) and jointly rule the kingdom. It was thus that the ten-year-old Ptolemy XIII and the eighteen-year-old Cleopatra VII succeeded to the throne of Egypt as man and wife. Two years later, during the year before Caesar reached Alexandria, Cleopatra had made an attempt to dislodge her half-brother from their joint throne. Little is known of this episode except that it failed, and she fled to Syria, where she and her allies raised an army. About the time that Caesar defeated Pompey at Pharsalus, she brought her troops along the coast and set up camp on Egypt's eastern edge. Her brother and his ministers hurried to the border with their own army, and were preparing to oppose her near Pelusium when Pompey arrived off the coast.

The decision of the King and his counselors to murder Pompey was born of the wish to curry favor with Caesar, and to avoid any possible retaliation by Pompey should they simply refuse him refuge. After removing Pompey's ring and beheading him, they left his body on the beach, where his former slave Philip cremated it and preserved the ashes for Cornelia. The day after Pompey's murder, Lentulus Crus, another of his generals who had escaped Pharsalus, and one of the Consuls of the previous year, arrived at Egypt's coast from Cyprus, unaware of what had happened, and was also lured to shore and put to death.

Caesar was on the Greek island of Rhodes when he learned, late in September, that Pompey had reached Cyprus. By now the VIth Legion and another he had summoned from the Greek mainland, both badly depleted, had caught up with him. He put them both, along with eight hundred cavalry, on board transports, and sailed immediately for Alexandria, thinking that Pompey would seek refuge in Egypt because of his previous connections there. He writes that he was not concerned about his safety, even though Egypt and Alexandria had supported Pompey, but he took with him ten fully manned Rhodian warships.

By the time he appeared off the Pharos island three or four days later, the Alexandrians had already absorbed the news from Pharsalus, but were surely not prepared for the victor to appear in their harbor. They must have been astonished to learn, perhaps in the same graphic way that Caesar did, that their King had just murdered the man he had so recently supported. Caesar's flagship was met by an Egyptian vessel carrying an emissary from the King, who presented him with the head of Pompey. In *The Civil War* Caesar is silent about this incident, but other historians have reported it, including Plutarch, who wrote that Caesar "turned away from him with loathing, as from an assassin; and when he received Pompey's signet ring on which was engraved a lion holding a sword in its paws, he burst into tears."[2] He ordered the head to be treated with veneration, and subsequently had it cremated and the ashes placed in a shrine dedicated to the purpose just outside the city. According to Appian, a native of Alexandria, the shrine stood until his day, two hundred years later.

If the King thought that his gift might dissuade another Roman from visiting Egypt, his hopes were frustrated when Caesar disembarked at the royal dock, preceded by the twelve lictors of a Roman Consul. The Alexandrian crowd, already hostile to Roman interference in Egyptian affairs, reacted with shouts of anger at the apparent slight to the Egyptian King. But the King's ministers ordered that Caesar be welcomed. He was given quarters in the luxurious royal palace on Cape Lochias overlooking the Great Harbor, and room was made for his troops in buildings near the palace grounds.

With Pompey dead, and Caesar's partisans and soldiers in control throughout the Roman world, except in Africa, there was no strategic reason for Caesar to remain in Egypt. He was, as usual, in need of funds to support his army, and he may have seen a chance to collect some of the money that the Egyptian kingdom still owed him and other Romans. He mentions nothing of this in his narrative, writing instead that he "had no alternative to staying" (*The Civil War* 3.107.1) because of the etesian winds blowing directly against the coast. Although it is well known that these northerly winds made sailing from Egypt difficult during the summer (it was late July by the modern calendar), Caesar knew that if he could hasten the end of Egypt's civil war, payments of some kind would be even more likely. He frames it in terms of the national interest: "Meanwhile, thinking that the dispute between the rulers was a matter of concern to the Roman people and to himself, because he was consul . . . he made it known that it was his decision that King Ptolemy and his sister Cleopatra should disband their armies and conduct their argument by judicial process before himself rather than by armed struggle between themselves" (*The Civil War* 3.107.).

He summoned King Ptolemy, now thirteen, to appear before him in Alexandria, and perhaps also his sister Cleopatra, although he does not say so. When it became known among the Alexandrians that Caesar was not only presuming to arbitrate between their rulers, but also making financial demands on the country, they indulged in a series of riots, during which several of his troops were killed. This hostility, and the fact that the King's army, though still camped at Pelusium, could easily be brought to Alexandria in a few days, persuaded Caesar that he might need more than the four thousand or so troops he had brought with him. He dispatched a fast ship to Domitius Calvinus in Asia to bring two more legions across to Alexandria.

In the meantime, the teenaged King and his advisor Pothinus both hurried to Alexandria when Caesar arrived, and began negotiations with him about the late King's will, the debt to Rome, and the question of who was to rule Egypt. As Caesar's hosts, the King and Pothinus made no secret of their unhappiness with his interference, reportedly supplying his soldiers with substandard food and using inferior crockery at the royal table to suggest that the country was being impoverished by his demands. Caesar writes that "while these matters were being disputed . . . news suddenly came that the king's army and all its cavalry were on their way to Alexandria" (*The Civil War* 3.109.1).

Entirely absent from his narrative is any hint of the notorious episode that thrust the name of Cleopatra into Roman history and into the consciousness of generations to come. Caesar mentions her name only twice, both times referring to her simply as Ptolemy's sister, but he would soon learn that she was more than someone's sister. Blocked at the border by the army of her brother-husband, who was now negotiating her fate with the most powerful man in the world, Cleopatra took a desperate gamble and arranged to be smuggled into Alexandria's Great Harbor at nightfall on a small boat. From the royal dock she was carried by her accomplice into the palace in a roll of bedding, and deposited at the feet of the astonished Caesar.

Presumably no seductive efforts were needed by either party, and their prompt sexual union should have surprised nobody. In his affairs with the

A bronze coin portrait of a teen-aged Queen Cleopatra struck in Alexandria a year or two before she and Caesar met. (Giraudon/Art Resource, NY.)

wives of his political associates, Caesar had already revealed a taste for dangerous liaisons, and Cleopatra would not be his last foreign queen. For her part, despite her later lurid reputation, Cleopatra was not promiscuous, just ambitious, and her situation was certainly precarious. Moreover, Caesar was a wealthy, virile, and powerful man. She may even have found him physically attractive.

Her own attractiveness is attested by the ancient writers, though no description survives by anyone who actually saw her, and coin portraits reveal a rather large mouth and the long hooked nose of her father. Despite her journey, her appearance was no doubt enhanced by the elaborate cosmetics, including lampblack, ochre, henna, white lead, and mulberry juice, for which Egyptian women were already famous. But her main appeal, it seems, was a youthful vitality and a compelling personality, accompanied by a seductive voice in which she could speak several languages. She was said to be the only Ptolemy in the two-hundred-year dynasty who could speak Egyptian. But as she had no Latin, the affair was apparently conducted in Greek, a language in which Caesar was fluent.

Cleopatra might have been an ideal counterpart of Caesar. She rode and hunted with her ministers and generals, and was said to be at home on the battlefield. They were both well educated, acutely intelligent, and politically shrewd. Caesar would also have been attracted by the age and luster of her name, which means "renowned in her ancestry" and had been borne by six Queens of Egypt before her. Her noble Macedonian lineage, preserved by persistent intermarriage, extended back to the illustrious Ptolemy I, whose mother may have been related to Alexander the Great. On top of that, she was one of the wealthiest women in the world, provided she could hold on to her share of the throne, which Caesar now undertook to assure.

When Caesar appeared at the next negotiation session with Cleopatra at his side, the thirteen-year-old King quickly perceived the new relationship and rushed from the room in a rage, and out of the palace into the street, crying out that he had been betrayed. This created an uproar among the Alexandrians, who were as ill-disposed toward Cleopatra as they were toward Caesar, and Roman troops were required to prevent the crowd from storming the palace. Nevertheless, the King and Pothinus returned to the bargaining table and later agreed, or pretended to agree, to Caesar's decision that Ptolemy XIII should share the throne with Cleopatra in the way that their father wished. It was a decision that would produce only a modest benefit to Rome and Caesar, but would almost certainly bring about an armed conflict, and cost him months of time and hundreds of troops.

In an effort to placate the King, the crowd, and the country, Caesar agreed to return to Egypt the island of Cyprus, which Rome had seized ten years earlier. Aside from the fact of his victory at Pharsalus, he was perhaps emboldened to do this because Antony, on returning to Italy after Pharsalus, had pressured the Senate to appoint Caesar to a second term as *dictator*. Receiving word of this in Egypt, Caesar appointed Mark Antony *magister equitum*, his second-in-command in Italy. But to the King's disappointment, Caesar declared Cyprus to be a separate kingdom, to be ruled by the two other members of the royal family, Arsinoë, aged about eighteen, and Ptolemy XIV, aged eleven, the younger siblings of Cleopatra and Ptolemy XIII. What Cleopatra thought about losing Cyprus to her younger sister and brother we do not know, but there can hardly have been good feelings among the four children of Auletes now living in the royal palace with the Roman *dictator*, one of whom shared his bed, while the other three schemed to get rid of him.

It was only now, according to the best evidence, that Pothinus and the King sent word to Achillas at Pelusium to bring his twenty-thousand-man army to Alexandria and put an end to Caesar's visit to Egypt. Because of the difficulty of crossing the swamps and lagoons of the Delta, this required a march of more than a hundred miles upriver to the area of modern Cairo, and then another along the Canopic Nile, its westernmost branch, to Alexandria. When Caesar finally learned of this move in mid-November, he immediately quarantined Pothinus, Arsinoë, and the two young Ptolemies, and ordered them to send word to Achillas to bring his army no further. He brought his own troops into the palace and its grounds, which covered more than a quarter of the city, and set up his command post in the theater of Dionysus, preparing to withstand an assault.

But Achillas knew he had every advantage over Caesar and, less than two weeks later, marched into Alexandria with his mercenary army, touching off the five-month conflict known as the Alexandrian War. Caesar and his four thousand troops were barricaded in the palace complex with limited supplies of food and water, and in control of only a portion of the dock that fronted on the Great Harbor. Although they easily turned back the first assault on the complex, it was quickly apparent that the key to the war, and to the Romans' survival, would be control of the Great Harbor and its narrow channel to the sea.

In their harbors the Egyptians had over seventy vessels, including fifty heavy warships—quadriremes and quinqueremes—that they had sent to help Pompey, and that had recently returned. Within hours troops from both sides rushed to the docks, where the Romans held back the Egyptians and burned almost all their ships, only a dozen or so escaping under the Heptastadion bridges and into the Eunostos Harbor.

The fire spread from the ships and burned a portion of the docks and nearby buildings, including some in which forty thousand rolls of papyrus were stored. Some ancient accounts of this incident have given rise to the claim that Caesar burned, either deliberately or accidentally, the renowned library adjacent to the Alexandrian Mouseion. In his exhaustive analysis of the ancient references to the burning of the library, E. M. Parsons concludes that this was not the case, and that the fire started by Caesar's troops burned only those papyrus rolls stored in a warehouse at the docks.[3] The library, in which the Greek geographer Strabo browsed two decades later, survived several hundred more years before being pillaged and burned by Roman Emperors, then Christians, and finally Arabs.

With the threat of the Egyptian fleet removed, Caesar now sent boatloads of marines to land on the eastern tip of the Pharos island and to take control of the remarkable forty-story Pharos lighthouse, which commanded the entrance to the Great Harbor. One of the seven wonders of the ancient world, this marble and limestone tower was financed by a wealthy Greek Alexandrian and completed in 279, during the reign of the second Ptolemy, after twenty years' work. For more than twelve hundred years, before it was badly damaged by an earthquake, it marked the entrance to the harbor for sailing ships approaching the flat and featureless coast of Egypt. Writers in the first century CE refer to a fire that was kept burning at its top, reflecting a bright light far out to sea by means of a polished bronze mirror.[4]

We may be sure that Cleopatra watched the burning of the fleet and the attack on the Pharos lighthouse with great concern from her window in the royal palace at the end of Cape Lochias. She was surely relieved when Caesar's marines captured the lighthouse after a short battle, and he gained control of both sides of the narrow entrance to the Great Harbor, insuring that vessels friendly to them could enter, should they ever arrive. Both he and Cleopatra had sent for reinforcements from their allies throughout the area, Caesar instructing Domitius Calvinus to bring a third legion, this time by land through Syria, and requisitioning troops, warships, grain, and artillery from Asia, Rhodes, and Cilicia. He also summoned archers from Crete, and even cavalry from Arab Nabataea in the desert of Palestina (their King still resented the humiliation of his people by Pompey).

In the meantime, the fighting reached a stalemate on the mainland after Caesar's troops put up barricades between buildings and dug ditches across streets to secure an area around the palace and its grounds. Achillas' troops took control of the rest of the city, pinning Caesar against the coast. Then Cleopatra's younger half-sister Arsinoë managed to escape from the palace with her chief advisor, the eunuch Ganymedes, and as she was the only royal at liberty, the Alexandrians were happy to proclaim her Queen of Egypt. Arsinoë and Ganymedes immediately began squabbling with Achillas over the best way to deal with Caesar, and from inside the palace Pothinus and the King smuggled encouraging messages out to Achillas, including information about Caesar's plans. But within a few days Caesar intercepted one of their couriers and learned that they were either plotting to escape or planning to kill him. Although he does not mention her, Caesar probably induced Cleopatra to issue an order as Queen for the execution of Pothinus.

After this paragraph, the text of *The Civil War* breaks off abruptly, Caesar apparently writing nothing more about the war. Where he was, when it was, and why it was that he stopped writing are unknown. He never returned to his narrative, and some have speculated that he was diverted by Cleopatra from any further literary labor. But it is more likely that after the death of Pompey and the events in Egypt he felt no further need to justify his actions. Fortunately, the story of the war is continued in a manuscript titled *Bellum Alexandrinum, The Alexandrian War*, that was long associated with Caesar's *Commentaries*, but that scholars now agree is by another hand. It is almost certainly the work of Caesar's aide Aulus Hirtius, the continuator of *The Gallic War*, who, some time in the year between Caesar's death and his own, diligently took up the story where Caesar had left it. Although Hirtius admits to being absent from the war in Egypt, he joined Caesar shortly afterwards and must have had the benefit of both his notes and his conversation.

Hirtius opens his history, a book one-quarter the size of *The Civil War*, with a list of the measures the Alexandrians were taking to escalate the war—arming their slaves, recruiting troops from all over the country, and bringing large quantities of arms, artillery, and supplies into the city. The Egyptians built ten-story siege towers, some being movable on wheels, and placed them in locations where their artillery could fire into Caesar's compound. For the first time in the Civil War, Caesar was himself under siege, holding a narrow strip of land in a harbor city, in the same situation as the Massiliots just a year before. He built his own towers and forts to house his artillery, and then extended his trenches to the south toward Lake Mareotis to gain access to fodder and drinking water from a marsh adjacent to the lake.

But in the narrow corridor of the city between the harbor and the lake, neither side could make much headway against the other, and the next phase of the war centered on the Alexandrians' attempts to cut off the Romans' drinking water. Their effort, however, was not to be supervised by Ptolemy's general Achillas. He and the new Queen, Arsinoë, quarreled over the conduct of the war, and she, after failing to take control of the army by means of bribes and bounties to the troops, resorted to the time-honored method of settling such questions among the Ptolemies, and had him murdered. In his place as commander of the army she put her own man Ganymedes.

It is not known how this Ganymedes came by his name, but it may have been a common one in Egypt for Greek eunuchs. For centuries in the Middle East and Greece, rulers had employed men who had been castrated, voluntarily or not, to guard the women of the royal household. Taking advantage of the importance of this assignment, many eunuchs had advanced to more responsible positions as tutors, chamberlains, and advisors. Those especially shrewd, like Pothinus and Ganymedes, had become prime ministers and generals. In the *Iliad* Homer describes Ganymedes as a shepherd boy so beautiful that Zeus snatched him from the earth to be his cupbearer, and he is later identified as the deity responsible for the earth's water, and thus the source of the Nile.

Alexandria's supply of drinking water came from wells, and from a canal outside the southern wall of the city that was fed by the Nile. With extensive digging, Ganymedes was able to block the conduits that carried water from the canal into the area the Romans occupied. But he also resorted to the extraordinary measure of setting up mechanical water wheels, turned by oxen, to pump large amounts of water out of the sea up to higher ground, and then release it into the same area. Within days the water in the wells the Romans were using became brackish and undrinkable, and this, combined with the general precariousness of their position, caused grumbling and even panic among Caesar's troops. But he responded by reassuring them, and suspended all other work, ordering wells to be dug around the clock. According to Hirtius, a single night's digging produced an abundance of fresh water, foiling Ganymedes' scheme.

In spite of these difficulties, Caesar may have preferred this kind of campaign to what he was accustomed to—camping in a rainy northern forest or marching through Thessaly in a hot summer. After a hard day on the battlements, he was able to retire to luxurious quarters overlooking a Mediterranean harbor, with Cleopatra waiting in the royal suite. But he also must have been exasperated with the time and effort it was taking to extricate himself from Egypt.

The next day brought even better news for the Romans when a boat arrived in the harbor with the message that Domitius Calvinus had reached the coast about eight miles to the west with a fleet of reinforcements. But since most of his ships were under sail, they had been prevented by easterly winds from reaching Alexandria and, after several days at anchor, were suffering for lack of water. Eager to have the troops and supplies Calvinus had brought, Caesar set out from the Great Harbor with all his vessels, but with only their oarsmen and crews, leaving all his fighting men to hold his position in the city. Later in the day, when Caesar had found Calvinus, and was towing his fleet toward Alexandria, Ganymedes learned that his opponent was on the open sea and without marines to defend him.

From the Eunostos Harbor the Egyptians put out to sea with the dozen or so warships they had remaining, including four quadriremes, all fully manned. When Caesar sighted them late in the afternoon, he was not, being without marines, ready for a sea battle, especially since nightfall would soon put him at a further disadvantage because he was in strange waters. Instead he brought the fleet to shore in a protected place where he thought he could spend the night unmolested. But one of his Rhodian warships anchored itself too far from the others, tempting the Egyptians to attack it, and obliging Caesar to send his warships to defend it. It was his first sea fight since he had sailed against the pirate fleet more than twenty-five years earlier, but he had not much fighting to do:

Battle was joined, with great commitment from the Rhodians; and although they were outstanding in every engagement in both technique and courage, at this moment above all they did not shirk the whole burden, to prevent their compatriots appearing responsible for any loss that occurred. A very favourable result was thus obtained. One enemy quadrireme was captured, another sunk, and two stripped of all their marines; in addition, on the other ships a very large number of the fighting men were killed. And if nightfall had not put an end to the battle, Caesar would have captured the whole enemy fleet. Since the enemy were thoroughly frightened by this disaster, and the contrary wind had fallen light, Caesar towed the merchant ships back to Alexandria behind his victorious warships. (*The Alexandrian War* 11.3–6)

Hirtius perhaps exaggerates the despair of the Egyptians. More determined than ever to crush the Romans, they immediately began rebuilding their navy by bringing out old vessels and refurbishing them, constructing new ones, and even stripping wood from their buildings for use as oars. Within a few weeks they had assembled a fleet of several dozen warships in the Eunostos Harbor, including twenty-two quadriremes, five quinqueremes, and many smaller open boats. For the Romans' part, they were greatly heartened by the arrival of

Calvinus with his cargo of grain, weapons, artillery, and a single legion of former Pompeian infantry, the XXXVIIth, of unknown size. Also in the convoy were twenty-five additional warships from Asia, Pontus, and Lycia. Although a straight-up sea battle with the Egyptians may not have been Caesar's preference, he could not let them blockade his harbor and prevent either his escape or his rescue. Early in January of 47 he loaded his thirty-four vessels with marines and led them out of the Great Harbor and eastward along the Pharos island to confront the Egyptian fleet.

Rounding the western tip of the island, Caesar deployed his fleet outside a line of shoals that extended across the wide mouth of the Eunostos Harbor. Inside the shoals, through which a single ship could pass only at a narrow gap in the center, the Egyptian fleet waited. On board the Rhodian flagship were Caesar and the Rhodian admiral, Euphranor, a man whom Hirtius praises as more like a Roman than a Greek because of his skill and courage. When Euphranor saw that Caesar hesitated to send a single file of ships through the gap against the Egyptians, he volunteered to take his ships through first, and promised that he would hold off the Egyptians until the rest could get through. Caesar praised his bravery and accepted the offer. The Greeks were the best sailors and the best sea fighters in the Mediterranean, and best among the Greeks were the Rhodians, with their speedy quadriremes.

The product of centuries of shipbuilding and sea fighting, the Rhodian quadrireme of this period was longer and broader than the typical trireme—as much as one hundred and eighty feet long and twenty feet wide—and sat lower in the water. With only two banks of oars instead of three, the quadrireme had fewer oars than the typical trireme, but more oarsmen (two to an oar), greatly improving its maneuverability. In preparation for battle, it would be stripped of its sails and rigging, which took up valuable space and were useful only for longer trips. Bolted to the hull at its front was a three-pronged ram that rode just above the water. Below deck, two hundred or so oarsmen sat on benches and pulled one hundred oars, which were arranged in two rows of twenty-five on each side of the ship.

On deck, the usual squad of twenty Rhodian marines would have been reinforced by at least as many Roman legionaries. Also on deck were half a dozen archers, one or two catapults and their operators, and a Rhodian invention, fire pots—iron kettles of burning wood that they could extend on poles and dump on the deck of an enemy warship. A crew of officers, junior officers, and deckhands ran the ship, assisted by specialists, such as a doctor, a carpenter, an oar binder, and an "olive-oil anointer," the man who issued olive oil to the oarsmen for rubbing down.

Euphranor himself promptly took four Rhodian war galleys through the gap, confronting twenty-two in the Egyptian front line. Using their typical sea-battle tactics, the Rhodians moved quickly through the enemy ships to their rear, and then turned to ram them from behind or, if they could flank them, from the side. For their size and weight, and with several hundred men on board, these oared vessels were surprisingly nimble. With a piping flute or the rap of a mallet sounding the timing of the stroke, they could reach top speed from a standing start in about thirty seconds, and a trained crew could spin its warship in little more than its own length. As Euphranor's ships rammed several Egyptians, more galleys shot through the gap, and the harbor was soon crowded with vessels, large and small, leaving little room to maneuver. Rowing skill gave way to strength and quickness with the javelin, sword, dagger, and shield. As Caesar's warships maneuvered close enough so their marines could board, Egyptian archers showered flaming arrows on them, and Caesar's archers and catapult shooters unloaded their own barrage of missiles.

We do not know if Cleopatra participated in the planning of this engagement, as she did in her later war with the Romans, but she must have watched the battle from her quarters in the palace, as did the boy-King from his. Throughout the city thousands of Alexandrians, civilians and soldiers, put aside their tools and weapons and stood on rooftops where they could see the bay. But the battle did not go the way they hoped. Fighting at close quarters, the Egyptians were no match for the Rhodian marines or Caesar's veteran legionaries, all fighting with the certain knowledge that if they lost control of the sea, they would be trapped and starved, or captured and killed.

As Hirtius points out, the Egyptians had the luxury of knowing that if they lost, they could try something else the next day. On this day, the combined Asian, Greek, and Roman fleet rammed and sank three Egyptian ships and captured two others and their crews, a quinquereme and a bireme. Unable to exit the harbor, the remaining Egyptian vessels scrambled for the docks, where catapult operators and archers, firing from buildings and piers, prevented the Romans from pursuing them. Having lost none of his own ships, Caesar led them all back around the Pharos island and into the Great Harbor. He had, for the time being, avoided a naval blockade and a possibly disastrous end to his Egyptian adventure.

It was probably about this time, perhaps when Caesar returned from the battle in the Eunostos Harbor, that Cleopatra announced that she was pregnant with their child. Naturally, Hirtius is silent on this subject, and, in fact, there is no mention of this pregnancy in any surviving text, nor of any child, until a vague reference to a son of Caesar in a letter of Cicero's two months after Caesar's death. Other than Julia, Caesar had fathered no children, but there is evidence that he hoped at one time to have a son. Presumably the couple decided to proceed with the pregnancy, although the timing was not the best. They no doubt agreed that if its parents survived their present circumstances, a child born to the Queen of Egypt and the ruler of Rome—a product of the royal Ptolemies and the patrician Julii—might have a brilliant future. But if any of them were to survive, Caesar knew that he would have to take control of the Pharos island, including the town in its center, and possibly the Heptastadion, and do so with the men and ships he already had.

Late in the month Caesar sent a flotilla of dozens of small craft across the Great Harbor and landed ten picked cohorts of infantry, the equivalent of a full legion, on the inland shore of the Pharos island. At the same time several of his heavy warships carried hundreds of legionaries to the outer, northern side of the island, where they struggled ashore through the waves and rocks to attack the walled town on the opposite side. For most of the day the men of Pharos fought the Romans in the streets and alleys of their town, hurling stones and shooting arrows from the doorways and rooftops of their houses and buildings. The Alexandrians sent "fire boats" filled with archers under the bridges into the Great Harbor and around the island, where they shot flaming arrows at Caesar's vessels. But they could not stop the Romans from finally overrunning the town and then the entire island. Caesar's troops killed a large number of Egyptians and took six thousand prisoners, while some of the defenders jumped into the harbor and swam to the docks. At the bridge between the Heptastadion and the island, the Romans built a fort, so that they held one end of the causeway, and the Alexandrians the other.

Caesar now moved quickly to capture the inner bridge at the other end of the Heptastadion, and thus gain control of all the water traffic between the harbors. But the shipborne attack he launched the next day turned into a disaster that nearly cost him his life. Approaching the inner bridge by boat, the Romans laid down a barrage of arrows and catapult missiles that drove the Egyptians off the Heptastadion and away from the bridge. Once this was done, three cohorts of infantry landed on the waterfront near the bridge and began constructing a barricade between the bridge and the mainland, and filling in the channel under it with boulders.

In the meantime, several of Caesar's warships moved nearer the Heptastadion, and many of the oarsmen and crew disembarked and clambered on it, some looking for a better view of the fighting and some wanting to get into it. When the Alexandrians in the Eunostos Harbor on the other side came up in their boats, the two groups began pelting each other with stones and arrows. Before long the Alexandrians landed some of their own troops farther out on the Heptastadion, and Caesar's crewmen were forced to scramble back to their ships. In the haste and confusion, many could not get on board and, instead, were chased along the causeway toward the inner bridge. When the Romans holding the barricade and the bridge against the Alexandrians on the mainland suddenly saw their ships' crews and oarsmen fleeing toward them, they thought they were surrounded.

What followed was a complete breakdown of the assault as the legionaries broke away from the barricade and rushed down to the water's edge, while the rowers and sailors struggled through the rocks and water to get to their ships, and those ships nearest the shore, now in danger of overloading, began to pull away into the harbor. On the Heptastadion himself, Caesar rushed among his troops exhorting them to stay and fight, but they had given themselves up to flight, and though most reached their ships and got away, and others swam out to other ships, many were drowned when their ships swamped, and others were caught and killed by the Alexandrians. When he could not stop the panicky retreat, Caesar got aboard his own small boat and then, as more troops boarded and it began to swamp, leaped off and swam out to another ship in the harbor. Hirtius is silent about this, but other historians report that he was showered with enemy arrows and missiles as he swam, holding a packet of papers above his head and towing his *paludamentum* in his teeth.

Although he escaped with his life, the battle cost Caesar four hundred infantry and at least as many oarsmen and sailors. The Alexandrians again took possession of the inner bridge, and added trenches and catapults for its defense, hauling up the rocks from the channel and regaining their access to the Great Harbor. They even captured Caesar's cloak, which he had lost in the water, and, in their delight with the outcome of the battle, displayed it as a trophy. But otherwise their victory had gained them little, and in order to break the stalemate they now sent emissaries to Caesar to say that they were unhappy with the leadership of Arsinoë and Ganymedes, and that his release of the boy King would help to bring about a peace.

Caesar had thought, in the early stages of this bizarre conflict, that he might benefit by holding the young Ptolemy hostage in the palace and keeping him separated from his army. But the intrigues of the royal family and their advisors had so muddled the situation that it now appeared to him that releasing the King could possibly lead to a truce, and even if it did not, another royal child in the Egyptian camp was not likely to improve their effectiveness. Also, as Hirtius admits, Caesar's own *dignitas* would be enhanced if he were fighting a king, and not a motley collection of refugees and mercenaries. Although the boy king pretended a fierce desire to remain in the palace with Caesar and his sister, on his release he immediately took up the prosecution of the war with the greatest fervor. He ordered yet another naval action against the Romans, this time an effort to intercept a convoy of supplies for Caesar that was approaching Alexandria along the coast from the east.

When Caesar learned of this early in March, he put the entire fleet under the command of his officer Tiberius Nero, father of the future Emperor Tiberius, and sent it out to protect the convoy. The battle took place at the mouth of the Canopic Nile, the now-dry branch of the river that reached the sea near the town of Canopus, today a ruin some ten miles east of Alexandria. Little is known of this episode except that Tiberius apparently brought his warships into the mouth of the river and there defeated an Egyptian squadron lying in wait for the convoy. His only loss was the ship carrying the valiant Euphranor, who led the attack. After ramming and sinking an Egyptian quadrireme, the Rhodian admiral perished when his own ship, pursuing another Egyptian ship, was surrounded and sunk.

The safe arrival of the convoy brought the news that a large army of Syrian, Jewish, and Arabian troops was approaching the Egyptian border under the command of Mithradates of Pergamon, the adopted son of Mithradates Eupator, whom Pompey had defeated fifteen years earlier. He was aided in this effort by two Jewish leaders, Hyrcanus, whom Pompey had appointed High Priest of Judaea, and a converted Arab, Antipater, his chief minister, both of whom had supported Pompey until Pharsalus, but now recruited thousands of troops in Judaea and its neighbors to help extricate Caesar from Egypt.

From the earliest times, the Pharaohs, the Persians, and then the Ptolemies had defended Egypt, for the most part with success, against land invasions across the narrow passageway at its northeastern corner, between the Mediterranean and Red seas. The key to this defense was the port of Pelusium, about fifteen miles east of the modern Suez Canal, which stood guard over the entrance to the Pelusiac branch of the Nile, as well as the land route. Here Ptolemy XIII had left a substantial garrison to hold off Cleopatra's army, but his advisors had either not foreseen, or had not adequately prepared for, the arrival of Mithradates. In less than a day his army surrounded and captured Pelusium, established a garrison there, and proceeded southward along the eastern

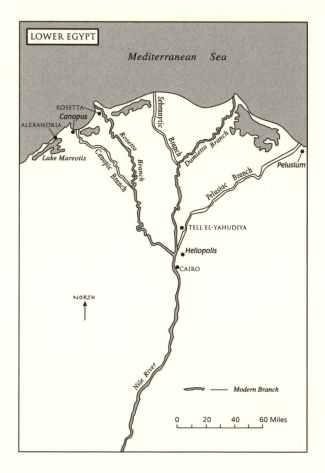

branch of the Nile to where it could be crossed. The army was spared much fighting by the presence of Antipater and his troops, who persuaded the Jewish settlements along the river to join Mithradates, or at least not oppose him.

At the same time the Egyptian high command dispatched a portion of its army from Alexandria up the western branch of the river to challenge Mithradates in the vicinity of modern Cairo before he could get around the apex of the Delta. According to Hirtius, some of the Egyptians rashly marched ahead, crossed the river, and attacked Mithradates where he had entrenched himself at the settlement identified by the Jewish historian Josephus as the Camp of the Jews, today an archaeological site called Tell el-Yahudiya, about eighteen miles north of Cairo. But when they failed to penetrate his camp, Mithradates led his troops out in a counterattack, chasing them back across the river and taking many lives. From there the relieving army made its way across the remaining Nile waterways until it emerged on the western edge of the Delta some seventy miles southeast of Alexandria.

The news of this engagement reached Caesar and Ptolemy simultaneously, and both immediately made ready to take their forces in Mithradates' direction, one to amalgamate their armies, the other to destroy the advancing army before that could be done. Unwilling to wait at Alexandria and fight Mithradates on one side and Caesar on the other, the Egyptians put all the troops they could spare onto galleys on the canal behind the city that connected with the western branch, and sent them upriver to find Mithradates.

Leaving a garrison sufficient to hold the palace quarter and the island, Caesar put the rest of his troops on ships and hurried out of the Great Harbor by night and to the east, toward the mouth of the Canopic branch, taking care that signal fires on each of his ships showed the direction he was taking. To the Egyptians it seemed that he intended to pursue the King's army up the river, but once he was out of sight of Alexandria, Caesar ordered the fires doused and the fleet turned around to the west. During the night he brought his ships back past the Pharos and some twenty miles beyond to a secluded part of the coast, where the army disembarked and began a trek to the southeast in search of Mithradates. The Egyptians, perhaps waiting to attack Caesar as he came up the Canopic branch, delayed just long enough that the Romans, after a three-day march, reached Mithradates before they did, and combined their armies for the last battle of the war.

The King and his army had taken an easily defended position on a hill overlooking the left bank of the western branch of the Nile, and protected on one side by a marsh, some seventy miles upriver from Alexandria. They had fortified a village adjacent to the camp, connecting the two with an earthwork, and had stationed all their archers and slingers on board ships on the river where they could not be attacked, and could protect the river side of the camp. Approaching the King's position, Caesar first attacked the fortified village with his entire army and captured it, forcing the Egyptians to retreat into their main camp. The following day he sent his infantry against two sides of the camp, but they were unable to make any headway, and those between the river and the camp came under heavy fire from both the ramparts and the ships. But when Caesar saw that a portion of the rampart overlooking a steep hill was only lightly defended, he ordered troops to attack there and, after meeting little resistance, they poured over the fortification in great numbers and stormed into the camp,

whereupon the Alexandrians, panic-stricken by the shouting and fighting on both sides of them, began to rush about in confusion . . . throughout the camp. This utter bewilderment of theirs fired the spirits of our troops to such a pitch that they captured the camp almost simultaneously in all sectors, though its highest point was the first to capitulate; and from that point our men rushed down and killed a vast number of the enemy. (*The Alexandrian War* 31, 2–3)

In their hurry to escape, some jumped off the ramparts into the surrounding ditch, and hundreds of others rushed to the river, where the teenaged King had already boarded his boat. As the Romans chased them to the water's edge, those who were able swam out to the boats, overloading and swamping several of them. When the royal barge failed to pull away from the bank quickly enough and numerous swimmers tried to board, it sank with the King on it, and he drowned. The remains of his army surrendered, and the war was over. Arsinoë was captured, but the fate of Ganymedes is unknown.

Without waiting for his infantry, Caesar hurried back to Alexandria and rode triumphantly through the city at the head of a troop of cavalry and into the royal compound, where the waiting Cleopatra was relieved to learn that her lover was victorious and her brother-husband dead. Caesar himself had reason to be relieved after six months on the wrong end of a siege, dodging and defensive the whole time, then calling for help for the first time in his life, and finally being rescued by a foreign army. According to Hirtius, crowds of somber citizens met Caesar in the streets and publicly resigned themselves to the Roman victory. To demonstrate to them that Ptolemy was genuinely dead, and could not return as a god (as was thought of anyone who disappeared in the Nile), he ordered the river dredged until the King's body was found, and then displayed the golden armor that his troops had stripped from it.

Toward the end of March of 47 Caesar restored a pregnant Cleopatra to the throne of Egypt, this time as co-regent with her remaining brother, the eleven-year-old Ptolemy XIV, whom she subsequently married. Caesar also deprived Arsinoë of Cyprus, returned the island to the Egyptian kingdom, and ordered her transported to Rome as a prisoner. The three children of Auletes were the last of the illustrious dynasty, but a new grandchild was only a few months away.

Once Caesar had disposed of these matters, he did not hurry away to pursue the Pompeians, who were still contending in the Adriatic, and were gathering an army in Africa. Instead, to the world's amazement, he lingered in Egypt with Cleopatra for two more months until early June. Suetonius writes that the lovers diverted themselves during these weeks with extravagant nightlong feasts and a lengthy cruise up the Nile on a luxurious barge, accompanied by a flotilla of several hundred boats.

There is no other information available about the cruise, but the Ptolemies were notorious for building outsized pleasure boats for Nile travel, and it is likely that Cleopatra's vessel was similar to one used by Ptolemy IV about one hundred and fifty years earlier. That particular royal barge was three hundred feet long, forty-five wide, sixty feet from waterline to rooftop, and double hulled in catamaran style. Built of cypress and what was then called Syrian cedar, it was luxuriously furnished in the Greek style, and decorated with carvings and inlays of ivory, copper, and gold. Hundreds of oarsmen and sailors manned the ship, while servants and slaves labored on two arcaded decks that included shrines, a winter garden, and a room large enough for twenty dining couches.

How far up the Nile this ancient houseboat took the couple is not known, but according to Suetonius it was not as far as they wanted. They were obliged to cut short their trip and turn back after the Roman troops accompanying them, most of whom had been at war for almost eighteen months, rebelled against any further travel in the opposite direction from Rome. It was perhaps while traveling on the river that Caesar resumed his correspondence with Cicero, who had written him a few months earlier to explain why he and Quintus had joined the Pompeians. No letter of Caesar's from Egypt survives, but Cicero later wrote to Terentia that Caesar's response was "quite a handsome one,"[5] leading him to hope that he would bear him no grudge.

To mark Caesar's brief presence in the historic city, Cleopatra ordered an enormous colonnaded structure, the Caesareum, incorporating both Pharaonic and Greek architectural features, erected on the Alexandrian waterfront. Nothing of this structure survives, but in 1996 French archaeologists discovered the remains of piers and streets from Ptolemaic Alexandria under sixteen to twenty feet of water on the eastern side of the Great Harbor. Granite columns, amphorae, and statues, including a granite sphinx with a head thought to be that of Ptolemy Auletes himself, have been raised from the harbor floor. By the Middle Ages, Cape Lochias, the royal palace, and most of ancient Alexandria's waterfront had fallen victim to earthquakes, fires, and the encroaching sea.

One priceless piece of physical evidence has been preserved of Caesar's Egyptian interlude—one of the few authentic representations of him. A tiny intaglio portrait in profile, carved in bluish gray chalcedony, came to light in Cairo in the 1960s. Caesar's face is lean and smooth, and resting on his head in a way that conceals his receding hairline is a laurel wreath in the Roman tradition, surmounted by a garland of flowers of the type favored in Ptolemaic Alexandria.[6]

The only other memento Caesar left in Alexandria, aside from the great loss of life and property, was the infant that Cleopatra expected to deliver in about three months. Although he could claim that he had preserved Roman *dignitas* in Egypt, and had collected some portion of an important Roman debt, nearly all historians, ancient and modern, agree that any benefit Caesar gained from his Egyptian adventure was far outweighed by what he lost. It is easy enough to catalog his losses. As an astonished Napoléon Bonaparte wrote in his analysis of Caesar's campaigns, he had given the Pompeians a nine-month respite from pursuit. In Pontus, his general Domitius Calvinus had lost a battle and had been forced to retreat because he had sent half his army to rescue Caesar. In Italy Caesar's inattention bred political squabbles, disgruntled legionaries, and popular unrest.

On the other hand, what he gained may have had nothing to do with the war, with politics, or with Rome. Could this seasoned politician and general have found in Cleopatra something he had always wanted—a female Caesar with whom he could produce an heir? Had he found something worth risking what he had won in two years of war? These questions could only be answered by Caesar himself, and he is silent.

Not until a full week of June had passed did Caesar yield to the demands of the war and, after a final farewell banquet, ride out of Alexandria at the head of a single legion, the VIth, now only a thousand strong, accompanied by Mithradates of Pergamon and his army. Leaving three legions to preserve the peace and safeguard Cleopatra, he led the army to Egypt's eastern border by way of the apex of the Delta, and into the no-man's-land between Egypt and Judaea. Before returning to Rome, he had one more Eastern King to deal with—Pharnaces, the adopted brother of the man who had come to his rescue, and who now rode beside him.

XII

Veni, Vidi, Vici

In the months after Pharsalus, several of the surviving Pompeian generals had gathered their remaining troops, recruited any others that would join them, and made plans to continue the war against Caesar wherever they could. After abandoning their campaign in the Peloponnese, Cato and his fleet had sailed into the eastern Mediterranean and somehow made contact with Pompey's fleeing ships, learning of his death. Cato turned toward Africa and landed near the prominent Greek city of Cyrene, today a cluster of ruins on a hill in eastern Libya. There he heard that Metellus Scipio, Labienus, and other Pompeians had been welcomed in Africa by King Juba, and had established a base at Utica. Cato took his ships to the west, but when his fleet was wrecked, he set out by land for Africa with an army of ten thousand troops. He arrived at Utica in time to support Scipio in his dispute with Attius Varus over who would command the Pompeian army, and to prevent any harm to the city, which Juba was still trying to punish for its support of Caesar. During Caesar's interlude in Egypt, the Pompeians and Juba assembled and trained a large army at Utica, and began sending their warships to harass Italian coastal towns and shipyards, and the Adriatic coast of Macedonia.

After Cato had abandoned Dyrrachium, Caesar's commander in Illyricum, Quintus Cornificius, had moved down and taken control of the city and the Macedonian coast. But one of Pompey's admirals, Marcus Octavius, remained in command of a large fleet of warships at Corcyra, and when Cornificius found that he was unable to prevent Octavius from attacking Caesarian garrisons and preying on his vessels in the Adriatic, he sent for assistance to Publius Vatinius, one of Caesar's commanders in Brundisium.

Vatinius was among Caesar's earliest confederates, serving with him as a tribune during his Consulship, and then as a general in the Gallic War. Although he was severely afflicted with gout at the time, he rounded up a small number of warships, outfitted some other oared vessels with rams, and then manned his makeshift fleet with veteran legionaries whom Caesar had left behind on the sick list. Using a quinquereme as his flagship, he sailed north in rough weather along the coast of Illyricum until he met the Pompeian fleet, which far outnumbered his own. Recognizing Octavius' quadrireme, he boldly raced forward to ram it, Octavius doing the same, and the two ships collided with such force that they stuck together. The other ships in each fleet crowded around, and in the ensuing battle Vatinius' marines, who were all experienced infantrymen, got the best of the Pompeians. Octavius lost the battle and his fleet, including his own ship, and spent some time in the water, but escaped in a small boat and the next day fled the area.

About a month after Vatinius had cleared the Adriatic of enemy warships, Caesar reached the coast of modern Israel with his single legion. It is likely that he traveled by land as far as Ascalon (modern Ashkelon) or Joppa (modern Tel Aviv), where he put his legion on board ship and continued up the coast, reaching Ake-Ptolemaïs (modern Akko) late in June. Along the way he met with the nominal rulers and would-be rulers in the region, settling disputes, imposing or forgiving taxes, and restoring or withdrawing kingdoms, land, favors, and privileges. To express his gratitude to the Jewish communities that had assisted him, he issued various decrees to reduce Roman exactions upon them. To reward Antipater for his help in the Alexandrian War, he appointed him Procurator of Judaea and conferred on him Roman citizenship, an honor that descended to his son Herod, the later King.

From Ake Ptolemaïs he sailed north to the port of Seleucia Pieria, now a set of ruins overlooking a silted-up harbor near the modern Turkish-Syrian border, and from there traveled the sixteen miles up the Orontes River, now Nahr al-Asi, to Antioch, the Syrian capital that had resisted the visit of Pompey the previous year. It was perhaps there, near the end of June, that he was joined by Aulus Hirtius, who brought him news from Rome, as well as the latest messages about a conflict that had developed in northern Anatolia during the early months of the Alexandrian War.

In the aftermath of the death of Mithradates Eupator fifteen years earlier, Pompey had allowed his son Pharnaces II to remain as King of Cimmerian Bosporus—what is now the Crimean peninsula. At the same time he had awarded the small kingdom of Lesser Armenia to Deiotarus, a Galatian prince who had helped defeat Mithradates. When Pompey sought his assistance at the outbreak of the Civil War, the aging Deiotarus supported him with six hundred Galatian cavalry, and then joined him when he fled Greece after Pharsalus. But while he and Pompey were busy with Caesar, Pharnaces brought an army around the eastern edge of the Black Sea, occupied Lesser Armenia, and then invaded Cappadocia. Deiotarus parted company with Pompey in Ephesus and, a few months later, possibly in mid-November, approached Domitius Calvinus, whom Caesar had left in command of Asia after Pharsalus, to beg for assistance against Pharnaces, who had overrun his kingdom.

Domitius saw that Pharnaces might later threaten the Roman province of Bithynia-Pontus, and offered to help Deiotarus, as well as King Ariobarzanes of Cappadocia, but he had only a single legion of captured Pompeians, the XXXVIth, having sent two others to Caesar in Egypt. He dispatched officers to recruit troops in Pontus and Cilicia and quickly assembled an army of four legions, including two Galatian legions and a troop of cavalry supplied by Deiotarus. Then Domitius sent a warning to Pharnaces to return to his own kingdom, and at the same time brought his army to where Pharnaces was camped near Nicopolis, now modern Susehri in eastern Turkey, the city that Pompey had built to commemorate his victory over Mithradates. When the two armies took up their positions in late December, Pharnaces asserted his right to reoccupy his father's kingdom, and urged Domitius to wait until Caesar arrived and to let him decide.

Although Domitius refused to relent or withdraw, his position was weakened when Pharnaces captured couriers with a letter from Caesar ordering Domitius to send still more troops to Egypt, and to come there himself without delay. Encouraged by this knowledge of pressure on Domitius, Pharnaces dug in and prepared to wait him out. Domitius decided that he had come too far to retreat and could wait no longer, and so ordered an attack on Pharnaces' camp across a broad front. But his motley army was stopped in the center and on the right, only the Roman XXXVIth Legion holding its ground on the left. Within a few hours his new recruits and Galatian legions had been cut to pieces, and the XXXVIth had to withdraw to the nearby hills. Domitius, Deiotarus, and their troops then retreated to the south, and Pharnaces advanced into Bithynia-Pontus in the same way that his father had invaded Asia forty years before, committing atrocities, notably castration, among Roman settlers.

In the meantime, that is, during the first few months Caesar spent in Egypt, Rome and Italy were racked by financial disruptions, commodity shortages, and a general confusion about the political situation. Caesar's attempts late in 49 to strike a balance between creditors and debtors had left the former dissatisfied and the latter angry. The debtors' cause was taken up by Caesar's admiral Publius Dolabella, a man with substantial debts who had attached himself to Caesar with the hope of erasing them. On returning from Pharsalus, he had arranged to convert himself from a patrician to a plebeian, and then won election as a Tribune of the Assembly. In this office he brought up legislation to reduce rents and abolish all debts, and gained substantial support, including, at first, that of Mark Antony himself.

For his own part, the Master of the Horse had aroused widespread disapproval after his return from Pharsalus by reverting to his habits of open carousing, drinking, and bullying of subordinates. On Caesar's instructions he prohibited all Pompeians from returning to Italy, the only exception being Cicero, whom he told to stay in Brundisium. An unforgiving Cicero later excoriated him in the Senate for his ostentatious arrival at Brundisium in October of 48, where he was met by his mistress, an actress/courtesan named Volumnia, and then his journey to Rome with his army in a caravan of looting, drinking, and violence. In the capital Antony seized property for himself and his cronies, abused citizens, and generally behaved like a boorish despot.

Finally, when Dolabella resorted to armed thugs to force passage of his bill, the Senate demanded he be restrained, and Antony brought a legion of infantry into the capital. Although Dolabella was an old ally, Antony's growing anger about his widely known intimacy with Antonia, Antony's wife of eight years (and first cousin), gave him another reason to move against him. In a pitched battle in and around the Forum, Antony's troops routed Dolabella's supporters, killing hundreds of them and eventually executing the last resisters by throwing them from the legendary Tarpeian Rock at the top of the Capitoline Hill, the traditional method of disposing of traitors.

Arriving in Antioch, Caesar "learnt from people who had arrived from Rome . . . that many matters there were being handled badly and incompetently and that no aspect of public life was running tolerably smoothly" (*The Alexandrian War* 65.1). No doubt he had been hearing these reports for several months, and he remained in Syria only a few days, rewarding those who had helped him and granting pardons to any Pompeians who approached him, including Quintus Cicero and his son, the brother and nephew of the orator. Although the situation in Rome clearly required his personal attention, the threat to Bithynia-Pontus by Pharnaces was too serious to be left for later. Early in July he appointed his distant cousin Sextus Julius Caesar Governor of Syria and sailed for Tarsus, capital of the Roman province of Cilicia.

Among the many Pompeians awaiting him there were Gaius Cassius, son-in-law of Servilia, and Marcus Brutus, who, having been the first to be forgiven after Pharsalus, now took the role of advocate for other Pompeians, notably for his brother-in-law Cassius. But he had not much arguing to do, as Caesar readily pardoned Cassius and all other Romans who asked, except those who had fought him again after being forgiven. After settling the affairs of the province, Caesar hurried north into Cappadocia and, after a march of two hundred and fifty miles, reached Comana Pontica, then an important religious center that survives today only in a cluster of scanty ruins near the village of Gümenek, about sixty miles from the Black Sea coast of northeastern Turkey.

As he approached Pontus, he was met by the Galatian King, Deiotarus, who presented himself bereft of kingly trappings and in mourning garb, as was the custom of defendants in court, and begged forgiveness for his active support of Pompey. Although Deiotarus was vigorously represented by Brutus, who may have been his creditor, Caesar agreed to absolve him only partially and, after administering a scolding, demanded that he supply cavalry and a legion of infantry for use against Pharnaces. Caesar was impressed with the force and boldness of Brutus' advocacy, but his long-standing affection for him may have been tested. It could have been on this occasion that Caesar made his famous remark about Brutus: "I do not know what this young man wants, but everything he wants, he wants very badly."[1]

Near the end of July, after the two legions of Domitius Calvinus joined his own depleted VIth Legion and Deiotarus' Galatians at Comana, Caesar began marching westward to engage Pharnaces. Envoys from the King brought him a gold crown, and entreated him not to advance with hostility, reminding him that Pharnaces had not supported Pompey (as had Deiotarus), and assuring him that Pharnaces would do whatever Caesar asked. Caesar rejected the crown, as well as a reported offer of marriage to Pharnaces' daughter, and accused Pharnaces of merely saving himself by not helping Pompey. He demanded the release of all Roman property and prisoners, the payment of tribute, and Pharnaces' withdrawal from Pontus.

The King replied that he would comply with Caesar's demands, but it was soon clear that he would not. Caesar continued marching toward him for several days until he reached the walled town of Zela, today's Zile in north-central Turkey. There he found Pharnaces camped on a high plateau about four miles north of town, the same plateau that his father, Mithradates Eupator, had camped upon before defeating a Roman general twenty years earlier. After spending a day or two south of town, Caesar suddenly broke camp at 2 A.M. on the morning of August 2, brought his army at dawn to an adjacent plateau less than a mile from Pharnaces, and began constructing his own fortified camp.

When Pharnaces immediately mustered his troops, marched them out of camp, and drew them up in battle lines on the slope of his hill, Caesar thought it only a show of force and, according to Hirtius, laughed to himself at the foolhardy display. But he was astonished to see the enemy army continue down the hill and across the ravine, and then up the steep hill at a steady pace directly at his camp. He ordered the trumpet signal for immediate battle, and his troops dropped their baskets and shovels and scrambled for their helmets, shields, and weapons. Before they could arrange themselves in battle lines, they were thrown into confusion by the sight of the King's chariots approaching them, each with long scythes attached to the ends of its axle. A volley of missiles from Caesar's archers and slingers halted the chariots, but behind them came the infantry, and in minutes thousands of soldiers were stabbing and slashing at each other all along the hillside.

Although Pharnaces achieved a certain surprise with his sudden attack, and his army was far larger than Caesar's, his troops labored under the serious handicap of charging and fighting uphill. Along a limited front, few ancient armies could succeed with such an approach. "The origin of our victory lay in the bitter and intense hand-to-hand battle joined on the right wing, where the veteran Sixth legion was stationed" (*The Alexandrian War* 76.1). In the center and on the left the defenders gained control more slowly, but gradually, over the course of the morning, Caesar's army pushed the King's troops back down the slope, many of them being knocked down by their comrades falling back upon them. As their front line collapsed, Pharnaces' troops dropped their weapons and ran back into the ravine and up the slope toward their own camp.

Against little resistance, Caesar's troops pursued them and then clambered up the hill themselves and assaulted Pharnaces' camp, which they overran after a short battle. The remainder of the King's troops they either killed or captured, but Pharnaces escaped to the sea with a few horsemen. Hirtius speculates that it was Pharnaces' arrogance and contempt for the Romans, perhaps fed by his easy victory over Domitius Calvinus' army the previous winter, a larger army than Caesar's at Zela, that led him to ignore a basic principle of ancient warfare and make his impetuous attack.

Whatever the reason, Caesar was elated by the sudden and surprising victory, and spontaneously distributed the King's captured treasure among his troops. In a letter to Rome in which he scoffed at Pompey's long campaign against Mithradates, Pharnaces' father, he turned a line from one of his favorite playwrights, Terence, into the succinct and triumphant phrase *veni, vidi, vici*, meaning that he approached his enemy, saw him, and defeated him, all in the same day, a boast that will forever accompany his name.[2]

Caesar's VIth Legion, which he had dispatched from Gaul to Spain in the first months of the war, and which had suffered losses of more than half its men while fighting at Ilerda, Dyrrachium, Pharsalus, and Egypt, he now released, allowing it to march on its own directly to the Hellespont, across the north of Greece on the Via Egnatia, and on to Italy. After releasing all the foreign troops as well, Caesar left a general and two legions to keep order in Pontus, and traveled himself with a cavalry troop southward into the province of Asia. Along the way he stopped to hear and decide local disputes, redraw boundaries, and reward or punish whomever he saw fit, in some cases collecting debts still owed Pompey from fifteen years earlier. As payment for his crucial help during the Alexandrian War, Caesar granted Mithradates of Pergamon extensive territory in Galatia, and named him King of Cimmerian Bosporus, which belonged to Pharnaces. Mithradates was expected to conquer it himself, but he could not, and was shortly defeated and killed by the prince Pharnaces had left in charge, and who had assassinated him when he returned from Zela.

In the meantime, all of Italy waited for Caesar's return. An impatient Cicero, who had been renting a house in Brundisium for almost a year, wrote to his friend Gaius Cassius, "Who could have expected that the main hostilities would have been so long held up by the fighting at Alexandria, or that this what's-his-name Pharnaces would menace Asia so formidably?"[3] Finally, near the end of August, the news of Pharnaces' quick defeat reached Rome, along with orders from Caesar to assemble troops in Sicily for the coming expedition to Africa. From Asia Caesar crossed to Mytilene and then sailed for Athens in the same way that Pompey had leisurely made his way homeward after conquering the East. Having supported Pompey in the Civil War, the Athenians were greatly relieved when Caesar declined to punish them, and even made large donations for the restoration of their city. Athens had withstood a long siege by Fufius Calenus, only surrendering after Pharsalus, and Caesar remarked in his address to the Athenian crowd that it was solely in deference to their dead, to the glorious achievements of their ancestors, that they were spared.

It was probably while Caesar was in Greece, about the first week of September of 47, that Cleopatra gave birth to a son whom she named Ptolemy Caesar, and whom the Alexandrians called Caesarion, "Little Caesar." We may be sure that the news of this birth aroused great interest as it gradually spread throughout the Roman world, but there is no mention of it in surviving letters or histories until after Caesar's death. That Cleopatra gave birth at all at this time has been a subject of dispute among scholars. She may have commemorated the event by issuing a series of intriguing coins in Cyprus, a territory that Caesar restored to her before he left Egypt. The coins depict her with an infant at her breast, but it is their date of issue that is the point of argument. The weight of evidence suggests that they were issued late in 47, although some scholars date them to 44 or even ten years later.[4]

Assuming that there was a birth in 47, it is likely that the news took several weeks to reach Caesar because it was so difficult for ships to sail out of Alexandria in the summer. There is no record that he ever acknowledged the child, but it is undisputed that he brought Cleopatra to Rome the following year, accompanied, we must assume, by her son. It is said that Antony and others later defended the boy as Caesar's, but the strenuous efforts of Octavius, Caesar's adopted son, to disprove this parentage once Caesar had died have tainted the record so as to leave it unreliable.

The circumstantial facts are no more help. There is a question whether Caesar was able to produce offspring at all after the birth of Julia, his only certain child, when he was about twenty-four. It is strange that no other children are attributed to him during thirty-four years of marriage to four different women and a lifetime of notorious sexual activity in an age when contraception and abortion were, at best, inefficient. (In contrast, Antony fathered at least ten children by five women.) It is just possible that Cleopatra, suspecting Caesar's infertility, contrived to become pregnant by someone else during the months they lived in the royal palace together. But against this unlikely scenario is the fact that the Ptolemaic Queens were not known to be promiscuous, and Cleopatra's only known lovers were Caesar and Antony, the latter fathering her three other children. Although most modern scholars accept the child as Caesar's, there are strong dissents, and the question remains undecided.[5]

From Athens Caesar traveled to Corinth, where he was moved to compassion by the remains of the rich and powerful city that a Roman general had destroyed a hundred years earlier. He would later order a reconstruction of the city and the establishment of a large Roman colony there, and in the last year of his life made plans for a ship canal to be dug across the Isthmus of Corinth, a project that was not completed until 1882. The short run from Corinth to Italy he made so quickly that his arrival at Tarentum on September 24 surprised everyone, including Cicero, who was waiting nervously at Brundisium, mindful that he was the most prominent ex-Pompeian in Italy. Plutarch describes the latest turn in this relationship of nearly forty years:

Finally the news came that Caesar had landed at Tarentum and was coming round by land from there to Brundisium. Cicero hurried out to meet him. He was not altogether without hope of the result, but he felt ashamed at having to test, as it were, the reactions of an enemy and a conqueror in front of so many witnesses. As it happened there was no need at all for him to do or say anything unworthy of himself. He was some way ahead

193

of the rest when Caesar saw him coming, and he immediately got down and embraced him and then took him along with him for a considerable distance, talking to him privately.[6]

Considering the zealous generals Caesar had already pardoned, Cicero had good reason to expect such a reconciliation, and a release from his exile in Brundisium. A few days later he sent word to Terentia to make preparations for his arrival at his villa (formerly owned by Sulla) in the resort town of Tusculum, fifteen miles southeast of Rome, today a few ruins on the ridge above Frascati. Caesar himself, still in the office of *dictator*, hurried to Rome, where his lieutenants were squabbling and violent gangs on either side of the debt issue roamed the streets. To restore order, he immediately decreed severe penalties for rioting, and then distributed grain, cooking oil, and money to the public (citizens only). Rather than punish the ineffective and dissolute Antony, he simply ignored him, and let his post of Master of the Horse expire when he relinquished the dictatorship later in the year.

With Dolabella he was kinder, and even agreed to some of his debt proposals by releasing tenants from payment of one year's rent, up to five hundred *denarii*. But further than that he would not go, and "when the multitude demanded an annulment of debts, he would not grant this, saying: 'I, too, owe large amounts.' "[7] But one way he raised money to pay what debts he paid was to extract large "loans" (as he called them) from wealthy *optimates*, neither party anticipating any repayment.

Before resigning the dictatorship, he filled all the magisterial offices with his supporters, either arranging their elections or appointing them outright, and did the same with ten *praetores*, as well as numerous augurs, priests, and lesser officials. He also arranged for his sixteen-year-old grandnephew Gaius Octavius to be elected to the position in the *collegium pontificum* left vacant by Lucius Domitius, just as he himself had been elected at a similar age. When he could find no more supporters from the Senatorial class, he filled out the depleted Senate with *equites* and centurions who had favored him or fought in his army. Passing over Antony entirely, he named as Consuls for the remainder of 47 the dependable Fufius Calenus, for his successes in Macedonia and Greece, and the resourceful Publius Vatinius, for his naval victories in the Adriatic. He continued his indulgence of Servilia's son Marcus Brutus by appointing him to govern the country's choicest province, Nearer Gaul. He also awarded Asia to one of her sons-in-law, Publius Servilius, and picked another, Marcus Lepidus, as his running mate on the ballot for the next year's Consuls, a ballot that contained no other candidates.

Besides handing out appointments, Caesar also confiscated and put up for auction all of Pompey's property and that of his generals and supporters. The heavily indebted Dolabella snapped up Pompey's villas at Formiae and at Alba Fucens, near today's Albe, while Antony was the high bidder for one in Rome, and another near Cicero's in Tusculum. In the spirit of victors taking spoils, neither expected to pay the high price he had offered, but they were surprised, and Antony angered, when Caesar held them to their bids. According to Cicero, however, Servilia picked up a Neapolitan estate for next to nothing.

Also about this time Antony divorced his straying wife Antonia and, perhaps at Caesar's urging, married the thirty-eight-year-old Fulvia, another of the politically active and strong-willed women who moved among the wealthiest and most powerful men in Rome. Fulvia was wealthy in her own right, as well as being descended from two old Consular families. In the words of Plutarch, she was "a woman who took no interest in spinning or managing a household, nor could she be content to rule a husband who had no ambition for public life: her desire was to govern those who governed or to command a commander-in-chief."[8] Her first husband had been the patrician political agitator Publius Clodius who, after years of rabble-rousing and demagoguery, was the victim of a notorious murder in the street in 52. In the next year Fulvia married another active politician, the Curio who suddenly became an ally of Caesar a few months before he crossed the Rubicon, and who later lost his army and his life in Africa. The marriage of Antony and Fulvia, her third into a noble family, was regarded as a sign that he was reforming his bad habits.

Although Caesar dealt with economic and political issues first, he was more worried about the rebellious legions that had been billeted for months in Campania. He needed them for the African campaign, but they had refused the pleas of their generals to go to Sicily until they were given the land and bonuses promised them after Pharsalus. Caesar first sent a spokesman to negotiate with them and offer further rewards after the campaign, but the troops shouted him down and stoned him, and he barely escaped with his life. A mob of soldiers marched on Rome to confront Caesar, but he refused to see them, and ordered Antony's troops to guard the city gates, as well as his own house. The confrontation turned into a riot, and before it was over, two Senators were dead, and thousands of infantry were bivouacked on the Campus Martius just outside the city.

The following day one of the most famous incidents of Caesar lore unfolded when he appeared suddenly on a platform in front of his troops, and demanded to know what they wanted. Their leaders, knowing that Caesar needed an army for Africa and hoping to pressure him into handing over their bonuses, replied that they wanted their release from service. Caesar's answer was curt and quick: "Why, of course, *Quirites* [Citizens]. What you say is right; you are naturally weary and worn out with wounds,"[9] and then at once released them all. The assembled legionaries absorbed these words in stunned silence. By deliberately calling them citizens instead of soldiers, something just short of an insult, and then abruptly dismissing them, Caesar scornfully declared that he no longer needed them. To complete the psychological ploy, he added that they would receive what rewards they had earned after he had won in Africa, and had celebrated a triumph with other troops. He turned and started down the steps of the platform.

Abashed and ashamed, and afraid that they would share neither the spoils of Africa nor the glory of a triumph, the mutineers shouted apologies and begged Caesar to relent. When he hesitated, there were further entreaties and then calls for the ringleaders to be punished. For a few moments Caesar stood on the steps until the full impact of his words had reached every spectator. Then he returned to the platform to say that he was grieved that it was the legion he had so often honored—the Xth—that had incited the rest. Therefore, he would dismiss this legion alone, and carry out the African campaign without it.

But the men of the Xth were "deeply hurt because Caesar seemed implacable towards them alone, and they requested him to have lots drawn and punish some of their number with death."[10] Caesar, however, having engineered a dramatic change in attitude, and needing every man who could fight, declined to punish any of them, and restored them all to the army. He would not be so forgiving the next time.

After ordering them all to Sicily, he left Rome near the end of November and arrived at Lilybaeum, the Sicilian port used for military expeditions to Africa, on December 17. Although he had his tent pitched on the beach to signal his eagerness to embark, he was forced to wait another week for his ships and troops to arrive and the weather to clear. Because of the shortage of vessels, he again allowed only indispensable baggage on board, and no slaves. Finally, on December 25, he set sail across the strait, followed by a fleet of galleys and sail-powered transports carrying six legions of infantry (five of new recruits and one of veterans), two thousand German, Gallic, and Spanish cavalry, and assorted bowmen from Syria and Crete. Additional troops, grain, and supplies were still being rounded up to follow later.

Against him, King Juba and the Pompeians had assembled fourteen legions of infantry and eighteen thousand cavalry, of whom about ten percent were Gauls and Germans brought from Pharsalus by Labienus, and the rest Numidians. Besides his four legions of Numidian infantry, Juba commanded numerous light-armed auxiliaries, slingers, and archers (mounted and on foot), as well as one hundred and twenty war elephants. Most of the Pompeian troops were quartered at Utica under the command of Metellus Scipio. On the eastern side of the province, Labienus patrolled the coast of today's Gulf of Hamemet with several thousand cavalry and infantry.

True to his habit, Caesar was undismayed by these numbers, according to the unknown author of a narrative titled *Bellum Africum, The African War*, the only surviving account of the campaign. This work was long attributed to Caesar and published with his *Commentaries*, but is clearly the work of another. Scholars speculate that the writer was a junior officer who was present throughout the campaign, but not a member of Caesar's inner circle. Although his vocabulary is limited and his style clumsy and monotonous, he is a keen observer, and his account agrees with the few other references to the war that have survived.

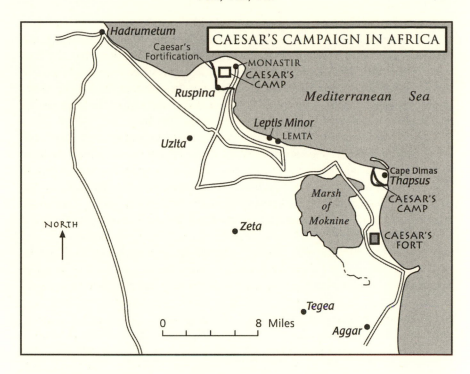

Avoiding the strongly fortified Utica, Caesar made for the southeastern coast and, after a three-day trip, entered, without opposition, the harbor at Hadrumetum, modern Sousse, with a part of his fleet, carrying three thousand infantry and one hundred and fifty Gallic cavalry. Because the town was held by a Roman general with two legions, and enemy cavalry was in the area, Caesar waited only two days for the rest of his fleet and, when it failed to arrive, led his army along the coast to the south. Over the next two days, as the Roman year of 707 ended (what we now call 47 BCE), Caesar moved his army about twenty miles south and camped near the coastal town of Leptis Minor, a mile from today's Lemta.

Because Caesar was careful to prevent any looting or violence against civilians by his troops, the natives and Roman settlers along the way supplied him with grain and other supplies, as did the residents of Leptis Minor. The next day another part of the convoy sailed into the harbor, but it carried less than two legions, bringing Caesar's invasion army to perhaps ten thousand men—still a dangerously small number to engage the enemy. He ordered the transports back to Sicily immediately to pick up more troops, and sent to Sardinia for more grain. He also sent instructions to his best admiral, Publius Vatinius, now freed of his Consular duties, to bring ten warships into the area to search for the rest of the convoy, and defend it against any attacks by Pompeian vessels.

Leaving a garrison of six cohorts at Leptis Minor, Caesar took the rest of his army a few miles back up the coast and built a substantial camp alongside the town of Ruspina on a promontory about two miles inland from the modern port of Monastir. For several more days the Romans waited anxiously for the remainder of the convoy, and occupied themselves with foraging in the countryside for grain. Finally, all but a few of the missing ships made the harbor with four legions of infantry and about two thousand cavalry.

Caesar's invasion army now totaled nearly thirty thousand men and thousands of animals, and he could not expect to feed them very long on the local supplies of grain and fodder. The next day he led a foraging expedition inland from Ruspina with three legions, dozens of archers, and four hundred horse. Before long his scouts reported that a large army was not far away, and shortly afterward a cloud of dust appeared on the horizon. After sending a summons back to camp for the rest of his cavalry and archers, Caesar advanced slowly and soon saw in the distance what proved to be the army of Labienus, the Pompeians' most talented tactician, who was now determined, after three years of war, to finally destroy his former general. To accomplish this, he had brought nearly ten thousand horsemen, including sixteen hundred Gauls and Germans, and eight thousand Numidians, as well as numerous slingers and archers, some mounted, and a large number of Numidian light-armed infantry.

Labienus deployed his infantry and cavalry in "a line of battle of remarkable length" (*The African War* 13.1) so that Caesar was forced to match its length by extending his three legions in a similar single line only a few ranks deep to avoid being flanked. To oppose the strong detachments of cavalry Labienus had put on his wings, he posted his own opposite them and, to delay combat as long as possible, put his archers out in front of everybody. Once the two armies were in position, Caesar simply waited, since he was badly outnumbered and hoping to be reinforced. Then the Pompeian cavalry on each wing began to move out around the ends of Caesar's line, and his own cavalry rode to stop them. At the same time Labienus' horsemen in the middle charged forward, while Numidian infantry moved among them, throwing their javelins. Whenever one of Caesar's cohorts charged, the cavalry retreated and the infantry moved to their left, attacking the advancing legionaries on their unshielded right sides as the cavalry surged forward again.

In response, Caesar ordered his infantry to stay in place, but the Pompeian cavalry on the wings began to drive his horsemen back, and then circle behind his infantry. As a rude ellipse began to form around Caesar's army, Labienus rode up behind his troops, encouraging them and, after taking off his helmet to show who he was, shouting insults into Caesar's ranks. One veteran shouted back, and flung his javelin at him with such force that it felled his horse, and he was thrown, but not injured.

Despite this temporary embarrassment, Labienus was now in a position to achieve his most heartfelt objective, as his Numidians completely surrounded Caesar's smaller army. In a desperate countermeasure, Caesar extended his line even further, until both armies were stretched so thinly across the plain that his troops on the wings were able to break through the cavalry lines that were flanking them, and split the Pompeian army in half. Then he ordered every second cohort to face about and charge the enemy at the rear. This particular maneuver had saved Caesar's Gallic army after an ambush by the Nervii ten years earlier, and according to the writer of *The African War*, it saved him again this time. His infantry was able to push back the light-armed Numidians, break out of the surrounding circle, and inflict heavy losses on Labienus' army.

Caesar was not strong enough to pursue, however, and began a measured withdrawal toward his camp. But before he could reach it, several thousand Numidian cavalry and infantry suddenly burst on the scene, at the head of whom rode Marcus Petreius, another survivor of Pharsalus who had made his way to Africa. It was late in the afternoon of a long day when both Pompeian armies attacked Caesar's rear guard, forcing him to halt and turn his legions to face them. Thousands of horses and men threw themselves against each other for the second time, Caesar riding among his troops, exhorting them to one more effort. None of the three ancient historians who treat the Battle of Ruspina mentions Caesar's reinforcements again, and they differ in their accounts of the battle's conclusion, but they agree that Caesar's troops eventually escaped to their fortified camp, whether because of their own heroic exertions, the early darkness of a late fall day, or the timidity of Petreius, who could count on execution if captured a second time.

After this near disaster, Caesar kept his army close to his camp near Ruspina, and extended its fortified earthworks in two directions to the sea, converting the promontory and its harbor into a secure compound of more than three square miles. Within two weeks of the battle Scipio arrived from Utica with his army of eight legions and three thousand cavalry, and joined Labienus and Petreius at a camp about three miles south of Ruspina. The next day his cavalry was roaming freely outside Caesar's compound, and no one was safe outside it without a heavy escort. Although he possessed ships and a harbor, Caesar was essentially pinned against the coast in the same position that he had occupied in Alexandria the year before—holding a narrow edge of coastline and waiting for reinforcements.

A short time later Scipio was the recipient of thirty-two African elephants that King Juba sent to him instead of coming himself, as he was occupied with an outlaw army that had invaded his kingdom. It seems, however, that Juba kept his experienced elephants and sent Scipio a group that had only recently been captured, and were not fit for use in battle. Elephants, both African and Indian, had been used in warfare for centuries by a variety of ancient armies, with mixed results. They were often deployed with great success to frighten opposing troops, especially horses, and could be fitted with a turret—a boxlike structure attached to the back—in which three or four archers or spearmen could stand and send their missiles down into enemy ranks. But elephants required careful training to accustom them to battle conditions and prevent them from stampeding when struck by missiles. After covering most of the elephants' bodies with light armor and padding, Scipio's men subjected them to a volley of stones from the front, and when they turned and ran, again peppered them from the other direction. Only by this laborious process, which sometimes took months, were they made ready for battle, and even then it was risky to use them.

About the third week in January, there was a dramatic improvement in Caesar's situation when a convoy he had been anxiously awaiting arrived in the harbor. Besides merchant ships filled with grain, hundreds of transports landed with the veteran XIIIth and XIV Legions, eight hundred Gallic cavalry, and a thousand archers and slingers. Caesar quickly sent the empty ships back for more troops, this time with orders to comb Italy for elephants.

Near the end of January, after a month in Africa, Caesar mounted his first offensive against Scipio with an army of nearly nine legions, including five of recruits, but with less than five thousand cavalry and auxiliary troops. Leading the entire army out of camp at Ruspina soon after midnight, he proceeded down the coast, then turned inland, and approached a line of hills that faced the town of Uzita, later called Uceta, and the camp of Scipio about a mile away. The Pompeians had fortified the town and had garrisoned it with Numidian troops. Labienus and his cavalry occupied another camp a few miles to the south and had established an outpost on the southernmost hill nearest their camp. While it was still dark, Caesar's troops took possession of the first three hills, all unoccupied, and before they could rest, he had them construct a three-mile-long earthwork across the front of the slope, halfway up, facing the town and the Pompeian camp.

Over the next two weeks, as Caesar moved his camp every few days, trying to gain a better position and edge closer to Scipio, his troops experienced the nadir of the African campaign. They had to build new earthworks and fortifications in each place, and so were constantly busy. Because they had sailed from Sicily without baggage and without slaves, very few had proper tents, and most slept under makeshift shelters of clothes or reeds that they had to put up themselves. Several heavy rainstorms, followed by hail and flooding, knocked down and washed away their tents, put out their fires, and ruined their food.

Aside from these hardships, Caesar's troops were apprehensive about the approach of King Juba with an enormous army to reinforce Scipio and Labienus. Instead of reassuring them, Caesar chose to heighten their fears, taking a calculated risk that the reality would not live up to the rumor: "You may take it from me that the King will be here within a few days, at the head of ten infantry legions, thirty thousand cavalry, a hundred thousand lightly-armed troops, and three hundred elephants. . . . You may as well stop asking questions and making guesses. I have given you the facts."[11]

He was borne out in his gamble when Juba arrived about the middle of February with three legions, eight hundred Gallic and Spanish cavalry, many Numidian horsemen and light-armed infantry, and thirty elephants. But Caesar's troops were plainly relieved at the sight of the vaunted Numidian army, and over the next several weeks desertions of many of Scipio's troops, and even some of Juba's officers and cavalrymen encouraged them further.

In the meantime, the IXth and Xth Legions, which had finally mustered at Lilybaeum, boarded their transports and set out from Sicily, while Caesar deployed forty war galleys in two fleets to find and escort them to port. It is probable that this convoy carried a number of elephants that Caesar's agents had rounded up from various *municipia* in Italy that kept them for entertainment. He ordered them fitted out with armor and turrets, and then gradually exposed to the army so that his troops and horses could become used to their appearance, their scent, and their trumpeting. Archers, slingers, and spearmen were shown how to attack them at the spots where they were vulnerable.

With the arrival of the troublesome Xth Legion, it came out that one of its tribunes, Gaius Avienus, had filled an entire vessel with his own slaves and pack animals, contrary to Caesar's orders. Caesar used this infraction as an excuse to muster all his officers and tribunes and publicly dismiss Avienus from the army, along with several others who had been active in the mutiny. After assigning them "only a single slave each" (*The African War* 54.9), he put them all on board a ship for Italy.

Around the middle of March, after spending six weeks threatening Uzita, Caesar abandoned his camp and took his entire army about twenty miles southeast to the vicinity of Aggar, an unidentified town near the coast in the middle of a fertile area where wheat, olives, vines, and figs were abundant. The three allied generals followed a few miles behind him, and for the next two weeks they and Caesar played a cat-and-mouse game of ambushes, feints, and night marches among half a dozen towns in the dry hilly country to the south and east of a broad and shallow salt water lake, today called the Marsh of Moknine, lying just inland from the sea. Each army's movements were dictated by its need for water, for grain and fodder, and above all for any position that would give it an advantage in battle.

Late in March another convoy reached Leptis Minor with four hundred cavalry, a thousand archers and slingers, and another four thousand infantry. Caesar now had, aside from those in garrison, thirty-five thousand infantry, four thousand cavalry with their auxiliaries, and two thousand archers and slingers. Although still outnumbered, he confronted the Pompeian generals with his entire army, but they were unwilling to fight except with a commanding advantage.

At the end of March Caesar conceived a plan that would force the allies not only to fight, but to do so within such a limited area that the seemingly numberless Numidian cavalry could not spread out and surround him. Between the eastern edge of the Lake of Moknine (today, Marsh of Moknine) and the seacoast, the town of Thapsus, a Pompeian stronghold and supply depot, perched on a promontory now called Ras, or Cape, Dimas. The lake blocked access to the town except by way of a corridor less than two miles wide running north and south along the coast.

Departing his camp at midnight to gain a few hours on the Pompeians, Caesar marched his entire army to the southern end of the coastal strip and then eight miles along the eastern edge of the lake to Thapsus, which elected to defend itself rather than surrender. After deploying his fleet to blockade the harbor at Thapsus, he camped just inland from the town, which was less than a square mile in area, and enclosed it with a crescent-shaped ditch and earth embankment from beach to beach.

The same morning, the three allied generals decamped and pursued him in an effort to prevent the capture of Thapsus. After spending the night in two camps about eight miles south of the town, they found their route along the coastal corridor to Thapsus blocked at its narrowest place by a fort manned by three of Caesar's cohorts. Seeing a chance to surround Caesar, Scipio detached his army and circled around the lake to attack him from the north, leaving Juba and his army in one camp and Afranius and Labienus with their cavalry in another at the south end of the lake. Again, Caesar was holding a narrow edge of coastline against a larger army, this one poised to attack him from two directions at once.

When he confirmed that the allies had divided their army, as expected, Caesar put veteran troops on board a portion of his warships and sent them along the coast north of Thapsus with orders to anchor close to shore, and to land in Scipio's rear when he signaled them. Leaving two legions of recruits to guard his camp, he then marched with the remainder of his infantry and cavalry a mile or so north between the lake and the coast. There he found most of the men of Scipio's eight legions deployed across the narrow corridor, although many troops were absent from the line and working feverishly to complete the camp entrenchments in the rear. On each of his wings Scipio had posted a troop of cavalry, as well as thirty-two elephants accoutered for warfare with armor and turrets. Caesar deployed his own legions in the customary three lines, with his newest recruits in the middle, and the veteran legions IX and X on the right, XIII and XIV on the left, and V, supported by archers and slingers, occupying an oblique fourth line on each flank to confront the elephants.

Caesar walked among his men, praising his veterans and reminding them of their gallant victories in the past, and encouraging the recruits to emulate their comrades and earn the same praise. As he was finishing his remarks, and waiting for the left end of his line to get into position, his commanders and his bodyguard urged him to signal the attack, as Scipio's troops were obviously in a state of agitation about the incomplete camp, and many had returned to work on it. Refusing to be rushed, Caesar shouted that he would not move until the line was ready, when

a trumpeter on the right wing, under pressure from the soldiers, suddenly began to sound the signal without orders from Caesar. The result was that the standards of all the cohorts began to move forward against the enemy, although the centurions turned round to face them and physically restrained their men from joining battle contrary to their commander-in-chief's orders—but to no avail. (*The African War* 82.3–4)

As it was futile to hold the troops any longer, Caesar signaled his assent to the attack, and rode up behind the front line as his infantry ran forward with their javelins poised. At the same moment Scipio's thousands of men and animals advanced against the front, and Caesar's archers and slingers on the flanks let loose a volley of arrows, stones, and lead bullets directly at the elephants. "At this the animals, terrified by the whistling of the slings and the impact of the stones and leadshot, turned about, trampled on the thickly packed ranks of their own men behind them, and rushed into the half-built gateways in the rampart" (*The African War* 83.2).

Within minutes the Numidian cavalry beside them, deprived of their protective mass, turned and galloped away, and Scipio's infantry, fearful of being overrun with no safe refuge behind them, halted their charge and edged backward. As Caesar's troops surged forward, Scipio's retreated, and then turned and ran for their camp, where men, horses, and elephants all struggled to get through the gates. Also at the gates were Caesar's pursuing infantry, who swarmed into the camp and massacred everyone they could catch, the great bulk of the Pompeians fleeing back around the lake along the route they had taken the day before.

While many of Caesar's legionaries chased them, the rest hurried back past the town and down the southern corridor, and attacked the two Pompeian camps at the south end of the lake. By the time Scipio's fleeing infantry reached Afranius' camp several hours later, they found him and Labienus gone, and the camp abandoned. Hurrying to Juba's camp, they found that he and his army had also disappeared, and Caesar's men in control of it. With no one to lead them (Scipio had disappeared) and no place to hide, the thousands of remaining Pompeians retreated to a nearby hill and signaled their surrender by lowering their weapons.

Far from capturing them, however, Caesar's legionaries, angered and frustrated by the arduous campaign, set upon them in a frenzy, and apparently slaughtered them all under Caesar's eyes, even as he begged them to spare them. The massacre of the Pompeians at Thapsus was the first time Caesar's troops had run amok against other Romans, and they even killed some of their own officers who they thought were collaborators. In all, ten thousand men in the allied armies died on the battlefield; the rest (there is no mention of prisoners), including all their generals, fled into the countryside to the west. Even though Caesar's reported loss of only fifty men is not credible, the Battle of Thapsus remains one of his most complete and stunning victories. Although he benefited, as he had in Spain, from his opponents' miscalculations and divided command, his adroit use of his troops and, finally, his inspired choice of the restricted terrain between the Lake of Moknine and the sea gave him the advantage he needed. Having divided a larger army in two and then luring each half into battle where it had no room to fight, he defeated it by attacking its most unstable element with troops he had trained for that purpose. Elephants were never again used in an African war, and gradually disappeared from ancient armies.

Caesar made one last effort to frighten the Pompeians inside Thapsus into surrender by arraying his captured elephants in front of the town walls, all fully equipped and armored. But after his personal appeal to the commander went unanswered, he dropped the effort and the next day paraded his army, giving cash rewards to his veterans and decorations for gallantry and merit to those who deserved them. He ordered three legions to blockade the town and sent two others against another Pompeian holdout to the south. With the flight of the allied armies and their leaders, there was now only one obstacle to his recapture of the province that Curio had lost some thirty months earlier. Nearly all the fleeing officers and troops were headed in the direction of the Pompeian stronghold at Utica, which, under the command of Marcus Cato, could be expected to mount a serious defense. Caesar dispatched a troop of cavalry ahead and started toward Utica with five legions of infantry.

XIII

The Last Campaign

In the days following the Battle of Thapsus in early April of 46—midwinter by the solar calendar—cold and rainy weather covered the African province. The numerous routes across the plains and hills were thronged with horsemen and foot soldiers hurrying north and west to whatever refuge they could find. The fleeing troops were, for the most part, without their officers and commanders, the four Pompeian generals having abandoned their troops and fled with small parties of horsemen in different directions.

The commander-in-chief, Metellus Scipio, whose legions had been routed near the coast, made his way to one of the ports to the north with some of his officers, and commandeered several warships to take them to Spain. Marcus Petreius cast his lot with King Juba, who fled with his horsemen directly to his kingdom, Numidia, and to his stronghold about eighty miles south of Utica, Zama Regia, a place that can no longer be identified. There the residents locked the gates and refused them admittance, not only because they had lost the war, but because Juba, when he had set out to fight Caesar, had threatened, if he lost, to burn all his treasure and possessions, as well as all the town's inhabitants, his family, and himself, on a huge pyre he had built in the center of town. After several days of futile pleading, and when the townspeople would not even release his family to him, he and Petreius retreated to one of his estates in the countryside.

At the same time hundreds of Pompeian fugitives arrived at Utica, and Cato, in command of the garrison, urged them and the residents to arm themselves and prepare to defend the city. But the residents and merchants of Utica had favored Caesar, and when they expressed a reluctance to fight him, most of the Pompeians, especially the Senators and their families, began preparations for their escape. When Cato realized that there would be no defense of the city, he bent his efforts to finding ships for those who wished to use them, but chose to stay himself. Caesar's Pompeian cousin, Lucius Caesar, proposed that he approach his kinsman and plead for their lives, but Cato would have no part of it, saying, "I do not wish to be beholden to the tyrant for one of his unlawful acts; and it is unlawful for him to spare, as though he were their master, the lives of men over whom he has no right to rule."[1]

Cato's calm demeanor and lack of fear impressed those around him, but when the discussion turned to Stoic philosophy, they and his son Marcus, perhaps about twenty-one at the time, became alarmed that he intended suicide, and hid his sword as a precaution. After a leisurely dinner and conversation with his friends, Cato retired to his room, taking with him a copy of the *Phaedo*, Plato's description of the last hours of Socrates, the most famous suicide in the ancient world. When he found his sword missing and demanded its return, his son and others rushed in and embraced him, and begged him not to think of taking his life. Far from reassuring them, he complained that instead of reasoning with him they were treating him as if he were insane, and preventing him from using his own judgment. At his insistence they all finally left, some in tears, none of them convinced that it was safe to leave him alone. Later in the night he persuaded a slave to return his sword, and then stabbed himself below the breastbone.

When a servant was alarmed by a noise from Cato's room, he aroused the household, and they all hurried in to find him on the floor, open-eyed and alive, but with a bloody gash across his stomach, from which his intestines were protruding. They brought in a doctor who restored the intestines, stitched up the wound, and applied bandages. Cato remonstrated with himself for his feeble blow, but allowed them to treat him, then thanked them for their attentiveness, and said he would sleep. " They then went away, taking his sword. . . . But although he gave the impression he was asleep, he silently tore the bandages off with his hand and undid the stitches of the injury. Like a wild animal, he enlarged the wound with his nails, opened up his stomach with his fingers, and tore his intestines out, until he died."[2]

Once it became known, the suicide of Cato shocked the Roman world, not only because of the pitiable details, but because he was the most respected and admired of all those involved in the war on either side. In a political climate of expedience, opportunism, and shifting loyalties, his *constantia* was legendary, although some called it obstinacy. Cicero admired his *integritas*, but thought he lacked tact and judgment. He was justly revered for his compassion, yet he stubbornly resisted any weakening of the selfish oligarchy that had ruled Rome for centuries. His choice of death over *clementia* was his last defiant insult to the man he loved to hate. Hearing of the suicide while he was hurrying to Utica, Caesar is said to have remarked, "O Cato, I grudge you your death, for you have grudged me [sparing] your life."[3]

Despite Caesar's frustration, he pardoned all Pompeian officers who approached him and, when he entered Utica about the middle of April, did the same for the townspeople who had opposed him. They did not escape his fine of fifty million *denarii*, however, which he ordered paid in six semiannual installments. It was perhaps not a coincidence that this was the same amount that Pompey had deposited in the state treasury on his return from the East in 62. How Caesar dealt with his distant cousin Lucius, who had served Pompey since the start of the war, is not certain. It appears that he forgave the young

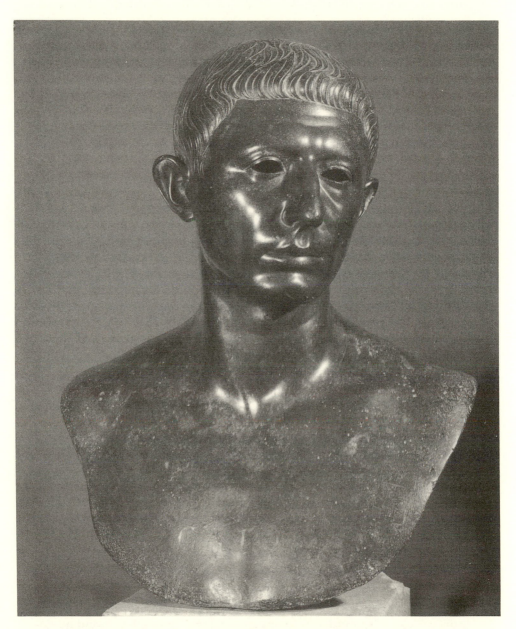

It was not until 1944 that this bronze bust of Cato the Younger, considered an accurate likeness, came to light in North Africa. (Archaeological Museum, Rabat, Morocco. Erich Lessing/Art Resource, NY.)

man, but that some of his soldiers did not, and later murdered him for an alleged offense.

Afranius and Faustus Sulla, after departing Utica with a thousand cavalry, fell into the hands of Publius Sittius, a renegade Roman officer who had fled to Spain to escape his debts fifteen years before, and then to Mauretania, where he had raised an outlaw army. After Caesar's landing in Africa in January, Sittius had allied himself with King Bocchus of Mauretania, and the two had invaded Numidia in support of Caesar, just as King Juba was preparing to join Scipio against him. Now Sittius had captured not only Afranius and Sulla, but Sulla's wife Pompeia, daughter of Pompey, and their children, and he brought them all to Caesar at Utica.

After four campaigns against Caesar, Afranius was still a loser, and his sins were manifest. Sulla and Pompeia were another matter. In the year of his first Consulship Caesar had thwarted their marriage with his scheme to marry his daughter to Pompey, and in 53 had proposed to Pompey that he marry Pompeia himself, Pompey declining. Although Faustus Sulla had fought him at Pharsalus, Caesar may have been willing to pardon him for the sake of his brother Publius, who had been one of his own generals. But he apparently acceded to the demands of his veterans, and ordered both Sulla and Afranius executed. Pompeia and her children he allowed to leave for Spain, to which her brothers, Gnaeus and Sextus, had already escaped.

In the meantime, after Juba and Petreius had been barred from Zama Regia, Caesar rode there with a troop of cavalry and took Juba's four-year-old son into custody. The boy's father and Petreius, both in their sixties, had no troops to defend them and, in fact, could find no one to help them escape. They both knew there would be no pardon, Petreius because he had already been spared in Spain three years earlier, and Juba because it was to him that Curio's head had been carried at the end of the first African campaign. They conceived, and then carried out, a bizarre pact to end their lives with swords, either at each other's hands or by their own, and who killed whom, or if another party took part, is not agreed upon by historians.

Pompey's father-in-law, Metellus Scipio, was aboard ship on his way to Spain with several of his officers when a winter storm drove them into the harbor of Hippo Regius, now Hippone, near Annaba on the Algerian coast. There they were surrounded and attacked by the fleet of Sittius and all their ships were sunk, Scipio reportedly either killing himself or perishing in the battle with all his companions. Another who did not escape was Juba's general Saburra, whose troops had surrounded and killed Curio. He had been left by Juba to defend Numidia, but Sittius attacked and defeated him, and he suffered the same fate as his victim. Caesar rewarded Sittius and King Bocchus by dividing western Numidia between them. Juba's Kingdom of Numidia he added to the African province, and named as its Governor one of his old cronies, Gaius Sallustius Crispus, whose name is preserved as Sallust, the well-known historian of the late Republic. Of the leading Pompeian generals, only the perseverant Labienus and Attius Varus escaped Africa, making their way to Spain, where they joined Pompey's sons.

It was perhaps during the following weeks that Caesar conducted a brief affair with Queen Eunoë of Mauretania, possibly with the consent of her husband, King Bogud, who later brought his army to Caesar's aid in the last battle of the war. Nothing else is known of this matter except Suetonius' report that Caesar gave numerous presents to both Eunoë and Bogud.

In mid-June of 46 Caesar sailed with his army to Sardinia, "one of his properties," a caustic Cicero wrote to Varro, "that he has not yet inspected."[4] From there he dispatched several legions to Spain to support his Governor against the Pompeians. After a long delay due to bad weather, he returned to Rome near the end of July for the fourth time since he had crossed the Rubicon. He had now personally fought and defeated the Pompeians in more than two dozen battles on land and sea in eight different countries, suffering his single serious setback at the end of the siege near Dyrrachium. He had been at war for three and a half years, and entered Rome with an authority over its affairs that no other Roman had ever enjoyed. His Senate accommodated him with a third term as *dictator*, this time for an unprecedented ten years, and declared a thanksgiving period of forty days.

Addressing the Senate and then the people, Caesar assured them of his good intentions, and that he would not behave as Marius and Sulla had when they had come to power. He reminded them that he had harmed no one who had not fought against him, and had even pardoned most who had, some a second time. Although it would be expensive to reward his troops, his conquest of Africa would bring ample supplies of wheat and olive oil to Rome, and there would be no new taxes.

In the following days the Senate, thinking perhaps that it had not done enough, bestowed on him the title of *praefectus moribus*, Prefect of Morals, an enhancement of the old office of Censor. It also commissioned a bronze statue of him to be mounted on a model of the world, as far as it was known, with an inscription identifying him as a demigod, an inscription that he later had removed. To this it added a flock of personal perquisites, such as the privilege of speaking first in the Senate, and of giving the signal at the public games and races held in the Circus Maximus. According to Cassius Dio, many other measures of this type were passed, but presumably they were too outrageous even for Caesar, and he declined them.

The *dictator* responded with his usual magnanimity, issuing pardons to many Pompeians and allowing them to return to Rome and in some cases to keep their property. Cicero, with the advantage of his position midway between the *dictator* and the Pompeians, worked busily to obtain pardons and restitution of property for those who were too fearful to approach Caesar in person; but he was impatient of the obsequies he was forced into on their behalf. To one of them, Quintus Ligarius, who had fought at Pharsalus, and again at Thapsus, but who was barred from Italy, he complained that in order to see Caesar he had to "put up with the humiliating and wearisome prelimi-naries of obtaining admission and interview. Your brothers and relations knelt at his feet, while I spoke in terms appropriate to your case and circumstances."[5]

In one extraordinary scene in the Senate, Caesar's father-in-law, Calpurnius Piso, broached the case of Claudius Marcellus, who, when he was Consul in 51, had sought the termination of Caesar's Gallic command. He had subse-quently fought in Pompey's army and was now languishing in exile at Myti-lene. His cousin Gaius Marcellus, who had bitterly opposed Caesar during his own Consulship in 50, but who had remained in retirement in Italy during the war, fell on his knees before Caesar and tearfully begged forgiveness for his cousin. At this, the entire Senate rose as one man in supplication for the par-don. Perhaps taken aback by this display, Caesar readily granted it, even though he had previously remarked about the acerbity of Claudius.

In the wake of this scene, after several Senators had expressed their personal thanks to Caesar, Cicero took to his feet and broke a six-year public silence by delivering a five-thousand-word speech, later published as *Pro Marcello*, that is notable for its catalog of fulsome flattery. Praising Caesar as an invincible gen-eral and the supreme conqueror of barbarian multitudes, Cicero called him a compassionate victor whose humanity and unheard-of *clementia* were even more admirable. Voicing his regret that his own repeated advocacy of a peace-ful settlement had gone unheeded, he urged Caesar to heal the wounds of war and work to restore the institutions of the Republic and suggested that he owed the country no less. There is no record of Caesar's response, but for the time being he showed no interest in relinquishing even a sliver of his power. It was during this period that he is reported to have remarked that Sulla, hav-ing voluntarily laid down the dictatorship, did not know the first thing about politics.

After a month of preparation, Caesar was at last free to celebrate the tri-umph he had been denied after his modest military success in Spain in 60. But that skirmish against the Celtiberians had now been superseded by a dozen campaigns in two major wars in every part of the Roman world. No Roman had celebrated more than two triumphs except Pompey, who had had his seal ring carved with three trophies to mark his triumphs in Africa (81), Spain (72), and Asia (61), suggesting a conquest of the entire Mediterranean world. In an obvious effort to top him, Caesar claimed, and the Senate approved, four sepa-rate triumphs to be celebrated on four different days for his victories against the Gauls, against the Egyptian King Ptolemy, against the barbarian army of King Pharnaces in Pontus, and against the Numidian King Juba. Because a tri-umph could be earned only by defeating a foreign foe, Caesar presented his Af-rican campaign as a defense of the province against an invasion by Numidia, and ignored the fact that he had injected himself into a civil war in Egypt. In fact, throughout the Civil War Caesar had pointedly refrained from announc-ing his victories over Roman generals and Roman troops, and had not even no-tified the Senate of the outcome of Pharsalus.

Besides the usual parade of Senators, soldiers, booty, prisoners, and musicians, each of the triumphs featured painted wood tableaux and statues depicting scenes and people from the conquered countries. In the Gallic triumph, the first and the most elaborate, the great rivers that Caesar had crossed were represented—the Rhône, the Rhine, and "*Oceanus*," the swiftly flowing river that was thought to circle the world. In the Pontic triumph a painting showing the fleeing King Pharnaces was followed by one bearing the words *veni, vidi, vici*. An image of the Pharos lighthouse was carried in the Egyptian triumph, as well as a painting showing the death of Achillas, murderer of Pompey, which drew jeers from the crowd. According to Appian, the African triumph alone included the death scenes of Pompeian generals, whom Caesar portrayed as joining with a foreign King to attack Roman soldiers. But the tableaux of Scipio stabbing and drowning himself, of Petreius killing himself at his table, and of Cato tearing at his stitches and bandages caused the crowd to groan in sympathy.

Nor were they pleased to see the teenaged Arsinoë, sister of Cleopatra, led through the streets in chains, an unusual sight that aroused great pity, as did the sight of the four-year-old Prince Juba walking among the captives. These two children Caesar later released unharmed; Arsinoë survived only a few years, but Juba II eventually married Cleopatra's daughter by Mark Antony and lived to become a respected historian. Another famous captive who marched in the Gallic triumph, the Arvernian chieftain Vercingetorix, who had waited in a dungeon more than five years since his surrender at Alesia, was not so lucky, and was strangled shortly after his appearance.

Behind the prisoners, in the midst of each procession, Caesar stood—painted, laureled, and crowned—in his triumphal chariot, drawn by four white horses, also wearing crowns, an honor last accorded a *triumphator* more than three hundred years earlier. The other occupant of Caesar's chariot was a slave who held a gold crown over Caesar's head and called out, "Remember that you are just a man," a ritual held over from the Etruscans, who used it to warn their kings of their mortality. Close by Caesar in the procession rode his sister's grandson, Gaius Octavius, now seventeen, whom he was grooming for a career similar to his own.

At the end of the last parade, and over the course of several days, tens of thousands of citizens were invited to sit down at twenty-two thousand tables where they were treated to a banquet of expensive delicacies, such as lampreys, and served imported wines. At a time when about three *denarii* were a day's pay for a laborer, each citizen received one hundred *denarii* and free rations of meat, grain, and olive oil. The greatest rewards Caesar reserved for his troops, who had been separated from their families for more than four years. After promising each of them a farm, he gave each legionary five thousand *denarii*, each centurion twice as much, and each military tribune twenty thousand.

Between and after the triumphal processions, Caesar entertained the Roman public as they had never been before with a variety of *spectacula* offered at different locations around the city. Just as his triumphs had outnumbered Pompey's, so his games and entertainments eclipsed all that had gone before, especially those Pompey had staged at his theater opening in 55. Caesar's engineers created an artificial lake adjacent to the Tiber, where thousands of oarsmen and marines in dozens of warships, dressed and ornamented to represent the navies of Egypt and Tyre, fought a mock naval battle. In the Circus Maximus, which Caesar had restored, as many as fifty thousand spectators watched young noblemen race chariots and horses and, on another occasion, a big-game hunt in which four hundred lions were set free in the central area, separated from the spectators by a water-filled ditch.

The Roman public had an intense interest in exotic wild animals, and had by this time already been shown hippopotamuses, crocodiles, leopards, rhinoceroses, and apes. But Caesar displayed an animal they had never seen—a giraffe, then called a *camelopardus*, a spotted camel, said to have been a gift from Cleopatra:

This animal is like a camel in all respects except that its legs are not all of the same length, the hind legs being the shorter. Beginning from the rump it grows gradually higher, which gives it the appearance of mounting some elevation; and towering high aloft, it supports the rest of its body on its front legs and lifts its neck in turn to an unusual height.[6]

The public's interest in strange animals was exceeded only by its penchant for watching violent fighting of all kinds among men and animals. Usually these were mock battles, such as one that Caesar staged in the Circus in which five hundred infantry, thirty cavalry, and twenty elephants fought on each side. But Caesar's games would have been a failure had he not offered (in honor of his daughter Julia) the customary fights to the death among gladiators, who had been housed and trained for the purpose. These usually took place among captives and others condemned to death, but in one display two Roman *equites* accoutered as gladiators fought to the death in the Forum itself in single combat.

Historians think that it was at about this time that Queen Cleopatra, her year-old son Caesarion, her twelve-year-old husband King Ptolemy XIV, and her royal court and retinue arrived in Rome at Caesar's bidding. The *dictator* installed her and her household in his villa outside the city limits on the far side of the Tiber, modern Trastevere, presumably to spare Calpurnia embarrassment. But it is possible that she and her party were spectators at the triumphs and entertainments of 46, and more likely that she was present at one of the more remarkable building dedications in the history of the Republic. Beginning as early as 54, while Caesar was in Gaul, his agents had been buying up property in the neighborhood of the Forum, and construction had begun on a building for the courts, the Basilica Julia, and on a new Senate House, the Curia Julia, both obviously intended to challenge Pompey's complex of buildings a few hundred yards away. Caesar's major architectural statement, however, was his Forum Julium, a large rectangular space fully two hundred yards in length, enclosed on three sides by buildings and arcades set off by columns of white marble from the new quarry at Carrara. On the fourth side stood a Corinthian-style temple, also of marble, dedicated to his legendary ancestor, Venus Genetrix, Venus the Mother, and in it stood her statue, as yet unfinished.

Statues of gods were nothing new in Rome, but what was unprecedented was that Caesar ordered a gilt-bronze statue of Cleopatra placed beside that of Venus Genetrix, clearly associating her with the founder and protecting Goddess of the Julian *gens*. The incident is significant in that Caesar not only implied that the Egyptian Queen was to be a part of his family, but also elevated a human being, for the first time in Rome, to the level of a goddess. Unusual as it was in Rome, this was in accord with Cleopatra's portrayal of herself in Egypt as a living incarnation of the Goddess Isis—the equivalent of Aphrodite to her Greek subjects, and of Venus to the Romans. For all that was suggested, there is no surviving record of any objection to Cleopatra's statue, and when the ceremony ended after dusk, a large crowd accompanied a flower-bedecked Caesar along the Sacred Way to the *domus publica*, escorted by a line of elephants carrying torches in their trunks.

Ironically, in the atmosphere of this indulgence, Caesar at the same time ordered the city's landlords to survey the number of citizens receiving free grain and then, presumably finding many foreigners and ineligible slaves on the lists, reduced it by more than half, setting an arbitrary limit of one hundred and fifty thousand receipients. He also imposed a set of sumptuary laws designed to curb the conspicuous luxuries that had become habitual among wealthy Romans. These included limits on the cost of burial monuments, and rules against wearing purple garments, displaying pearls, riding in litters (with exceptions for young women), and consuming certain rare and expensive foods. "To implement his laws against luxury he placed inspectors in different parts of the market to seize delicacies offered for sale in violation of his orders; sometimes he even sent lictors and guards into dining rooms to remove illegal dishes, already served, which his watchmen had failed to intercept."[7] Such laws had a long history in Roman society, but they were no more effective under Caesar than they had been in the past, and he admitted that once he was out of the country, they were rarely enforced.

The reform that was by far the most important to the modern world (and the only one to endure) was Caesar's correction of the Roman calendar to conform, and to remain in conformity, with the solar year and the four seasons. On the advice of the Greek astronomer Sosigenes, Caesar decreed a new year of 365¼ days to begin the following January, and instituted a new calendar of four thirty-day and seven thirty-one-day months, and a twenty-eight-day February to be augmented by a single day every four years. The month of Mercedonius having already been added during 46, he ordered another sixty-seven days inserted between November and December, lengthening the year to 445 days.

What came to be called the Julian calendar began on January 1 of the Roman year 709 *ab urbe condita,* within a day of what we now calculate was January 1 of the year 45 before the birth of Christ. Caesar's new calendar was inscribed on stone (fragments of some forty copies survive), and displayed in public places throughout Italy and the provinces. The new Julian year proved to be only eleven minutes longer than the actual solar year calculated by modern astronomers, and the calendar, with a minor correction in the sixteenth century to omit certain leap-year adjustments, remains in use today.

In the fall of 46, after a busy summer of honors, triumphs, entertainments, dedications, and legislation, Caesar was called upon to deal with one more threat, this time from the sons of Pompey and their allies in Spain. After the surrender of Varro in the fall of 49, Caesar had installed Quintus Cassius as Governor of Further Spain. Cassius proved to be so greedy and corrupt that within a year most of the people of means in his province detested him, and many of his troops began transferring their allegiance to new commanders, one of whom declared his intention to regain the province for Pompey.

After surviving an assassination attempt, Cassius appealed for help to King Bogud of Mauretania and to Lepidus, Governor of Nearer Spain, both of whom sent troops to oppose the mutineers, who by now comprised nearly three legions. The generals reached a stalemate after some desultory fighting in the region just south of Corduba, and just as Gaius Trebonius arrived from Rome to replace him, Cassius was allowed, by common consent, to leave the province. He began a dangerous sea voyage to Rome from Malaca, modern Malaga, in February of 47 with a cargo of money and booty, reaching Tarraco on the eastern coast a few days later. The next day, while attempting to leave the harbor in rough weather, he was caught between heavy ocean swells and the strong current from the Ebro River. When his ship foundered in the river's mouth, he drowned.

Trebonius brought the province under his tentative control, but the mutinous commanders feared that Caesar would eventually punish them, and secretly sent a plea to Scipio in Africa for assistance. Later in the year, just before Caesar landed in Africa, Scipio responded by dispatching thirty ships and two thousand conscripted troops toward Spain under the command of Pompey's elder son Gnaeus. This army sailed from Utica along the coast and, after attacking a town in Mauretania and being driven off, landed in the Balearic Islands opposite Nearer Spain and captured them. But Gnaeus fell ill, and his troops were still there in April of 46 when news of the loss of Africa reached the Pompeian sympathizers in Further Spain. When this was followed two months later by word that Caesar had dispatched several legions in their direction, they ousted Trebonius and began organizing a Pompeian army to seize the province.

In the meantime, the fugitives from Africa—Sextus Pompey, Attius Varus, Labienus, and the few troops following them—were arriving in the neighborhood of Corduba, and joined the newly formed army. When Gnaeus Pompey finally recovered, he joined the other Pompeians, who elected him their commander. The combined army, augmented by hundreds of Roman soldiers who had surrendered with Afranius in 49, now amounted to thirteen legions, four of which were veteran (two had deserted Cassius), while the rest were made up of refugees, freed slaves, and new conscripts. With this army the Pompeians took control of most of the province, while Caesar's generals in the area, Quintus Pedius (his nephew) and Quintus Fabius Maximus, avoided battle and sent a series of couriers to Rome with requests for assistance.

Caesar had hoped that his troops in Spain could dispose of the Pompeians without his help, and for several months only sent reinforcements, but when the pleas became more urgent, finally determined to go himself. Early in November of 46, after placing Italy in the charge of Marcus Lepidus as Master of the Horse, he left for Spain by land with a troop of horsemen. Apparently alerting nobody that he was coming, and traveling at a grueling pace of fifty miles a day, he surprised ally and foe alike when he arrived in southern Spain twenty-seven days later. Five legions of infantry followed him, and three awaited him in Spain, as well as some light-armed local infantry and thousands of horsemen that had been recruited in the region.

The single surviving contemporary account of the second Spanish campaign is a narrative titled *Bellum Hispaniense, The Spanish War*, an anonymous work that has been called "perhaps the most illiterate and exasperating book in classical literature."[8] It is marred by numerous colloquial expressions, a limited vocabulary, and uncertain grammar that leaves many passages unintelligible. The author was apparently a combatant in Caesar's army below the officer level who had little understanding of the overall campaign or strategy, but a detailed knowledge of individual events and battle sites. His literary shortcomings, however, are counterbalanced by the high value of his eyewitness account.

Gnaeus Pompey had established his main depot at Corduba, the provincial capital, and had assigned his younger brother Sextus to hold it with two legions. With the rest of his army Gnaeus laid siege to Ulia, now called Monte Mayor, about seventeen miles to the south, a stronghold that had remained loyal to Caesar. To lure Gnaeus into battle, Caesar approached Corduba from the south, but found his way blocked by the Baetis River, now the Guadalquivir, a hundred yards wide and too deep to ford. With the only bridge controlled by the enemy, Caesar built a second bridge downstream from the first, crossed the river, and deployed his troops in three camps around the walls of the city. Sextus sent word to his brother that he needed help, and Gnaeus, on the point of capturing Ulia, abandoned the siege and hurried north to Corduba.

When he arrived, he camped south of the river, and Caesar attempted to build an entrenchment to deny him access to the permanent bridge and to Corduba, Gnaeus building his own to head Caesar off. After numerous skirmishes between the armies in which many were killed, Caesar tried to provoke

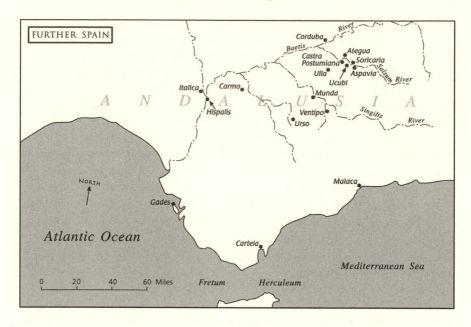

Gnaeus to fight a larger action, but the latter refused, knowing that his green troops could not stand up to Caesar's veterans. Caesar finally decided that he could not take Corduba without a prolonged siege and led his army back across the bridge by night, leaving his camp fires burning and Gnaeus unaware of where he was going. By morning he reached another Pompeian stronghold, Ategua, the remains of which have been found on a hill now called Teba la Vieja about fourteen miles southeast of Corduba.

Ategua, which was known to have a large supply of grain, was also heavily defended, and occupied a strong position overlooking the plain of the Salsum River, now called the Guadajoz. Caesar's troops encircled it with a ditch and bank, and began constructing a terrace of logs similar to that at Massilia so that a battering ram could be put to its walls. It was only when this work had begun that Gnaeus learned where Caesar had gone, and even then he chose not to pursue him, instead entering Corduba to resupply his troops and give them some respite from the bitter winter weather. But a day or two later he brought his army through the hills to the vicinity of Ategua and attacked one of Caesar's outposts under cover of a thick morning mist, inflicting many casualties. He refrained, however, from approaching the town or provoking a serious battle.

Meanwhile Caesar's *catapultae* were bombarding Ategua from every direction, and the defenders, without artillery of their own, were vainly trying to set fire to his towers and terrace. When they realized that Gnaeus was not attacking the besiegers, the townspeople clamored to surrender, but the Pompeian troops refused, afraid that they would be massacred. Nevertheless, when Caesar's sappers demolished a section of the wall, several surrender offers emanated from the town. Caesar rejected them all, even though his troops were still unable to break in. The dissension within the town led the commander to condemn those who urged surrender, and to order them all butchered, and their bodies thrown over the wall. This was only one example of the cruelty in which both sides indulged during this campaign, with numerous spies, scouts, messengers, and random civilians suffering stabbing, crucifixion, beheading, cut throats, or loss of their hands. But the failure of all the defenders' attempts to set fire to the siegeworks or to break out of the town, and the inability of Gnaeus to force Caesar to lift the siege, finally persuaded the garrison commander to give up. Caesar accepted his terms, and on February 19 took possession of Ategua after a siege of four weeks.

During the next month Gnaeus and his legions retreated to the southwest, maneuvering among the hills of the region now called Andalusia, while he sent messages to various towns exhorting them to resist Caesar. But he refused a head-on battle and confined himself to hit-and-run cavalry attacks and nighttime skirmishes. As his dwindling prospects gradually became apparent throughout the area, several towns simply refused to admit him, more than one of which he ordered burned. But as town after town surrendered to Caesar, morale in Gnaeus' army fell so low that desertions to Caesar became common, including many officers.

About the middle of March Gnaeus brought his army to a plain below the fortified hill town of Munda, and built his camp on the rising ground outside its walls. Caesar followed him and camped on the plain about five miles away, on the other side of a stream that ran across it.

Among the most famous of Civil War sites, Munda's location has been debated by historians and archaeologists for at least a hundred years. In the 1970s a team of Spanish archaeologists concluded that the ruins of Alhonoz, a fortress on a deserted hill about thirty-five miles due south of Corduba, marked the site of the ancient town. The hill overlooks the Río Genil, called in Roman times the Singilis River, which crosses a broad plain, and in this, as well as in all other topographical details, the site agrees with the description given in *The Spanish War*.[9]

In his position on the rising ground before Munda, with the walled town accessible behind him, Gnaeus had probably picked the best locale to fight the battle with Caesar that he knew he must. Although some of his eleven legions were of questionable quality (two remained at Corduba), he had a core group of trained Roman infantry who had deserted Cassius or had crossed to Spain after Thapsus. To support them, he had about six thousand light infantrymen, nearly as many auxiliary troops, and perhaps another six thousand cavalry under the command of Labienus. Accompanying this army of perhaps seventy thousand fighting men were the usual thousands of grooms, slaves, and servants.

On the other side of the plain, Caesar commanded eight legions, of which four were veterans of several campaigns, two others had fought in Africa, and two were of recruits. Nine thousand cavalry, including a corps of Numidians brought to Spain by King Bogud, and an unknown number of auxiliary infantry rounded out Caesar's fighting force at somewhat less than sixty thousand men.

According to the author of *The Spanish War*, the weather was calm and sunny on the day after Caesar reached the plain—March 17, according to the new Julian calendar. He was preparing to move on, perhaps to besiege Urso, modern Osuna, about a day's march away, when his scouts reported that Gnaeus had arrayed his army in battle formation on the slope in front of Munda long before dawn. Just as his father had at Pharsalus, he invited Caesar to advance and fight uphill, and this time Caesar did not hesitate, immediately ordering the flag displayed to signal a battle. During the next several hours he brought his army two or three miles across the plain and stopped at the modest river running through the middle of it. There he waited for the Pompeian army to descend to level ground, but Gnaeus was not as bold as his father had been, or perhaps was not beset with the same advice, and his troops remained on the slope.

With the right side of his line anchored by the Xth Legion, and the rest of the army, including the IIIrd and the Vth Legions, deployed to the left of them, Caesar continued through marshy ground, crossed the stream, and approached the base of the foothills where Gnaeus' army waited. There he called a halt, greatly frustrating the men in the front line, who were eager to attack. In the words of the eyewitness soldier, "The delay made the enemy keener, thinking that it was fear which prevented Caesar's forces joining battle" (*The Spanish War* 30.5). Suddenly thousands of Gnaeus' troops, no doubt impatient after hours of waiting, rushed, shouting, down the hill, as Caesar's charged upward, bellowing with zeal for the pitched battle they had sought for months.

No less than ten ancient historians devote at least a sentence, some several paragraphs, to the Battle of Munda, but they all appear to derive from just two eyewitness accounts, that of Aulus Hirtius, which is lost, and that of the anonymous author of *The Spanish War*. Although there are contradictions among them, there is agreement that the battle, which raged undecided for several hours, may have been the most fiercely fought of the entire Civil War. Most report some version of a story that Caesar, when he saw his line giving way and the battle slipping out of control, jumped from his horse, tore off his helmet, and rushed into the ranks "like a madman . . . where he seized hold of those who were fleeing . . . and dashed this way and that through the ranks with glances, gestures, and shouts" to rally his men.[10] According to Appian, he snatched a shield from a soldier and ran toward the enemy, shouting to his officers that if they were defeated, "this will be the end of my life and of your campaigns."[11]

This display seemed to inspire his troops, and when the men of the Xth Legion began to force the enemy back, Caesar ordered King Bogud and his Numidian horsemen to attack on the Pompeian left flank, perhaps sending them directly toward Gnaeus' camp. In response to this, Labienus, in command on his right flank, detached several cohorts of infantry and sent them across the rear of the Pompeian line to hold off the cavalry. This movement behind them caused those in Gnaeus' front line to think that a retreat was under way, and they gradually began to withdraw. Caesar pressed his advantage by urging his men to attack again, and the withdrawal mushroomed into a confused and headlong rush to escape. As the Pompeians fled in a crowd to their camp and into the town, Caesar's troops pursued and slaughtered them by the thousands, until the only survivors were those barricaded inside Munda. The anonymous writer on the scene reports that his fellow soldiers piled up a rampart of corpses around the fortress, fixing the javelins and shields of the dead on its top, and impaling their heads on swords, to frighten those inside into surrender. In the aftermath, only a few horsemen escaped—among them Gnaeus Pompey.

For the fourth time in the war, and the second time in Spain, Caesar had totally routed a Pompeian army, the deaths mounting on each occasion, this time including those of Attius Varus and the persistent Labienus. The outcome was no doubt heavily influenced by the lack of experience and poor morale of Gnaeus' troops. But once again, just as at Pharsalus and at Thapsus, Caesar's generalship was a crucial element, although, just as at Ruspina and in the harbor of Alexandria, he may have relied too heavily on his *fortuna*. He is reported to have admitted as he left the battlefield that he had often before struggled for victory, but that this was the first time he had had to fight for his life. He did not know that it would be his last battle of any kind.

There are no reliable casualty statistics from Munda, the thirty-three thousand Pompeian, and one thousand Caesarian, dead reported in *The Spanish War* being discounted by historians, but there were enough to make it one of the costliest battles of the war for both sides. The subsequent mop-up and pursuit followed the pattern of previous victories. After seeing to it that Varus and Labienus were buried properly, Caesar left an officer to besiege Munda, and then marched to Corduba, where he found that Sextus had fled, leaving those inside the city divided on the question of surrender. A brief siege, abetted by Caesarian sympathizers within, was sufficient to breach the gates and allow his troops to conduct another slaughter, sparing some for slavery.

From Corduba Caesar hurried off to attack Hispalis, some seventy miles down the Baetis River. After the Pompeian garrison refused to surrender, Caesar surrounded the city and prepared for a siege, but he was concerned about the destruction that an extended battle might cause. He relaxed the siege somewhat, allowing the defenders to conduct raids outside the walls. He then sent his cavalry to surround and kill them, and thus captured the city intact. From there he proceeded further down the river to Gades, which he also captured after a short battle. Shortly afterward the garrisons at Munda and Urso capitulated, as did the other major towns in the province.

In the meantime, Gnaeus had reached his naval base at Carteia, about four miles east of modern Gibraltar, but found his supporters there in such a state that he did not trust them to carry him to safety. He finally set out in a small boat, but sustained a wound to his foot in an accident, and had to go ashore. A party of Caesar's cavalry picked up his trail and pursued him into the woods, where he took refuge in a cave after exhaustion and his injury allowed him to go no further. When they found him, he refused to surrender, and they killed him. A few days later, when Caesar returned to Hispalis after receiving the surrender of Gades, he found the head of Gnaeus Pompey *filius* displayed in the square.

With this grisly image of his opponent still fresh in the minds of his audience, Caesar summoned an assembly of the people and delivered a lengthy scolding for their ingratitude. He complained bitterly that after his many kindnesses to the province in 69 when he was *quaestor*, again when he was Consul, and finally when he had defeated the Pompeians in 49, they had responded by attempting to murder and then overthrowing Cassius, and then sheltering and supporting the Pompey brothers. Unfortunately, the text of *The Spanish War* breaks off abruptly just as Caesar reaches the height of his tirade. Other historians tell us, however, that he refrained from pillaging or killing, limiting his penalties to heavy fines, confiscations of land and valuables, and the sale of prisoners into slavery. The pursuit of Sextus, who had managed to escape entirely, he left to one of his lieutenants. Pompey's last son, however, was never captured, and before long had rallied an army of diehard Pompeians and was harassing provincial towns on the east coast.

A few weeks later Caesar was joined in Spain by Gaius Octavius, who had been too ill to accompany him to Spain the previous winter. During the following month, before they began the trip to Rome, the two of them traveled throughout both provinces, Caesar receiving renewed assurances of loyalty in various cities. At Carthago Nova, modern Cartagena on the southern coast, as well as at several other towns in both provinces, Caesar made plans to establish colonies to which he would send thousands of indigent Romans for the purpose of easing congestion and reducing public expenditures in the capital.

At some time during the Spanish campaign, perhaps in the weeks after the battle of Munda, Caesar composed the last literary work he would offer to the public, an angry polemic in response to a work issued by Cicero the previous year. At the urging of Marcus Brutus, Cicero had composed and published an extended eulogy of Cato (widely read, but no longer extant) in which he praised his foresight, his efforts to prevent the war, and his courage for refusing to accept its outcome. He described "the hero of Utica" as one of the few men who was greater than his reputation. Two other eulogies appeared about the same time, one by Brutus himself, who in a few months would marry Porcia, Cato's daughter.

Caesar had written to Cicero complimenting him on the style of his pamphlet, but he could hardly help resenting a eulogy of the man who, more than any other, had expressed the *optimate* opposition to him from the beginning of his career. Before returning from Spain, Caesar issued his retaliation, titled *Anticato* (also lost), in which he attacked Cato on moral grounds, portraying him as an eccentric drunkard and miser. He described Cato's opposition to him as simple personal enmity and resentment over his failure to win the Consulship. Stubborn, oligarchic, and reactionary Cato might have been, but his moral superiority to Caesar was patent to everyone, and Caesar was widely vilified for this overheated response. A Catonian cult developed and flourished well into the next century, especially among Stoics, and his suicide became the exemplar for similar acts under the Emperors to come. To top it off, Cato's family added to his name a commemoratory *cognomen*, Uticensis, that forever identified him with his defiant act.

The news of Caesar's victory at Munda reached Rome during the latter half of April. In June, when it was learned that he was on his way home, many leading Senators, including Mark Antony, Gaius Trebonius, and Marcus Brutus, traveled to Narbo Martius to welcome him. Caesar greeted Antony warmly and invited him to share his carriage for the journey back to the capital, apparently restoring him to favor after ignoring him for two years.

Ironically, it was just at this time that he might have had reason to distrust his wayward lieutenant. There is some evidence that in Narbo Martius Trebonius broached to Antony the idea that it was time to put an end to the *dictator*, an idea to which he made no response, but which he failed to reveal to Caesar. Whether or not this actually occurred, it is clear that such an idea was already circulating, not among Caesar's enemies, but among those closest to him.

XIV
The Ides of March

Even before Caesar's last return to Rome late in the summer of 45, his deputies, Lucius Balbus and Gaius Oppius, promoted a flurry of new titles, honors, and celebrations for the victor of Munda. Beginning with a simple act of news manipulation, they withheld word of the victory in Spain until the eve of April 21 so that it could be celebrated in conjunction with the traditional birthday of the Roman Republic. After inflating the usual thanksgiving period to fifty days, the Senate declared Caesar Consul for ten years and *dictator* for the fourth time. The designation *imperator,* from which the word "emperor" later derived, was made a permanent attachment to his name, a title that was to descend to his sons, if any, as well as to his grandsons. Also decreed were inscriptions, busts, and sacrifices, a new temple to Freedom, and a new palace for Caesar on the Quirinal Hill. Among the statues of him the Senate ordered erected was one inscribed "To the unconquerable god," the first suggestion that another Roman besides the mythical founder-king Romulus was to be raised to godly status. The Senate proclaimed him *parens patriae,* father of the country, and authorized him to wear the triumphal purple *toga picta* at all official events, and the laurel wreath of victory at all times.

Among the most extraordinary measures discussed in the Senate, certainly at the instigation of Caesar's agents, was one to change the name of the seventh month of the year, then called Quintilis, to Julius, in honor of his birthday on the thirteenth. Quintilis, or fifth, was originally the fifth month of the archaic Roman year that began in March. The Senate designated Caesar's birthday a festival day and approved the name change, to take effect the following year. At the opening of Caesar's ten-day victory games, the *ludi Victoriae Caesaris,* which he had established the year before to celebrate his victory at Thapsus, an ivory statue of him was carried alongside that of the Goddess Victory in a parade from the Capitol to the Circus Maximus, an innovation that spectators found offensive. In a letter to Atticus, Cicero may have expressed the general mood when he wrote that "the people are behaving splendidly in refusing to applaud Victory because of her undesirable neighbor."[1]

But for all the cynicism, there was general relief in the capital about the outcome at Munda, and not only because the end of the war brought a general easing of prices. For the six months following Caesar's departure for Spain,

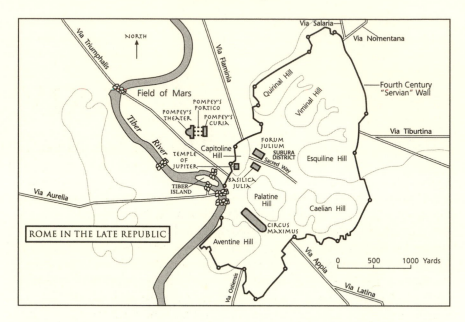

there had been considerable anxiety among those whose positions, property, and lives depended on who returned victorious to Rome. Except for a few die-hard Pompeians, the members of this class preferred that it be Caesar, whatever his faults, who would wield supreme power, rather than the violent Gnaeus Pompey, who might conduct a reign of terror in the manner of Marius and Sulla. Gaius Cassius, who had commanded a fleet for Pompey before being pardoned by Caesar, had written to Cicero in January that he would rather have the "old, easygoing master than try a cruel new one. You know what a fool Gnaeus is, how he takes cruelty for courage."[2]

Cicero was certainly familiar with the rashness of Gnaeus, and he considered himself personally fortunate that it was Caesar and not Gnaeus that he would have to answer to. Because of a series of distressing events within his own family, the previous twelve months had been among the most difficult in his life. Since just after the beginning of the war, and during his absence abroad, his relationship with his wife Terentia had been strained, apparently because of her, or her financial advisor's, mismanagement of his funds. Even during his uncomfortable stay in Brundisium he had discouraged her from visiting, writing that "it is a long and unsafe journey, and I do not see what good you can do if you come."[3] But his daughter Tullia, who was having her own marital problems, made the journey, and father and daughter spent several months of the summer together. His return to Tusculum and to Terentia late in 47 had brought to a head the friction between them, and some time in 46 he divorced her. Also in 46, presumably at Tullia's behest, he sent the unstable Dolabella notice of her divorce from him, her third husband, after four years of marriage. Although Cicero was relieved by the termination of both his own and his daughter's unhappy marriages, he was now responsible for repaying Terentia's dowry, and for obtaining a refund of Tullia's dowry from her spend-thrift ex-husband, as well as taking over her upkeep.

Toward the end of 46, nineteen-year-old Marcus *filius,* perhaps in connection with his parents' divorce, had demanded a large allowance and either a house of his own in Rome, or permission to accompany Caesar and his cousin Quintus on the coming campaign in Spain. Although the boy had already shown a military flair (he had served in Pompey's cavalry at Pharsalus), Cicero wrote to Atticus that he refused the second option because of how it might look to the Pompeians. The following spring he sent Marcus to study philosophy at Athens and to board with Atticus, even though he had complained that the boy showed no aptitude for scholarship.

About the time that Caesar left for Spain, the sixty-year-old Cicero married Publilia, a beautiful teenaged girl whose considerable fortune he had been named to manage as trustee. Those around him gave different reasons for the marriage. A possible political motive is suggested by the fact that the bride's family were supporters of Caesar; Terentia put it down to an old man's infatuation; to others it was simply a matter of Cicero's restoring his fortune, which had suffered during his absence from Italy, and was now under increased pressure. Whatever the reason, the marriage lasted only a few months, reportedly because of Publilia's hostility toward Cicero's beloved Tullia, who was pregnant again at the time.

The thirty-year-old Tullia bore Dolabella's son in January of 45, but never recovered from the birth, and in a matter of weeks she was dead, the baby surviving only a few more months. Cicero was overcome with grief at the loss of his Tulliola, the one human being for whom he never had a word of criticism. He retreated to his villa on the tiny promontory of Astura, today Torre Astura near Anzio, and poured out his sorrow in a composition he called *Consolatio,* which survives only in fragments. To his dearest correspondent he wrote, "Atticus, everything is over with me, everything, and has been long enough, but now I admit it, having lost the one link that held me."[4] Among the many letters of consolation he received was one from another father, Caesar—who had also lost a daughter, even younger—written two or three weeks after the battle of Munda.

Despite these tribulations, the period following Cicero's return to Tusculum at the end of 47 was the most productive of his entire career. During the following three years he published a series of discourses and dialogues that helped introduce Greek ideas to the Romans, and ultimately to the rest of the Western world. During 46 alone, besides his eulogy of Cato, he wrote four works on oratory, two of which he dedicated to Marcus Brutus, and in the next two years published several philosophical and religious works that affected both Christian doctrine and Renaissance humanism. In fact, no writer in any language had more influence upon European literature than Cicero. The literary styles of both Cicero and Caesar had individual impacts on the writing of Latin prose for many centuries to come, and remain staples wherever the Latin language is taught.

Caesar himself did not arrive in northern Italy until September, and when he did so, he bypassed the sweltering capital and rode on to his estate near Lavicum, now Labici, about thirty-five miles southeast of Rome. He had been under arms and on the march for all but a few months of the last five years, and the constant demands of war had begun to affect his health. Coin portraits made a few months later showed a gaunt face, sunken cheeks, and a much-lined neck. On several occasions during his lifetime he had suffered what appeared to be epileptic seizures, including one on the battlefield at Thapsus, and in the next two years he reportedly suffered several incapacitating episodes, described by witnesses as dizziness or fainting spells.

In the relaxed and rural atmosphere of the Alban Hills he composed another will in which he adopted Octavius as his son, thus conferring on him his own name and its particular mystique. To the Roman people he bequeathed the gardens at his estate across the Tiber, and to each citizen a gift of seventy-five *denarii,* the equivalent of a month's wages for an ordinary workman. Three-quarters of the rest of his immense personal fortune Caesar left to Octa-

One of the few authentic coin portraits of Caesar, issued a few months before his death, when he was *dictator* for the fourth time. (Bibliothèque Nationale, Paris, France. Giraudon/Art Resource, NY.)

vius, and the remaining quarter to his elder sister's son and grandson. He included words of gratitude for Antony and Decimus Brutus, naming both secondary heirs, but mentioned neither Cleopatra nor Caesarion. (Roman law forbade any foreigner from inheriting assets of a Roman citizen.)

When he returned to Rome at the end of September, preparations had just been completed for his fifth triumph, which he celebrated without any pretense that it was a victory over a foreign enemy. According to Plutarch, there were no illusions about who had been defeated, and the parade of marching soldiers, musicians, and wagonloads of booty offended the Romans, especially those with the slightest affection for Pompey, more than anything else Caesar had done. Although a statue of Pompey was restored to the Curia Pompei behind his theater, the public was well aware that it was Caesar who had all but destroyed the family, and had even ousted Pompey's widow Cornelia from the family estate in the Alban Hills. Respect for the triumph was not enhanced when Caesar allowed both Quintus Pedius and Quintus Fabius Maximus, two of his generals in Spain, to also celebrate triumphs, even though, as subcommanders, they were not entitled to them.

What role Cleopatra and her family played in any of these festivities is simply unknown. Her appearance with Caesar at any time during these months would certainly have been mentioned by historians, but there are only general references to her presence in Rome. This is probably due in part to the determined effort by Octavius in the fifty years after Caesar's death to minimize or conceal his relationship with Cleopatra as much as possible. Little about her survives from the next one hundred and fifty years of Latin literature until Suetonius' biography, in which he noted that Caesar allowed her to name her son Caesarion. He also mentioned that some later historians said that the boy closely resembled Caesar in features, as well as in gait.

Cassius Dio claimed that Caesar "incurred the greatest censure from all because of his passion for Cleopatra. . . . For she had come to the city with her husband and settled in Caesar's own house, so that he derived an ill repute on account of both of them."[5] He added that at some time during this period, the Senate, no doubt at Caesar's instigation, formally declared her and her husband friends and allies of the Roman people. What Caesar had in mind for Cleopatra is not clear, and it is possible that he eventually intended to marry her. Supporting this notion is a report that one of Caesar's agents later claimed that he had, under "instructions," drafted a law that would have allowed Caesar to marry as many women as he wished, "for the procreation of children."[6] Nothing else is known of such a law.

It is likely that the Romans were by turns fascinated and offended by Caesar's mistress—a young and exotic Egyptian queen living in their capital, who would perhaps exert a pernicious, oriental influence on their married *dictator*. Cicero apparently had some modest involvement with her, possibly on a literary matter, but his few short references to her in his letters (all after Caesar's death) are primarily complaints about *superbia,* her haughtiness. Some historians ascribe Caesar's movement toward absolutism and ruler worship to Cleopatra's example, and there were rumors in Rome that he planned to move the capital to Troy or to Alexandria. In other respects, Cleopatra (and Egypt) may have had a positive effect on Caesar and the Romans. His reform of the calendar and his plans for public libraries in Rome certainly emanated from Alexandria, and probably also his employment of four Greek geographers to produce a map of the world.

During the remaining months of 45, Caesar plunged into the work of administering the largest political entity that had yet appeared in the Western world. As *dictator,* he gave orders, and a compliant Senate issued decrees, that touched on every aspect of domestic and foreign affairs, and ranged from mundane to grandiose. Perhaps the most far-reaching and significant was the unprecedented resettlement of tens of thousands of Roman citizens, primarily freedmen and their descendants, in a dozen new and expanded colonies from Spain to Bithynia. This mammoth effort eventually involved some eighty thousand citizens, and significantly reduced the poor and near-poor population in the capital. Among those transported and settled at government expense were entire legions of Caesar's troops, with colonies of veterans and their families being placed at Narbo Martius, Arelate, and Carthage, which he now ordered rebuilt, just a hundred years after Scipio Aemilianus had destroyed it.

By resettling native Romans throughout the provinces, Caesar enforced the idea that a citizen of Rome carried his status, privileges, and protection wherever he lived or traveled in the Mediterranean world. The colonization also had the effect of Romanizing the provinces, bringing the religion, culture, and attitudes of Romans to the edges of what was beginning to be called an empire. Along the same lines, Caesar extended Latin rights, that is, Roman citizenship, to local magistrates and officials—the native upper class—in additional cities in Further Gaul, Sicily, and Spain.

Other reforms were directed toward improving social and economic conditions in the capital, such as a tariff on foreign goods, and a new law that created an early form of legal bankruptcy. Other acts had a less public purpose. When the Senate authorized him to create new patrician families, a power previously exercised only by the ancient kings, Caesar immediately raised the Octavii, the plebeian *gens* of his adopted son, to the status of patrician.

The Senate he enlarged from six hundred to nine hundred men, appointing many who were totally unlike the traditional Roman Senator, including centurions, former scribes, the foreign born, and sons of freedmen. For the first time, men from "beyond the Alps" were made Senators, and among the class-conscious nobility there were numerous complaints about Caesar's newcomers. Jokes were told about semicivilized Gauls, wearing the baggy pants peculiar to the Celts, finding their way to Rome and asking directions to the Senate House. Caesar brushed off the jibes, remarking that if even bandits and cut-throats had defended his honor as his Gallic appointees had, he would have shown his gratitude in the same way.

But his addition of a few hundred families to the nobility did nothing to change the narrow and constricting oligarchy that had ruled Rome for centuries; he only expanded it slightly, and set himself above it. He did not modify the makeup of the voting centuries or the method of counting votes so as to allow all citizens to actually vote, and to have their votes count. Nor did he remove the property requirements for public offices, or endow them with salaries so they could be held by other than the wealthy. And, of course, he did nothing to allow women any type of citizenship, and nothing about slavery. To be fair, there was little or no agitation for any of these reforms (Cicero would have hated them), and had Caesar implemented a single one, the reaction of the aristocracy would have been even swifter than it was.

If Caesar's initiatives were not democratic, they were bold and energetic. It seems, however, that despite his unfettered authority and limitless resources, Caesar may not have cared much for governing. Within a few months of returning to Rome, he had begun assembling troops and making preparations for another campaign, this one to the East. His reported targets were the newly powerful King Burebista in Dacia, the area of modern Romania, and the dreaded Parthians, who had destroyed a Roman army and murdered Marcus Crassus eight years earlier, and were now threatening the province of Syria. After instructing his officers to begin ferrying sixteen legions and ten thousand cavalry across the Adriatic, Caesar began arranging for the right men to be in charge at Rome during the three years he expected to be on campaign. He decided that he and Mark Antony would serve as Consuls for the coming year, with Publius Dolabella to take his place when he left the country. For the following two years he designated four others, among them Aulus Hirtius and Decimus Brutus.

Caesar had relinquished his own ten-year Consulship after celebrating his triumph, and then had engineered the election of his generals Gaius Trebonius and Quintus Fabius Maximus as Consuls for the remainder of 45. His arbitrary manipulation of the Consulship reached an acme when he learned on the last day of December that Maximus had suddenly died the night before. Caesar hurriedly assembled the voters and had Gaius Caninius, a loyal general who had served him since the Gallic War, elected to serve out the last hours of the term. Thus was the *gens* Caninia, most likely the descendants of a dog breeder, raised to the nobility. From Cicero came the bitter comment: "The Consul's vigilance was extraordinary. Throughout his entire term of office he never closed an eye! You find such things laughable, for you are not on the spot; if you were here to witness, you would have to weep."[7]

For all his disapproval, however, Cicero still shared many common interests with the *dictator* that had nothing to do with politics. During December, while on an inspection trip through Campania, Caesar notified Cicero that he wished to visit him at his country house near Puteoli, today's Pozzuoli on the

Bay of Naples. Hosting the *dictator* was no easy task, as he customarily traveled with a bodyguard of two thousand Spanish soldiers, as well as a large retinue of friends, servants, slaves, and hangers-on. Fortunately for Cicero, the troops were billeted on a nearby estate, but he felt it necessary to post guards to protect his property from being overrun. Although he claimed to have enjoyed a convivial lunch with Caesar, at which they confined their conversation to literary matters, his comment to Atticus was "But my guest was not the kind of person to whom you say 'Do come again when you are next in the neighborhood.' Once is enough."[8]

Throughout Cicero's correspondence of 45 and 44 are numerous negative reactions, both his and others, to the acts and attitude of the *dictator,* and they were not limited to Caesar's enemies. Earlier in the year, Caesar's appointee as Governor of Achaea had written to Cicero on the occasion of Tullia's death: "Think how fortune has dealt with us up to now. All that man should hold no less dear than children—country, honor, respect, and rank—has been snatched from us,"[9] not unusual sentiments among Cicero's other correspondents. By now it had become clear, if it had not been clear before, that upon becoming literally *domitor mundi,* conqueror of the world, Caesar had no intention of restoring the Republican institutions that he had claimed to be defending five years before at the Rubicon. For the great majority of the common people, however, this made no difference. Caesar at least brought order, peace, and economic stability. It was the aristocracy, long accustomed to sharing the government among themselves, who could not tolerate his seizure of every shred of authority and privilege.

A surprising detail about the attitude of many Senators comes from the *Roman History* of Cassius Dio:

When they had begun to honor him, it was with the idea . . . that he would be reasonable; but as they went on and saw that he was delighted with what they voted—indeed he accepted all but a very few of their decrees—different men at different times kept proposing various extravagant honors, some in a spirit of exaggerated flattery and others by way of ridicule. . . . Others, and they were the majority, followed this course because they wished to make him envied and hated as quickly as possible, that he might sooner perish.[10]

This might have been the motivation for some of the new honors, titles, and personal privileges that the Senate bestowed on Caesar in a single session toward the end of the year. These included the Consulship for life, and the creation of a new cult of Jupiter Julius, over which a special priest (Mark Antony) was to preside and supervise sacrifices in Caesar's honor. For his personal comfort and decoration, the Senate presented him with a raised couch on which to recline in the orchestra of the theater, a golden wreath adorned with jewels to wear at the games, and a golden throne on which to sit while presiding over the Senate.

When they had finished, the most prominent members sought him out to personally inform him of what they had done, followed by the rest of the Senate and a large crowd of people. In a notorious scene described by at least seven ancient historians, the Senators found Caesar sitting in his Forum Julium reading documents in the vestibule of the Temple of Venus. All accounts agree that Caesar remained seated as the Senators addressed him, thus conspicuously insulting them in front of their junior colleagues and the watching crowd. The incident provoked immediate indignation and was widely reported as an insult to Rome's most prestigious body and, by implication, to the people themselves. The negative reaction caused Caesar's spokesmen to offer excuses for his behavior, ranging from momentary dizziness to an attack of diarrhea, but these were ridiculed when Caesar was seen shortly afterward walking to his residence.

Further indignation flared up over several public incidents a short time later suggesting that Caesar wanted nothing less than to be *rex*, King of the Romans. If there was a single principle that the entire spectrum of the governing class agreed upon, from populist to oligarch, it was that there should be no king in Rome. In the way of many ancient and modern societies, the Romans treasured the moment in their history when they had overthrown their king—in their case, and most often, a tyrant—and set up a government that was answerable, if only marginally, to a body of voters, no matter how limited that body might be.

During January of 44, a wreath of the type worn by the ancient Kings was found on a bust of Caesar that had been set up on the *rostra*, and two of the people's tribunes ordered it removed and the culprit jailed. Shortly afterward, the same tribunes apprehended and held for trial a man who had addressed Caesar as *rex* as he was returning to Rome on the Via Appia after a festival. Caesar's well-known reply *"Caesarem se, non regem esse"* ("I am Caesar, not king"), as reported by Suetonius, has been interpreted by scholars in two different ways. One view is that it was a simple rejection of the notion that he was a king, but others hold that Caesar cleverly evaded the issue of the kingship by assuming that the speaker was calling him Rex, an existing name of a Roman family, and correcting him with his own family name.

Whatever Caesar meant, he apparently interfered with the tribunes in some way, and then became furious when they publicly complained that they had been prevented from performing their duties. He hauled them before the Senate, accused them of scheming to discredit him, and demanded their punishment. When the Senate obediently removed them from office, an illegal act unknown in Rome for nearly a century, there were cries of outrage from the crowd outside the Senate. Some called the tribunes "Brutuses," a reference to the legend of the courageous Lucius Junius Brutus, one of the first pair of Roman Consuls who, more than four centuries earlier, had led the revolt that toppled the last Tarquin King. This particular tale has been discounted by modern historians, but it was not only real, but a vivid example of a patriotic act to the

Romans of Caesar's day, and especially to Marcus Brutus, who regarded himself as a descendant of Junius.

Caesar displayed a certain sensitivity to these feelings the next month at the annual Lupercalia, the Wolf Festival, in which Antony (now Consul) participated as the leader of the feverish and nearly naked priests of the Luperci, who ran around the Palatine Hill and through the Forum in a fertility ritual many centuries old. Approaching the *rostra* where Caesar was seated on his gilded chair, Antony held up a crown and shouted, "The people offer this to you through me," and tried to place it on his head. Although Caesar was already clad in full monarchical regalia—the jewelled and golden laurel wreath, the purple robe, and high red shoes (both affected by the ancient Kings), he brushed the crown aside three times, each time to increased applause from the crowd.

In some versions of this incident, which is reported by many ancient writers, it is claimed that Caesar and Antony planned it beforehand, and that, had the crowd approved, Caesar would have accepted the crown and, presumably, the Kingship. Instead he declared, "Jupiter alone is King of the Romans," and ordered the crown placed on the statue of Jupiter in the Capitol, ordering the public record to show that he had refused the kingship offered by the people through the Consul. Nevertheless, in the telling words of Suetonius, "From that day forward he lay under the odious suspicion of trying to revive the title of king."[11]

It was perhaps only the title *rex* that the Senate was unwilling to bestow, since it had granted Caesar virtually every power of a king, and early in February of 44 proclaimed him *dictator perpetuus*, dictator for life, a sinister and unprecedented concept that acknowledged no hope of the restoration of Republican institutions. His portrait had already been stamped on coins, the first in Rome of a living person, and the new title promptly appeared alongside it.

The cumulative effect of these events now reached a level of extreme frustration for the aristocracy. They were evidently willing to accept the supremacy of Caesar in all matters of state, based on his overwhelming military power. They had suffered the same on several other occasions in his lifetime. They, or most of them, were even willing to put up with Caesar's special privileges, his pompous and redundant titles, and his obnoxious statues. But the *superbia* and contempt he displayed for the Senatorial leaders in the Forum Julium was personally offensive, and moved many of them to fury. And when he finally flirted with the hated monarchy, the ultimate taboo, he gave the aristocracy a powerful symbol of tyranny on which to focus.

It was perhaps in the latter half of February that a small group of Senators agreed among themselves that they would kill the *dictator*. The four leaders of this group, if not Caesar's closest associates, were all holders of high office to which he had recently raised them. More than that, the two most prominent conspirators were the son and son-in-law of Servilia, Caesar's most enduring mistress. Gaius Cassius, a *praetor* in 44, may have been the first to articulate the idea, approaching his fellow *praetor*, Marcus Brutus, to whose sister Junia he was married, and urging him to serve his country with a patriotic act. Despite the fact that both had been forgiven after Pharsalus, and were in line to be Consuls in 41 according to Caesar's plan, they were dismayed by Caesar's growing tyranny and adamantly opposed to anything resembling a king. Cassius, especially, was unhappy with Caesar's shuffling of men and titles, and angered that he was not offered a command in the coming campaign against the Parthians, whom he had fought in 53.

The motives of Brutus were more complex. His hatred of Pompey, his father's murderer, is well known; but it is possible, despite Caesar's indulgent treatment of him all his life, that the straitlaced Brutus resented even more the man who used his mother as a mistress. He shared this disapproval with his uncle Cato, whose lifelong opposition to Caesar, and whose martyr's death, had a profound effect on him. Even so, Brutus had prospered under Caesar since Pharsalus and had earned his praise as Governor of Nearer Gaul, the coveted office Caesar had given him in 46, perhaps to spare him fighting in Africa against his uncle. After that, Brutus seemed reconciled to Caesar, and even joined the group that traveled out to Narbo Martius to meet him after Munda.

But something changed in the following months, and several modern historians of the Roman Republic have suggested that a woman may have been the cause.[12] When he returned to Rome from Nearer Gaul in June of 45, Brutus suddenly divorced his wife Claudia, and within a few weeks married his cousin Porcia, Cato's widowed daughter, a marriage that Servilia furiously opposed. Porcia came to the marriage with more than a little anti-Caesarean baggage. Her first husband had been Caesar's lifelong rival and enemy, Marcus Bibulus, who had died on one of Pompey's warships off the coast of Macedonia early in 48, leaving a young widow and a baby. The devoted and strong-willed Porcia no doubt influenced Brutus for the rest of his short life.

It was said that Brutus kept a diagram on the wall of his house showing his direct descent on his father's side from Junius the founder of the Republic, as well as his mother's descent from a similar liberator. His passionate feeling for this tradition was strongly enforced by various anonymous placards and graffiti posted around the capital, exhorting him to emulate his storied ancestors.

By early March of 44 Brutus was deeply involved in discussions about when and where the conspirators would strike. Whether or not Porcia encouraged him to act, Brutus behaved like any Roman *pater familias* and kept the plot from her, but was beset with such anxiety and fitful sleeping that she became concerned about his health. In his biography of Brutus, Plutarch recounts the famous scene, later dramatized by Shakespeare in *Julius Caesar*,[13] in which she deliberately cut her leg with a manicuring knife to demonstrate that she was brave enough to share his secret and to keep it:

Brutus, I am Cato's daughter, and I was given to you in marriage not just to share your bed and board like a concubine, but to be a true partner in your joys and sorrows. . . . [w]hat proof can I give you of my love if you forbid me to share the kind of trouble that demands a loyal friend to confide in . . . ? I know that men think women's natures too weak to be entrusted with secrets, but surely a good upbringing and the company of honorable men can do much to strengthen us, and at least Porcia can claim that she is the daughter of Cato and the wife of Brutus. . . . [N]ow I have put myself to the test and find that I can conquer pain.[14]

The startled Brutus embraced her and revealed the plot. According to Plutarch, who cites as his source a *Life of Brutus*, no longer extant, by his stepson Bibulus, Porcia nearly lost her nerve as the day approached. She kept the secret, of course, but two years later became a widow a second time when Brutus took his own life at Philippi in the same way her father had taken his at Utica.

The two other main conspirators, Gaius Trebonius and Decimus Brutus, had been members of Caesar's high command as far back as the Gallic War. The former had been Consul for three months at the end of 45, and Caesar had just appointed him Governor of Asia for the current year. Decimus Brutus he had just named Governor of Nearer Gaul and Consul-designate for 42. Besides being one of the generals closest to Caesar, Decimus had a cadre of gladiators in the capital that he was training for a public event, who might be needed for protection after the act. On the surface, neither man had good reason to complain of Caesar's treatment, but they may have been jealous of others promoted ahead of them, and it is likely that they, too, had been offended by Caesar's aspirations to be king.

According to the sources, the conspirators discussed the merits of including two others in the plot. All but one were inclined to bring in Antony, but Trebonius objected because of Antony's failure to support the notion when he had raised it the previous year. When the suggestion was made that they do away with Antony as well, Brutus dissuaded them, saying that if they killed only Caesar, they would be called heroes for removing a tyrant, but if they did more than that, they would be accused of acting out of personal enmity and to avenge Pompey. Brutus also apparently convinced the others that Cicero was too old and timid to take part. During the first two weeks of March dozens of additional Senators joined the plot, fueled by *inimicitia*, their hatred of Caesar, and the number eventually reached as many as sixty, of whom sixteen are known by name.

The conspirators were hurried into action because of Caesar's imminent departure for the East, which was planned for March 18. The immediate impetus for the deed was a report that a prophecy about the coming Parthian campaign had been extracted from the Sibylline Books, a collection of verse oracles in which the Romans set great store, and that guided their actions from time to time. Lucius Cotta, one of the keepers of the books, and another cousin of Caesar's mother, had found a prophecy that the Parthians could only be conquered by a king. It was rumored that he planned to ask the Senate to insure a victory in the East by conferring on Caesar the title of King, but only of the provinces. Brutus and the others were determined to vote against this measure, but, fearing the consequences, decided that they must act before the next meeting of the Senate, scheduled for the Ides of the month, which for March was the fifteenth, the last before Caesar's Eastern campaign.

Because of the notoriety of the Ides of March, more information about it has accumulated than about any other date in Roman history. Accounts of ancient writers are filled with tales of omens, prophecies, warnings, and alarms, most of which are discounted by modern historians. But Suetonius' assertion that "unmistakable signs warned Caesar of his assassination"[15] is very likely true. When he was told of a plot against him by Antony and Dolabella, two well-known epicures and ladies' men, he is said to have replied, "It is not these sleek, long-haired fellows who frighten me, but the pale, thin ones,"[16] referring to Brutus and Cassius (Shakespeare's "lean and hungry" Cassius).

But the excess of warnings may have led him to discount them. When he was warned specifically against Brutus, he scoffed at the notion that Brutus could not wait for him to die. He was well aware of his own unpopularity, however, and on one occasion, when he saw Cicero impatiently waiting for an interview with him, observed that this most easygoing of men no doubt detested him. Although he was obviously a tenacious survivor, Caesar had always taken enormous risks, and Cicero had, only two years before, quoted him as saying, "Satis diu vel naturae vixi, vel gloriae" (whether for nature or for glory, I have lived long enough).[17] Enlarging on this Stoic notion, he professed a loathing for a lingering end. His last remark on this subject came at a dinner at the home of Marcus Lepidus on the evening of March 14, a dinner attended by Decimus Brutus. When the conversation turned to a discussion of the best way to die, Caesar declared emphatically, "Let it come swiftly and unexpectedly."[18] As if to emphasize this attitude, he dismissed his extensive Spanish bodyguard early in March, and went out among the public, borne on his customary litter, entirely approachable and careless of his safety.

On the morning of the Ides of March, the Senate convened at dawn, as was the custom, in Pompey's Curia, adjacent to his theater, and waited for Caesar to appear. Among the stories that surround this day is one that Caesar's wife Calpurnia awoke from such a frightening nightmare (she dreamt that she held his murdered body) that she implored him not to go. According to various accounts, Caesar was impressed enough to offer the sacrifices that were customary after such a dream in order to appease the gods and learn their will. When the results of these were unfavorable, Caesar remained at home and considered not attending the meeting. But when the Senate had been waiting five hours, and word came that Caesar might not come, the conspirators became alarmed. They sent Decimus Brutus to his house to persuade him to appear, which he did, and shortly before noon Caesar made his entrance and proceeded to the podium.

As a precaution against the interference of Antony, a man of great physical strength, Gaius Trebonius kept him in conversation outside the hall. When Caesar had taken his seat, about a dozen of the leading conspirators gathered around him, each with a dagger hidden in the case in which he carried his writing stylus. By prearrangement, Lucius Cimber, Caesar's designated Governor of Bithynia, began speaking to him about his brother's recall from exile. As Cimber leaned forward, he pulled Caesar's toga down from his shoulder, signaling the attack, and Publius Casca, from behind, struck a glancing blow at the seated Caesar's neck. Caesar jumped up and turned to him, striking back with his stylus, shouting that this was violence. But then the daggers came from every side, the assassins stabbing wildly, some wounding others, as Caesar twisted one way and then another to avoid them. But they had agreed that each would take part, and two dozen dagger blows struck him as he slumped, bleeding, to his knees, drawing his toga over his head, and then fell dead at the foot of a statue of Pompey.

In the space of seconds, the invincible general, the Consul and *dictator* for life, the would-be King and god yet to be were all extinguished—the most startling murder in Roman history. The general who had risked the open sea in winter, had slipped out of half a dozen traps, and had scrambled, swum, or galloped away from death or capture in seven different countries was struck down in public, in his own capital, and in front of waiting Senators whom he had put in office. Suddenly gone were all the honors, titles, and kingly trappings, and suddenly, six months after Caesar's last triumphant return to Rome, the Roman world was upside down.

Among the stunned assembled Senators was Cicero, who later wrote in the first account we have of Caesar's death that Brutus saluted him with his bloody dagger and then stepped forward to address the Senators. But in the crowd of shouting, churning men no one was listening, and instead all rushed to the doors— Caesar's assassins and his foes fearing his troops, his supporters fearing that they were next. In another minute the hall was empty, and the bleeding body lay alone, as if no one dared approach it, until some of Caesar's slaves arrived to carry it away.

It is almost certain that Caesar's famous words "You too, my child?" allegedly addressed in Greek to Brutus, were never spoken. Virtually all modern historians reject the incident, and the only two ancient writers who report it, Suetonius and Cassius Dio, do so with reservations (Cassius Dio is notorious for copying Suetonius). What can be said for the remark is that it has the ring of truth—that Brutus was like a son to Caesar, and that in the instant of his death, it would have been a profound shock to see the boy he doted on become the man who murdered him. What gave the story credibility for so long was the widespread belief that Brutus was actually Caesar's son, born of Servilia early in their extended affair. Only in this century has it been shown that Brutus was born when Caesar was fifteen, long before the affair began.[19]

Brutus and the other assassins, many of them still smeared with Caesar's blood, ran the half-mile to the Capitoline Hill and to the Temple of Jupiter, where they sought refuge, as well as assurance from the gods that they had acted rightly. They were afraid of Antony's retaliation and of Lepidus, who commanded the only legion in the capital.

But Caesar's two most powerful allies, his co-Consul and his Master of the Horse, were far from mounting a response, and had sought refuge in strangers' houses. People ran in all directions as the news of Caesar's murder spread across the city; no one felt secure, and no one knew what would happen next. The streets and public areas grew quiet as shops shut down and doors were bolted. In the nearly empty Forum there was silence and bewilderment.

A few hours later Brutus and Cassius went down into the Forum and attempted to address a curious crowd that had gathered, but when they inspired only silence, they hurried back to the Capitol, where they were protected by Decimus' gladiators. That evening a group of sympathizers visited them, including Cicero and Dolabella, who was already wearing the *toga praetexta*, the white toga bordered with a band of purple that was the mark of the Consulship that Caesar had promised him. Cicero was asked to negotiate with Antony, but he refused, saying that Antony would agree to anything as long as he was threatened, but otherwise was unreliable.

Later in the evening a deputation finally met with Antony, who had barricaded himself in his house (formerly Pompey's), and his response was that they would hear from him in the morning. The assassins stayed the night in the Capitol, and before dawn Lepidus brought his troops from the Tiber island where they were stationed, and deployed them in the Forum. He and Balbus wanted the killers captured, but Hirtius counseled caution. It was now that the impulsive Antony, so long the misbehaving boy of Roman politics, regained the steady hand that he had always shown on the battlefield, and took control of the highly charged negotiations. He ordered a notice posted that the Senate would meet the next day, March 17.

The following morning Antony convened the Senate near his home in the Temple of Tellus, which he surrounded with troops. When many members urged him, he invited the assassins to attend, knowing they would not come. In their absence, the debate that followed revealed a general feeling of relief, and approval of what had been done. When Caesar's partisans demanded that the killers be punished, the rejoinder came that he had been a tyrant and had been justly murdered, as was the tyrant's due.

Then, after much discussion, the Senators agreed that before they could decide the justice of the deed, they had to first decide if Caesar had been a tyrant. At this point Antony introduced the question of Caesar's edicts and appointments. If Caesar was declared a tyrant, he said, then all his actions were illegal and his appointments void. In the words of Appian of Alexandria, "They all immediately leapt to their feet and started shouting and protesting against

The masculine features of Mark Antony are unmistakable on this gold coin issued a few yars after Caesar's death. His fellow Triumvir Octavian is pictured on the reverse. (Bibliothèque Nationale, Paris, France. Giraudon/Art Resource, NY.)

submitting themselves to further elections or to the popular choice instead of holding on firmly to what they had already got."[20]

The result of Antony's proposition was a decree confirming every act and word of Caesar's until the moment of his death, thus assuring that no one would lose his present office, or the one picked for him by Caesar for the future. Antony had already, on the night of Caesar's death or the next, taken sole possession of all of Caesar's papers and a large sum of money, after a hurried visit to Calpurnia. The former he would use selectively to justify anything he did; with the funds he would buy allies, votes, and legions. Another motion brought by Antony was enthusiastically passed, this time with no debate—the abolition for all time of the office of *dictator*.

Now the fate of the assassins caused a lengthy argument that could not be resolved until Cicero proposed that they imitate the Athenians, and do what they had done after a similar murderous upheaval. He suggested a general amnesty for all that had occurred—Caesar's tyranny and his murder—and acceptance of the current state of things. The vote for this was unanimous, and the assassins were invited to join the meeting. This they did, but not before the children of Antony and Lepidus were taken to the Capitol as hostages. That evening the sudden ruptures of the Ides of March were papered over at banquets where Caesar's supporters and assassins entertained each other.

The Senate met again the next day to decide the remaining contentious questions of the will and the funeral. Those who wanted Caesar's will destroyed and his property confiscated were opposed by those who expected to benefit from his bequests. The conspirators wanted Caesar's body thrown into the Tiber, the customary disposition of a criminal. Others thought a quiet, private ceremony was best, but Calpurnia's father demanded a funeral in keeping with Caesar's legitimate office of *pontifex maximus*. Antony again took the initiative and, against the violent objections of Cassius, coolly steered the Senators to approve a public reading of the will, followed by a state funeral and a burning of the body beside the tomb of Caesar's daughter on the Campus Martius. He was no doubt aware that public sympathy for Caesar would be aroused by these displays, and that he would be the beneficiary.

Two days later, early on March 20, Caesar's closest and highest-ranking friends, surrounded by a cadre of his troops with their javelins reversed, bore his body on a funeral litter through a crowd along the Sacred Way and to the *rostra* in the Forum. Preceding them were musicians, mimes, and dancers, many of whom had lately performed in Caesar's triumphs. Professional mourners, and actors wearing wax masks of his father and other ancestors followed them. Calpurnia and her relatives walked behind the litter, and behind them Caesar's friends, slaves, and servants, all in mourning garb. On the *rostra* a large, gilded model of Caesar's Temple of Venus had been erected, in which the bearers placed his body, resting on a funeral couch—a mattress on a frame of wood inlaid with ivory and draped with gold and purple cloth. On a pillar in the model temple they hung the bloody robe in which he had died.

In the ceremony that followed, shouts of grief and anguish rose from the crowd as actors recited lines from Greek and Roman plays referring to the *clementia* Caesar had offered, but was denied himself. Then a herald read his will, provoking cries of sympathy at his public gifts, and groans of disapproval when the name of Decimus Brutus was pronounced. (It is highly unlikely that any of the assassins were in the crowd.) This was followed by a reading, interspersed with Antony's comments, of the Senate's edict confirming all of Caesar's acts, and conferring on him divine and human honors.

The speech that Antony then made was in all probability a short but emotional eulogy, rather than the elaborate oration reported by several ancient writers, and brought to rhetorical perfection by Shakespeare many centuries later.[21] When his account of Caesar's generosity, and of his many acts of mercy, began to have an impact on his audience, Antony picked up the garment that Caesar had been wearing when he was killed and held it up before the crowd. Just as he unfolded it to show the holes the daggers made, a wax model of Caesar's body was raised on a pole and slowly rotated to show the two dozen wounds about his head and torso. We do not know what Antony said at this moment, but it may well have been akin to Shakespeare's famous lines:

You all did love him once, not without cause;
What cause withholds you then to mourn for him?[22]

Accounts of the funeral differ in detail about what happened next, but they agree that the Forum crowd grew agitated and then belligerent as Antony continued speaking. Finally, a few rushed forward, brusquely took the couch with Caesar's corpse, and carried it down from the *rostra* to the pavement of the Forum, where they set it on fire. As the couch and body began to burn, the excited crowd fed the flames with benches from the Forum and furniture from nearby shops, as well as trappings and insignia from the funeral, and pieces of their own clothing. When the corpse had been consumed, a mob of "slaves and beggars,"[23] in Cicero's phrase, took flaming brands from the fire and ran to set the houses of the assassins on fire. According to some accounts, mourners kept vigil beside the funeral pyre throughout the night, and were joined by groups of Roman Jews, who revered Caesar as their benefactor.

A single ancient writer, Cassius Dio, reports that Caesar's freedmen took up his bones and ashes and placed them in the family tomb. The spot in the Forum where his corpse was burned became a hallowed place where his successor later built a Temple of Caesar, traces of whose cement foundation can be discerned today. Less than a mile away, beside the Via di Torre Argentina, today's visitor can see the remains of several huge stone blocks that formed the podium of the Curia Pompei, the precise place where Caesar died.

Portions of structures that Caesar built have been identified in the ancient Forum area, but it is his words and deeds that have carried his name into the modern era. Many historians have called him the greatest man that Rome produced, and have argued that his combined achievements in historical writing, in politics and oratory, and on the battlefield have never been matched. Certainly no other figure in ancient times, perhaps no one in all of history, succeeded as he did in all that he attempted. His single failure was that he could not bring himself to share his power or find a way to govern Rome judiciously. Although his achievements are indisputable, they are colored by the usual contradictions and paradoxes of a complex personality. His two *Commentaries* are masterpieces of military narrative, and his Attic style is justly famed for its unadorned simplicity. But *The Gallic War* has been called "the one example in literature of an impersonal autobiography."[24] It is devoid of the humanity of Tacitus or the charm of Herodotus. More important, Caesar's dry and unemotional writing conceals a masterpiece of self-serving history, primarily intended to persuade and justify, rather than report.

As a military leader, Caesar was the bold and unpredictable genius of his time, pursuing the Gauls and Britons with great energy and using his heavily armed and efficient legions with *celeritas* and *improvisum*. But he added nothing new to Roman military science, and prevailed most often out of sheer persistence. As a tactician he was brilliant, but his many narrow escapes were often the result of his carelessness and inattention to logistics. His greatest assets in the Gallic War were Roman wealth, with which he bought great quantities of weapons, troops, and warships, and Roman technology, which furnished him with bridges, advanced artillery, and sophisticated siegecraft. Throughout his career he suffered minimally from mutinies and desertions, and inspired his troops with a combination of attention to their needs, strict discipline, and personal courage and charisma.

His cruelty to barbarians was standard practice for the time, but his *clementia* for Romans was so unusual that it amazed his enemies and gained him great public favor. Of the four or five Roman generals who seized the Republic by force in its last fifty years, only Caesar did so without butchering his opponents. Although his legionaries fought and killed their Roman enemies, his generosity toward his countrymen prevented tens of thousands of injuries and deaths, and much destruction of property. This won troops, towns, and allies to his side.

As a politician, Caesar was utterly pragmatic and formed partnerships and coalitions as readily with enemies as with friends. He lobbied both the public and his peers with great effectiveness, and used gifts, appointments, bribes, and threats with consummate skill. Besides these traditional tactics, he used obscure laws with imagination and made significant innovations, such as the daily recording of the Senate's deliberations. But when he turned to illegality and violence in his first Consulship, he created the politician's nemesis—devoted and lifelong enemies. His sparing of these enemies on the battle-field—Cicero called it his *insidiosa clementia*[25]—only caused rancor and resentment. He was killed by men he had forgiven, but who hated him.

What he could not achieve politically, he did by force of arms. But even after systematically defeating every enemy, wherever they opposed him, and attaining unprecedented power, he failed to legitimate it. He was unable to use it in a way that his peers would tolerate, in a way that did not outrage them. His failure was not that of a bloody tyrant, but of a humane man intoxicated with power. For all his success on the battlefield and in politics, Caesar failed as a statesman because he had no vision of how Rome should function, except at his bidding, and allowed no one to govern it but himself. For the next five hundred years his successors would adhere to his example.

Epilogue
Cicero

In contrast to his grudging tribute to Pompey on his death in 48, Cicero reacted to Caesar's murder with satisfaction, if not elation, and his letters during the following weeks referred to the good that had been done. "Nothing so far gives me pleasure except the Ides of March," he wrote to Atticus in April.[1] Although he claimed that his single regret was that Antony was not dead too, he acknowledged that the deed had left the government unstable and the public confused.

It may have been that the assassins were among those most confused, and in the days after Caesar's funeral, those who had not fled to their country homes took care to hide themselves and protect their families and property. Although they had not been arrested, they were no doubt surprised at the hostile reaction among a great many Romans. Even those who were not part of the plot, but only sympathetic to it, were vilified and attacked, and Cicero had to defend his own home on the Palatine Hill from arsonists. One unlucky soul, the poet Helvius Cinna, was mistaken for another Cinna who had made a bitter speech against Caesar the day before the funeral, and was literally torn to pieces by a mob.

Within a few weeks, as Antony and Dolabella asserted their Consular authority, Trebonius and Decimus Brutus retreated to the provinces assigned to them by Caesar, the former to Asia and the latter to Nearer Gaul. Despite a law requiring Marcus Brutus and Cassius, as *praetores*, to remain in the capital, Antony allowed them to seclude themselves in the country. The main motivation behind the conspiracy, personal hatred of Caesar, began to dissipate after his death, and none of the conspirators had a plan for what was to happen next. Although the Senate had satisfied itself with its amnesty, there was still widespread indignation over Caesar's murder, and agitation to punish the assassins continued.

As senior Consul and engineer of the compromise, Antony took control of the Senate, armed with Caesar's secret plans, which he refused to make public. Deeply suspicious of him, Cicero saw no advantage in attending and little chance of a return to normal Republican government. Reconciliation between those he called the "Liberators" and those outraged at Caesar's murder seemed an impossibility. To Atticus he quoted a mutual friend as saying, "If a man of Caesar's genius could find no way out, who will find one now?"[2] He left Rome for his villa on the coast and considered a trip to Athens to visit his son, and to attend the Olympic Games.

In response to sporadic rioting, Antony summoned six thousand troops from Campania, a number that was widely considered many more than necessary. It became clear that he was choosing which of Caesar's edicts to enforce and adding others for his own benefit. His main interest was in buying loyalty with gifts of land to Caesar's veterans and the poor, and with payments and favors for his friends and supporters. Cicero remained in close contact with events in the capital, and when he heard that Antony was selling state privileges, emptying the treasury, and tampering with the judicial system, he complained to Atticus that the tyranny had survived the tyrant. Before the end of May he wrote: "So there's no sense any longer in consoling ourselves with the Ides of March. We have shown the courage of men and the policy, believe me, of children. The tree has been felled but not uprooted, and you see how it is sprouting."[3]

What Cicero could not have imagined was that in less than four years Antony would again emulate Caesar and begin a liaison with Cleopatra that would make that of the *dictator* seem like a childish fling. Just a month after the Ides of March, Cicero mentioned in a letter that Cleopatra had fled Rome. A few weeks later he reported a rumor about her that has led some historians to suggest that she had suffered a miscarriage, possibly of Caesar's second child.[4] Although other scholars maintain that there was no miscarriage at all, and that Cleopatra bore her first child by Caesar after his death in 44, the best evidence indicates that Caesar's child—Ptolemy Caesar—was now almost three years old.[5]

Nothing is known of Cleopatra's reaction to Caesar's death except that she, her family, and her court left Rome within a month and returned to Egypt. Her half-brother–husband, the fourteen-year-old Ptolemy XIV, did not survive the year. The assertion of Josephus that she poisoned him is very likely true, as he would have been a threat to Caesarion, the fifteenth and last Ptolemy. After disposing of her husband, Cleopatra had no King with whom to reign, as required by Egyptian tradition, and so made the infant, Ptolemy Caesar, King of Egypt. Her subsequent marriage to Antony and their suicides in the aftermath of Actium fourteen years later are well known. Ptolemy XV outlived his mother by only a few days. In July of 30, as Caesar's adopted son closed in on the royal household in Alexandria, Cleopatra sent his sixteen-year-old natural son fleeing into southern Egypt. He may have made his way as far as Ethiopia before assassins found and killed him.

Octavius' metamorphosis from eighteen-year-old protégé of the *dictator* to one of the rulers of the Roman world began about two weeks after the Ides of March when he received a message in Apollonia from his mother Atia (Caesar's niece) urging him to come to Italy at once, that Caesar had been killed. He left immediately, but because he thought that Caesar's killers might be hunting him, he landed surreptitiously south of Brundisium. There he learned that he was heir to Caesar's fortune and his name, that the assassins were in hiding, and that he was in no danger. He traveled up to Puteoli, where his mother and stepfather urged him to stay away from Rome and out of politics. But the young man continued on to the capital, after stopping to visit Cicero, and arrived there late in April, where he was welcomed with great interest and enthusiasm by Caesar's partisans and his troops.

Over the next several months Octavius gradually asserted himself as Caesar's heir, willingly embracing the name that Caesar had prescribed for him in his will—Gaius Julius Caesar Octavianus. Although he chose not to use Octavianus, he was customarily called Octavian to avoid confusion with the dead Caesar until he changed his name to Augustus nearly two decades later. He also suggested by his words and actions that he would be not only Caesar's namesake, but his political, as well as financial, heir. When he took a strong position against the murderers of Caesar, he tapped a well of public feeling, attracting sympathetic attention and praise, as well as the backing of Caesar's wealthy friends.

He confronted Antony about Caesar's money, said to amount to twenty-five million *denarii*, claiming that it was needed to pay for Caesar's bequest to the people. Antony perceived the threat to his position that a well-financed son of Caesar would pose, and refused to turn over any money. He also blocked the special meeting of the Assembly that was required to formally approve Caesar's adoption of Octavian. As the two began to criticize each other, it soon became clear that Antony had a formidable rival.

Now the assassins and their followers also came into conflict with Antony as he sought public approval by praising Caesar and seeking to enhance his memory. Early in June he also moved to prevent any dilution of his political strength after he left the Consulship at the end of the year. In the annual allocation of provincial commands for the coming year, the Senate had, in April, assigned Antony to Macedonia, but he now decided that to be in such a distant place when an opposing faction might attempt a coup was not to his advantage. Bypassing the Senate, which was opposed to the idea, he hurried an illegal vote through the Assembly in June that deprived Decimus Brutus of his command in Nearer Gaul and gave the province to Antony for a six-year term, along with the four legions that had been stationed in Macedonia. He then arranged for Dolabella's tenure in Syria to also run for six years. The next month the Senate assigned Brutus to govern Crete and Cassius to govern Cyrene, a province west of Egypt, both unimportant posts.

During the summer Antony and Octavian began a serious competition along several fronts to win the backing of the public, the allegiance of the army, and the support of the the Senate. Various military units aligned themselves with one or the other in exchange for money, gifts, and promises. Antony used his troops to threaten the Senate; Octavian countered by offering Senators protection with his own. Both used the public's affection for Caesar as a way of winning popularity, Antony proposing that Caesar be declared a god and issuing a coin showing him mourning Caesar's death. He held public games in Caesar's honor and resurrected the Senate's forgotten decree changing the name of Quintilis to Julius. Octavian put on his own commemorative games and on Caesar's birthday, Julius 13, distributed money to the public.

In August Antony finally broke with the assassins and, after an acrimonious exchange of letters with Brutus and Cassius, issued a violent threat against them. Both left Italy for the East, where less than two years later they would perish in the last battle with Caesar's avengers. But popular feeling began to turn against Antony because of his autocratic behavior, and many Senators were afraid to vote against him, or even attend the Senate meetings, because his troops were always present. Hoping that Cicero could somehow halt the drift toward a military confrontation, his friends in the Senate persuaded him to return to Rome, and at the end of August he appeared in the capital, where an enthusiastic crowd welcomed him.

Antony was anxious for a senior statesman of Cicero's standing to lend credibility to his legislation, and made a point of asking him to attend the Senate's meeting on September 1, when special honors for Caesar were on the agenda. But Cicero was conspicuously absent, pleading fatigue from his recent journey. Antony flew into a rage and made an angry speech against him, threatening to send troops and have him brought by force. He was finally dissuaded from this unprecedented act and, after bullying the Senators into voting a semireligious thanksgiving to the dead Caesar, left for his country home.

The next day Cicero appeared in the Senate for the first time since the tumultuous session following Caesar's murder. When the presiding Consul, Dolabella, called on him, Cicero entered upon the most courageous political battle of his life with a formal oration, restrained and mild in tone, but highly critical of Antony for his actions during the previous five months. Scolding him for his threats against him, Cicero charged him with using Caesar's private notes as excuses for self-serving edicts. Urging him to abide by the agreement of March 17, he warned him against the fate suffered by the last person who had ruled by fear. It was the first of fourteen speeches Cicero would direct against Antony during the next eight months. He later termed them *Philippics* in reference to a series of orations by Demosthenes, three hundred years earlier, warning the Athenians against Philip II of Macedon.

Later in September Antony called a meeting of the Senate, which he demanded that Cicero attend, and responded with a series of violent accusations against him, including the charge that he was responsible for Caesar's death. Cicero was again absent, as were many others, frightened by Antony's troops stationed around the building. After that, both Octavian and Antony began openly recruiting troops, Antony traveling to Brundisium the next month to take charge of the four legions he had ordered to return from Macedonia. Octavian sought recruits throughout the country and appealed to Caesar's veterans to honor their oath to him. He also sought out Cicero, just as Caesar had, and asked for his counsel and support. Cicero now found himself in the same position between Antony and Octavian that he had been in between Caesar and Pompey. While he deplored Antony's illegal tactics and promotion of Caesar, he suspected that Octavian in power might be an even worse tyrant, and even more vengeful against the Liberators.

In October Cicero drafted a second speech, one that was not delivered in the Senate nor published until much later, but that he circulated to Atticus and other friends. The twenty thousand-word *Second Philippic* is perhaps the most famous—and most scathing—political diatribe ever written. In it Cicero responded in detail to Antony's accusations, and then delivered a lengthy and intemperate catalog of his public and private misdeeds. Condemning Antony's use of armed force, Cicero asserted that he would have killed him himself if he had been among the conspirators, and warned that others would now be inspired to do so.

Despite Cicero's invective, it was real events that dictated Antony's moves, and after two of his Macedonian legions defected to Octavian, he chose to gather what troops he had and leave Italy. At the end of November he marched with three legions into Nearer Gaul, which Decimus Brutus, the Governor named by Caesar, refused to surrender. But Brutus commanded only two inexperienced legions and dared not risk an open battle, so he barricaded himself and his troops inside Mutina, modern Modena, which Antony then put under siege.

The next month Cicero finally cast his lot with Octavian, who had by now raised five legions, almost all veterans. In his *Third Philippic* Cicero urged the Senate to take military action against Antony, and championed Octavian as the man to do it. He also urged Antony's assassination on whoever would do it. With his assent, the Senators gave the nineteen-year-old Octavian a seat in the Senate, and dispensation to stand for the Consulship ten years before the legal age. Early in February of 43 the Senate declared war on Antony, and the next month instructed the Consuls for the year, Aulus Hirtius and Vibius Pansa (previously designated by Caesar), to lead an army into Nearer Gaul against him. Now strong enough to refuse subordination to any other general, Octavian joined them at the head of his own army.

In April the four armies fought two battles two weeks apart in the vicinity of Mutina, and Decimus Brutus, with the help of the Senate's and Octavian's forces, delivered a beating to Antony, who retreated across the Maritime Alps into southern Gaul. Losses were heavy on all sides, and Caesar's longtime aide, Aulus Hirtius, was killed and Pansa mortally wounded. In his *Fourteenth Philippic*, the last that is extant, Cicero praised the dead Consuls and called for a public thanksgiving of fifty days. By now there were a quarter of a million men under arms, a larger number than ever before in Roman history, a great many of them new recruits. But no general was sure of his troops, and no faction was sure of its generals, as legions defected and commanders changed sides or refused to fight.

In the aftermath of the Ides of March, Marcus Lepidus, another loyal Caesarian, had pledged his support to Antony and had been rewarded with the office of *pontifex maximus*, which he held in conjunction with the provinces of Further Gaul and Nearer Spain. He had since then organized ten legions in his provinces, and now joined Antony in southern Gaul, creating the largest army in the country. The Senate declared them both public enemies, but it was still suspicious of Octavian, and awarded the triumph for Mutina to Decimus Brutus, as well as control of the legions assigned to pursue Antony.

With both of the year's Consuls dead, Octavian now began openly lobbying for the Consulship, and delayed marching against Antony and Lepidus. According to Caesar's designation, Decimus Brutus was to be one of the Consuls for the following year, and Marcus Brutus and Cassius for the year after that. Octavian reacted strongly against the prospect of Caesar's assassins being in control of the government, and was reluctant to ally himself with them against Antony, who had never wavered in his support for Caesar.

At the end of July Octavian sent a deputation of four hundred centurions to Rome to demand the Consulship for him, money for themselves, and a lifting of the ban against Antony. Cicero persuaded the Senate to reject the idea, but just weeks later Octavian marched on Rome with eight legions. Cicero and the Senate attempted to organize troops to oppose him, but they instead defected to him, and Octavian easily occupied the capital. He promptly seized the treasury and distributed the money to his troops that the Senate had promised. Before the end of August the Senate was forced to hold a Consular election, and the voters replaced the dead Hirtius and Pansa with Octavian and his cousin Quintus Pedius. The new Consuls set up a special court to try the assassins, who were condemned to death *in absentia*. After Octavian excused him from attendance in the Senate, Cicero left Rome for the last time, retreating to his place in Tusculum, where his brother Quintus joined him.

During the summer Antony and Lepidus had combined their forces into an army of more than thirty legions, and in September brought it over the Alps into Nearer Gaul. In the same month Octavian marched north with eleven legions, ostensibly to attack them, but once again purpose dissolved into pragmatism, and they began to negotiate. Late in October Antony, Octavian, and Lepidus met at Bononia, now Bologna in the Po Valley, and agreed that their interests would be best served, and the pursuit of Caesar's assassins best accomplished, if they joined forces. In the same way that Caesar, Pompey, and Crassus had joined in 59 (and in the same province), they formed an unassailable Triumvirate and divided among themselves the Western Roman world that they controlled. And just as Pompey had married Caesar's daughter, Octavian betrothed himself to Clodia, daughter of Fulvia, Antony's wife.

The three generals returned to Rome and each entered it separately with a bodyguard and a single legion. A meeting of the Assembly was hurriedly called, and the voters, surrounded by troops, passed a law granting the Triumvirate absolute authority for five years, thus restoring the equivalent of a dictatorship just twenty months after abolishing it. The new *dictatores* were commissioned to pursue Brutus and Cassius and the rest of Caesar's assassins. From this legal dictatorship by committee proceeded a bloody purge of the upper classes even more devastating than that of Sulla forty years before, and unprecedented in Roman history. The Triumvirate published a list of enemies—three hundred Senators and two thousand *equites*—who were to forfeit their lives and property. Enormous bounties were offered, and freedom in the case of a slave, to those who brought in the heads of the proscribed. Even though Cicero had opposed Octavian's Consulship, the man who called himself Caesar's son was inclined to spare him. But Antony insisted that his name be on the list and, in fact, condemned both Cicero brothers and their sons.

Although the clash between Cicero and Antony had only spilled into the open during the past year, the enmity between them may have begun two decades earlier, in 63, the year of the conspiracy of Catiline. After the five conspirators had been tried and found guilty by the Senate, Cicero, as Consul, had ordered them all executed and their property confiscated. One of them was Antony's stepfather, and his death made Antony's mother a widow for the second time. Another old quarrel surely worked against Cicero. There is evidence that Fulvia urged his death on Antony because of his public attacks on her first husband Publius Clodius after he was tried and acquitted of sacrilege in 61.

As the hunting down and killing of the proscribed began, Cicero and his brother Quintus decided to flee to Macedonia, and started toward the villa at Astura. Somewhere along the way they separated, and Quintus went to his own home, perhaps to get money, or to find his son. But within a day he and the twenty-three-year-old Quintus *filius* were found and killed.

Cicero reached the coast and went on board a boat, but after a few hours became seasick and put in to shore. Now he changed his mind and started out on the road toward Rome, hoping that Octavian would forgive and spare him. After traveling fifteen miles or so, he changed his mind again and stopped at Astura, where he spent the night. The next day he was persuaded to flee after all, and went by boat down the coast to his place at Formiae. After he had rested there awhile, his servants began to carry his litter back to the beach to continue his journey. Only a few minutes later the two men sent by Antony to kill him reached his house, and when they overtook Cicero's party, he ordered his servants to put his litter on the ground. In the words of Plutarch:

He himself, in that characteristic posture of his, with his chin resting on his left hand, looked steadfastly at his murderers. He was all covered with dust; his hair was long and disordered, and his face was pinched and wasted with his anxieties—so that most of those who stood by covered their faces while Herennius was killing him. His throat was cut as he stretched his neck out from the litter. He was in his sixty-fourth year.[6]

On Antony's orders, Cicero's head was brought to him in Rome and fastened up on the *rostra* in the Forum, as were those of other victims of the purge. In Cicero's case, however, the hands that wrote the *Philippics* were also displayed. It had been almost forty years since he and Caesar had stood in the crowd in the Forum and watched Pompey wave from his triumphal chariot. Since then all three had earned great honors, wealth, and power, and a place in history. In the 60s they had warily supported each other until Cicero turned against the First Triumvirate. Then Caesar and Pompey grew jealous and suspicious of each other and, in the guise of defending the Republic, resorted to war to maintain their *dignitas*. But the man who valued the Republic most of all urged peace on them, and refused to fight. In the end it made no difference. All three suffered the same fate—*ferroq nex*, violent death by steel—unarmed, undefended, and alone.

Notes

I. SULLA AGAINST CAESAR

1. Michael Grant, *History of Rome* (New York: Charles Scribner's Sons, 1978), p. 185.

2. Plutarch, *Sulla* 31, in *Fall of the Roman Republic*, translated by Rex Warner (Harmondsworth, U.K.: Penguin Books, 1958).

3. Ibid., 2.

4. Cassius Dio, *Roman History*, translated by Earnest Cary (Cambridge, Mass.: Harvard University Press, 1954), 36.24. Cassius Dio, a native of Bithynia who became a Roman Senator and later a Consul, wrote in about 200 CE.

5. Plutarch, *Pompey* 14, in Warner, *Fall of the Roman Republic*.

6. H. S. Versnel, *Triumphus* (Leiden: E. J. Brill, 1970), pp. 55–57, 79, 92.

7. Whether Caesar was actually married to Cossutia is disputed, but most modern scholars conclude that he was. The best discussion is in M. Deutsch, "Caesar's First Wife," *Classical Philology* 12 (1917), pp. 93–96.

8. Suetonius, *Divus Julius* 45, in *The Twelve Caesars*, translated by Robert Graves and revised by Michael Grant (Harmondsworth, U.K.: Penguin Books, 1979). See also Plutarch, *Caesar* 1 and Cassius Dio, *Roman History* 43.43.4.

II. ROME AND ITS NEIGHBORS

1. On the earliest settlement of Rome and eruptions of Monte Cavo, see Michael Grant, *History of Rome* (New York: Charles Scribner's Sons, 1978), pp. 7–8; Tim Cornell, *The Beginnings of Rome* (London: Routledge, 1995), p. 48.

2. On the myths of early Rome and the founding of the city, see Cornell, *Beginnings of Rome*, pp. 80, 94, 103; Grant, *History of Rome*, p. 21.

3. Michael Grant, *The Etruscans* (New York: Charles Scribner's Sons, 1980), pp. 60–85; Massimo Pallottino, *The Etruscans*, translated by J. Cremona (Harmondsworth, U.K.: Penguin Books, revised edition, 1978), pp. 64–81.

4. "Roma" of Etruscan origin: H. J. Wolff, *Roman Law* (Norman: University of Oklahoma Press, 1951), p. 8. General Etruscan influence on Rome: Jacques Heurgon, *The Rise of Rome to 264 B.C.*, translated by James Willis (Berkeley: University of California Press, 1973), pp. 137–55; Grant, *History of Rome*, pp. 11–14; *Etruscans*, pp. 37–39; Tim Cornell and John Matthews, *The Roman World* (Alexandria, Va.: Stonehenge Press, 1991), p. 23. Etruscan origin of chariot racing: E. Rawson, "Chariot-racing in the Roman Republic," *Papers of the British School in Rome*, n.s. 49 (1981), pp. 1–2. Etruscan origin of the Roman naming system: Alexander Humez

and Nicholas Humez, *A B C et Cetera* (Boston: David R. Godine, 1985), p. 146. Etruscan origin of the Latin alphabet: Andrew L. Sihler, *New Comparative Grammar of Greek and Latin* (New York: Oxford University Press, 1995), pp. 20–21. Etruscan origin of Roman numbers: Paul Keyser, "The Origin of the Latin Numerals 1 to 1000," *American Journal of Archaeology* 92 (1988), pp. 541–42.

5. Cornell, *Beginnings of Rome*, pp. 199–207; Cornell and Matthews, *Roman World*, p. 28; Grant, *History of Rome*, pp. 15–17.

6. Plutarch, *Pyrrhus* 21.9, in *Lives*, translated by B. Perrin (London: William Heinemann, 1920).

7. On the type and size of the population in Caesar's time, see Cornell and Matthews, *Roman World*, p. 28.

8. Matthias Gelzer, *The Roman Nobility*, translated by R. Seager (Oxford: Blackwell, 1969), p. 52.

9. On the living conditions of the Roman poor, see P. A. Brunt, *Italian Manpower, 225 B.C.–A.D. 14* (London: Oxford University Press, 1987), p. 385; Jérôme Carcopino, *Daily Life in Ancient Rome*, translated by E. O. Lorimer (1940; reprint, Harmondsworth, U.K.: Penguin Books, 1986), chapter 2; Z. Yavetz, "The Living Conditions of the Urban Plebs in Republican Rome," *Latomus* 17 (1958), pp. 500–517.

III. POMPEY AND CICERO CONQUER ROME

1. Arthur Keaveney and J. A. Madden, "Phthiriasis and Its Victims," *Symbolae Osloenses* 57 (1982), pp. 87–99.

2. Appian, *The Civil Wars*, translated by John Carter (Harmondsworth, U.K.: Penguin Books, 1996), 1.105.

3. On the origin of Caesar's *cognomen*, see E. G. Sihler, *Annals of Caesar* (New York: G. E. Stechert and Co., 1911), p. 3; Pliny the Elder, *Natural History*, translated by H. Rackham (Cambridge, Mass.: Harvard University Press, 1938–63), 7.47; Aelius Spartianus 2, in *Scriptores Historiae Augustae*, translated by David Magie (Cambridge, Mass.: Harvard University Press, 1921–32).

4. Suetonius, *Divus Julius* 49, in *The Twelve Caesars*, translated by Robert Graves and revised by Michael Grant (Harmondsworth, U.K.: Penguin Books, 1979).

5. Cicero, *Brutus*, translated by G. L. Hendrickson (London: William Heinemann, 1939), p. 252.

6. Plutarch, *Caesar* 3, in *Fall of the Roman Republic*, translated by Rex Warner (Harmondsworth, U.K.: Pengiun Books, 1958).

7. Suetonius, *Divus Julius* 45.

8. The only evidence for the data of the birth of Julia is that she married Pompey in 59. The early modern biographers of Caesar place her birth in 83, when Caesar was seventeen. More recent biographers, including Michael Grant, *Julius Caesar* (New York: McGraw-Hill, 1969), p. 81, and Matthias Gelzer, *Caesar: Politician and Statesman* (Cambridge, Mass.: Harvard University Press, 1968), p. 21, place it in 76.

9. *Psalms of Solomon* 2.1, translated by R. B. Wright in *The Old Testament Pseudepigrapha*, edited by James H. Charlesworth (Garden City, N.Y.: Doubleday and Co., 1983–85), vol. 2, p. 651.

IV. THE ROAD TO GAUL AND BACK

1. Plutarch, *Cato Minor* 24, translated by George Cozyris (unpublished).

2. The ancient sources are contradictory about the sequence and timing of the formation of the First Triumvirate, as are the opinions of modern historians. I have adopted the conclusions of John Carter in his introduction to Caesar, *The Civil War, with the Anonymous Alexandrian, African, and Spanish Wars* (Oxford: Oxford University Press, 1997), p. xvii.

3. Caesar's Consulship is discussed in Cassius Dio, *Roman History*, translated by Earnest Cary (Cambridge, Mass.: Harvard University Press, 1954) 38.1–8; Suetonius, *Divus Julius* 18–23, in *The Twelve Caesars*, translated by Robert Graves and revised by Michael Grant (Harmondsworth, U.K.: Penguin Books, 1979); Plutarch, *Pompey* 47–48, in *Fall of the Roman Republic*, translated by Rex Warner (Harmondsworth, U.K.: Penguin Books, 1958); Lily Ross Taylor, "On the Chronology of Caesar's First Consulship," *American Journal of Philology* 72 (July 1951), pp. 254–68; Taylor, "The Dating of Major Legislation and Elections in Caesar's First Consulship," *Historia* 17 (1968), pp. 173–93.

4. Cicero, *Letters to Atticus* 2.13, translated by James Sabben-Clare, *Caesar and Roman Politics, 60–50 B.C.* (London: Oxford University Press, 1971), p. 21.

5. The notion that Julia's actual jilted fiancé was Marcus Brutus, thus supplying him with another motive to hate Pompey, gained credence during the twentieth century, but was effectively refuted by J. Geiger, "The Last Servilii Caepiones of the Republic," *Ancient Society* 4 (1973), pp. 154–56.

6. R. A. Bauman, *Women and Politics in Ancient Rome* (London: Routledge, 1992), pp. 75–76.

7. Cicero, *Letters to His Friends*, translated by D. R. Shackleton Bailey (Harmondsworth, U.K.: Penguin Books, 1978), 7.1.

8. A modern account of the Thames crossing and Caesar's campaign in Hertfordshire can be found in R. Jiménez, *Caesar Against the Celts* (New York: Sarpedon, 1996), chapter 8.

9. The complicated issue of Caesar's command is discussed succinctly by John Carter in his introduction to Caesar, *The Civil War*, pp. xvi–xxi; and in Matthias Gelzer, *Caesar: Politician and Statesman* (Cambridge, Mass.: Harvard University Press, 1968 ed.), pp. 127, 151, 170.

10. Caesar, *The Battle for Gaul*, translated by Anne Wiseman and Peter Wiseman (Boston: David R. Godine, 1980), 7.15.

11. The four families were the Metelli, the Scipiones, the Claudii Marcelli, and the Cornelii Lentuli. See Ronald Syme, *The Roman Revolution* (Oxford: Oxford University Press, 1952), pp. 43–44.

12. The date and method of publication of *The Gallic War* have long been debated by scholars. Some argue that a single book was issued at the end of the first year of the war (58), and one each year thereafter (T. Hastrup, "On the Date of Caesar's Commentaries on the Gallic War," *Classica et Mediaevalia* 18 [1957], p. 74; and Barry Cunliffe and Peter Wiseman, Introduction to *The Battle for Gaul*, p. 9); others that the entire work was issued at the beginning of 51 (Gelzer, *Caesar*, p. 171) or late in 51 (Michael Grant, *Julius Caesar* [New York: McGraw-Hill, 1969], p. 152).

V. ACROSS THE RUBICON

1. Charles Beeson, "Text History of the Corpus Caesarianum," *Classical Philology* 35 (1940), pp. 113–15; V. Brown, *The Textual Transmission of Caesar's Civil War* (Leiden: E. J. Brill, 1972), p. 1.

2. Caesar, *The Civil War, with the Anonymous Alexandrian, African, and Spanish Wars*, translated with an introduction and notes by John Carter (Oxford: Oxford University Press, 1997), 1.8.1. All subsequent quotations from, and references to, these works will be identified in parentheses in the text by work, book, chapter, and sentence number, rather than cited as footnotes.

3. H. Philipp, "Eine Gedenktafel Mussolinis am Rubicon," *Petermanns Geographische Mitteilungen* 79 (1933), pp. 180–81. Giuseppe Nanni, "Biografia di un fiume: La secolare disputa per il Rubicone," *Le Vie d'Italia* 58 (March 1952), pp. 388–92.

4. Suetonius, *Divus Julius* 32, in *The Twelve Caesars*, translated by Robert Graves and revised by Michael Grant (Harmondsworth, U.K.: Penguin Books, 1979). In Appian, *The Civil Wars*, translated by John Carter (Harmondsworth, U.K.: Penguin Books, 1996), 2.35, the phrase is, "let the die be cast."

5. Plutarch, *Caesar* 32, in *Fall of the Roman Republic*, translated by Rex Warner (Harmondsworth, U.K.: Penguin Books, 1958); Appian, *The Civil Wars,* 2.35. The lost *Historiae* of Asinius Pollio is discussed, with further references, in C. C. Coulter, "Pollio's History of the Civil War," *Classical Weekly* 46 (1952), pp. 33–36. A more recent analysis of the sources is Robert A. Tucker, "What Actually Happened at the Rubicon?" *Historia* 37 (1988), pp. 245–48.

6. Cicero, *Letters to Atticus,* translated by D. R. Shackleton Bailey (Harmondsworth, U.K.: Penguin Books, 1978), 7.12.2.

7. The circumstances and motivation for Labienus' defection are discussed in W. Blake Tyrrell, "Labienus' Departure from Caesar in January 49 B.C." *Historia* 21 (1972), pp. 424–40; Ronald Syme, "The Allegiance of Labienus," *Journal of Roman Studies* 28 (1938), 113ff.; Graham Wylie, "Why Did Labienus Defect from Caesar in 49 BC?" *Ancient History Bulletin* 3 (1989), pp. 123–27.

8. Appian, *The Civil Wars* 2.35.

9. Cicero, *Letters to Atticus* 7.21.

10. Ibid., 7.22.

11. Both quotations, ibid., 8.1.

12. Ibid., 8.11C.

13. Ibid., 8.4.

14. Ibid., 8.13.

15. B. H. Liddell Hart, *Strategy* (New York: Praeger, 1954), p. 54.

VI. THE FIRST SPANISH CAMPAIGN

1. "I am not merely distressed": Cicero, *Letters to Atticus,* translated by D. R. Shackleton Bailey (Harmondsworth, U.K.: Penguin Books, 1978), 9.6.4. "I grieve that I am not participating": ibid., 9.9.2. "The one thing": ibid., 9.10.2. "Meanwhile not a line": ibid., 9.10.2. "This dishonor": ibid., 9.10.6.

2. Ibid., 9.11A.

3. Cicero, *Letters to Atticus* 9.18, in L. P. Wilkinson, *Letters of Cicero: A Selection in Translation* (New York: W. W. Norton, 1968), p. 119.

4. Appian, *The Civil Wars,* translated by John Carter (Harmondsworth, U.K.: Penguin Books, 1996), 2.40.

5. Cicero, *Letters to Atticus,* translated by D. R. Shackleton Bailey, 10.8B.

6. Cicero, *Letters to His Friends,* translated by D. R. Shackleton Bailey (Harmondsworth, U.K.: Penguin Books, 1978), 14.7.2.

7. Peter Connolly, *Greece and Rome at War* (Mechanicsburg, Penn.: Stackpole Books, 1998), pp. 238–39.

8. Other followers included "actors and actresses, seers, and holy men." Ramsay MacMullen, "The Legion as a Society," *Historia* 33 (1984), pp. 444–45.

9. Polybius, *The Rise of the Roman Empire,* translated by Ian Scott-Kilvert (Harmondsworth, U.K.: Penguin Books, 1979), 6.27–38; Connolly, *Greece and Rome at War*, pp. 135–39.

10. J. Hornell, *Water Transport: Origins and Early Evolution* (Cambridge: The University Press, 1946), pp. 112, 147.

11. The largest horses of ancient times were approximately 14–15 hands (4'10"-5'2") at the withers, according to S. Piggott, *Wagon, Chariot, and Carriage* (London: Thames and Hudson, 1992), Chapter 3. Date and origin of stirrup: ibid., pp. 89–90.

VII. THE SIEGE OF MASSILIA

1. On the construction, size, and origin of the Massilian wall, see M. Euzennat, "Ancient Marseille in the Light of Recent Excavations," *American Journal of Archaeology* 84 (1980), pp. 133–40.

2. Size and appearance of triremes: Lionel Casson, *Ships and Seamanship in the Ancient World* (Princeton: Princeton University Press, 1971. Reprint, with new material. Baltimore: Johns Hopkins University Press, 1995), pp. 82, 235. Bronze ram: Lionel Casson, *The Ancient Mariners* (Princeton: Princeton University Press, 2nd ed., 1991), pp. 135–36.

3. Configuration of ancient warships: John S. Morrison, *The Ship: Long Ships and Round Ships: Warfare and Trade in the Mediterranean 3000 BC–500 AD* (London: Her Majesty's Stationery Office, 1980), pp. 34–35. Crew of trireme: Chester G. Starr, *The Influence of Sea Power on Ancient History* (New York: Oxford University Press, 1989), pp. 22–23.

4. Vernard Foley and Werner Soedel, "Ancient Oared Warships," *Scientific American* 244, 4 (April 1981), p. 154.

5. Werner Soedel and Vernard Foley, "Ancient Catapults," *Scientific American* 240, 3 (March 1979), pp. 150–54; E. W. Marsden, *Greek and Roman Artillery: Historical Development* (Oxford: Clarendon Press, 1969), pp. 86, 93, 169.

6. Peter Connolly, *Greece and Rome at War* (Mechanicsburg, Penn.: Stackpole Books, 1998), p. 276; Barbara Tuchman, *The March of Folly* (New York: Ballantine Books, 1985), pp. 44–45.

VIII. CURIO IN AFRICA

1. Pliny the Elder, *Natural History*, translated by H. Rackham (Cambridge, Mass.: Harvard University Press, 1938–63), 5.1.

2. Caelius Rufus in Cicero, *Letters to His Friends*, translated by D. R. Shackleton Bailey (Harmondsworth, U.K.: Penguin Books, 1978), 8.4.

3. Caesar, *The Battle for Gaul*, translated by Anne Wiseman and Peter Wiseman (Boston: David R. Godine, 1980), 8.8.

4. Appian, *The Civil Wars*, translated by John Carter (Harmondsworth, U.K.: Penguin Books, 1996), 2.47.

5. Plutarch, *Pompey* 65, in *Fall of the Roman Republic*, translated by Rex Warner (Harmondsworth, U.K.: Penguin Books, 1958).

6. Ibid., 64.

IX. THE CAMPAIGN IN MACEDONIA

1. Cassius Dio, *Roman History*, translated by Earnest Cary (Cambridge, Mass.: Harvard University Press, 1954), 41.47.3.

2. Appian, *The Civil Wars*, translated by John Carter (Harmondsworth, U.K.: Penguin Books, 1996), 2.57.

3. E. C. Echols, "The Ancient Slinger," *Classical Weekly* 43, 15 (March 27, 1950), pp. 227–30.

4. Appian, *The Civil Wars* 2.61. In his description of the Dyrrachium campaign in *Der Feldzug von Dyarrhachium* [sic] (Wien: Seidel and Sohn, 1920), pp. 254–55, archaeologist George Veith writes that troops under his command in Albania in the First World War were forced by hunger to eat "chara," although they were forbidden to do so. They boiled the roots and found them sharp to the taste, though not unwholesome, if thoroughly slaked.

5. Cicero, *Letters to Atticus*, translated by D. R. Shackleton Bailey (Harmondsworth, U.K.: Penguin Books, 1978), 11.3.3.

6. Plutarch, *Caesar* 39, in *Fall of the Roman Republic*, translated by Rex Warner (Harmondsworth, U.K.: Penguin Books, 1958).

7. Ibid.

X. THE BATTLE OF PHARSALUS

1. J. D. Morgan, "Palaepharsalus—The Battle and the Town," *American Journal of Archaeology* 87 (1983), pp. 23–54.

2. Ramsay MacMullen, "The Legion as a Society," *Historia* 33 (1984), p. 446.

3. Suetonius, *Divus Julius* 30.4, translated by M. Gelzer in *Caesar: Politician and Statesman* (Cambridge, Mass.: Harvard University Press, 1968), p. 240.

4. Appian, *The Civil Wars*, translated by John Carter (Harmondsworth, U.K.: Penguin Books, 1996), 2.85.

5. Cicero, *Letters to Atticus*, translated by D. R. Shackleton Bailey (Harmondsworth, U.K.: Penguin Books, 1978), 11.6.

XI. THE ALEXANDRIAN WAR

1. Michael Grant, *From Alexander to Cleopatra* (New York: Charles Scribner's Sons, 1982), p. 257.

2. Plutarch, *Pompey* 80, in *Fall of the Roman Republic*, translated by Rex Warner (Harmondsworth, U.K.: Penguin Books, 1958).

3. Edward A. Parsons, *The Alexandrian Library* (Amsterdam: The Elsevier Press, 1952), pp. 288–319.

4. Peter Clayton and M. Price, editors, *The Seven Wonders of the Ancient World* (London: Routledge, 1988), pp. 138–57; Don Miguel de Asin, "The Pharos of Alexandria: Summary of an Essay in Spanish, with Architectural Commentary by Don M. Lopez Otero," *Proceedings of the British Academy* 19 (1933), pp. 277–93; J. Marlowe, *The Golden Age of Alexandria* (London: Gollancz, 1971), p. 62.

5. Cicero, *Letters to His Friends*, translated by D. R. Shackleton Bailey (Harmondsworth, U.K.: Penguin Books, 1978), 14.23.

6. A photograph of this portrait can been seen on p. 140 in Michael Grant, *Caesar* (Chicago: Follettt Publishing Co., 1974).

XII. *VENI, VIDI, VICI*

1. Plutarch, *Brutus* 6.2, in *Makers of Rome*, translated by Ian Scott-Kilvert (Harmondsworth, U.K.: Penguin Books, 1965).

2. A full discussion of the phrase is found in Monroe Deutsch, "Veni, Vidi, Vici," *Philological Quarterly* 4 (1925), pp. 151–56; also H. W. Gilmer, "Caesar's Thrasonical Boast," *Philological Quarterly* 4 (1925), p. 157.

3. Cicero, *Letters to His Friends*, translated by D. R. Shackleton Bailey (Harmondsworth, U.K.: Penguin Books, 1978), 15.15.2.

4. Michael Grant, *Cleopatra* (London: Weidenfeld and Nicolson, 1972), p. 85; J.P.V.D. Balsdon, "Cleopatra," review of Hans Volkmann, *Cleopatra*, *Classical Review* 10 (1960), pp. 68–71.

5. For arguments on both sides of the question, see Hans Volkmann, *Cleopatra*, translated by T. J. Cadoux (London: Elek Books, 1958), pp. 73–80; Grant, *Cleopatra*, pp. 83–85; Sarah Pomeroy, *Women in Hellenistic Egypt* (New York: Schocken Books, 1984), pp. 25–26; J.P.V.D. Balsdon, "The Ides of March," *Historia* 7 (1958), pp. 86–87.

6. Plutarch, *Cicero* 39.3, in *Fall of the Roman Republic*, translated by Rex Warner (Harmondsworth, U.K.: Penguin Books, 1958).

7. Cassius Dio, *Roman History*, translated by Earnest Cary (Cambridge, Mass.: Harvard University Press, 1954), 42.50.4.

8. Plutarch, *Antony* 10.1, in *Makers of Rome*, translated by Ian Scott-Kilvert (Harmondsworth, U.K.: Penguin Books, 1965).

9. Cassius Dio, *Roman History* 42.53.3.

10. Appian, *The Civil Wars*, translated by John Carter (Harmondsworth, U.K.: Penguin Books, 1996), 2.94.

11. Suetonius, *Divus Julius* 66, in *The Twelve Caesars*, translated by Robert Graves and revised by Michael Grant (Harmondsworth, U.K.: Penguin Books, 1979).

XIII. THE LAST CAMPAIGN

1. Plutarch, *Cato the Younger* 66, in *Selected Lives and Essays*, translated by L. R. Loomis (Roslyn, N.Y.: Walter J. Black, 1951).

2. Appian, *The Civil Wars*, translated by J. M. Carter (Harmondsworth, U.K.: Penguin Books, 1996), 2.99.

3. Plutarch, *Cato the Younger* 72.

4. Cicero, *Letters to His Friends*, translated by D. R. Shackleton Bailey (Harmondsworth, U.K.: Penguin Books, 1978), 9.7.2.

5. Ibid., 6.14.

6. Cassius Dio, *Roman History*, translated by Earnest Cary (Cambridge, Mass.: Harvard University Press, 1954), 43.23.

7. Suetonius, *Divus Julius* 43.2, in *The Twelve Caesars*, translated by Robert Graves and revised by Michael Grant (Harmondsworth, U.K.: Penguin Books, 1979).

8. A. G. Way, editor and translator, *Caesar: Alexandrian, African and Spanish Wars* (Cambridge, Mass.: Harvard University Press, 1955), p. 305.

9. Location of Munda: Antonio Caruz Arenas, "La última campaña de César en la Bética: Munda," in J. F. Rodríguez Neila, editor, *Andalucia en la antiguedad. Actas del I Congreso de Historia de Andalucia* Vol. 3 (Cordoba: Publicaciones del Monte de Piedad y Caja de Ahorros de Cordoba, 1978), pp. 143–52. For a different location, see T. Rice Holmes, *The Roman Republic and the Founder of the Empire* (Oxford: Clarendon Press, 1923), vol. 3, pp. 544–47.

10. Florus, *Epitome of Roman History*, translated by E. S. Forster (London: William Heinemann, 1984), 2.13.82.

11. Appian, *The Civil Wars* 2.104.

XIV. THE IDES OF MARCH

1. Cicero, *Letters to Atticus*, translated by D. R. Shackleton Bailey (Harmondsworth, U.K.: Penguin Books, 1978), 13.44.

2. Cicero, *Letters to His Friends*, translated by D. R. Shackleton Bailey (Harmondsworth, U.K.: Penguin Books, 1978), 15.19.4.

3. Ibid., 14.12.

4. Cicero, *Letters to Atticus*, 12.23.

5. Cassius Dio, *Roman History*, translated by Earnest Cary (Cambridge, Mass.: Harvard University Press, 1954), 43.27.3.

6. Suetonius, *Divus Julius* 52, in *The Twelve Caesars*, translated by Robert Graves and revised by Michael Grant (Harmondsworth, U.K.: Penguin Books, 1979).

7. Cicero, *Letters to His Friends* 7.30.

8. Cicero, *Letters to Atticus* 13.52.

9. Cicero, *Letters to His Friends* 4.5, translated by M. Gelzer in *Caesar: Politician and Statesman* (Cambridge, Mass.: Harvard University Press, 1968), p. 300.

10. Cassius Dio, *Roman History* 44.7.

11. Suetonius, *Divus Julius* 79.

12. Lily Ross Taylor, *Party Politics in the Age of Caesar* (Berkeley: University of California Press, 1961), p. 175; J.P.V.D. Balsdon, "The Ides of March," *Historia* 7

(1958), pp. 92–94; Michael Grant, *Julius Caesar* (New York: McGraw-Hill, 1969), p. 254.

13. William Shakespeare, *Julius Caesar* II, i.

14. Plutarch, *Brutus* 13, in *Makers of Rome*, translated by Ian Scott-Kilvert (Harmondsworth, U.K.: Penguin Books, 1965).

15. Suetonius, *Divus Julius* 81.

16. Plutarch, *Brutus* 8. The Shakespeare phrase is in *Julius Caesar* I, ii, 192–95.

17. Cicero, *Pro Marcello* 25, in *Selected Political Speeches,* translated and edited by Michael Grant (Harmondsworth, U.K.: Penguin Books, 1989), p. 290.

18. Suetonius, *Divus Julius* 87.

19. Brutus as Caesar's son: Plutarch, *Brutus* 5; Appian, *The Civil Wars,* translated by John Carter (Harmondsworth, U.K.: Penguin Books, 1996), 2.112. That Decimus Brutus and Publius Dolabella may have been sons of Caesar is suggested in Ronald Syme, "No Son for Caesar?" *Historia* 29 (1980), pp. 430–25, and "Bastards in the Roman Aristocracy," *Proceedings of the American Philosophical Society* 104 (1960), pp. 323–27.

20. Appian, *The Civil Wars* 2.129.

21. The ancient reports of Antony's speech are found in Suetonius, *Divus Julius* 84; Plutarch, *Brutus* 20; Plutarch, *Antony* 14.2, in *Makers of Rome*, translated by Ian Scott-Kilvert (Harmondsworth, U.K.: Penguin Books, 1965); Appian, *The Civil Wars* 2.142–48; Cassius Dio, *Roman History* 44.36–52. Their accuracy is discussed at length in Monroe Deutsch, "Antony's Funeral Speech," *University of California Publications in Classical Philology* 9, 5 (April 1928), pp. 127–48, and George Kennedy, "Antony's Speech at Caesar's Funeral," *Quarterly Journal of Speech* 54, 2 (April 1968), pp. 99–106.

22. William Shakespeare, *Julius Caesar* III, ii, 107–8.

23. Cicero, *Letters to Atticus* 14.10.

24. Edith Hamilton, *The Roman Way* (New York: W. W. Norton, 1964), p. 72.

25. Cicero, *Letters to Atticus* 8.16.2.

EPILOGUE: CICERO

1. Cicero, *Letters to Atticus,* translated by D. R. Shackleton Bailey (Harmondsworth, U.K.: Penguin Books, 1978), 14.6.1.

2. Ibid., 14.1.

3. Ibid., 15.4.2.

4. John H. Collins, "On the Date and Interpretation of the *Bellum Civile,*" *American Journal of Philology* 80 (1959), p. 127; Michael Grant, *Cleopatra* (London: Weidenfeld and Nicolson, 1972), pp. 95–96.

5. J.P.V.D. Balsdon, "Cleopatra," review of Hans Volkmann, *Cleopatra, Classical Review* 10 (1960), pp. 68–71; Balsdon, *Julius Caesar* (New York: Atheneum, 1967), pp. 141, 159. Caesarion's birth date in September 47 is established in Grant, *Cleopatra,* pp. 83–84.

6. Plutarch, *Cicero* 48, in *Fall of the Roman Republic*, translated by Rex Warner (Harmondsworth, U.K.: Penguin Books, 1958).

Selected Sources

ANCIENT SOURCES

Appian. *The Civil Wars*. Translated by John Carter. Harmondsworth, U.K.: Penguin Books, 1996.

Caesar. *The Battle for Gaul*. Translated by Anne Wiseman and Peter Wiseman. Boston: David R. Godine, 1980.

———. *Caesar's War in Alexandria*. Edited by Gavin Townend. Wauconda, Ill.: Bolchazy-Carducci Publishers, 1988.

———. *The Civil War, with the Anonymous Alexandrian, African, and Spanish Wars*. Translated with an introduction and notes by John Carter. Oxford: Oxford University Press, 1997.

Cassius Dio. *Roman History*. Translated by Earnest Cary. Cambridge, Mass.: Harvard University Press, 1954.

Cicero. *Brutus*. Translated by G. L. Hendrickson. London: W. Heinemann, 1939.

———. *Letters of Cicero: A Selection in Translation*. Edited and translated by L. P. Wilkinson. New York: W. W. Norton, 1968.

———. *Letters to Atticus*. Translated by D. R. Shackleton Bailey. Harmondsworth, U.K.: Penguin Books, 1978.

———. *Letters to His Friends*. Translated by D. R. Shackleton Bailey. Harmondsworth, U.K.: Penguin Books, 1978.

———. *Selected Political Speeches*. Edited and translated by Michael Grant. London: Penguin Books, 1989.

Florus. *Epitome of Roman History*. Translated by Edward S. Forster. London: William Heinemann, 1984.

Lucan. *Lucan's Civil War*. Translated by P. F. Widdows. Bloomington: Indiana University Press, 1988.

Pliny the Elder. *Natural History*. Translated by H. Rackham. Cambridge, Mass.: Harvard University Press, 1938–63.

Plutarch. *Lives*. Translated by B. Perrin. London: William Heinemann, 1920. Contains *Pyrrhus*.

———. *Selected Lives and Essays*. Translated by L. R. Loomis. Roslyn, N.Y.: Walter J. Black, 1951. Contains *Cato the Younger*.

———. *Fall of the Roman Republic*. Translated by Rex Warner. Harmondsworth, U.K.: Penguin Books, 1958. Contains *Caesar, Pompey, Crassus, Cicero, Sulla, Marius*.

———. *Makers of Rome*. Translated by Ian Scott-Kilvert. Harmondsworth, U.K.: Penguin Books, 1965. Contains *Brutus, Antony*.

Polybius. *The Rise of the Roman Empire.* Translated by Ian Scott-Kilvert. Harmondsworth, U.K.: Penguin Books, 1979.

Suetonius. *The Twelve Caesars.* Translated by Robert Graves; revised by Michael Grant. Harmondsworth, U.K.: Penguin Books, 1979. Contains *Divus Julius.*

Velleius Paterculus. *Compendium of Roman History.* Translated by F. W. Shipley. Cambridge, Mass.: Harvard University Press, 1924.

Vitruvius. *On Architecture.* Translated by Frank Granger. London: William Heinemann, 1934.

SECONDARY SOURCES

Adkins, L., and R. A. Adkins. *Handbook to Life in Ancient Rome.* New York: Facts on File, 1994.

Africa, T. W. "The Mask of an Assassin: A Psychohistorical Study of M. Junius Brutus." *Journal of Interdisciplinary History* 8 (1978), pp. 599–626.

Alexander, Michael C. *Trials in the Late Roman Republic 149 BC to 50 BC.* Toronto: University of Toronto Press, 1990.

Asin, Don Miguel de. "The Pharos of Alexandria: Summary of an Essay in Spanish, with Architectural Commentary by Don M. Lopez Otero." *Proceedings of the British Academy* 19 (1933), pp. 277–93.

Avery, H. C. "A Lost Episode in Caesar's Civil War." *Hermes* 121, 4 (1993), pp. 452–69.

Babcock, Charles L. "The Early Career of Fulvia." *American Journal of Philology* 86, 1 (1965), pp. 1–32.

Badian, E. "The Date of Pompey's First Triumph." *Hermes* 83 (1955), pp. 107–18.

———. *Studies in Greek and Roman History.* Oxford: Blackwell, 1964.

———. *Lucius Sulla: The Deadly Reformer.* Sydney: Sydney University Press, 1969.

Balsdon, J.P.V.D. "The Ides of March." *Historia* 7 (1958), pp. 80–94.

———. "Cleopatra." Review of Hans Volkmann, *Cleopatra, Classical Review* 10 (1960), pp. 68–71.

———. *Julius Caesar.* New York: Atheneum, 1967.

———. *Life and Leisure in Ancient Rome.* New York: McGraw-Hill, 1969.

Bauman, R. A. *Women and Politics in Ancient Rome.* London: Routledge, 1992.

Beeson, C. "Text History of the Corpus Caesarianum." *Classical Philology* 35 (1940), pp. 113–25.

Bevan, E. R. *A History of Egypt under the Ptolemaic Dynasty.* London: Methuen, 1927.

Bishop, M. C., and J. C. Coulston. *Roman Military Equipment.* London: Batsford, 1993.

Bloch, R. *The Origins of Rome.* New York: Praeger, 1960.

Bonaparte, Napoléon. *Précis des guerres de César.* 1836. Reprint. Napoli: Jovene, 1984.

Bosworth, A. B. *Conquest and Empire: The Reign of Alexander the Great.* Cambridge: Cambridge University Press, 1988.

Brunt, P. A. *Italian Manpower, 225 B.C.–A.D. 14.* London: Oxford University Press, 1971; reissue, with a postscript, 1987.

Burns, Alfred. "Pompey's Strategy and Domitius' Stand at Corfinium." *Historia* 15 (1966), pp. 74–95.

Carcopino, Jérôme. *Daily Life in Ancient Rome.* Translated by E. O. Lorimer. 1940. Reprint. Harmondsworth, U.K.: Penguin Books, 1986.

Caruz Arenas, Antonio. "La última campaña de César en la Bética: Munda." In J. F. Rodríguez Neila, editor, *Andalucia en la antiguedad: Actas del I Congreso de Historia de Andalucia.* Vol. 3, Cordoba: Publicaciones del Monte de Piedad y Caja de Ahorros de Cordoba, 1978.

Casson, Lionel. *The Ancient Mariners.* Princeton: Princeton University Press, 2nd ed., 1991.

———. *Ships and Seamanship in the Ancient World.* Princeton: Princeton University Press, 1971. Reprint, with new material. Baltimore: Johns Hopkins University Press, 1995.

Chevallier, Raymond. *Roman Roads.* Berkeley: University of California Press, 1976.

Clarke, M. C. "Lucius Domitius Ahenobarbus." Ph.D. dissertation, University of California, Berkeley, 1930.

Clarke, M. L. *The Noblest Roman.* Ithaca, N.Y.: Cornell University Press, 1981.

Clayton, Peter, and M. Price, ed. *The Seven Wonders of the Ancient World.* London: Routledge, 1988.

Coggins, Jack. *The Fighting Man.* Garden City, N.Y.: Doubleday, 1966.

Collins, John H. "Caesar and the Corruption of Power." *Historia* 4 (1955), pp. 445–65.

———. "On the Date and Interpretation of the *BellumCivile*." *American Journal of Philology* 80 (1959), pp. 113–32.

Connolly, Peter. *Greece and Rome at War.* Mechanicsburg, Penn.: Stackpole Books, 1998.

Cornell, Tim. *The Beginnings of Rome.* London: Routledge, 1995.

Cornell, Tim, and John Matthews. *The Roman World.* Alexandria, Va.: Stonehenge Press, 1991.

Coulter, Cornelia C. "Pollio's History of the Civil War." *Classical Weekly* 46 (1952), pp. 33–36.

Cowell, F. R. *Cicero and the Roman Republic.* London: Sir Isaac Pitman and Sons, 1948.

Crawford, Michael. *The Roman Republic.* Cambridge, Mass.: Harvard University Press, 2nd ed., 1993.

D'Arms, J. H. *Romans on the Bay of Naples.* Cambridge, Mass.: Harvard University Press, 1970.

Davies, Roy W. "The Roman Military Diet." *Britannia* 2 (1971), pp. 123–41.

———. *Service in the Roman Army.* David Breeze and Valerie A. Maxfield, editors. Edinburgh: Edinburgh University Press, 1989.

Delbrück, Hans. *Warfare in Antiquity.* Translated by Walter J. Renfroe, Jr. Reprint. Lincoln: University of Nebraska Press, 1990.

Deutsch, Monroe E. "The Plot to Murder Caesar on the Bridge." *University of California Publications in Classical Philology* 2, 14 (January 1916), pp. 267–78.

———. "Caesar's First Wife." *Classical Philology* 12 (1917), pp. 93–96.

———. "The Women of Caesar's Family." *Classical Journal* 13 (1918), pp. 502–14.

———. "The Apparatus of Caesar's Triumph." *Philological Quarterly* 3 (1924), pp. 257–66.

———. "Pompey's Three Triumphs." *Classical Philology* 19 (1924), pp. 277–79.

———. "Veni, Vidi, Vici." *Philological Quarterly* 4 (1925), pp. 151–56.

———. "Caesar's Triumphs." *Classical Weekly* 19, 13 (January 25, 1926), pp. 101–6.

———. "Antony's Funeral Speech." *University of California Publications in Classical Philology* 9, 5 (April 1928), pp. 127–48.

———. "Caesar's Son and Heir." *University of California Publications in Classical Philology* 9, 6 (October 1928), pp. 149–200.

———. "I Am Caesar, Not Rex." *Classical Philology* 23 (1928), pp. 394–98.

———. "Caesar and Mucia." *Philological Quarterly* 8 (1929), pp. 218–22.

Echols, E. C. "The Ancient Slinger." *Classical Weekly* 43, 15 (March 27, 1950), pp. 227–30.

Epstein, David F. "Caesar's Personal Enemies on the Ides of March." *Latomus* 46 (1987), pp. 569–70.

Euzennat, M. "Ancient Marseille in the Light of Recent Excavations." *American Journal of Archaeology* 84 (1980), pp. 133–40.

Foley, Vernard, and Werner Soedel. "Ancient Oared Warships." *Scientific American* 244, 4 (April 1981), pp. 148–63.

Forster, E. M. *Alexandria*. Garden City, N.Y.: Anchor Books, 1961.

Fraser, P. M. *Ptolemaic Alexandria*. Oxford: Clarendon Press, 1972.

Fritz, Kurt von. "The Mission of L. Caesar and L. Roscius in January 49 B.C." *Transactions and Proceedings of the American Philological Association* 72 (1941), pp. 125–56.

———. "Pompey's Policy before and after the Outbreak of the Civil War of 49 B.C." *Transactions and Proceedings of the American Philological Association* 73 (1942), pp. 145–80.

Fuller, J.F.C. *Julius Caesar: Man, Soldier, and Tyrant*. [New York]: Minerva Press, [1969, c. 1965].

Gabriel, Richard A., and D. W. Boose. *The Great Battles of Antiquity*. Westport, Conn.: Greenwood Press, 1994.

Gabriel, Richard A., and Karen S. Metz. *From Sumer to Rome: The Military Capabilities of Ancient Armies*. Westport, Conn.: Greenwood Press, 1991.

Geiger, J. "The Last Servilii Caepiones of the Republic." *Ancient Society* 4 (1973), pp. 143–56.

Gelzer, Matthias. *Caesar: Politician and Statesman*. Cambridge, Mass.: Harvard University Press, 1968.

Gershenson, Daniel E. " 'Kai su, teknon': Caesar's Last Words." *Shakespeare Quarterly* 43, 2 (Summer 1992), pp. 218–19.

Gilmer, H. W. "Caesar's Thrasonical Boast." *Philological Quarterly* 4 (1925), p. 157.

Goar, R. J. *The Legend of Cato Uticensis from the First Century B.C. to the Fifth Century A.D.* Bruxelles: Collections Latomus, Vol. 197, 1987.

Goldsworthy, Adrian. *The Roman Army at War, 100 BC–AD 200*. Oxford: Clarendon Press, 1996.

Gordon, H. L. "Marcus Porcius Cato Uticensis." Ph.D. dissertation, University of California, Berkeley, 1930.

Grant, Michael. *Julius Caesar*. New York: McGraw-Hill, 1969.

———. *The Roman Forum*. New York: Macmillan, 1970.

———. *Cleopatra*. London: Weidenfeld and Nicolson, 1972.

———. *The Jews in the Roman World*. New York: Charles Scribner's Sons, 1973.

———. *The Army of the Caesars*. New York: Charles Scribner's Sons, 1974.

———. *Caesar*. Chicago: Follett Publishing Co., 1974.

———. *History of Rome*. New York: Charles Scribner's Sons, 1978.

————. *The Etruscans*. New York: Charles Scribner's Sons, 1980.

————. *A Social History of Greece and Rome*. New York: Charles Scribner's Sons, 1992.

————. *A Guide to the Ancient World*. New York: Barnes and Noble, 1997.

Greenhalgh, Peter. *Pompey, the Roman Alexander*. London: Weidenfeld and Nicolson, 1980.

————. *Pompey, the Republican Prince*. London: Weidenfeld and Nicolson, 1981.

Grimal, Pierre. *The Civilization of Rome*. New York: Simon and Schuster, 1963.

Gwatkin, W. E. "Pompey on the Eve of Pharsalus." *Classical Bulletin* 33 (1957), pp. 39–41.

Hackett, Sir John, ed. *Warfare in the Ancient World*. London: Sidgwick and Jackson, 1989.

Hadas, Moses. *Sextus Pompey*. New York: Columbia University Press, 1930.

Hamilton, Edith. *The Roman Way*. New York: W. W. Norton, 1964.

Hammond, N.G.L. "The Western Part of the Via Egnatia." *Journal of Roman Studies* 64 (1974), pp. 185–94.

Hansen, M. H. "The Battle Exhortation in Ancient Historiography: Fact or Fiction?" *Historia* 42, 2 (1993), pp. 161–80.

Harris, William V. *Ancient Literacy*. Cambridge, Mass.: Harvard University Press, 1989.

Haskell, H. J. *This Was Cicero*. Greenwich, Conn.: Fawcett Publications, 1964.

Heuzey, L. *Les opérations militaires de Jules César: Étudiées sur le terrain par la Mission de Macedoine*. Paris: Hachette & Co., 1886.

Hillman, Thomas P. "Strategic Reality and the Movements of Caesar, January 49 BC." *Historia* 37, 2 (1988), pp. 248–52.

Holloway, R. R. *The Archaeology of Early Rome and Latium*. London: Routledge, 1994.

Holmes, T. Rice. *The Roman Republic and the Founder of the Empire*. 3 vols. Oxford: Clarendon Press, 1923.

Hopkins, Keith. "Brother-Sister Marriage in Roman Egypt." *Comparative Studies in Society and History* 22 (1980), pp. 303–55.

Horsfall, N. "The Ides of March: Some New Problems." *Greece and Rome*, n.s. 21 (1974), pp. 191–99.

Hughes-Hallett, L. *Cleopatra: Histories, Dreams, and Distortions*. New York: Harper and Row, 1990.

Huzar, Eleanor G. *Mark Antony*. London: Croom Helm, 1986.

Hyland, Ann. *Equus: The Horse in the Roman World*. New Haven: Yale University Press, 1990.

Johnston, Mary. *Roman Life*. Chicago: Scott, Foresman and Co., 1957.

Jones, A.H.M. *Augustus*. New York: W. W. Norton, 1970.

Judson, H. P. *Caesar's Army*. New York: Biblo and Tannen, 1961.

Kahn, A. D. *The Education of Julius Caesar*. New York: Schocken Books, 1986.

Keaveney, Arthur. *Sulla, the Last Republican*. London: Croom Helm, 1982.

————. "Young Pompey: 106–79 BC." *L'Antiquité Classique* 51 (1982), pp. 127–37.

Keegan, J., and R. Holmes. *Soldiers*. London: Hamilton, 1985.

Kennedy, George. "Antony's Speech at Caesar's Funeral." *Quarterly Journal of Speech* 54, 2 (April 1968), pp. 99–106.

Korfmann, M. "The Sling as a Weapon." *Scientific American* 229, 4 (October 1973), pp. 34–42.

Leach, John. *Pompey the Great*. London: Croom Helm, 1978.

Liddell Hart, B. H. *Strategy*. New York: Praeger, 1954.

Lintott, A. W. *Violence in Republican Rome*. Oxford: Clarendon Press, 1968.

Lord, L. E. "The Date of Julius Caesar's Departure from Alexandria." *Journal of Roman Studies* 28 (1938), pp. 19–38.

MacMullen, Ramsay. *Roman Social Relations, 50 B.C. to 284 A.D.* New Haven: Yale University Press, 1974.

———. "The Legion as a Society." *Historia* 33 (1984), pp. 440–456.

Marlowe, J. *The Golden Age of Alexandria*. London: Gollancz, 1971.

Marsden, E. W. *Greek and Roman Artillery: Historical Development*. Oxford: Clarendon Press, 1969.

———. *Greek and Roman Artillery: Technical Treatises*. Oxford: Clarendon Press, 1971.

Martin, Paul M. "Le jour où César a franchi le Rubicon." *L'Histoire* 130 (February 1990), pp. 68–70.

McEvedy, C., and R. Jones. *Atlas of World Population History*. New York: Facts on File, 1978.

McLeod, W. "The Range of the Ancient Bow." *Phoenix* 19 (1965), pp. 1–14.

Messer, W. S. "Mutiny in the Roman Army in the Republic." *Classical Philology* 15 (1920), pp. 158–75.

Morgan, J. D. "Palaepharsalus—The Battle and the Town." *American Journal of Archaeology* 87 (1983), pp. 23–54.

Morrison, J. S. *The Ship: Long Ships and Round Ships: Warfare and Trade in the Mediterranean 3000 BC–500 AD*. London: Her Majesty's Stationery Office, 1980.

———. *Greek and Roman Oared Warships*. Oxford: Oxbow Books, 1996.

Nanni, Giuseppe. "Biografia di un fiume: La secolare disputa per il Rubicone." *Le Vie d'Italia* 58 (March 1952), pp. 388–92.

Napoléon III. *History of Julius Caesar*. London: Cassell, Peter, and Galpin, 1865–66.

Nelson, R. B. *Warfleets of Antiquity*. Goring-by-Sea, U.K.: Wargames Research Group, 1973.

O'Connor, Colin. *Roman Bridges*. Cambridge: Cambridge University Press, 1993.

Ogilvie, R. M. *The Romans and Their Gods in the Age of Augustus*. New York: W. W. Norton, 1969.

O'Sullivan, Firmin. *The Egnatian Way*. Newton Abbot, U.K.: David and Charles, 1972.

Parsons, Edward A. *The Alexandrian Library*. Amsterdam: Elsevier Press, 1952.

Pauly, A. F. von, and G. Wissowa. *Paulys Realencyclopädie der classischen Altertumswissenschaft*. Stuttgart: A. Druckenmüller, 1964–75.

Peaks, Mary Bradford. "Caesar's Movements Jan. 21 to Feb. 14, 49 B.C." *Classical Review* 18 (1904), pp. 347–49.

Peddie, John. *The Roman War Machine*. Stroud, Gloucester: Alan Sutton Publishing, 1994.

Pelling, C.B.R. "Pharsalus." *Historia* 22 (1973), pp. 249–59.

Philipp, H. "Eine Gedenktafel Mussolinis am Rubicon." *Petermanns Geographische Mitteilungen* 79 (1933), pp. 180–81.

Pomeroy, Sarah. *Women in Hellenistic Egypt*. New York: Schocken Books, 1984.

Potter, T. W. *Roman Italy*. Berkeley: University of California Press, 1987.

Radke, G. "Römische Strassen in der Gallia Cisalpina und der Narbonensis." *Klio* 42 (1964), pp. 299–317.

Rawson, Beryl. *The Politics of Friendship: Pompey and Cicero*. Sydney: Sydney University Press, 1978.

Rawson, Elizabeth. *Cicero: A Portrait*. Revised ed., Ithaca, N.Y.: Cornell University Press, 1983.

Rickman, Geoffrey. *The Corn Supply of Ancient Rome*. Oxford: Clarendon Press, 1980.

Rivet, A. L. *Gallia Narbonensis*. London: B. T. Batsford, 1988.

Rodgers, W. L. *Greek and Roman Naval Warfare*. Annapolis: United States Naval Institute Press, 1937.

Rowland, R. J. "The Number of Grain Recipients in the Late Republic." *Acta Antiqua* 13 (1965), pp. 81–83.

Russell, James. "Julius Caesar's Last Words." In B. Marshall, editor, *Vindex Humanitatis: Essays in Honour of John Huntly Bishop*. Armidale, New South Wales: University of New England, 1980, pp. 123–28.

Sabben-Clare, James. *Caesar and Roman Politics, 60–50 B.C.* London: Oxford University Press, 1971.

Scullard, H. H. *The Elephant in the Greek and Roman World*. London: Thames and Hudson, 1974.

———. *Festivals and Ceremonies of the Roman Republic*. Ithaca, N.Y.: Cornell University Press, 1981.

Seager, Robin. *Pompey, a Political Biography*. Berkeley: University of California Press, 1979.

Seyrig, H. "Un portrait de Jules César." *Revue Numismatique*, ser. 6, 11 (1969), pp. 53–54.

Shackleton Bailey, D. R. *Cicero*. London: Duckworth, 1971.

Shelton, Jo-Ann. *As the Romans Did*. New York: Oxford University Press, 2nd ed., 1998.

Sihler, E. G. *Annals of Caesar*. New York: G. E. Stechert and Co., 1911.

Smith, R. E. "The Conspiracy and the Conspirators." *Greece and Rome*, n.s. 4 (1957), pp. 58–70.

Smith, William, ed. *Dictionary of Greek and Roman Geography*. Boston: Little, Brown and Co., 1870.

Soedel, Werner, and Vernard Foley. "Ancient Catapults." *Scientific American* 240, 3 (March 1979), pp. 150–60.

Speidel, M. Alexander. "Roman Army Pay Scales." *Journal of Roman Studies* 82 (1992), pp. 87–106.

Speidal, Michael P. "The Soldiers' Servants." *Ancient Society* 20 (1989), pp. 239–47.

Starr, C. G. *The Roman Imperial Navy, 31 B.C.–A.D. 324*. New York: Barnes and Noble, 2nd ed. 1960.

Stillwell, Richard, ed. *The Princeton Encyclopedia of Classical Sites*. Princeton: Princeton University Press, 1976.

Stoffel, Colonel Eugène G.H.C. *Histoire de Jules César, Guerre civile*. 2 vols. and atlas. Paris: Imprimerie Nationale, 1887.

Storch, Rudolph H. "Relative Deprivation and the Ides of March: Motive for Murder." *Ancient History Bulletin* 9, 1 (1995), pp. 45–52.

Sullivan, R. D. *Near Eastern Royalty and Rome, 100–30 BC.* Toronto: University of Toronto Press, 1990.

Sumner, G. V. "A Note on Julius Caesar's Great Grand-father." *Classical Philology* 71 (1976), pp. 341–44.

Sutherland, C.H.V. *Roman Coins.* London: Barrie and Jenkins, 1974.

Sydenham, E. A. *The Coinage of the Roman Republic.* London: Spink, 1952.

Syme, Ronald. Review of *Caesar: Politician and Statesman* by M. Gelzer. *Journal of Roman Studies* 34 (1944), pp. 92–103.

———. *The Roman Revolution.* Oxford: Oxford University Press, 1952.

———. "No Son for Caesar?" *Historia* 29 (1980), pp. 422–37.

Talbert, Richard J. A., ed. *Atlas of Classical History.* London: Routledge, 1988.

Taylor, Lily Ross. "Caesar's Early Career." *Classical Philology* 36 (1941), pp. 113–32.

———. "On the Chronology of Caesar's First Consulship." *American Journal of Philology* 72 (July 1951), pp. 254–68.

———. "The Rise of Julius Caesar." *Greece and Rome,* n.s. 4 (1957), pp. 10–18.

———. *Party Politics in the Age of Caesar.* Berkeley: University of California Press, 1961.

———. "The Dating of Major Legislation and Elections in Caesar's First Consulship." *Historia* 17 (1968), pp. 173–93.

Teggart, F. J. "Caesar and the Alexandrian Library." *Centralblatt für Bibliothekswesen* 16 (1899), pp. 470–75.

Tucker, Robert A. "What Actually Happened at the Rubicon?" *Historia* 37 (1988), pp. 245–48.

Ulrich, R. "Julius Caesar and the Creation of the Forum Julium." *American Journal of Archaeology* 97 (1993), pp. 49–80.

Versnel, H. S. *Triumphus.* Leiden: E. J. Brill, 1970.

Volkmann, Hans. *Cleopatra.* Translated by T. J. Cadoux. London: Elek Books, 1958.

Von Hagen, V. W. *The Roads That Led to Rome.* Cleveland: World Publishing Co., 1967.

Walter, Gérard. *Caesar.* Translated by Emma Craufurd. London: Cassell and Co., 1953.

Ward, Allen M. "Caesar and the Pirates." *Classical Philology* 70 (1975), pp. 267–68.

———. "Caesar and the Pirates II." *American Journal of Ancient History* 2 (1977), pp. 26–36.

Warry, J. G. *Warfare in the Classical World.* London: Salamander Books, 1980.

Watson, G. R. *The Roman Soldier.* Ithaca, N.Y.: Cornell University Press, 1969.

Webster, G. *The Roman Imperial Army of the First and Second Centuries AD.* London: A. & C. Black, 1985.

Weinstock, Stefan. *Divus Julius.* London: Oxford Clarendon Press, 1971.

Wistrand, Erik. *Caesar and Contemporary Roman Society.* Göteborg: Kungl. Vetenskaps- och Vitterhets-Samhället, 1979.

Wylie, Graham. "Why Did Labienus Defect from Caesar in 49 BC?" *Ancient History Bulletin* 3 (1989), pp. 123–27.

———. "The Road to Pharsalus." *Latomus* 51 (1992), pp. 557–65.

Yavetz, Z. "The Living Conditions of the Urban Plebs in Republican Rome." *Latomus* 17 (1958), pp. 500–517.

Index of Persons

Subentries are arranged in rough order of occurrence, rather than in alphabetical order. All dates are BCE unless otherwise indicated.

General Index